Historical Sociology
and World History

Global Dialogues: Developing Non-Eurocentric IR and IPE

Series Editors: John M. Hobson, Professor of Politics and
International Relations, University of Sheffield and L.H.M. Ling,
Professor, Milano School of International Affairs, Management,
and Urban Policy, The New School.

This series adopts a dialogical perspective on global politics, which focuses on the interactions and reciprocities between West and non-West, across Global North and Global South. Not only do these shape and re-shape each other but they have also shaped, made and remade our international system/global economy for the last 500 years. Acknowledging that these reciprocities may be asymmetrical due to disparities in power and resources, this series also seeks to register how 'Eastern' agency, in tandem with counterparts in the West, has made world politics and the world political economy into what it is. While this series certainly welcomes purely theoretically-based books, its primary focus centres on empirical rethinking about the development of the world political system and the global economy along non-Eurocentric lines.

Titles in the Series

Islam and International Relations: Exploring Community and the Limits of Universalism by Faiz Sheikh.

Historical Sociology and World History: Uneven and Combined Development over the Longue Durée, edited by Alexander Anievas and Kamran Matin.

Historical Sociology and World History

Uneven and Combined Development over the *Longue Durée*

Edited by
Alexander Anievas and Kamran Matin

ROWMAN &
LITTLEFIELD
INTERNATIONAL

London • New York

Published by Rowman & Littlefield International Ltd
Unit A, Whitacre Mews, 26-34 Stannary Street, London SE11 4AB
www.rowmaninternational.com

Rowman & Littlefield International Ltd.is an affiliate of Rowman & Littlefield
4501 Forbes Boulevard, Suite 200, Lanham, Maryland 20706, USA
With additional offices in Boulder, New York, Toronto (Canada), and Plymouth (UK)
www.rowman.com

British Library Cataloguing in Publication Data
A catalogue record for this book is available from the British Library

ISBN: HB 978-1-7834-8681-6
       PB 978-1-7834-8682-3

Library of Congress Cataloging-in-Publication Data Is Available
ISBN 978-1-78348-681-6 (cloth : alk. paper)
ISBN 978-1-78348-682-3 (paperback : alk. paper)
ISBN 978-1-78348-683-0 (electronic)

∞™ The paper used in this publication meets the minimum requirements of American
National Standard for Information Sciences—Permanence of Paper for Printed Library
Materials, ANSI/NISO Z39.48-1992.

Printed in the United States of America

Dedicated to Turkey's Academics for Peace

Contents

Acknowledgements   ix

1   Introduction: Historical Sociology, World History and
    the 'Problematic of the International'   1
    Alexander Anievas and Kamran Matin

2   Uneven and Combined Development: 'The International'
    in Theory and History   17
    Justin Rosenberg

3   The Conditions for the Emergence of Uneven and
    Combined Development   31
    Neil Davidson

4   The Uneven, Combined and Intersocietal Dimensions
    of Korean State Formation and Consolidation over the
    Longue Durée: 300–1900 CE   53
    Owen Miller

5   Combination as 'Foreign Policy': The Intersocietal Origins
    of the Ottoman Empire   73
    Kerem Nişancıoğlu

6   Revisiting the Transformation of the Nineteenth Century
    and the 'Eastern Question': Uneven and Combined
    Development and the Ottoman Steppe   93
    Jamie Allinson

7   Asian Sources of British Imperial Power: The Role of the
       Mysorean Rocket in the Opium War   111
       Luke Cooper

8   Rejecting the 'Staples' Thesis and Recentring Migration:
       A Comparative Analysis of 'Late Development'
       in Canada and Argentina   127
       Jessica Evans

9   Navigating Uneven and Combined Development:
       Britain's Africa Policy in Historical Perspective   149
       William Brown

10 The Impact of the 'Global Transformation' on Uneven
       and Combined Development   171
       Barry Buzan and George Lawson

11 The Ethiopian Revolution: A World-Historical Perspective   185
       Fouad Makki

12 Uneven and Combined Development in the Sociocultural
       Evolution of World-Systems   205
       Christopher Chase-Dunn and Marilyn Grell-Brisk

13 Navigating Non-Eurocentrism and Trotskyist Integrity
       in the New Trotskyist IR of World History   219
       John M. Hobson

14 The Stakes of Uneven and Combined Development   239
       David L. Blaney and Naeem Inayatullah

Conclusion: Rethinking Historical Sociology and World History:
Beyond the Eurocentric Gaze   251
Alexander Anievas and Kamran Matin

Bibliography   257

Index   291

About the Contributors   303

Acknowledgements

The editors would like to acknowledge the support of the series editors John M. Hobson and L.H.M. Ling, and Anna Reeve, Dhara Patel and Michael Watson at Rowman and Littlefield International. In addition, the editors would wish to thank the constructive comments provided by the anonymous reviewers which helped shape the overall direction of the volume. They would also like to extend their deepest gratitude to the contributors of this book for their intellectual and personal generosity. Finally, Alexander Anievas would like to acknowledge the generous funding and support provided by the Leverhulme Trust while completing this manuscript.

Chapter 1

Introduction

Historical Sociology, World History and the 'Problematic of the International'

Alexander Anievas and Kamran Matin

The classical sociology tradition has long been criticised for offering a conception of 'the social' abstracted from its wider intersocietal context. The 'methodological internalism' inherited from this intellectual tradition has in turn lent itself to Eurocentric modes of enquiry in which modernity is conceived as endogenously and autonomously emerging within Europe—or even more narrowly, England—from which it subsequently spread to the rest of the world at varying times and tempos. From such perspectives, we find the flowering of the Renaissance (Burkhardt 1990), the emergence of absolutism and the modern state system (Teschke 2003), the origins of capitalism and the 'rise of the West' (Jones 1981; Brenner 1985; Landes 1998) as exclusively European phenomena: immanent properties of the uniqueness of European development itself. Europe is thus not only conceived as auto-generative and self-sustaining, but also as the permanent 'core' and 'prime mover' of world history. This is a view of European development as autopoietic. As a result, dominant *theoretical* understandings of world history have been constructed with non-European societies and agents largely absent, even when they are recognised as being *empirically* important to the stories we tell (cf. Anievas and Nişancioğlu 2015). Missing in these Eurocentric accounts, then, is any theoretical comprehension of 'the international' as a thick space of interconnection and co-constitutive societal differentiation: a conception of intersocietal systems as necessarily marked by, and generative of, alterity, hybridity and non-linear forms of development.

Recently in the fields of International Relations (IR) and historical sociology, a thriving new research program has emerged specifically addressing these two intersecting problematics of 'the international' and Eurocentrism building upon Leon Trotsky's notion of uneven and combined development. This volume brings together a number of scholars working within these

1

fields in offering critical reflections on the potential of uneven and combined development as an intellectual basis for a non-Eurocentric social theory of 'the international'. It does so through a series of theoretically informed and empirically rich analyses of socio-historical change, political transformation and intersocietal conflict in world history over the *longue durée*.

In what follows, we further flesh out the issues and debates revolving around the twin problematics of 'the international' and Eurocentrism. We offer an exposition of the theory of uneven and combined development, while addressing some of the central lines of debate within the contemporary literature. We then move in Section IV to position the various chapters in relation to the above-noted problematics.

It is worth noting here that in putting together this volume we aim to pursue two main goals. The first, more explicit one is that the volume should act as a catalyst for further critical discussion and debate on and theoretical re-articulations of the central role of intersocietal relations— and extra-European societies in particular—in the making of world history. Our second, more implicit goal is to show the intellectual potentials of the idea of uneven and combined development for acting as a bridge between the fields of historical sociology and world history. For although contemporary world historians have also been centrally concerned with intersocietal interactions and differentiation in history there has been little dialogue between world history and historical sociology in IR as distinct but cognate fields. We reflect on the roots of this problem and the ways in which uneven and combined development can contribute to its solution in the concluding chapter.

To these ends, we offer the idea of uneven and combined development as a framework uniquely suited to theoretically and empirically 're-orient' (Frank 1998) extant conceptions of world history and 'the international'. In particular, we argue that uneven and combined development provides a *generative* research programme that opens up new theoretical and empirical vistas through which to analyse world history anew.

THE LEGACY AND LACUNA OF THE CLASSICAL SOCIOLOGY TRADITION

Over the past four decades or so, scholars of historical sociology have provided a wealth of new and exciting works analysing world history. From multi-volume studies, such as those provided by Perry Anderson (1974a; 1974b), Michael Mann (1986; 1993; 2012; 2013), Immanuel Wallerstein (1974; 1980; 1989; 2011), W. G. Runcimen (1983; 1989; 1997) and Kees van der Pijl (2007; 2010; 2014), to the many works of Jack Goldstone

(1991; 2002; 2008), Theda Skocpol (1979; 1994), John M. Hobson (1997; 2004; 2012) and Charles Tilly (1984; 1993; 2004), historical sociological approaches have offered a number of important insights and novel analytical frameworks for examining world history over the *longue durée*. Particularly significant here is the persistent question of the theoretical standing of *intersocietal relations*—or 'the international'—that many of these historical sociological works have sought to address and the zones of engagement and cross-fertilisation this has inspired with the field of IR.[1]

Engagements with the 'problematic of the international' have time and again taken centre stage in historical sociology and IR as they have sought to overcome the problems bequeathed by classical sociology's singular notion of 'society' conceived in abstraction from the conditions of societal multiplicity and interactivity (see, among others, Nisbet 1969; Berki 1971; Skocpol 1973; Barker 1978; Giddens 1985; Mann 1986; Halliday 1987; Bertram 1990; Linklater 1990; Hobson 1998; Hall 1999; Teschke 2005; Rosenberg 2006; van der Pijl 2007; Davenport 2013). As far back as 1965, Gianfranco Poggi noted how modern sociology had primarily taken shape around the 'study of the inner structure and dynamics of social units'. It was therefore marked by a 'learned incapacity' to theoretically incorporate the distinct causal dynamics and behavioural patterns emergent from the interactive co-existence of multiple societies and states (Poggi 1965, 284). For the guiding methodological assumption of the classical sociology tradition was that the growth and change of society 'should be explained with reference to its internal constitution' (Tenbruck 1994, 74). While the interactions between societies may not be viewed as entirely 'inconsequential', they are 'in principle insignificant for sociology, since its effects on the essential process [are] seen as negligible'. It was this 'conception of the *internal history of societies* that underlies the rise of sociology' (Tenbruck 1994, 74, emphasis added). Similarly, surveying the vast field of classical sociologists from Karl Marx and Ferdinand Tönnies to Émile Durkheim and Talcott Parsons, Richard Bendix (1967, 306–7) concluded that '[f]or all their diversity' the classical sociology tradition has tended to 'treat societies as "natural systems"' whereby 'social change consists of a process that is internal to the society changing'. This absence of any intellectual tradition of international theory is replicated in Classical Political Philosophy, rousing Martin Wight's (1966) oft-cited question: 'Why is there no international theory?'

The problem of how to theorise international relations inherited from the classical sociology tradition has led a number of contemporary historical sociologists and IR scholars to abandon any unitary notion of society. They have instead invited us to revisualise processes of long-term social change and transformation in terms of intersecting 'webs' and 'flows' operating across, and irreducible to, individual societies, or contextualising social development within wider 'intersocietal systems' (see, for example, Giddens 1985; Mann 1986; Runciman 1989; Shaw 2000). While marking definite advances in approaching macro-historical analysis, such moves towards assigning a more central status to intersocietal relations and dynamics have all too often involved either an 'extra-social' or reductionist conception of 'the international'. In other words, existing historical sociological approaches have oscillated between realist[2] reifications of 'the international' as a timeless supra-social sphere or reductive theorisations of its distinct causal properties through some form of 'domestic analogy': a visualisation of 'the international' as a reimagining of domestic society *writ large* (Bull 1966). Consequently, the theoretical divide between 'sociological' and 'geopolitical' modes of explanation persists as neither perspective *theoretically* transcends classical sociology's original conception of society in the ontologically singular (cf. Rosenberg 2006). This methodological dichotomy and the myriad problems it has generated have been at the heart of recent debates within the field of IR, where historical sociology has secured a vocal, albeit still marginal, place (see, *inter alia,* Hobson 1998; Buzan and Little 2000; Halliday 2002; Rosenberg 2006; Bigo and Walker 2007; Matin 2007; van der Pijl 2007; Chernilo 2010; Bhambra 2010; Hobson, Lawson and Rosenberg 2010; Teschke 2014; Anievas and Nişancioğlu 2015; Bieler, Bruff and Morton 2015; Buzan and Lawson 2015).

While historical sociologists have provided new vistas from which to revisualise grand-scale social change and development over the *longue durée*, the intellectual lacuna of 'the international' persists as few scholars have offered any systematic theoretical apparatus capable of incorporating the coexistence and interaction of multiple societies as a distinct sphere of developmental dynamics and social causality (but see van der Pijl 2007). As such, intersocietal relations remain theoretically undigested since it is not clear what is 'the international' rendered in substantive historical and sociological terms. That is to say, we have yet to see the formulation of a genuinely international historical sociology (Rosenberg 2006 and chapter in this volume).

MISSING: A NON-EUROCENTRIC SOCIAL THEORY OF 'THE INTERNATIONAL'

The residual methodological internalism of historical sociological approaches entailed in this continuing absence of 'the international' in theory intersects with a second key line of debate within the contemporary social sciences: the problem of Eurocentrism.[3] Indeed, one can arguably view the latter as a consequence of the former in the sense that the conception of social change and transformation as an *immanent* property of societies has led to interpretations and theoretical analyses of the predominant sites and driving forces of such historical processes as an exclusively European affair. Relatedly, through the comparative method, we find the distinct forms and paths of European development posited as ideal-type abstractions and/or normative benchmarks with which all other examples are contrasted and ultimately judged a 'deviation'. Consequently, the particularities of European development are projected in one form or another on to the 'extra-European' world, thereby elevating the European experience into a *universal* stage of development through which all societies must pass, albeit at different times, places and velocities. The false sense of universality generated by such Eurocentric modes of enquiry has been the bane of social theory since its inception (cf. Anievas and Nişancioğlu 2015).

So what then constitutes Eurocentrism as such? At the core of Eurocentrism lies the claim that modern development across the world consists of a series of discrete re-enactments of modernity's endogenous development in Europe. This is a view of modern world history as a play with one stage and one actor. As noted, this claim is rooted in classical sociology's foundational assumption that the character of a society's development is determined by its internal structures and agents. The self-contained conception of autopoietic development—the autonomous emergence and reproduction of particular social orders—embedded in the 'pernicious postulate' (Tilly 1984) of this singular abstraction of 'the social' simultaneously entails both an internalisation and globalisation of modern capitalist development in Europe (Amin 1989). This is effectuated by the subordination of *space* to *time* through a double-movement.[4] Different geopolitical spaces are conceptually decoupled from the particularities of their internal developmental processes, while being simultaneously enclosed and homogenised within an abstract universal history derived from the concrete internal history of one such geopolitical space: Europe. The constitutive and causal significance of political multiplicity is thereby dissolved into a European temporality refashioned as 'the universal'. In this respect, Eurocentrism combines 'internalism' (Tenbruck 1994) and 'historicism' (Chakrabarty 2008) producing what can be termed 'monadic sociology' (Matin 2007)—a mode of analysis that arguably remains hegemonic within the social sciences, operating across a wider variety of different theoretical traditions despite its many critics.

Two critical alternative approaches to Eurocentrism that have become particularly influential include 'multiple modernities' (Eisenstadt 2000) and 'late postcolonialism' (Bhaba 1994; Spivak 1994). Both approaches reject European development as the epitome of modernity, whilst emphasising the fundamentally plural nature of the modern experience. These are two crucial components to the formulation of a non-Eurocentric perspective which resonates with the framework of uneven and combined development offered in this volume. However, the 'multiple modernities' and 'late postcolonialism' perspective each face real difficulties in fully transcending Eurocentrism. The Weberian sociological framework of the multiple modernities approach retains the static comparative methodology fitted with ideal-type abstractions that renders 'the international' a contingent externality to its theoretical premises. This in turn attenuates the constitutive role of (geo)politics and intersocietal relations attendant to the globalisation of modern world history. The approach therefore lends itself to a culturalist/relativist mode of inquiry that is preoccupied with questions pertaining to the specificity of each instance of modernity leaving Eurocentrism's internalist method largely intact (Eisenstadt 2000, 2; Masud and Salvatore 2009, 45).[5] By contrast, late postcolonialism interrogates the interactive construction of 'colonial modernity' through an explicitly internationalist method (Dabashi 2006, xi–xii). Yet, its poststructuralist hostility towards general theory and universal categories arrests the translation of its powerful critique of Eurocentrism into an alternative non-Eurocentric social theory (Dirlik 1999, 1994; Matin 2013a; Anievas and Nişancioğlu 2015). Thus, while multiple modernities and late postcolonial scholars have been highly successful at impeaching Eurocentrism, they have not yet decisively supplanted it (cf. Matin 2013b, 2–3).

FOUND: THE IDEA OF UNEVEN AND COMBINED DEVELOPMENT

The long forgotten idea of uneven and combined development, we argue, offers a theoretical framework that avoids these pitfalls and overcomes Eurocentrism. The term was first coined by the Bolshevik revolutionary Leon Trotsky (2008) to explain the 'peculiarities of Russian development' which led to the world's first socialist-inspired revolution—a revolution which took place within the most economically 'backward'[6] and ideologically reactionary state in Europe at the time. Trotsky's views on the possibility of Tsarist Russia moving straight to socialism were in stark contrast to predominant positions within the Second International that the socialist revolution in Tsarist Russia had to wait for the bourgeois 'stage' to complete itself (Davidson 2015a).[7] And, for Trotsky, the ability of Russian society to 'skip' a few stages of the historical process was inherently conditioned by its international context (what Trotsky termed the 'whip of external necessity'). The 'law' of uneven and combined development essentially constituted the historical sociological foundations for Trotsky's strategy of permanent revolution, capturing both a real historical process and its conceptual comprehension in thought (cf. Davidson 2012 and this volume). But, moreover, implicit in Trotsky's idea of uneven and combined development was a fundamental redefinition of the very logic and concept of development itself: one embedded with a 'more-than-one' ontological premise.

This long hidden potential of Trotsky's concept in furnishing a historical sociological theory of 'the international' was taken up by Justin Rosenberg in his Deutscher Prize lecture of 1994 entitled 'Isaac Deutscher and the Lost History of International Relations' (Rosenberg 1996) and, more systematically and ambitiously, over a decade later in an article titled 'Why Is There No International Historical Sociology?' (2006).[8] Over the subsequent two decades since Rosenberg introduced the idea as the basis for a social theory of 'the international', it has witnessed an unprecedented intellectual renaissance representing, as Neil Davidson puts it in this volume, 'perhaps the most dramatic reversal of fortune ever undergone by any concept from within the Classical Marxist tradition'. Having been lifted from a relatively obscure concept confined to the Trotskyist left, where even there it remained at the outer-margins of discussion, 'uneven and combined development is now part of the standard theoretical apparatus available to those working in International Relations and to some extent in the social and political sciences more generally' (Davidson, this volume).[9] Indeed, the idea's revival has not only been witnessed in IR and historical sociology,[10] but also within—and often in dialogue with—other fields such as history (van der Linden 2007; Tooze 2014; 2015; Eley 2015), world literature and cultural studies (cf. Mukherjee 2009; Brennan 2014; Warwick Research Collective 2015; Christie and Degirmencioglu 2016). So what is uneven and combined development?

The conceptual core of uneven and combined development, as further elaborated upon by Rosenberg (2006), is threefold.[11] First, unevenness posits multiplicity and differentiation as a general ontological condition of social existence. Second, unevenness *ipso facto* conditions and is reconditioned by processes of change within and across interacting societies. This interactive process ontologically blurs the analytical distinction between the 'internal' and 'external', and by extension the 'traditional' and 'modern', as it necessarily generates particular 'combinations' of its own component parts, continuously generating new iterations and dynamics of unevenness.

Crucially, combined development is an open-ended and politically charged process. It involves lived agents, differentially located within a complex structure of uneven power relations, borrowing and adapting available resources in order to create 'new' social orders or reform existing ones—a process wrought with unintended consequences. The category of combination thereby denotes how social structures and relations within particular human geographies are shaped by and constituted through their interactions. Such interactions are in turn generative of unique amalgams of 'native' and 'foreign', 'traditional' and 'modern', social forms. Third, this intrinsically 'uneven' and 'combined' character of social change finds its concrete expressions in historical processes of 'development'. Development is, of course, among the most controversial and Eurocentric concepts in the social sciences (cf. Nisbet 1969; Escobar 1995; Nederveen Pieterse 2001). In Trotsky's formulation, however, development is neither unilinear nor homogenous/homogenising but interactively multilinear. In this respect, the theory reconceptualises the (re)productive activities of human collectivities that are implicated in their mutually constitutive relations. These relations in turn produce differentiated societal outcomes and underpin 'processes of directional change over time, which can be theorised by analysing the causal properties of particular structures of social relationships' (Rosenberg 2007, 330).

A few important clarifications are in order here. Uneven and combined development has been often used interchangeably and conflated with the concept of 'uneven development' (see also, Davidson chapter in this volume). However, the two categories are quite distinct. 'Uneven development' conceptualises differential development within different parts of a country, or between different countries, regions and economic sectors. It has been extensively used to describe the unequal pace and depth of economic and political 'modernisation' in the Global South (cf. Emmanuel 1972; Amin 1977; Arrighi 2007), as well as in examining the differential production of space— uneven geographical development—under capitalism (e.g. Harvey 2006; Smith 2008). But there are two crucial differences between the two concepts. First, 'uneven development' is derived from the internal dynamics of capitalism. It therefore obscures the causal significance of societal multiplicity and international relations central to uneven and combined development. And second, 'uneven development' does not capture conditions of hybridity. In its more complex renditions it connotes the 'articulation of modes of production' whereby capitalist and non-capitalist forms hierarchically coexist but remain internally coherent (Foster-Carter 1978; Laclau 1971).

Relatedly, the order of the concepts uneven and combined is quite significant as a number of scholars often refer to Trotsky's idea as 'combined and uneven development'. But, again, the two are in fact distinct. As Trotsky himself made clear (1979, 556, emphasis ours), 'I would put uneven before combined, because the second *grows out* of the first and *completes it*'. The reasoning behind this order is drawn out by Davidson (2012, 295) when discussing the specific theoretical innovation of 'combined development' which Trotsky coined in seeking to overcome the 'inability of uneven development to fully encapsulate' a number of phenomena (such as the hyper-fusion of the most 'archaic and contemporary forms' within a society), which 'appears to have made Trotsky search for a new concept, with a new name, *starting from and incorporating uneven development but deepening its content*'. The implications of this point are particularly relevant in the contemporary debates on uneven and combined development vis-à-vis theorising 'the international'.

For the more commonly used term combined and uneven development, as Rosenberg notes (2005, 68–69fn28), 'invokes a general condition in which a range of societies, at different levels of development, interact (or are "combined") in a single geopolitical system'. This interactive component of combined development is important, but it does not by itself capture the 'yet deeper' dimension entailed in Trotsky's original use of the concept which captured how the unevenness of development became a 'causal mechanism of "combined development"': that is, the production of a 'hybrid' social formation consisting of 'a changing amalgam of pre-existent "internal" structures of social life with external socio-political and cultural influences' (Rosenberg 2005, 68–69fn28; 2006, 324). Hence, while 'combined and uneven development' *describes* a general condition, it does not theorise it.

By contrast, the notion of uneven and combined development draws attention to, and theorises how, forms and patterns of combination are conditioned by and rooted within the overall unevenness of human development. As such, the combinations of different modes of production do not simply denote their co-existence within a concrete social formation, but rather their reproductive interpenetration and fusion in ways violating any preformed theory of their 'laws of motion'. That is to say, a combined development represents more than the sum of its parts: Tsarist Russia, to take Trotsky's classic example, was neither feudal nor capitalist, but both and more. Taking Trotsky's concept of combined development seriously means that there has never existed any pure or 'normal' model of development since each and every society's development has always already been interactively 'overdetermined', creating a plurality of different sociological amalgamations. The universal condition of combined development in effect means there has never been a 'pre-combined' social formation (Rosenberg 2006). Hence, the very unevenness and combination of historical development resists any kind of abstracted conceptions of European history—or any history, for that matter—that can be used as the privileged 'benchmark' to normatively judge or comparatively contrast with others.

The question of whether 'unevenness' and 'combination' are universal conditions also lies at the heart of current debates over the spatio-temporal range and theoretical and explanatory remit of the idea of uneven and combined development. This debate has broadly split between two positions: one that restricts uneven and combined development to the industrial-capitalist period and primarily applicable to 'late-developing' states (e.g. Ashman 2009; Davidson 2009; Kiely 2012; Davidson this volume; Evans this volume); and, a second that extends the idea to include the pre-capitalist epoch, whilst maintaining the qualitative variations uneven and combined development takes in different historical eras (Matin 2007; Rosenberg 2006; 2010; Anievas 2014, chapter 2; Anievas and Nişancioğlu 2015; Allinson 2016;

and see the chapters by Rosenberg, Miller, Cooper, Hobson, and Chase-Dunnand Grell-Brisk in this volume). This second approach, its advocates argue, is both more consistent with Trotsky's original idea (Matin 2013b, 17; Rosenberg 2013b; cf. Davidson this volume) and, more importantly, provides a deeper theoretical foundation for a non-Eurocentric international historical sociology; one that challenges the idea of the endogenous formation of capitalist social relations in England (e.g. Brenner 1985) by highlighting the constitutiveness of 'the international' to the emergence and expansion of capitalism. Such approaches do not deny the specifically European form of capitalist modernity nor that capitalism first took root in Europe (cf. Anievas and Nişancioğlu 2015). Rather, they argue that to truly 'provincialize Europe' (Chakrabarty 2008) requires not simply a theory of capitalist modernity, but a *general* social theory that goes beyond a mere phenomenology of capital's expansion and comprehends capital itself as a product of the interactive multiplicity of the social (Matin 2013a). While there is growing empirical support for such claims regarding the fundamental significance of intersocietal relations and non-Western agency in explaining the rise of capitalist modernity (Hodgson 1993; Moore 1997; Hobson 2004; Bhambra 2007), critics nonetheless argue that such processes more properly belong to the realm of 'uneven development' not 'combined development', which is a phenomenon that only emerged after capitalism was established (Davidson 2009; Davidson this volume).

In the above-noted ways, the idea of uneven and combined development offers a potential means of theoretically and methodologically displacing Eurocentrism (cf. Matin 2007; 2013b; 2013c; Shilliam 2009a; Hobson 2011; Anievas and Nişancioğlu 2013; 2015; Nişancioğlu 2014; Nilsen 2015; Allinson 2016). By positing the differentiated character of development as its 'most general law', Trotsky's concept of unevenness provides a necessary corrective to any ontologically singular conception of society and resulting unilinear conceptions of history that underpin Eurocentric accounts. By positing the intrinsically interactive character of this multiplicity, combined development in turn challenges the methodological internalism of Eurocentric approaches propounding there has never existed any pure or normative model of development (Anievas and Nişancioğlu 2015). As such, the theory rejects Eurocentrism's reified conceptualisation of the universal as an *a priori* property of an immanently conceived homogeneous entity. For the 'historical reality' of uneven and combined development (Trotsky 1972, 116) is a universally operational causal context whose ontological fabric is simultaneously generative of, and shaped by, intersocietal difference (Matin 2013a). A world in which the specificities of any given society represents 'an original combination of the basic features of the world process' (Trotsky 1962, 23)—a 'social amalgam combining the local and general' (Trotsky

1969, 56) that is 'nothing else but the most general product of the unevenness of historical development, its summary result, so to say' (Trotsky 1962, 24). Such a perspective thereby allows for a conception of 'the universal' that is radically amenable to and constituted by alterity (Matin 2013a).

ORGANISATION OF THE BOOK

In their different ways, the contributions to this book build upon the framework of uneven and combined development in confronting the twin problematics of 'the international' and Eurocentrism highlighted in this introduction. In chapter 2, Justin Rosenberg sets out the historical context and general parameters of the intellectual and real-world challenge of 'the international' and the way in which it was confronted by Trotsky who responded by formulating the notion of uneven and combined development. Rosenberg then considers the proper scope of the concept's spatial and temporal remit and argues for a more general conception of the idea that extends beyond the capitalist epoch. He contends that it is only through this more general conception that uneven and combined development can fundamentally reabsorb 'the international' into social theory and decisively supplant Eurocentrism. The chapter concludes with an examination of the relevance of the idea of uneven and combined development for twenty-first century world politics.

In contradistinction to Rosenberg's transhistorical conception of uneven and combined development, in chapter 3 Neil Davidson makes the case for a more historically limited understanding of Trotsky's idea. He does so through an investigation of the *historical* origins of uneven and combined development—a process fundamentally rooted in the rise and violent spread of industrial capitalism to 'late' developing states—and Trotsky's attempt at comprehending this process in *theory*, which distinguished his idea from earlier notions of 'uneven development'. Davidson concludes by addressing the argument that the historically restricted conception of uneven and combined development is inherently susceptible to Eurocentrism.

In chapter 4, Owen Miller traces the emergence and consolidation of the Korean state over the course of some 1,600 years. Moving beyond prevailing Eurocentric and 'stagnation/progress dichotomy' approaches characterising the existing historiography, Miller demonstrates how the Korean state was shaped and strengthened through a process of uneven and combined development in which ideas, institutions and technologies were transmitted and adopted from neighbouring polities and were combined into novel forms and at varying tempos. Miller shows how this internationally sensitive account of Korean state formation provides significant insights into the historical evolution and transformation of tributary modes of production and the differentiated trajectories of non-European processes of state formation.

In chapter 5, Kerem Nişancıoğlu problematises conventional Eurocentric approaches to the study of the Ottoman Empire which neglect its dynamism and invoke essentialist conceptions of its history derived from its purportedly internal *sui generis* characteristics. Critically deploying the theory of uneven and combined development, Nişancıoğlu provides an alternative non-Eurocentric account of the origins and evolution of the Ottoman state and society that reveals a far more complex, dynamic and historically contingent process marked by a complex amalgam of social relations derived from a multiplicity of geographically distinct yet interactive origins. More specifically, Nişancıoğlu demonstrates the causal significance of 'the international' in the formation of the Ottoman Empire and the ways in which the geopolitical flux of thirteenth- to fifteenth-century Anatolia was marked by the interactive combination of the sociological remnants of Inner Asian nomadism, Seljuk Empire and the Byzantine Empire, which generated the developmental conditions in which the peculiar characteristics of the Ottoman Empire emerged.

In chapter 6, Jamie Allinson turns to late Ottoman history and the 'social origins of the Middle East' through a critical examination of the complex impact of Ottoman reforms during the early to mid-nineteenth century on the regions that became part of southern Syria and Jordan. Allinson shows how the Ottoman's recourse to mimetic reforms under the whip of capitalist Europe gave rise to a particular form of combined development in which a (geo)politically inflected process of primitive accumulation transformed the central extractive relationship of the taking of 'brotherly' tribute (*khuwwa*) by pastoral nomads without polarising the vertical institution of the tribe. The chapter thereby demonstrates the significance of non-European agency within a process of mimetic but mediated primitive accumulation consciously articulated and implemented by the Ottoman rulers themselves.

While Miller, Nişancıoğlu and Allinson's analyses problematise Eurocentric approaches to histories outside 'the West', Luke Cooper's chapter examines a crucial non-Western dimension of the rise of British imperial power, which was a key *coercive force* behind the internationalisation of industrial capitalism. Through a critical deployment of the idea of uneven and combined development, Cooper's revisionist account uses the story of the Mysorean rocket to show how in confronting the power of Indian polities Britain appropriated and adapted their antecedent military technologies, which came to partially underpin Britain's imperial ascent. British emulation of the rocket following their defeat by the Indian Kingdom of Mysore in 1780 was key to their subsequent decimation of Qing naval forces in 1841 leading to victory in the First Opium War and the consequent 'opening of China' to colonial-commercial interests. Highlighting the importance of Asia for Britain's developmental 'leap-frogging' during the 1780–1840 period, Cooper's analysis foregrounds the causal significance of interactions with the non-capitalist world for the formation of capitalism as a genuinely global system.

In chapter 8, Jessica Evans examines migration as a crucial mechanism of the differential incorporation of non-capitalist societies into the capitalist world market. Drawing on the theoretical insights of Political Marxism and uneven and combined development, Evans offers a potent critique of the 'staples thesis' of economic development in settler colonies. In doing so, she demonstrates how the Great Atlantic Migrations of the nineteenth century served as a distinct mechanism of 'combined development' in which migrant populations' reproductive strategies interacted with those conditioned by the prevailing social property relations in the colony, resulting in differential processes of class formation while inducing different incentives to revolutionise the production process. Evan therefore argues that migration must be understood in terms of both the social relations of production that conditioned variable paths of emigration as well as those which prevailed in and varied across New World destinations, thus contributing to the divergent and amalgamated trajectories of capitalist transformations amongst the settler colonies.

In chapter 9, William Brown intervenes in recent debates on Britain's post-1997 Africa policy, which have focused on the continuities and parallels between Britain's contemporary 'liberal imperialism' and its nineteenth-century forays into Africa, which has informed comparisons between China's contemporary involvement on the continent and the late-nineteenth-century 'scramble for Africa'. Brown demonstrates that these debates under-emphasise the developmental dynamism of the relationship between Africa and the wider world. He shows that the interactive developmental processes resulting from Europe's domination of Africa altered the context and at least some of the content of the intersocietal relations involved. Thus, Brown argues, contemporary studies repeat earlier debates about imperialism, which located its causes either in the geopolitical machinations of European powers, or in the inner logic of (capitalist) European societies thereby excluding the role of African societies in shaping the pathways of European imperialism. Building upon key components of the theory of uneven and combined development, the chapter shows how contemporary policy conundrums have their roots in these international dimensions of African history.

In chapter 10, Barry Buzan and George Lawson focus on the impact of the nineteenth century 'global transformation' on the process of uneven and combined development and draw on the concept in fashioning a non-Eurocentric account of macro-historical change. Buzan and Lawson show how the global transformation led first to a much more uneven and combined world order, and subsequently to a less uneven but increasingly combined world order. This intense period in the history of uneven and combined development produced a highly centred, core-periphery global order during the nineteenth century and much of the twentieth century. However, during the late twentieth and especially early part of the twenty-first century, this order has, they argue, been giving way to an increasingly decentred global order, still highly combined, but with a marked diffusion in the distribution of the modern 'mode of power'. The result, Buzan and Lawson claim, is a reduction in the extreme unevenness of power, wealth and status that characterised the initial phases of global modernity.

In chapter 11, Fouad Makki provides an international account of the Ethiopian revolutions of 1974 and 1991, which transformed the social and political structure of the country, respectively. Makki challenges the nationalist-culturalist frameworks of the existing literature on the revolutions and provides an alternative account based on the idea of uneven and combined development that foregrounds the international dimensions of these revolutions and thus theoretically re-casts the disjuncture between the consciously socialist, anti-capitalist project of the key revolutionary agents and the actual outcomes of the revolutions, which embodied the basic contours of capitalist modernity. This disjuncture, Makki argues, was itself an outcome of a world-historical context strategically marked by material and cultural interconnections.

In chapter 12, Christopher Chase-Dunn and Marilyn Grell-Brisk marry the insights of World-Systems Analysis with uneven and combined development in analysing the sociocultural evolution of particular world-systems over the *longue durée*. Focusing on interpolity interaction networks (world-systems) central to semiperipheral development, Chase-Dunn and Grell-Brisk show the centrality of semiperipheral polities to the adaptation of technologies and organisational forms that facilitated conquest and empire-formation and expanded and intensified exchange networks. Sociocultural evolution can thus only be explained if polities are visualised in their interactive (uneven and combined developmental) relations with each other since the Palaeolithic Age. This is substantiated through an analysis of the differential forms of semiperipheral development in two small world-systems in prehistoric California. The chapter also surveys various cases of semiperipheral 'marcher states' that conquered older core polities and formed larger empire states. The chapter concludes with an examination of contemporary forms of semiperipheral 'catch-up' development catalysing innovative systemic change with reference to the BRICS (Brazil, Russia, India, China and South Africa), which have recently come to challenge the centrality of the United States, Europe and Japan, thus demonstrating the continuing impact of processes of uneven and combined development within the modern world-system.

In chapter 13, John M. Hobson focuses on the potential problems of Eurocentrism and ahistoricism in the contemporary IR literature on uneven and combined development through a critical reading of the works of Anievas,

Nişancioğlu and Matin. In so doing, Hobson engages with the above-noted debates on the historical scope of uneven and combined development and their bearings on the issue of Eurocentrism/non-Eurocentrism, on the one hand, and whether a 'non-Eurocentric Trotskyism' remains within or breaks with Trotsky's original conception of uneven and combined development, on the other. Hobson defends an extended conception of uneven and combined development as key to fully transcending Eurocentrism. He concludes with an analysis of various 'West-East' interactions during the Medieval epoch in demonstrating that while in this period there was no *singular global logic* of uneven and combined development, it did nonetheless operate at various regional and trans-regional levels.

Commenting upon the chapters in this volume and the broader debates surrounding them, David L. Blaney and Naeem Inayatullah reflect in chapter 14 upon the potentials and pitfalls of the theory of uneven and combined development in fully overcoming the problem of Eurocentrism. They recognise the importance of the insights gleaned from this perspective in superseding analytically 'internalist' and normatively Eurocentric conceptions of development. Nonetheless, they take issue with the retention of the concept of development in Trotsky's idea. This move, they argue, risks replacing the logic of capitalism with a broader notion of human development, which potentially effaces the presence of multiple and different cosmologies and forms of life in the cultural encounters involved in, and constitutive of, capitalist modernity. They therefore propose 'cultural encounters' as a better conceptual anchorage for the study of historical change and call for a more direct engagement with the ethical and political implications of uneven and combined development.

In the concluding chapter, Anievas and Matin take 'stock' of the contributions to this volume in furthering a more explicit and constructive dialogue and exchange between the fields of historical sociology and world history. Reflecting upon the deeper sources of their mutual neglect, they show how the relational and plural ontology of uneven and combined development might act as productive bridge between these two intellectual traditions, which have recently converged around a shared concern in displacing the methodological internalism and Eurocentrism of earlier approaches to world history and historical sociology. With these concerns and more in mind, Anievas and Matin then outline a number of new and promising avenues for future research.

NOTES

1. For good surveys of the relationship between historical sociology and IR, see Hobden and Hobson (2002), Bhambra (2010) and Hobson, Lawson and Rosenberg (2010).

2. By 'realism' we are referring to realist IR theory not the philosophy of science.

3. For overviews of the debates on Eurocentrism in social and IR theory, see Gruffydd Jones (2006), Bhambra (2007) and Hobson (2012).

4. The following paragraphs partly draw on Matin (2013b, 2).

5. As M. Kamal Pasha (2010, 220) suggests, this problem also marks the 'alternative modernities' approach (Gaonkar 1999).

6. According to Baruch Knei-Paz (1978, 63), Trotsky's use of the concept of 'backwardness' was not intended as a 'moral judgement'. Rather, for Trotsky, 'backwardness' demarcated a 'clear social and historical uniqueness' which terms such as 'less developed' or 'under-developed' do not convey (see further Matin 2013b, 18). Whether Trotsky fully overcame the Eurocentric assumptions so often inscribed in the use of the idea of 'backwardness' is nonetheless open to debate (see, for example, Cooper's chapter in this volume). For a recent attempt to reformulate the concepts of 'backward' and 'advanced' on firmer non-Eurocentric grounds, see Anievas and Nişancioğlu (2015, 55–56).

7. But see the collection of contemporary Marxist writings in Day and Gaido (2009) that somewhat problematises the view that Trotsky was alone in arguing for the strategy of permanent revolution.

8. Justin Rosenberg's PhD supervisor, Fred Halliday, must also be given credit as he had also used uneven and combined development in conceptualising modern revolutions (esp. Halliday 1999). Nonetheless, within Halliday's work, the idea remained something of an after-thought; Halliday never systematically integrated the concept into his theoretical understandings of revolutions thereby never realising the potential of uneven and combined development as a social theory of 'the international'. As far as we are aware, the first IR scholar to explicitly draw on Trotsky's idea in theorising world politics was Robert Gilpin (1981, 177–80)—though in his work the concept played a marginal role.

9. For some notable discussions of uneven and combined development over the intervening period, see Horowitz (1969), Mandel (1970), Novack (1972), Romagnolo (1975), Knei-Paz (1978), Deutscher (1984), and Elster (1986).

10. For an extensive list of this contemporary literature, see https://unevenandcombineddevelopment.wordpress.com/.

11. The following paragraphs partly draw on Matin (2013a, 370).

Chapter 2

Uneven and Combined Development

'The International' in Theory and History

Justin Rosenberg

The idea of uneven and combined development (UCD) was originally formulated by the Russian revolutionary, Leon Trotsky, in the early twentieth century.[1] Largely neglected for several decades, it has recently undergone a significant revival, with over 70 articles about it being published in the last ten years alone.[2] Arguably this newfound popularity reflects the properties of the idea itself—for it is at once both simple and yet profound. The simplicity can be grasped if one considers the phrase itself, which draws together three claims about the human world.

- The world is **uneven**: it contains not one but many societies of many different kinds, different levels and stages of development, some stronger and richer than others and so on;
- This is not just a comparative fact about the world. Because these societies co-exist, they also interact with each other—their existence is **combined**;
- And this interaction is itself a key driver of historical **development** and change. So much so, that we cannot understand the world if we do not factor it in.

This summary perhaps also makes it clear why the current revival has been occurring predominantly in the field of international relations (IR). After all, it would be hard to imagine an idea that does more to emphasise the importance of IR for understanding the world around us. And yet, stated on its own in this way, the idea can also appear to be simply obvious. How then is it profound? Why all the fuss about 'uneven and combined development'? In order to answer these questions, we need to recall the context of the idea: we need to know what problems it solves, so that we can see how powerful it can be.

This chapter seeks to meet these needs by setting out the idea in four parts. First, we shall provide the general context, so we can see what the problem is that this idea addresses—the problem of the international. Then, we shall recall how this problem first presented itself to Trotsky and how it led him to produce the idea of uneven and combined development. Third, we must consider the question of how big an idea this is: does it relate only to the modern world, or did Trotsky stumble upon something that applies to human history as a whole? And finally, we shall return to the present day and ask what this idea can tell us about the world in the twenty-first century.

THE PROBLEM OF THE INTERNATIONAL

The international dimension of human affairs is all around us. Nobody who read the newspapers in 2014 could have missed the souring of relations between Washington and Moscow over Syrian chemical weapons, or the Edward Snowden affair, or events in Ukraine; they could watch the wrangling among Eurozone states over economic policy and bail-outs; they would know about French military interventions in sub-Saharan Africa and so on. International politics, it seems, are always in the news.

But the international dimension is not only something 'out there' in the military and political struggles between states. It is also part of a population's domestic public consciousness of itself as a national society. This too can be readily seen in the media. It shows up in the endless stream of *comparisons* through which people are continually placing their own society in an international setting in order to criticise it, or boast about it or make demands on it in some way. People compare: rates of economic growth, or manufacturing productivity or monetary inflation; standards of education or other public services; and levels of social justice and democracy. In all these cases, and more besides, politicians, think tanks, academics and campaigning organisations of all kinds are continuously comparing how things are done in other societies, and what can be copied and applied to improve things in their own society to prevent it from falling behind.

And of course societies do not relate to each other only through comparison. They are also materially *interdependent* in all kinds of ways. Even the fresh fruit and vegetables in a typical supermarket come from all over the world. But that is only the start. Modern industrial economies depend extensively on both importing and exporting goods and services of all kinds. Indeed, globally, '[t]he sum of exports and imports is now higher than 50% of global production' (Nagdy and Roser 2015). Cut these off, and many societies would grind to a halt.

Finally, even the things that appear as most distinctively national achievements often turn out to be in part the result of *interactions* between societies.
Nothing could seem more English than the English language: and yet we know
that it is actually a mixture of the Latin, Saxon, Norse and French languages
among others. And those different ingredients are not just linguistic influences: they are the sedimentation in language of the influence of the Romans,
Saxons, Vikings and Normans on British social and political history too.

And this point can apply to some very large things indeed. In 1620, Francis
Bacon, the English philosopher and father of modern scientific method, wrote
that the modern world was marked off from the past by the impact of three
main inventions: gunpowder, the printing press and the magnetic compass.
Between them, he wrote, these inventions had done more than any empire or
religion to lift Europe out of the darkness of the Middle Ages (Bacon 1960,
118). Unknown to Bacon, all three of these had originated in China and had
been transferred to Europe through processes of indirect trade and communication (Hobson 2004, 123, 185, 186). So, even the rise of the West that did so
much to shape the modern world was in part interactively produced.

Now, all these examples suggest three basic things about the significance
of the international dimension. First, the fact that the world is divided into
many countries is a major and enduring feature of social reality. Second, the
consequences of this fact reach right down into making individual societies
what they are internally too. And finally, it therefore follows that if one sets
out to build a social theory to explain what happens in the world, then these
two facts—that society is multiple and interactive—should be part of the
theory itself.

Once again, all this must appear simply obvious: who could possibly be so
remiss as to build a general theory of social change without explicitly incorporating this interactive dimension? And yet if we try to answer this question,
we soon discover what is meant by 'the problem of the international'.

There are many different approaches to social theory, but most of them rest
in some way on ideas produced by the tradition of Classical Social Theory,
which in turn is dominated by three thinkers in particular: Karl Marx, Max
Weber and Emile Durkheim. These authors knew, of course, that the world
contained many countries. And Marx in particular wrote a great deal about
the international politics of his day. And yet none of them, not even Marx,
made the co-existence and interaction of multiple societies part of their
model of what societies are and how they change. Nor is this just a point
about Classical Social Theory. Many writers today argue that as a result of
that original lacuna, modern social science continues to suffer from what
is called 'methodological nationalism'—that is, unwittingly thinking about
societies as if they really were self-contained entities. The most famous

post-war historical sociologist, Theda Skocpol, launched her career with an article that was partly about this problem, and which contained a section entitled: 'Wanted: an Intersocietal Perspective' (1973, 28). Twenty years later, Zygmunt Bauman argued that this remained 'a most urgent task faced by sociology' (1992, 65). And in 1994, Friedrich Tenbruck pointed out—no doubt for the hundredth time—that by failing to include the international, modern social theory was hopelessly contradicted by what he called 'the well-known, massive facts of history', because we all know that societies do not exist in isolation (1994, 87).

Now, one might expect that this problem would have been solved long ago by the existence of IR as a discipline. After all, IR is all about relations *between* societies. Unfortunately, however, IR has allowed itself to become part of the problem. How so?

Kenneth Waltz, arguably the most influential international theorist since the Second World War, put it like this: 'Students of international politics have had an extraordinarily difficult time casting their subject in theoretical terms' (Waltz 1990, 21). IR students today might think this claim outdated. For it was made at the very moment when IR was experiencing a dramatic widening of its theoretical horizons. From the late 1980s onwards, traditional realist, liberal and Marxist approaches were being joined on the stage by numerous new theories: critical theory, constructivism, neo-Gramscianism, feminism, poststructuralism, postcolonialism and so on. As a result, IR theory today is a very crowded field. And yet Waltz never changed his mind. For him, most of the approaches studied as 'international theories' were nothing of the kind. Instead they were theories of domestic society that people were using to think about international affairs. Such theories, argued Waltz, are not useless, because domestic factors do play a large role in how governments behave internationally. But they cannot be the whole story, because at the international level states also have to deal with each other. And if one's basic model of reality excludes that political multiplicity and its effects, then it cannot avoid wrongly reducing those effects to purely domestic causes.

What Waltz was identifying here is of course the knock-on effect in IR of the original problem of 'methodological nationalism' that goes all the way back to Classical Social Theory. But how (apart from importing numerous 'reductionist' theories) did IR itself become part of the confusion? The answer is that when Waltz saw there was a problem with social theories and the international, his response was not to fix the problem. It was to turn away and produce a completely separate theory of what they had excluded—namely geopolitics. And he advised everyone else to do the same: 'Students of international politics will do well to concentrate on separate theories of internal and external politics until someone figures out a way to unite them' (Waltz 1986, 340).

The trouble was that, brilliant though his new theory was, it was as incomplete in its own way as those he had criticised. They comprised theories of society without the international; and he now produced a theory of the international without society. As a result, there now existed *two* self-contained kinds of theory, neither of which was able to connect to the other. And yet even Waltz agreed that they must be put back together at some point: 'I don't see any logical reason why this can't be done…. However, nobody's thought of how to do it. I've thought about that a lot. I can't figure out how. Neither can anybody else so far' (Waltz 1998, 379–80).

UNEVEN AND COMBINED DEVELOPMENT

One could be forgiven for thinking that this problem—of how to integrate the international into a theory of social change—is a purely intellectual one with no bearing on the challenges people face in the real world. That, however, would be a mistake. For Leon Trotsky, growing up in nineteenth-century Russia, it had a directly political consequence. At the turn of the century, Trotsky joined the movement for radical change. But this movement was caught up in a mismatch between theory and reality that had a paralysing effect on its political strategy.[3] This mismatch in turn was all about the missing international dimension. And it was Trotsky's response to it that produced the idea of UCD.

For any political movement that wishes to change the world, it helps to have a theorisation of the existing situation—a roadmap that explains both the dynamic of change and how the political movement fits into it. The Russian Marxists had such a map, which they took from the *Communist Manifesto* of 1848. There, Marx and Engels, using England as an example, had mapped out how the industrial revolution was transforming society and what that meant about the future. All societies, they wrote, contain within them the seeds of change. In England in the seventeenth century, this had produced a revolution that ended feudalism and introduced a new kind of society—capitalism, presided over by a liberal state. Over time, capitalism was transforming society into two opposing classes of people: owners and workers (bourgeois and proletarians). The struggle between these two would eventually create the conditions for a further revolution through which a third kind of society, socialism, would emerge.

For Trotsky and his fellow Marxists, this socialist revolution was already imminent in the West. And the Russian state too was on the verge of collapse. And yet Russian society did not look anything like it was supposed to according to the roadmap. The Russian state was still under the control of a semi-feudal ruling class, because Russia had never experienced a bourgeois revolution. The bourgeoisie, which ought to have overthrown it long ago, was far too weak to do so, not least because, in a bizarre twist of history, it was the semi-feudal state that was leading the process of industrialisation. The Russian working class was far too small to play the revolutionary role envisaged by Marx, and yet, partly because its employers were not liberal capitalists but a highly repressive police state, it was already *more* revolutionary than its counterpart in more advanced England. Russian industry, meanwhile, still had a long way to go to catch up with England, and yet what there was of it, having being very recently built, was actually more technologically *modern* than most English industry. And yet this super-modern industry was sprouting up in the midst of a sea of peasants who still made up the vast majority of the population.

It is no wonder that the Russian Marxists were paralysed: the roadmap could not tell them where they were. Right up to April 1917, Lenin, who six months later would be leading a communist revolution, was convinced that such a thing was impossible in Russia because it had not even experienced its bourgeois revolution yet (Davidson 2015a, 302).

It was this practical conundrum that Trotsky solved by adding the international into social theory. He argued, in effect, that the contrasting social structures found in the *Communist Manifesto* and the early twentieth-century Russian state were not unrelated to each other. Not only were they based on actual societies that had interacted with each other in real time; but it was the interaction that produced the differences between them. And by tracing out how this had happened, Trotsky not only resolved the political dilemma of the Russian Marxists; he also produced what Theda Skocpol called 'an inter-societal perspective', and what Kenneth Waltz could not work out how to put together: a theory of society that was at the same time an international theory.

Before going any further, it is important to pre-empt a possible misunderstanding. Marxism has often been criticised for possessing a teleological (and hence unilinear) view of history.[4] And it might therefore be assumed that overcoming this limitation would be of purely local significance, devoid of any wider implications beyond Marxism itself. Nothing could be more misleading. In the early post-war decades, Modernisation Theory was probably the most influential social theory in the US social sciences. One of its most famous early exponents was Walt Rostow who published a book in 1960 called *The Stages of Economic Growth: A Non-Communist Manifesto*. And it was just that: a blueprint for how Third World societies could modernise and become like the West. The major criticism that has always been made of Modernisation Theory is that it was a unilinear roadmap that could not understand how Third World societies were actually changing. And in fact a strong critique of this unilinearity grew up around the work of a Russian émigré called Alexander Gerschenkron.

Now, Gerschenkron never references Trotsky, but their arguments are so similar that it is very hard not to conclude that Trotsky's writing formed a major unacknowledged influence on Gerschenkron's most famous work, *Economic Backwardness in Historical Perspective* (Gerschenkron 1962; see also Selwyn 2012). Meanwhile, Walt Rostow went on to become US National Security Advisor during the Vietnam War. And another modernisation theorist, Samuel Huntington, published an article which claimed that American carpet bombing of the Vietnamese countryside was historically progressive, because it was forcing people off the land and into the cities, which was a necessary step in the modernisation of societies (Huntington 1968a). What all this shows is that, on the one hand, the politics of unilinear theories of history do not belong to the Marxists alone. And on the other, Trotsky's idea may already have played an undercover indirect role in the critique of unilinear thinking in the West.

Let us turn now to the original idea itself. Trotsky's exposition of 'uneven and combined development' is scattered across his writings.[5] But we can use these fragments to reconstruct the core of the idea as follows. His foundational move was to change the starting point of social theory. Instead of focusing on a single society—as in the roadmap—he began instead with the unevenness of world development: namely the fact that the world is made up of many different societies of different sizes and kinds and levels. And he pointed out that when industrial capitalism first emerged in Western Europe at the end of the eighteenth century, its first effect was to radically deepen this unevenness by suddenly making European states much more powerful than the rest. And because all these societies co-existed concretely in real time, this deepening unevenness produced a 'whip of external necessity' (Trotsky 1932, 5) that compelled the ruling elites of other societies to change course and try to follow the path of development now pioneered by the industrial societies.

But how could they ever catch up in time? Russia was so far behind that it would take several hundred years for it just to arrive at the conditions that had produced the industrial revolution in England. However, it turned out that Russia did not *need* to repeat English development, because unevenness also produced a second international effect that Trotsky (1932, 5) called 'the privilege of historic backwardness'. Once again, precisely because late developers *co-exist* with more advanced societies, they can directly import the achievements of those other societies and use them without having to reinvent them for themselves. In this way, they leap over intermediate stages of development that would otherwise have been necessary, massively compressing and accelerating the process.

Thus we now have two sources of change that render unilinear change impossible; indeed they break all the rules of how development would happen if there was only one society in the world. And sure enough, as a result of

these two sources, Russia's industrialisation (like China's today) was proceeding much faster than England's had done. However, Russia was not
turning into another England. And this brings us to the third effect of multiple
societies, namely 'combined development'.

Recall that unevenness involves the co-existence of societies that might be
at completely different stages of internal development. What this meant in the
case of Russia was that the 'whip of external necessity' imposed itself at a
time when there did not even exist a politically independent middle class that
was strong enough to overthrow the semi-feudal Czarist state. But *someone*
had to respond to the external pressure. And when the Czarist state used the
'privilege of historic backwardness' to build a modern industrial sector, its
purpose was not to create a Western liberal society. It was to extend its own
survival. Thus, the techniques of capitalist industry were now (quite unlike
in England) being combined with an anti-liberal, semi-feudal form of state.
A quite new kind of society was being produced. And Trotsky called this
interactive process of change: 'combined development'.

Once Trotsky grasped the logic of this situation—the way that different
temporalities of development were being spliced unpredictably into each
other—he was able to use it to explain all the peculiarities of Russian development that had so confused the Marxist revolutionaries. But how did that
solve the *political* dilemma they were faced with?

The answer is that combined development turned out to have three meanings. There was the combination of different *stages* of development that
resulted from the importing of advanced technologies into a pre-industrial
society. There was also the combination of different *types* of society, as capitalism fused with different pre-existing social structures in different countries. But there was also a kind of combination of these different *countries*
themselves into a larger whole. For by importing all these ideas and resources
and technologies, Russia was unavoidably becoming integrated into a wider
interconnected structure of capitalist *world* development—but one that was
itself now modified by the inclusion of Russia into it.

Trotsky (1962, 9) called this wider structure 'the social structure of humanity'. And what he saw was that the more capitalism expanded beyond its
original heartlands, the more its global structure was coming to include unstable
hybrids like Russia. Thus, instead of the world as a whole turning into an enormous version of the Marxist roadmap, it was itself becoming an unstable, interconnected hybrid. And although there was indeed no way a revolution in Russia
could produce a socialist society, it might, thought Trotsky, because of all these
interconnections, trigger the long overdue revolution in the advanced countries.

In effect, Trotsky was arguing that just as the global transition to industrial
capitalism was uneven and combined, so too would be the *further* transition
beyond capitalism. In that scenario—an intersocietal scenario—the Russian

revolution, which was unstoppable anyway, finally made political sense. And all the vicissitudes and horrors of twentieth-century 'communism' should not blind us to the intellectual achievement of this idea: for Trotsky had produced an intersocietal theory of social change.

BACKWARDS INTO WORLD HISTORY

How big an idea is 'uneven and combined development'? The question must be faced because most writers argue that it applies only in the modern period of capitalist development that it was initially designed to explain (Ashman 2009; Davidson 2009). But if UCD applies only to one kind of society, then it would not be a general solution for incorporating international relations into social theory. And we do need such a general solution, because we know that throughout history societies have interacted with each other in all kinds of ways. Written records of interactions between political entities are among 'the oldest legible documents' that survive, dating from over four thousand years ago (Bozeman 1994, 21; Watson 1992, 24ff). And in fact Trotsky (1932, 5) himself says at one point that 'unevenness is the most general law of the historic process'. Trotsky never elaborated on this comment, but we can see what it means if we simply take a snapshot of world development at any point in history.

Imagine, for example, a map of the world in 1530 which used different colours to indicate the different kinds of society co-existing at the time.[6] The irregular pattern of colours would immediately reveal that the biggest fact about this world, viewed as a whole, really is its radical unevenness. For it would form a tapestry in which several different kinds of human society, which had emerged at different points in history, are co-existing in real time. One colour might denote the great state-based power centres of the day (European, Ottoman, Safavid, Mughal, Ming, etc.), each of them rooted in a different regional civilisation, having different histories, different cultural worldviews and different ways of organising politics and society. But the world was not only composed of states and empires. A second colour would mark the vast areas of Asia, Arabia and North Africa that were occupied by nomadic pastoralists—tribal societies in constant motion with the seasons, living off their herds of livestock. A third would indicate those parts of the world still covered by communities of settled farmers organised in family and tribal groupings of the kind that preceded the original emergence of state organisations. And a fourth would be needed for the huge areas (especially in the Americas and Australasia) that were still composed of hunter-gatherer groups.

And of course these different societies were interacting with each other. The nomadic peoples of the Eurasian steppe-lands periodically erupted in great campaigns of conquest that could overwhelm the surrounding civilisations—a perennial 'whip of external necessity' (Wolf 1982, 32–4). When Marco Polo visited China in the thirteenth century, he found it had been completely conquered by the Mongol nomads.

And there were also interactions *among* the civilisations of the time. The transmission of inventions indirectly from China to Europe has already been mentioned. But by the time of this snapshot, Europe had also received an infusion of ancient Greek learning from the Arab world that helped stimulate the Renaissance. And in 1530, the Iberians were conquering America and unlocking huge resources of silver and gold that would buy them into the Indian Ocean trade of Asian societies that were still much wealthier than Europe. So, multiplicity and interaction played a major role in the rise of the West (Hobson 2004; Anievas and Nişancioğlu 2015). And Trotsky's idea therefore provides an antidote to Eurocentric versions of modern world history (Matin 2013a).

Going further back, Trotsky's own society of Russia originated in a fusion between two completely different types of society. In the tenth century, a branch of the Scandinavian Vikings called the Rus settled in what is now Ukraine, in order to secure their trade with Constantinople, the capital of the Byzantine Empire. It was from this relationship that the first Russian state was born, and from which it received the Cyrillic alphabet, the Greek Orthodox religion and the Byzantine code of commercial law. Kiev did not have to reinvent these artefacts of Byzantine civilisation—it accessed them ready-made through the 'privilege of historic backwardness' (Bozeman 1994, 327ff).

In fact, the importance of interaction reaches all the way back to the very earliest known civilisation. Ancient Sumer was built on a flood plain, which was ideally suited to agriculture but was completely lacking in the metals and timber and precious stones that became central to Sumerian city life. All these had to be imported through interactions with surrounding communities (McNeil and McNeil 2009, 50; Smith 2009, 25).

Why go back so far? And what do all these examples tell us? First, they tell us that Trotsky was right: uneven and combined development really is a universal in human history, and should therefore always have been part of our basic model of the social world. Second, they also show that the whip of external necessity and the privilege of historic backwardness are repeatedly generated across history as routine effects of the multiplicity of societies. Through these effects, uneven development underlies two of the most elemental problematics in human affairs: the problematic of security and the problematic of cultural difference.

And finally, what does all this show us about IR? Here we must be careful. We cannot say it shows that inter*national* relations extend all the way back in history, because nation states are modern. But the claim that needs to be made here is actually even bigger than this. These examples show us what the international really is. It is not just a by-product of modern capitalism. It is the form taken today by a central feature of human history: namely the fact that social existence has been multiple and interactive right from the start.

FORWARDS TO TODAY

How then is Trotsky's idea relevant to the world in the twenty-first century?

We need not look far to find really striking examples of combined development today. In Saudi Arabia, a tribal system of politics has been grafted onto an industrialising society, so that the state, which owns the wealth of society, is itself the property of a 7,000-strong extended family of princes. The forcing together of the old and the new rarely comes in more extreme forms than this. And yet a significant fraction of the world's energy supply rests on this peculiar political hybrid (and the events of 9/11 and after showed just how unstable and destabilising this hybrid could be). In China, a Communist government presides over the most rapid and enormous process of *capitalist* industrialisation ever seen—creating in the process the second largest industrial economy in the world. And in Iran, a theocratic revolution that has no precedent in Shia Islam, let alone the textbooks of Western social theory, has been locked in a confrontation with the great powers over its use of advanced nuclear technology. Because we live with these examples every day, we forget how truly remarkable they are. Their peculiarities could never be explained by internal development alone—intersocietal pressures and opportunities have created these hybrids and woven them into 'the social structure of humanity'. They are a sign of the need for Trotsky's idea in contemporary social analysis.

But what about 'the social structure of humanity' itself? What is the overall shape of uneven and combined development in the world today? Arguably, the key here remains what it has been for more than two centuries now: namely the radical unevenness in space and time of industrialisation as a global process. In the nineteenth century this unevenness suddenly unbalanced world development and led to an unprecedented world domination by one region—Europe. But it also created a geopolitical roller coaster inside Europe as late developers like Germany and Russia caught up with Britain, but on the basis of very unstable socio-political structures created by their combined development. In the twentieth century, the contradictions of this regional unevenness produced first the two world wars and then, as a direct outgrowth of the case first analysed by Trotsky, the Cold War which dominated world politics right up to the 1990s.[7] In the twenty-first century, with the long-delayed industrialisation of the Asian giants, this same historical unevenness of world development is finally bringing an end to the Western Age of world history as we have known it (Buzan and Lawson 2015).

At the centre of this process is China, a country that endured a whip of external necessity so intense and prolonged that it has been named 'the century of humiliations'. Using the privilege of historic backwardness, Chinese industrialisation is now occurring on an even more accelerated, compressed scale than the other late developers before it. And like others before it, Chinese combined development is also scrambling and reshuffling the sequence of stages set out in the roadmap. Capitalist industrialisation organised by a semi-feudal Czarist monarchy was peculiar enough. But capitalism presided over by a Communist state is surely the most peculiar, most paradoxical combination so far.

Furthermore, its impact on the social structure of humanity today is one of *the* central themes of contemporary world affairs, in at least two key ways. By producing the sudden rise of China as a great power, uneven development is driving a geopolitical revolution as the United States hurries to disentangle itself from Europe and the Middle East in order to concentrate on its famous 'pivot to Asia'. At the same time, a new structure of economic interdependence has grown up that has already had major consequences for world development. As we know, from the 1990s onwards, China's export-oriented model of development produced a tidal wave of cheap products that counteracted inflationary tendencies in Western economies. In addition, Chinese purchases of US treasury bonds helped to keep US interest rates lower than they would otherwise have had to be to finance the trade deficit. The net result of this was surely an extension of the global economic boom of the 1990s, and arguably much higher levels of sovereign and private debt when that boom finally collapsed in 2007–2008. The claim is not that China caused the crash. It is rather that international uneven development, with its deflationary effects and global trade imbalances, is a key ingredient of the economic crisis we are still living through today.

It is in the nature of UCD that complex, dialectical relationships form between advanced and rapidly developing societies. Through these relationships, different social formations are both newly produced and woven together into a historically specific 'social structure of humanity'. And the future of world affairs then arises not from a pure model of any single type of society but from the shape and consequences of these global patterns of combined development.

In the light of all these examples (ancient as well as modern) we can now formulate UCD not just as a claim about the nature of historical process but also as a distinctive *method* of analysis. The elements of this method are given in the sequence of terms making up the phrase itself: **uneven, combined, development**. Thus, when seeking to explain any given event or phenomenon, we first use the concept of *unevenness* to invoke the international dimension: what is the wider intersection of different forms and temporalities of development that frames the context of this event or phenomenon? Second, we specify the empirical consequences of that intersection. What pressures of 'external necessity' does it produce for the societies involved? Conversely, what additional possibilities does it generate for social change, over and above those arising from their internal structures? And how are the particular features and temporalities of different societies therefore being concretely *combined* by the historical process? Third, we ask what unique dynamic of combined *development* arises from this dialectical process, and how far its 'peculiarities' explain the event or phenomenon we are trying to understand.

But has this method not simply replaced the false logic of 'internalism' (Tenbruck 1994) with an equally false 'externalist' assumption (that 'the international' explains 'the domestic')? Worse, does it not detach external factors from any historically specific context and 'ontologize' them into transhistorical logics that operate independently of the kinds of society involved? By asserting a 'universal law of unevenness', and deriving a general 'whip of external necessity' and 'privilege of historic backwardness', has UCD not simply reified 'the international'? (Teschke 2014).

The danger looks real—until we hold it up to the actual method of UCD just outlined. For every conjuncture of uneven development is necessarily made up of the particular social formations themselves, with their unique 'domestic' characteristics as they co-exist at a given point in their own inner histories. The causes arising from these internal structures are not replaced by external ones; instead, they are rescued from the fallacy of unilinear thinking by being relocated in a wider field of causation that now includes the *conjunction* of social formations, as well as their inner make-up. In this respect, UCD leads to *more* historical specificity, not less: for it requires the empirical identification not only of a particular social formation itself but also of the shifting configurations formed at any moment by its co-existence with others.

Who truly wishes to return to a form of theorising that does not include the interactive dimension that arises from these configurations? And yet how can this be avoided unless we incorporate the fact of multiplicity and interaction into our conception of social development itself?

CONCLUSION

One final point remains to be made. It is a point that carries us away from the global political economy. And yet it is also, if anything, even larger in its implications. We suggested earlier that international relations is the distinctive form that UCD takes in the modern world. But the logic of the idea is that it cannot be the only such form—or to put it another way, UCD enables us to track the significance of the international far beyond the normal subject matter of IR itself. This is because the multiplicity of societies entails inter-actions not only of politics and economics and technologies, but of every other dimension of social existence too. It includes ideas, religions, literature, music, cinema and all the other ways that humans construct their worlds cul-turally as well as in physical and organisational ways.

It follows that some version of Trotsky's idea can be used to map the role that intersocietal influences play in all the different national traditions of these cultural processes. And if we use it in this way, it will surely reveal that—culturally as well as politically—the interactive multiplicity of human societies is not only a constraint and (sometimes) a threat, but it is also a fun-damental source of creative change and innovation in human history.

Like World-Systems Theory or Postcolonial Theory, UCD is thus an idea whose application is not limited to any one field. In principle, it can speak right across the social sciences and humanities. For all these disciplines study social practices and processes that are formed in the context of multiple interacting societies. And this thought points to an ironic conclusion: the final wisdom of the idea of UCD, an idea which can do so much to make intelli-gible the subject matter of IR, may be that to grasp the full significance of the international, we shall have to embrace much more than the discipline of IR.

NOTES

1. This chapter is an edited version of a Professorial (Inaugural) Lecture delivered at the University of Sussex on 26 February 2014. I am grateful to the editors for numerous helpful suggestions in the course of preparing it for publication. The third section ('Backwards into History) and the first three paragraphs of the fourth ('Forwards to Today') have already appeared in 'IR in the Prison of Political Science'. *International Relations* 30(2), June 2016.

2. For a comprehensive bibliography of contemporary writings on UCD, see www.unevenandcombined.com.

3. For the political context of Trotsky's thought, see Deutscher (1954) and Knei-Paz (1978).

4. For critical discussions of this charge, see Erik Olin Wright (1983) and Ellen Wood (1995).

5. Many of the relevant fragments have been assembled into a *Trotsky Digest*, which is available on the 'selections' page of www.unevenandcombined.com.

6. The following discussion is based on an actual map, 'The World, AD 1530', which can be found in *Atlas of World History*, by John Haywood, Sheriffs Lench: Sandcastle Books 2006, p. 4.01.

7. For applications of UCD to the causes of the First World War, see Anievas 2013, Green 2012 and Rosenberg 2013a.

Chapter 3

The Conditions for the Emergence of Uneven and Combined Development

Neil Davidson

Two of the most important contributions of Leon Trotsky to Marxism are his strategy of 'permanent revolution' and what he called the 'law' of 'uneven and combined development'. The two are connected in that the latter was intended to *explain* the conditions of possibility under which the former could take place, first in Russia, then other countries in which similar conditions prevailed, starting with China. Above all, uneven and combined development was intended to explain the unprecedented revolutionary militancy of the working classes in these countries (Trotsky 1977, 907). Until recently, however, these innovations had not received comparable levels of scrutiny. Trotsky's version of permanent revolution—there were several others—was the subject of intense controversy since he proposed it in 1905–1906; his own concept of uneven and combined development, first unveiled in 1932, was barely discussed at all. Why did it receive so little attention hitherto? Why is it receiving that attention now?

Trotsky stated his position relatively briefly in *The History of the Russian Revolution* (1932) and never systematically returned to the subject in subsequent writings. Indeed, apart from a handful of fragmentary comments, usually in the context of other subjects, his entire theoretical discussion can be found in chapter 1 and appendix 2 of *History*. There are, of course, perfectly comprehensible reasons for the priorities which Trotsky adopted in relation to his literary activities. He was trying, with minimal resources, to build opposition to the overwhelming dominance of Stalinism in the world socialist movement, and his subject matter was largely dictated by the practical requirements of that task. His commitment to rebuilding the revolutionary movement, however, deprived him of the opportunity to elaborate several theoretical positions, of which uneven and combined development was the most important. There is therefore some truth in the comment by two critics that, 'Trotsky's concept of uneven and combined development ... remained only a sketch' (Post and Wright 1989, 35).

This would have mattered less if, after Trotsky's death, the movement he left behind had shown any inclination to develop his theoretical legacy. The problems of political direction which it experienced were partly due to a post-war situation objectively unfavourable to revolutionary politics. But many Trotskyists compounded their difficulties by combining extreme departures from Trotsky in practice, notably in their seemingly endless search for substitutes for the working class as a revolutionary agency, with an equally extreme unwillingness to develop the theoretical positions adopted by Trotsky at the end of his life: to do so was 'revisionism'.

Not all of Trotsky's followers displayed such an un-Marxist fidelity to the letter of his work; but even those who did not tended to focus on permanent revolution at the expense of uneven and combined development. Again, this emphasis is perfectly comprehensible in the political context of the time. For over 40 years after the Second World War liberation movements in the colonial and neo-colonial world were dominated by Stalinist, nationalist and populist politics. The most urgent task for revolutionaries was therefore to argue for permanent revolution as a strategic alternative, rather than devote scarce intellectual resources into further exploring the process which made it possible, the existence of which could be taken for granted. Typical in this respect is an otherwise important book by Michael Löwy called *The Politics of Combined and Uneven Development*. The first part is perhaps the most accurate and detailed exposition ever made of permanent revolution, but the promise of the title remains unfulfilled. Löwy devotes precisely three out of two hundred and thirty-one pages to the subject—unmentioned in the index—whose political implications he seeks to discuss (Löwy 1981, 52, 89–90).

Outside of the ranks of Trotskyism proper, a type of academic Marxism influenced by it emerged late in the 1970s, largely around the *New Left Review* (NLR), where a number of the editors were members of the International Marxist Group, the British organisation recognised by the Fourth International. Editor Perry Anderson himself posed Trotsky as an alternative to Western Marxism in his book on that subject, but famously used an Afterword to point to problematic concepts within the Classical Marxist tradition, among which was permanent revolution, the possibilities of which Anderson described as 'unproven'. Uneven and combined development, however, did not even feature as a problem (Anderson 1976, 96–97, 118–19). For many academic Marxists even this level of critical engagement seemed extraordinary, while non-Marxist academics either treated Trotsky's theories with hostility or else never registered them at all (see, e.g., Hirst 1985, 5; Nisbet 1969, 296–97; Wertheim 1974, 23, 69). Since the very few academics to have discussed uneven and combined development conspicuously failed to understand it, their collective neglect of the subject may seem no great cause for regret; but the need to defend revolutionary thinkers from misrepresentation has often provided the necessary stimulus to clarify and extend their thought. In the case of uneven and combined development, this was rarely necessary.

Or at any rate, it was rarely necessary until the last decade of the twentieth century, when the status of uneven and combined development began to change out of all recognition. Quite unexpectedly, the source of the revaluation was precisely the world of academic Marxism which had hitherto largely ignored it. Awarded the Deutscher Memorial Prize in 1994 for *The Empire of Civil Society*, Justin Rosenberg took the occasion of the Prize Lecture to argue that uneven and combined development provided no less than 'the key to the lost history of international relations' (Rosenberg 1996, 9, and 6–10 more generally). The two subsequent decades have seen perhaps the most dramatic reversal of fortune ever undergone by any concept from within the Classical Marxist tradition, much of it due to the efforts of Rosenberg. From being a concept confined to the Trotskyist left, and on the margins of discussion even there, uneven and combined development is now part of the standard theoretical apparatus available to those working in international relations (IR) and to some extent in the social and political sciences more generally.

The efflorescence of interest in uneven and combined development has not of course gone unchallenged, with some scholars denying that there is anything distinctive or even Marxist about it at all:

> Trotsky's theory of combined and uneven development, which has recently been revived to deal with the phenomenon of 'the international' … remains anchored in an economic reductionism. The very notion of 'backwardness' is only acceptable and meaningful as an economic category, and once the component of permanent revolution is removed, what remains is a de-subjectified sociology of catch-up industrialisation for which we do not need Marxism. (Van der Pijl 2010b, 19)

I will in due course try to show that these criticisms of uneven and combined development are wrong, but Van der Pijl has nevertheless correctly identified the role it is now expected to play. Even before Rosenberg's initial 1996 intervention, Michael Burawoy argued that uneven and combined development was valuable as a general exemplar, demonstrating 'the superiority of the methodology of research programmes over the methodology of induction as a mode of advancing social science' (Burawoy 1989, 796). For Rosenberg, it offers the more specific possibility of overcoming two symmetrical absences within the social and political sciences, that of 'the international' from historical sociology and that of 'the historical' from IR (Rosenberg 2007, 479). More recently, two key figures in the current debates, Alexander

Anievas and Kerem Nişancioğlu, have found uneven and combined development itself to be a methodology 'or set of epistemological coordinates', which both draws on a prior 'ontology of human development ... irrespective of historical context' and points towards a theorisation of 'concrete historical processes, be they epochal or conjunctural' (Anievas and Nişancioğlu 2015, 58). Is there anything that this super-concept *cannot* do? Trotsky himself did not make such excessive claims for it and seems to have regretted even describing it as a 'law'. Shortly after the term appeared in print for the first time in 1932, he himself shied away from doing so, writing: 'As a law it is rather vague; it is more of a historical reality' (Trotsky 1972a, 116). The new enthusiasts for his concept have been less willing to recognise that it has any limits in space or time.

More than anything else, Marxists in IR have seen uneven and combined development as providing, not only historical sociology, but Marxism itself with a hitherto missing theory of 'the international'. It is not clear what such a theory could involve from *any* theoretical perspective, given that intersocietal interaction has taken radically different forms and has produced radically different results in different historical periods. Is there a single theory of 'the international' which could account for them all? As we shall see, uneven and combined development is something much more specific and chronologically bounded, but in any case it is being proposed as an imaginary solution to a non-problem. For while it is true that Marxism does not have a theory of the international, it is not evident to me that it requires one. Like his Enlightenment forerunners, above all Adam Smith, Marx was perfectly aware that societies did not exist in isolation from each other and, as we shall see in the discussion of uneven development below, took account of this in his substantive analyses. Marxism *can* provide a solution to methodological or ontological deficiencies of the social and political sciences, but it is necessary to first recognise that these are inevitable given the very existence of the academic disciplines themselves.

At its best, the Enlightenment was able to present an integrated view of human development, above all through its master-discipline, political economy. The turn away from science in bourgeois thought, which Marx dated to the 1830s, saw the splintering of that unity into a series of more or less arbitrarily defined subject disciplines, with 'sociology' attempting—from the very beginning in consciously anti-Marxist ways—to replace the abandoned wholeness of Enlightenment thought. But from the moment it was conceded that a subject called 'economics' could be isolated and treated as a separate area of knowledge this attempt was doomed to fail as an explanation of the social world, although it was of course a tremendous success in providing ideological justifications for it (Davidson 2005b, 11–12; Davidson 2015c, 160–65).

Classical Marxism attempted to resist the fragmentation, which is why, as David Harvey points out, 'disciplinary boundaries make no sense whatsoever from the Marxist standpoint. The technical division of labour is obviously necessary but its social representation is to be rejected'. Marx, for example, 'did not disaggregate the world into "economic", "sociological", "political", "psychological", and other factors. He sought to construct an approach to the totality of relations within capitalist society' (Harvey 2001, 77–78).

Perhaps the clearest explanation of the concept of totality has been given by Bertell Ollman: 'Few people would deny that everything in the world is related to everything else—directly or indirectly—as causes, conditions, and results; and many insist that the world is unintelligible save in terms of such relations. Marx goes a step further in interiorising this interdependence within each element, so that the conditions of existence are taken to be part of what it is' (Ollman 2003, 139). Ollman makes his case in highly abstract form, but it can be concretised. Take 'international relations' or, to be more precise, take one of the subject areas which is discussed under this disciplinary heading: the relationship between the nation-state system (a 'part') and capitalism (the 'whole'). As I have argued elsewhere, it is possible to work through the mediations from the two basic components of the mode of production, the exploitation of wage labour by capital and the competition between many capitals, to the nation-state system without reductionism, or recourse to theories of either historical contingency or intersecting but separate logics (Davidson 2016, 187–220).

What, if anything, does totality have to do with uneven and combined development? The latter concept was an attempt to give concrete expression to what totality might mean within particular 'backward' territories at the moment when industrial capitalism was pushing outwards from the core of the system under the pressure of inter-imperialist rivalry. Combined development is not a process in itself, so much as the *result* of the prior process of uneven development. The latter does indeed operate at the level of the international; but the former cannot because part of what determines the form taken by any particular example of combined development is the response to it by the state and—for better or worse—states are multiple and territorially demarcated from each other, and not international, far less global entities.

THE CLAIMS OF TRANSHISTORICITY

Anievas and Nişancioğlu have written that 'history and theory … are mutually intertwined and reinforcing' (2015, 58). I agree, and this is particularly relevant in the case of uneven and combined development, since the term signifies both a historical *process* and a *conceptualisation* of that process.

In this chapter I am concerned with the circumstances in which the former emerged, but, to write of 'emergence' is to assume that there was a time in history during which uneven and combined development did not exist, that a moment occurred when it became possible, and that a period followed in which the process could—and perhaps still can—be observed in operation.

Trotsky's own views are ambivalent on the subject, although in his most substantive discussions he takes a 'modernist' position, in which uneven and combined development is given a highly restricted chronological compass. In chapter 1 of *History* Trotsky describes combination as involving a mixture of 'archaic and more contemporary forms'. The latter term could conceivably be interpreted in relative terms, except that in the context 'contemporary' clearly means, 'the recent past and present'. Elsewhere in the same work, however, he is more explicit, describing the 'combined development of backward countries' as 'a peculiar mixture of backward elements with the most modern' (Trotsky 1977, 27, 72). But it is precisely this limited conception of uneven and combined development which is being challenged in some of the most interesting contemporary work on the subject (for a rare exception, see Ashman 2009). It is of course perfectly possible for a more capacious notion of uneven and combined development to be valid regardless of Trotsky's own views on the subject one way or the other: theories have an internal logic independent of the theorist. The issue here is whether this is actually the case.

I do not believe that it is. Until the advent of capitalism, societies could borrow from each other, influence one another, but were not sufficiently *differentiated* from each other for elements to 'combine' to any effect. In fact, it was the advent of *industrial* capitalism which initiated both 'the great divergence' between West and East, and—for the first time in history—the overwhelmingly unidirectional impact of the former on the latter which followed. As Rosenberg himself makes clear: 'Imperial China sustained its developmental lead over several centuries; yet the radiation of its achievements never produced in Europe anything like the long, convulsive process of combined development which capitalist industrialization in Europe almost immediately initiated in China' (Rosenberg 2007, 44–45). The detonation of the process of uneven and combined development certainly required sudden, intensive industrialisation and urbanisation. Burawoy is therefore right to describe uneven and combined development as a product of 'the timing of industrialisation in relation to the history of world capitalism' (Burawoy 1985, 99). The immense difference between industrial capitalism and previous modes of production meant that, from the moment the former was introduced, combination became *possible* in a way that it had not been hitherto; but the structural dynamism of industrial capitalism compared to previous modes of production also meant that combination became *inescapable*, as all aspects of existing society registered the impact on them, to differing degrees, of this radically new means of exploitation. 'In contrast to the economic systems that preceded it', wrote Trotsky, 'capitalism inherently and constantly aims at economic expansion, at the penetration of new territories, the conversion of self-sufficient provincial and national economies into a system of financial interrelationships' (Trotsky 1974b, 15). What is decisive is that former levels of stability are disrupted by the irruption of industrial capitalism and all that it brings in its wake: rapid population growth, uncoordinated urban expansion, dramatic ideological shifts.

Rosenberg's position on this has significantly changed since his first intervention in 1996, his more recent work treating the process of uneven and combined development as transhistorical, rather than confined to one period: 'because historical development has always been both plural and interactive, Trotsky's idea may be applied much more widely in historical analysis' (Rosenberg 2013b, 572). Using examples from the Russian state after 800 CE, he has highlighted what he regards as three aspects of combination. First, how 'the course of Russian development was "combined" in the sense that at every point it was causally integrated with a wider social field of interacting patterns of development'. By this he means that Russia was subject to 'inter-societal causality', an environment in which the endless interplay of other states or social forces shaped the country's internal structure in a way that could never be completed. Second, combination also involved 'structures' which 'extended beyond Russia itself'. Among such structures Rosenberg includes 'regional political orders, cultural systems and material divisions of labour'. The third, 'yet deeper' dimension is the consequence of the first two, the creation of a 'hybrid' social formation in which 'a changing amalgam of pre-existent "internal" structures of social life with external socio-political and cultural influences'. Consequently, there 'never existed a "pre-combination" Russia'; at every point its existence was traversed by these influences: 'combined development identifies the inter-societal, relational texture of the historical processes within which the shifting meanings of the term "Russia" crystallized and accumulated'. In general terms, Rosenberg invites us to 'abandon at the deepest theoretical level any notion of the constitution of society as analytically prior to its interaction with other societies' (Rosenberg 2006, 321–25).

Anievas and Nişancioğlu (or at least the former) have also changed their position over the years, although they have always agreed with Rosenberg that uneven and combined development should be seen as a 'general abstraction' applicable throughout human history like 'labour' or 'class'—which is, of course, precisely the point at issue. They do, however, prefer the term 'transmodality' to 'transhistoricity', as this 'highlights the ways in which it only operates *in* and *through* historically distinct modes of production, which provide the explanations for the specific dynamics, scales and qualitative forms of unevenness and combination' (Anievas and Nişancioğlu 2015, 61, 62). The overall conclusion is, however, effectively the same as Rosenberg's: uneven and combined development is not specific to the capitalist era— although Anievas has qualified this assessment in an individually written study, where he notes that in the pre-capitalist period 'occurrences were qualitatively different: irregular, episodic, and thus often not systematized' (Anievas 2014a, 53).

What, concretely, is being claimed here? Take the three components of uneven and combined development set out in Rosenberg's argument from Russian history, but considered in more general terms: societies never exist in isolation at any point in human history, but always interpenetrate each other through, for example, conquest, trade or migration; societies exist in international relationships, for example, as subjects of an empire, as components of a military alliance, or through adherence to a common faith; and consequently, societies always embody fusions of quite different institutions and practices, embodying different levels of development. These are all defensible claims and Anievas and Nişancioğlu show how they can be put to work in the excellent historical case studies of which most of their book, *How the West Came to Rule*, consists. I regard their substantive arguments as having enriched our understanding in a number of fields, and this is also true of other writers who, from similar positions, have made detailed case studies of individual states, notably the recent works by Jamie Allinson (2016) on Jordan and by Kamran Matin (2013c) on Iran. The difficulty I have is that virtually all the conclusions reached in these works would remain unaltered even if every reference to uneven and combined development was removed. On this basis a concept intended to encapsulate a particular international historical process becomes transformed into a term applicable to virtually any situation in which societies interact with and mutually influence each other, as in this discussion of the Neolithic by David Steel: 'In Europe the phase was based on the spread of exogenous technological elements that had for a long time developed elsewhere, hence CAUD [*i.e. uneven and combined development—ND*] is applicable' (Steel 2010, 149–51).

Are we then simply dealing with an example of conceptual overstretch? Extension is not necessarily *over*extension. The concept of 'hegemony', for example, evolved from being a long-standing description of geopolitical domination by a particular state, to being a strategy of Russian Social Democracy by which the working class would lead the peasantry in the 'bourgeois-democratic' revolution, to being Gramsci's much more general term for the way in which the bourgeoisie was able to maintain its rule over the working class by securing its acceptance of the existing order (Anderson 1976–77, 15–34; Thomas 2009, 56–71, 220–28). But across these modifications in meaning, a common theme is still retained, developing rather than abandoning the original concept: leadership, whether exercised by a state over other states, or a revolutionary class over its allies, or a ruling class over the subordinate classes. Contrast the fate of 'hegemony' with that of 'capital', a concept from bourgeois political economy which was similarly adopted and modified by Marxists, initially by Marx himself. In recent years, it has been subject to fundamental extensions through the attachment of pre-fixes such as 'social', 'cultural', 'intellectual', 'natural' or 'human', to the point where it no longer has any connection to the original object of competitive accumulation, but is simply a metaphor for anything of emotional or reputational value (Fine 2010; Hodgson 2014).

But if uneven and combined development has been subject to overextension then, as I suggested earlier, Trotsky himself is at least partly responsible. For Rosenberg, Anievas and Nişancioğlu could legitimately point to a small number of texts in which Trotsky endorses a subordinate transhistorical or transmodal interpretation. The most famous of these is in his last major work, *The Revolution Betrayed*, where he wrote: 'The law of *uneven* development is supplemented throughout the whole course of history by the law of *combined* development' (Trotsky 1937, 300). But this would not be the only time in the history of historical materialism where a Marxist theoretician has been subjected one of their own concepts to inappropriate overextension. More or less contemporaneously with Trotsky, Gramsci was doing precisely this to his notion of 'passive revolution'. From a relatively narrowly focussed means of identifying bourgeois revolutions from above, such as the Italian Risorgimento of the 1860s, it came to encompass virtually any regime of capitalist reorientation, such as Fascism in Italy, or transformation of the labour process, such as Fordism in the United States. But as Alex Callinicos points out, there are real difficulties in applying the same term to both revolutions leading to the domination of the capitalist mode of production and to subsequent changes which do not lead to any 'systematic transformation' but which, like Fascism and Fordism, are '*counter*-revolutionary projects which seek to manage the structural contradictions of the capitalist mode of production'. By referring to different phenomena under the same name, Gramsci's own multiple uses of passive revolution render the concept incoherent. Extended still further by his followers, it loses all specificity and 'runs the risk of just becoming another way of referring to the dynamism and flexibility of capitalism' (Callinicos 2010, 498, 505).

Trotsky did far less stretching of uneven and combined development than Gramsci did of passive revolution but, in any event, Rosenberg does *not* rely on the handful of passages in which Trotsky takes a similar view to defend his interpretation of the former concept. Instead, he effectively argues that Trotsky did not understand, or at least pursue, the logic of his own position:

Trotsky asserted that combined development was an intrinsic, emergent property of uneven development. And he also claimed (rightly, we decided) that uneven development was a 'universal law'. The phenomenon of combined development must therefore also have a more general existence. If so, however, it is not one that Trotsky ever fully explicated. (Rosenberg 2006, 319)

Elsewhere Rosenberg claims that Trotsky's position involves a 'two-step process of abstraction' whose proper subject is 'the laws of history in general', but that this has been obscured. How?

During the first step, the general significance of inter-societal interaction for historical development appears to have been momentarily conflated with the specific (dynamic and universalising) properties of capitalism. And the consequences of interaction, which in fact can be observed across human history, have then appeared (quite misleadingly) to derive their very existence from characteristics particular to capitalism. But universality and interaction are not the same thing. The fact that capitalist society has uniquely universalising (and technologically dynamic) properties does not at all entail that precapitalist development was not interactive. On the contrary, it is the fact that all development—even capitalism—includes this interactive dimension arising from unevenness which explains the phenomenology of modern combined development here apparently derived by Trotsky from capitalism alone. And sure enough, Trotsky himself, despite the apparent conflation, proceeds to take the second step by now invoking 'the laws of history'. (Rosenberg 2013b, 587)

At this point, Rosenberg partially quotes what is probably the most famous passage in *History*. Here is the passage in its entirety:

The privilege of historic backwardness—and such a privilege exists—permits, or rather compels, the adoption of whatever is ready in advance of any specified date, skipping a whole series of intermediate stages. From the universal law of unevenness thus derives another law which for want of a better name, we may call the law of combined development—by which we mean a drawing together of the different stages of the journey, a combining of separate steps, an amalgam of archaic with more contemporary forms. (Trotsky 1977, 27–28)

Rosenberg then continues: 'Modern combined development must therefore be a particular, if particularly intense, instance of a phenomenon (arising from societal multiplicity) which is generic to the historical process per se. This clarification is the only way to make Trotsky's observations about different historical periods consistent with each other'. He then adds in footnote: 'After all, Trotsky himself presents Russian development as having been shaped by both a "whip of external necessity" and a "privilege of historic backwardness" long before the emergence of capitalist society in the West' (Rosenberg 2013b, 587).

As a general rule, when writers begin to argue that, although a particular thinker appears to be taking one position, they are really taking another, a degree of scepticism is usually in order. This is a strategy regularly used by writers in the Political Marxist tradition, for example, when they assert that Marx actually meant the opposite of what he repeatedly said about the primacy of the productive forces in social development (e.g. see Davidson 2012, 155–58). Rosenberg's position is more defensible, given the ambiguities in Trotsky's own writing to which I have already referred, but is nevertheless misleading. For one thing, Rosenberg reverses the order in which Trotsky presents his argument. As the above quotation shows, the latter begins with 'a law of history' (uneven development) and ends with an *outcome* of that law (combined development). Rosenberg effectively argues that, because uneven development produces 'combination' throughout history, the formation of the latter also constitutes a universal 'law'. Now it is perfectly correct to say that (to use Rosenberg's term) 'interaction' between societies takes place throughout history—it is highly unlikely that anyone has ever seriously doubted this—but 'interaction' is not what Trotsky means by 'combination'. It is rather that, in a particular and historically unprecedented ('contemporary', 'modern') context, uneven development produces a social form ('uneven and combined development') which has not previously existed: universal processes can give rise to singular outcomes.

CAPITALISM, EUROCENTRISM AND UNEVEN DEVELOPMENT

Virtually everyone engaged in these debates accepts that, throughout history, 'the whip of external necessity' in the form of economic or military competition has forced those societies capable of doing so to adopt certain manufacturing technologies, military techniques, or state structures at their highest levels of existing development, rather than undergo the entire process of development which led to that point. This is precisely what constitutes 'the advantages of backwardness'. In this respect, uneven development is a genuinely transhistorical process. It was first identified, if not named, by figures in the eighteenth-century German, French and Scottish Enlightenments, then picked up in the nineteenth-century by both Russian Populists and Marx and Engels, before becoming a generally accepted component of Second International thought around the time Trotsky was entering political life. Given that the first articulation of uneven development in this sense that I have been able to discover (a 1712 letter by Leibniz to Peter the Great), was written 220 years before Trotsky took it as the starting point for his concept of combined development, it is remarkable how many commentators continue to conflate the two (e.g. see Davidson 2006, 10–20; Davidson 2012, 287–89; Davidson 2015b, 155–65). The current over-extensions of uneven and combined development repeat the same error by fixing that label on processes which properly belong to the province of uneven development.

For Marx and Engels, unevenness had two aspects. One should by now be familiar. In his 1847 review of a book by Frederick List, Marx specifically rejected the idea that every nation had to repeat the same experience and argued instead that it might be possible for nations to draw on what others had accomplished in their areas where they were most advanced: 'To hold that every nation goes through this development [*of industry in England–ND*] internally would be as absurd as the idea that every nation is bound to go through the political development of France or the philosophical development of Germany. What the nations have done as nations, they have done for human society' (Marx 1975, 281). The other was where relatively advanced societies either conquered the more backward or colonised empty territories, but in both cases imposed the highest level of development possible at the time, higher than those societies they left behind. For example, Marx noted that in terms of 'completeness and systematic elaboration', 'the feudalism introduced into England [*i.e. by the Norman Conquest*] was more perfect in form than that which arose spontaneously in France' (Marx 1973, 490). After 1066 England went from being a territory which had barely emerged out of the Asiatic mode to being the most rigorous and centralised feudal state in Europe. In one of his last letters Engels pointed out that 'the ephemeral kingdom of Jerusalem' established by the Crusaders in the twelfth century was 'the classic expression of the feudal order' precisely because it had been planted in a territory where feudalism had no native roots (Engels 2005, 565). They do not seem to have considered that capitalism might also develop in this way. Why not?

In his preparatory notes for *Capital*, Marx wrote: 'Some determinations belong to all epochs, others only to a few' (Marx 1973, 85). As an example of this, Marx and Engels noted that 'history becomes world history' only as a result of the spread of capitalism (Marx and Engels 1976, 50–51). There have been relatively few modes of production. The illusion of multiplicity is generated by treating variations among those 'Asiatic' societies transitional from primitive communism to class society—'nomadism' for example—as if they were based on fully fledged modes of production. In fact, with the exception of the very few societies based on the slave mode of production, there were only two other types of pre-capitalist society and these both involved modes of production in which a surplus was extracted from a class of peasants: the feudal and tributary modes. There were important differences between them, both in the nature of the respective ruling classes—local landowners in the case of the former and a state bureaucracy in that of the latter—and in terms of how these ruling classes organised themselves; but, because they were both based on the exploitation of the same class, most pre-capitalist societies seem to have involved elements of both, with one or the other achieving dominance at different times (Davidson 2012, 539–551; Davidson 2015b, xii–xvii, chapters 2 and 3; Haldon 1994, 63–69; Wickham 2005, 57–61). Those cases which were the purest examples of one variant or the other (e.g. feudal England or tributary China) had quite different possibilities for capitalist development.

Some theorists have argued that to argue in this way is Eurocentric, since it allegedly ignores both the timing and extent of the Eastern influence on Western development, perhaps even the way in which Western capitalism was only made possible by colonialism (Bhambra 2011, 678; Hobson 2011, 164). These claims lack all specificity in outcomes as we are ushered across the centuries from England, to Britain, to Western Europe, to Europe as a whole, and to the West in general. But the central claim is in any case factually wrong. On the one hand, some Western European states, notably Spain and Portugal, certainly plundered South American and parts of Asia from the late fifteenth century onwards, but they were *not* the original sites of capitalist development for much the same reason that the Chinese, Mughal and Ottoman tributary empires were not: the existing states—absolutist in the Peninsular cases—were strong enough to block or, as in the case of Spanish rule over Catalonia, at least temporarily retard capitalist development. On the other hand, modernising elites in Italy, Germany and Japan (the latter of which is of course in 'the East') were able to overthrow the existing states in the 1860s and make the transition to capitalism in highly compressed timescales, but they only acquired their empires *after* the transition was complete. Only for a handful of states or territories in Western Europe—sequentially, the United Netherlands Provinces, England, Catalonia, Scotland and France—could it seriously be argued that their initial development on a capitalist basis was aided by expansion beyond Europe.

One of these authors, John M. Hobson, has adopted the transhistoric interpretation of uneven and combined development—and inadvertently revealed some of the problems with this approach—to argue that it applies to Britain, which should be seen as 'the classic case of late industrialisation', rather than Russia. By 'late', Hobson means that, down to 1800, Britain was less developed than China and by 'uneven and combined development' he means this: 'Britain was only able to industrialise because it actively borrowed and imitated so much of that which had underpinned China's industrial and agricultural revolutions some 700 and 1100 years earlier, respectively. And it also emulated various methods that had been pioneered in India, which was enabled in large part through the British colonial presence there'. He concludes that 'at no point in the rise of European capitalism in its *longue durée*

(800–1800) could we describe its development as purely "self-made" under conditions of "even and separate development"' (Hobson 2011, 163–65).

Hobson constantly elides the distinction between development and *capitalist* development—his vagueness about the latter is illustrated by the outlandish notion that the transition to capitalism in Europe began in 800, at a time when feudalism had still to be consolidated across most of the continent. But Britain was not 'developing' in some generic sense, but in terms of the way in which it was increasingly dominated by the capitalist mode of production, which China was not. It is important to know the number of Africans transported to the Americas as slaves, or to know the amount of cotton transported from India to the North of England as material for manufacture; but these did not *lead* to changed social relations of production in a handful of areas in Western Europe where this actually took place. On the contrary, they were able to feed expansion in these areas only because social relation of production had *already* been transformed. External factors may have allowed space for these changes to take place without interruption—this is precisely what Anievas and Nişancioğlu argue (2015) in relation to the conflict between the Hapsburg and Ottoman Empires—but that is an enabling condition, rather than a causal factor.

The emergence of the original group of capitalist states extended for the 300 years between the outbreak of the Dutch Revolt in 1567 and the completion of German Unification in 1870. Comprising less than twenty states in all, very few of them made the transition to industrial capitalism, as it were, 'organically': 'Only a minority of countries has fully gone through that systematic and logical development from handicraft through domestic manufacture to the factory, which Marx subjected to such detailed analysis' (Trotsky 1940, 41). And some of these 'countries' were either stateless nations like Catalonia or federal territories like the northeastern states of the United States. Of the remainder, only England—the second capitalist state to emerge, following the United Netherlands Provinces—shows the pattern of capitalist development in its classic form, which is why Marx used it to illustrate his abstract model of capitalist production in *Capital* (Marx 1976, 90, 876).

Capitalism in England was certainly a product of *uneven* development. Anievas and Nişancioğlu have argued that the 'privilege of backwardness' and the 'disadvantages of priority' were respectively allocated to Europe— or at least North-Western Europe—and the Ottoman Empire (Anievas and Nişancioğlu 2015, 104–6, 146). Like these authors, I reject Political Marxist claims for the supposedly unique development of capitalism in England, but it is clear that capitalism developed more powerfully than anywhere else in Europe, the most relevant comparison being with France. 'Sufficiently near to the most advanced feudal societies to have high levels of technical resource at her disposal', writes Guy Bois, '[England] was also sufficiently underdeveloped to have escaped the consequences of the fossilization of social relations which feudal reorganization induced'. As Bois explains (1985, 114), 'the relative backwardness of England's social evolution as compared to France was to prove its trump card in the transition from feudalism to capitalism'. Far from England being emblematic of Western uniqueness or superiority, it was backward even *within* Europe.

Marx himself drew attention to the way in which England was then able to benefit from the experience of countries which had earlier undergone incomplete transitions to capitalism, starting with the Italian city-states:

> The different moments of primitive accumulation … are systematically combined together at the end of the seventeenth century in England; the combination embraces the colonies, the national debt, the modern tax system, and the system of protection. These methods depend in part on brute force, for instance the colonial system. But they all employ the power of the state, the concentrated and organised force of society, to hasten, as in a hothouse, the process of transformation of the feudal mode of production into the capitalist mode, and to shorten the transition. (Marx 1976, 915–16)

Both the date ('the end of the seventeenth century') and the reference to the role of the state are central here. The capitalist state in England was consolidated at the completion of the bourgeois revolution in 1688, at a time when its economy was still dominated by agrarian, mercantile and financial capital. The significance was twofold: industrial capitalism arose within the context of a society where the state was already dedicated to the accumulation of capital; and that state had a far greater capacity for absorption and renovation under pressure than rival pre-capitalist states (Stone 1983, 18–19). In other words, the extent to which Britain, or perhaps England, appeared to represent an *ancien régime* was an indication of its adaptive modernity, rather than the opposite.

The internal pressures to which England was subject were in any case containable because of the extended timescale in which industrialisation took place. But the experience of subsequent countries was not just different from that of capitalist England, the difference was *caused* by its prior existence, which altered the conditions under which subsequent capitalist industrialisation took place. Their pace of development was also relatively faster, partly because of the urgency of acquiring the attributes of capitalist modernity, partly because the long period of experiment and evolution, characteristic of the Dutch and English pioneers, could be dispensed with. The gradual, dispersed and unplanned nature of the process in England had implications for both the structure of the working class and the nature of the class struggle, both of which are in stark contrast to the forms these took later under actual conditions of uneven and combined development. Workplaces remained relatively small, until very late in the nineteenth century. As a result, trade union struggles were typically defensive of traditional or at least transitional forms of labour (Calhoun 1982, 55, 60, 140; Zmolek 2013, 509–792).

The experience of the second wave of capitalist industrialisation was quite different. By the middle decades of the nineteenth century, the pressure of military and commercial competition between the actual or aspirant great powers forced at least some of those which were still absolutist or tributary states to adopt the current stage of development achieved by their already capitalist rivals, if were to have any chance, not only of successfully competing, but of surviving at the summit of the states-system. In very compressed timescales they had been able to adopt the socio-economic achievements of Britain to the extent that they became recognisably the same kind of societies, without necessarily reproducing every characteristic of the Anglo-Saxon pioneer: where backwardness remained it tended to be in the nature of the political regimes led by monarchs or emperors supported by a landowning aristocracy.

The process of industrialisation and, consequently, the character of the class struggle took respectively more intense and explosive forms. In the first wave, which consisted of the United Netherlands, England and possibly France, class differentiation took place *prior* to industrialisation. In the second wave, which included Germany and Japan, the transition to capitalism was 'virtually contemporaneous' with industrialisation which was forced on the state by external pressures, leaving the bourgeoisie relatively weak and with less room for manoeuvre in terms of making concessions to working class movements (Looker and Coates 1986, 98–101, 112–13). Compare Scotland and Prussia to England. By the early nineteenth century, the enormous tension produced by industrialisation was heightened in both cases by undemocratic state forms, and expressed itself in moments of sharp class struggle, above all the 1820 general strike in the former and the 1848 revolution in the latter. 'Scotland entered on the capitalist path later than England,' wrote Trotsky in 1925, 'A sharper turn in the life of the masses of the people gave rise to a sharper political reaction' (Trotsky 1974a, 37). Similarly, he wrote of the consequences 'when the productive forces of the metropolis, of a country of classical capitalism ... find ingress into more backward countries, like Germany in the first half of the nineteenth century' (Trotsky 1972b, 199). But because these societies *did* make the transition to the ranks of the advanced societies, either as a component part of another national formation (Scotland/Britain) or the centre of one (Prussia/Germany), these moments passed with the tensions that caused them. The key point is that in both cases *the state was transformed*, along the same lines as in England, but over a much more compressed period of time, in order to direct rapid industrialisation and contain the social tensions which it produced.

But not even the impact of industrial capitalism is sufficient to explain the historically unique, combined outcome of uneven development in the nineteenth century. By the outbreak of the First World War membership of the dominant states was essentially fixed. Those states which were capable of achieving parity with, or even superiority to those which had undergone first wave industrialisation, had done so. But there were two other aspects of uneven development, both identified by Lenin in *Imperialism: The Highest Stage of Capitalism* (1916). One was the *ongoing* rivalry between the great powers, which involved them constantly trying to overtake each other in a contest for both economic and geopolitical supremacy that would continue as long as capitalism itself. This rivalry led in turn to the other aspect: the developed imperialist states collectively but competitively asserting their dominance over two other types, described by Lenin as 'the colonies themselves' and 'the diverse forms of dependent countries which, politically are formally independent but in fact, are enmeshed in the net of financial and diplomatic dependence', like Argentina and Portugal (Lenin 1964, 263–64). It was only at this point in history that the limits of uneven development were reached.

THE TIMES AND SPACES OF COMBINATION

The final factor leading to the emergence of uneven and combined development was the *response* to this irruption within those areas which were soon to be designated as 'backward', the *extent* to which they could take advantage of the 'privilege of backwardness'. 'Historical backwardness does not imply a simple reproduction of the development of advanced countries, England or France, with a delay of one, two, or three centuries', noted Trotsky: 'It engenders an entirely new "combined" social formation in which the latest conquests of capitalist technique and structure root themselves into relations of feudal or pre-feudal barbarism, transforming and subjecting them and creating peculiar relations of classes' (Trotsky 1976b, 583). Unlike Italy or Germany in the 1860s, these areas were unable to complete the process of 'catching up and overtaking' the earliest group of capitalist states.

The process is perhaps best illustrated by the only Asian country to undertake comparable development during that period. 'In Japan', Trotsky wrote in the 1930s, 'we observe even today ... correlation between the bourgeois character of the state and the semifeudal character of the ruling caste' (Trotsky 1976a, 66). The former outweighed the latter. Indeed, Christopher Bayly (2004, 104) has drawn attention to the similarities between the British and Japanese states after 1868. Between 1870 and 1914, both consciously emphasised the role of their monarch-emperors, the pre-existing symbolism of the crown being used to represent national unity against two main challenges: external imperial rivalry and internal class divisions. Both were capitalist states that could be strongly contrasted with feudal-absolutist Austria-Hungary or Russia, even down to the role of the emperor and empresses: 'Russia represented the opposite pole to Japan within the spectrum of authoritarian monarchy—no corporate regime strategy, much depending on the monarch himself' (Mann 1988, 200). The state structure was crucial, as in many respects Japanese development was far more rapid than Russia's, as Trotsky himself noted:

> Even late-developing Russia, which traversed the same historic course as the West in a much shorter length of time, needed three centuries to get from the liquidation of feudal isolation under Ivan the Terrible, through the Westernizing of Peter the Great, to the first liberal reforms of Alexander II. The so-called Meiji Restoration incorporated in a matter of a few decades the basic features of those three major eras in Russia's development. At such a forced pace, there could be no question of a smooth and even cultural development in all fields. Racing to achieve practical results with modern technology—especially military technology—Japan remained ideologically in the depths of the Middle Ages. The hasty mixture of Edison and Confucius has left its mark in all Japanese culture. (Trotsky 1972c, 291)

Backward areas were able to 'unblock' themselves to the extent of making sectional advances in quite specific areas, but were unable to reproduce the overall experience of the advanced; above all the pre-capitalist state remained untransformed. Trotsky emphasises the partial nature of these adoptions throughout *History*:

> Russia was so far behind the other countries that she was compelled, *at least in certain spheres*, to outstrip them.... The absence of firmly established social forms and traditions makes the backward country—*at least within certain limits*—extremely hospitable to the last word in international technique and international thought. Backwardness does not, however, for this reason cease to be backwardness. (Trotsky 1977, 507, 906, my emphasis)

But within these spheres and limits backward societies could attain *higher* levels of development than in their established rivals: 'At the same time that peasant land-cultivation as a whole remained, right up to the revolution, at the level of the seventeenth century, Russian industry in its technique and capitalist structure stood at the level of the advanced countries, and *in certain respects* even outstripped them' (Trotsky 1977, 30; my emphasis).

There were essentially three ways by which combined development came into effect. The first was where feudal-absolutist or tributary states, like Russia or Turkey, were forced under pressure from the Western powers to partially modernise for reasons of military competition. As Trotsky noted, 'the Great War, the result of the contradictions of world imperialism, drew into its maelstrom countries of *different* stages of development, but made the same *claims* on all the participants' (Trotsky 1972b, 199). In Russia this involved both partial agrarian reform and limited industrialisation. Factories using the manufacturing technology characteristic of monopoly capitalism were established in order to produce arms with which to defend feudal absolutism. Here the state acts as an obstacle to the 'revolutions from above' necessary to allow 'catch-up' development in any overall sense. Trotsky noted as a general proposition: 'The [backward] nation ... not infrequently debases the achievements borrowed from outside in the process of adapting them to its own more primitive culture' (Trotsky 1977, 27). In some cases, adaptation is merely decorative, as the Balkan states which were formerly part of the Ottoman Empire (Trotsky 1980b, 83); but even in Russia, 'the state, which was largely staffed by landlords, could never displace those landlords and reallocate the agricultural surplus to industry' (Schwartz 2000, 96). As a result, while 'modern bourgeois republics ... manage their internal tensions ... backward Russian society bursts apart, with contending upper classes and raging lower classes' (Stinchcombe 1978, 76).

The second space of uneven and combined development was occupied by states like China or regions like the post-Ottoman Arab Middle East that had been broken by imperialist pressure. Instead of being directly colonised, these were allowed to disintegrate while the agents of foreign capital established areas of industrialisation under the protection of either their own governments or local warlords. Colonial rule often throws societies backward, as in the case of British-occupied Iraq. Ruling through the Hashemite monarchy after 1920, the regime deliberately rejected any attempts at modernisation, except in the oil industry. Instead, it reinforced disintegrating tribal loyalties and semifeudal tenurial relationships over the peasantry (Gowan 1999, 167). Nevertheless, even within this overall context of enforced backwardness, combined development was visible in the urban centres of oil production (Batatu 1978, 481–2). Combined development was not only experienced in the workplace, but in the entire texture of urban life where capitalism took hold. Shanghai was in the vanguard in terms of both production and consumption. It had textile mills before anywhere in the Southern states of the USA and by 1930 was home to the largest mill in the world; the first cinema in Shanghai opened only 5 years after the first large cinema opened in San Francisco (Pye 1981, xv).

The third space comprised the actual colonies. Not every colonised country experienced uneven and combined development, although ironically, those that did not tended to be those that had escaped colonisation. Ethiopia, for example, 'was a social formation that contained social relations analogous to feudalism', but until the Italian invasion of 1935 and the British occupation of 1941, 'this pre-capitalist system remained almost untouched' (Halliday and Molyneux 1981, 65 and 54–74 more generally). Once the race of imperial territory began in earnest during the closing decades of the nineteenth century, it became necessary for strategic reasons to seize territories which were often of no value in themselves—indeed, which were often net recipients of state expenditure—but which were necessary in order to protect those territories which *were* of economic value, like India (Hobsbawm 1987, 67–69). These territories tended to remain untransformed. But in the latter type of territory, 'transformation' often simply involved consolidating pre-capitalist forms in more easily governable ways, rather than establishing capitalist social relations in any sense: 'Nomads, herdsmen, hunter-gatherers, or even peasants who moved around frequently or indulged in practices such as "slash and burn" cultivation were a nuisance to colonial states and other emerging political authorities which wanted regular taxation' (Bayly 2004, 299). By 1914, these ways of life had been 'eroded' and many of these peoples 'uprooted':

> In some cases, as in the Pacific and the Americas, populations had been slaughtered by white invaders and reduced by disease in a broader replay of the devastation of the *conquista* of the sixteenth century in Spanish America. Elsewhere, as in South and East Asia and parts of Africa, former nomads and 'tribal' people had been forced to settle either as poor share-croppers or penned in to become a pool of migrant labour. (Bayly 2004, 481)

But even in this type of context, industrialisation took place. The British in India were unwilling to allow full-scale industrialisation in case it produced competition for its own commodities, but was prepared to sanction it in specific circumstances for reasons of military supply or where goods were not intended for home markets—a form of 'licenced industrialisation', particularly in textiles (Bayly 2004, 182; Osterhammel 2014, 663).

For Trotsky, the most important consequence of uneven and combined development in all three spaces, but especially in the first two, was the enhanced capacity it gave the working classes for political and industrial organisation, theoretical understanding and revolutionary activity: 'When the economic factors burst in a revolutionary manner, breaking up the old order; when development is no longer gradual and "organic" but assumes the form of terrible convulsions and drastic changes of former conceptions, then it becomes easier for critical thought to find revolutionary expression, provided that the necessary theoretical prerequisites exist in the given country' (Trotsky 1972b, 199). As an example of this he drew attention to the greater implantation of Marxism among the working classes of Russia than in that of Britain. In the case of Russia itself, 'the proletariat did not arise gradually through the ages, carrying with itself the burden of the past, as in England, but in leaps involving sharp changes of environment, ties, relations, and a sharp break with the past. It was just this—combined with the concentrated oppressions of czarism—that made Russian workers hospitable to the boldest conclusions of revolutionary thought—just as the backward industries were hospitable to the last word in capitalist organization' (Trotsky 1977, 1220). Describing the situation prior to the Russian Revolution of 1917, Gareth Stedman Jones has contrasted 'the revolutionary maturity of the Petrograd proletariat, uniquely concentrated in the most advanced factories of the capitalist world' with Britain, 'the most advanced capitalist country', where 'the structure of the metropolitan working class still looked back to pre-industrial divisions of skill and status': 'A few large plants were lost in an ocean of small workshops' (Stedman Jones 1984, 346). Tim McDaniel is therefore correct to note that the militancy of Russian workers was 'the product of leadership by a militant proletarian core of advanced workers employed in modern industry', not 'traced largely to disorientated workers of peasant origin and to young recruits into industry' which emphasises the '"spontaneity" and unpredictability of worker militancy ... denying to it the coherence and ultimate rationality ascribed by Trotsky' (McDaniel 1991, 125).

CONCLUSION

In conclusion, I think it is impossible to treat uneven and combined development seriously without foregrounding what it was intended to explain. Anievas and Nişancioğlu point out (2015, 300–1fn64) that Rosenberg and I have both argued that it can be detached from the strategy of permanent revolution. We do so, however, for rather different reasons. In Rosenberg's case, it is because he has a transhistorical conception of uneven and combined development in which permanent revolution is plainly irrelevant for the vast bulk of human history in which capitalism, and consequently a combination of the bourgeois and socialist revolutions was not in prospect anywhere. In my case, it is because I see permanent revolution as involving two factors, uneven and combined development and an unaccomplished bourgeois revolution; but now that the bourgeois revolutions have all been accomplished—by which I simply mean that there are no longer any pre-capitalist states awaiting transformation into centres of capital accumulation—then the era of permanent revolution has also passed. Socialist revolution per se is still feasible and it is likely that it is more likely to break out where conditions of uneven and combined development prevail, but it is difficult to conceive of how one can talk of leaping over stages when there are no longer any pre-capitalist stages left (Davidson 2015b, 140–44). Does uneven and combined development not usually involve what Burawoy calls 'the combination of the capitalist mode of production with pre-existing modes' (Burawoy 1985, 99)? It can, but it can also involve the destabilising effect of capitalist industrialisation and urbanisation on hitherto relatively stable agrarian communities. 'A political prognosis cannot pretend to the same exactness as an astronomic one', as Trotsky once noted (1973, 73). Nevertheless, if I was asked to predict where a future revolution was most likely to erupt, it would be the state where Trotsky first detected uneven and combined development outside Russia, and which is now experiencing its second coming: China (Davidson 2015b, 179–87). To historicise the emergence of combined development does not mean that we should assume it will come to an end, since this seems unlikely as long as capitalism and consequently uneven development persist; it does mean, however, that our primary focus should be, as Trotsky's was, on its *effects*.

Chapter 4

The Uneven, Combined and Intersocietal Dimensions of Korean State Formation and Consolidation over the *Longue Durée*

300–1900 CE

Owen Miller

Until recently attempts to analyse the history of Korea prior to the twentieth century have tended towards two frameworks: stagnation or progress. In response to this there has been a tendency to abandon any form of long-term historical analysis or to argue that concepts developed to analyse the history of Europe or other parts of the world cannot be applied to East Asia. This chapter will instead argue that the analytical concepts of unevenness, combination and intersocietal development can be usefully employed to develop a historical sociology that moves decisively beyond the stagnation/progress dichotomy and Eurocentric historiography.

Korean history represents a relatively small part of human history, taking place on a peninsula at one end of the Eurasian continent, in certain ways peripheral to the core zones of human civilisation over the last two thousand years. However, its wider relevance will hopefully be apparent in the fact that certain similar problems arise when studying any country or region outside of Europe. The central problem that has confronted historians of Korea over the past 120 years has been how to account for Korea's apparent backwardness and, ultimately, its fall into the clutches of Japanese imperialism. While this problem might be a near universal one for countries that experienced colonial rule in the nineteenth and twentieth centuries, what makes the Korean experience somewhat unusual is that the immediate counterexample with which it was repeatedly compared was not Europe but rather its neighbour, Meiji Japan. By showing that it was possible for a non-European country to escape colonialism and find its own route to capitalist modernity, the Japanese case threw Korea's perceived failure into sharper relief.

Furthermore, for Japan as an aspiring imperial power, the apparent backwardness and stagnation in Korean history provided ample justification for its annexation of the country in 1910. Subsequently, after liberation from colonial rule in 1945, for nationalists in both North and South Korea, the stigma of backwardness was something to overcome. It is significant that these different approaches to the problem of Korean backwardness all remained firmly locked within the framework of methodological nationalism and were either implicitly or explicitly Eurocentric, in that they assumed Europe as the source of modernity and progress and measured Korea (like other parts of the world) against that yardstick. They also both remained fixed in the simple and dichotomous framework of advanced/backward, which implied, either implicitly or often quite explicitly, a set of fixed historical stages that must be followed in a certain order.

How then do we step outside of the simplistic paradigm of advanced and backward, stagnation and progress, to build a picture of human societies developing over time in both their specific complexity and universality? This chapter will seek to reconceptualise the problem of backwardness within a different methodological framework; that of uneven and combined development, although here I will also use the terms divergence and convergence, which I think better capture the nature of long-term historical processes. Alongside this methodology I will employ a particular understanding of Marx's concept of mode of production—centred around the concept of the tributary mode of production—which has important implications for uneven and combined development in the premodern world. After outlining the problem at hand within this new framework, I will use it to examine a series of events and processes over the course of 1,600 years of Korean history, from the early state formation period to the late nineteenth century, paying particular attention to the patterns of divergence and convergence between the premodern historical trajectories of Korea, Japan and China.

Before moving to that analysis, however, this chapter will examine how historians, and particularly Korean Marxists, have tried to address the problem of backwardness, in order to provide a historiographical basis for the rest of my argument.

THE ABNORMAL HISTORY OF KOREA

By the late nineteenth century, the paradigm of Eurocentrism and Orientalism was firmly established in Europe, but it was also being replicated in new forms around the world (Amin 1989). Thus, beginning in the second half of the nineteenth century, Japanese ideologues and historians sought to create a version of the Europe/Asia dichotomy within East Asia itself, based on what one might call a 'Little Divergence' between the supposedly progressive, feudal, market-oriented history of Tokugawa Japan (1603–1868) and the stagnant, Asiatic, state-dominated history of Qing China and Chosŏn Korea. This intellectual project coincided with two streams in nineteenth-century Japanese thought and policy: the desire to 'leave Asia' (*Datsu-A ron*) and the desire for empire, the latter of which was realised in 1895 with Japan's acquisition of Taiwan as its first modern colony.[1]

Thus the context in which Korean Marxists sought to understand Korean history was one where they were faced with a choice between two forms of Eurocentric theory. On the one hand, there was the contradictory Eurocentric-but-universalist paradigm of 'five stages', inherited from Second International Marxism, and later given Stalin's seal of approval. On the other, there was the Eurocentric-but-particularist Asiatic mode of production (AMP), which turned out to be very influential in East Asia (Fogel 1988).[2] In the 1930s and 1940s, most Korean Marxists took the latter option and focused on explaining what they saw as the particularity and backwardness of Korea's historical society via its 'Asiatic' features.

In the 1930s, a local version of the international AMP debate developed within colonial Korea among a number of Marxists, including Yi Ch'ŏngwon, Kim Kwangjin, Yi Pungman, Chŏn Sŏktam, Moritani Katsumi and Paek Namun, the man now considered by many to be the 'father' of Korean Marxist historiography. Essentially their views came down to two positions. One, advocated by Yi Ch'ŏngwon, and to some extent Paek Namun, was that Korean history prior to capitalism had passed through all the necessary stages (primitive communism, slavery, feudalism) but that these stages were in some way untypical and had an 'Asiatic' character. Paek, for example, argued that the primitive communist stage in Korean history was abnormally long, while feudalism developed slowly and had an 'Asiatic form' (Paek 1933, 25). Yi argued that the term Asiatic was 'not a geographical category' but rather a 'special historical category' developed by Marx that could be applied to Russian history as much as to Korean. However, when he lists the attributes of an Asiatic society as 'a feudal or semi-feudal social formation based on patriarchal agriculture; stagnating development; general ignorance; poverty; autocracy; and serfdom' his argument becomes circular. The term Asiatic is supposed to provide a scientific explanation for stagnation, but at the same time stagnation becomes one of its main characteristics (Yi Ch'ŏngwon 1935).

The second position, advocated by historians like Yi Pungman and Chŏn Sŏktam, argued that the lack of progress in Korean history could be explained by its lack of a fully fledged slave stage. Chŏn claimed that despite slavery being a prominent feature of most of Korea's premodern history from the Three Kingdoms period (c. fourth century CE to 668 CE) onward, in all periods slave labour was only one form of labour and never the dominant form

(Chŏn 1949, 22; cf. Miller 2011). The significance of this was that in Europe slave-owning societies such as ancient Greece and Rome had destroyed the remnants of the communal mode of production through the enslavement of a large part of the population. In Korea meanwhile, according to Chŏn, this process was much delayed and led to a backward form of feudalism. Yi Pungman also claimed that the reasons lay 'in the incomplete nature of the transition from primitive communal society to slave society and the similarly malformed transition from slavery to feudalism which meant that feudal society was not able to develop sufficiently'. Like Yi Ch'ŏngwon, he tended to use the Marxist term Asiatic as an explanation for backwardness, writing that it was 'precisely this "Asiatic stagnation" that forced Korea to bear the fate of a backward society' (Yi Pungman 1948, 1).

After liberation in 1945 historians in both North and South Korea shifted towards approaches to the Korean past that attempted to erase backwardness altogether in favour of some form of 'internal development' (*naejaejŏk palchŏn*). As in other postcolonial countries, North Korean Marxists adopted the Stalinist orthodoxy, asserting the law-governed 'normality' of Korean history and searching not for the origins of backwardness but for the 'sprouts of capitalism'. These historians—including some such as Chŏn Sŏktam who had previously held a completely opposite view—now argued that Korea had passed through all necessary stages prior to capitalism and had been independently developing its own indigenous capitalism and even showing signs of social change that would lead to a bourgeois revolution (Petrov 2006). Not only North Korean historians but South Korean nationalist and progressive historians too saw Korean history as having followed a 'normal' path that was then thrown off course and 'distorted' by Japanese imperial aggression and colonisation. Still today in both countries the search for evidence of Korean history's progressive character and the signs of internal social and economic development that can match the European model are fundamental to contemporary Korean historiography.[3]

While their aims in writing the history of Korea were diametrically opposed, the explanations for Korean backwardness advanced by Japanese colonial historians and Korean Marxists were surprisingly similar. In both cases they located the 'abnormality' of Korean history in the lack or underdevelopment of a historical stage, whether *Stadtwirtschaft*, feudalism or the slave mode of production. For the Marxists this abnormality and backwardness could be explained more 'scientifically' with the use of the term Asiatic, derived from a small fragment of Marx's writing. However, their argument tended to become circular, with the existence of stagnation itself explaining stagnation. What colonial historians, Korean Marxists and post-liberation nationalist or progressive historians all had in common was a Eurocentric notion of what was a 'normal' historical pathway. This path consisted of a fixed set of historical stages that could not be skipped, with a definite end point (capitalist modernity, the modern nation state or communism). All these approaches reveal a paradigm, centred around rigid dichotomies of progress/stagnation and normal/abnormal, that is ill-suited to grasp the rich complexity of a single country's history, let alone that of a region or larger field of human history.

RECONCEPTUALISING THE PROBLEM OF KOREAN HISTORY

In this section I will draw on elements of Marxist historical thought in order to build a framework for approaching Korean history, while eschewing the tropes of abnormality, lack and backwardness. I will do this with reference to the Korean case before moving on to a more concrete examination of some of the processes and dynamics of Korean history up to the late nineteenth century. However, my intention is that the framework I outline here can be a useful contribution to the more general discussion of Marxist historical sociology and pre-capitalist societies outside of the north Atlantic region.

First of all, what is the core problem that a new methodological and theoretical framework for pre-capitalist Korean history seeks to address? While for Yi Pungman the key question was how to account for Korean backwardness, from our current standpoint this is inadequate, largely because it tends to reinforce the rigid and static dichotomy of advanced/backward. Moreover, when we consider that since 1945 both Koreas achieved remarkable industrial development and accelerated social change, to focus only on backwardness in this way seems anachronistic. If we are fundamentally seeking to understand Korea's particular historical trajectory, a more apposite research question might be, how did Korean, Japanese and Chinese historical trajectories diverge from each other over the 1,600-year period from 300 CE to 1900 CE? The framework underlying this question is one that assumes the universality of unevenness, and human history as a constant pattern of divergences and convergences within fields of interconnected polities and societies at different scales. In other words, it is a framework founded on the method of uneven and combined development (Trotsky 1962), supplemented by the concepts of divergence and convergence, which help to capture the historicity of unevenness and combination.

However, the starting point of my framework will not be uneven and combined development but rather Marx's concept of mode of production, as this is crucial to any development of Marxist historical sociology. In the first half of the twentieth century, this analytical concept was much abused, and generally came to be understood as a theory of historical stages, much like the theories developed by other nineteenth-century historians and sociologists such as Karl Bücher. Once Marxist historians discovered that it was difficult to apply a fixed set of five historical stages to all of human history, various debates over periodisation ensued, such as the one between advocates of the five stages model and partisans of the Asiatic mode of production. One response to this problem has been for historians to make the mode of production concept more descriptive and less analytical, giving rise to a plethora of modes—beyond primitive communism, slave, feudal and capitalist—that match more closely the actual political and institutional features of historical societies.[4] The response of John Haldon and Eric Wolf, on the other hand, has been to take the concept in the other direction, to emphasise its utility as an abstraction that serves to guide a research programme rather than describe a concrete society (Haldon 1995, 93–94). This is the approach I will take here.

The formulation of the tributary mode of production (TMP) advanced by Haldon, Wolf and Samir Amin returns to Marx's core definition of a mode of production as the means by which surplus is extracted from the direct producers.[5] The TMP concept strips away institutional and political aspects of a particular society and focuses on the fact that in pre-capitalist class societies surplus was appropriated from the direct producers by 'non-economic' coercion.[6] This serves to avoid the problems inherent in a concept of mode of production that might be understood to include particular culturally or geographically specific features (Asiatic mode of production) or could be misunderstood to encompass political and institutional forms, as the feudal mode of production often is. However, this particular concept of mode of production does more than provide terminological clarity: what is most significant is the role it plays as a guide for a research programme.

What this means in practice is that it encourages the historian to ask certain historical questions and pushes us to look for the answers in certain places. So, if all pre-capitalist class societies have essentially been shaped and constrained by the same fundamental social relations, centred around coercive extraction, then how do we account for the great unevenness of pre-capitalist societies, their constant divergence and convergence? Wolf argued that the different forms of class society found in the few thousand years of human history before capitalism occupy a 'continuum of power distributions', with relatively centralised, bureaucratic states at one end, decentralised 'feudal' societies at the other and many possible forms in between (Wolf 1982, 80). Haldon has gone a step further than this in showing how such an insight can become the basis for a research programme, since for him the differences in the way ruling class power is distributed in different societies and the constantly shifting balance of different forms of extraction within societies reflects the ongoing struggle over surplus among different elements of the ruling classes (Haldon 1995).[7] The most obvious way in which this takes concrete historical form is through struggles between states and aristocracies, something that will be amply illustrated in the next section. Rather than focusing on the question of whether tax or rent might represent two different modes of production, this conception of the TMP sees tax and rent as forms of extraction within a constantly shifting struggle between different parts of the non-producing class. In fact, in most historical class societies, the situation has been very complicated, with tax, rent and other forms of coercive extraction, such as slavery and corvée labour, all co-existing. In addition, each of these forms of extraction can themselves be complex and diverse, being paid in cash, in kind or in specialised tribute goods; with aristocrats farming taxes, or paying them themselves; states collecting rents on state or royal-owned estates; and both aristocracies and states owning slaves and levying corvée. All of these forms have existed at various points in Korean history, and for most of Korean history prior to capitalism, they have co-existed. The particular complex of forms of extraction that can be found at a particular point in the history of a society therefore reflects the current state of the struggle for surplus among the segments of the non-producing class. Here Jamie Allinson has pointed out an analogy with the way that capitalist societies are shaped and driven by the constant competition among many capitals, the difference being that in tributary societies the 'division lies not between units competing via the market but between central and local control of the coercive power by which surplus is extracted' (Allinson 2016, 46).

How then does this understanding of premodern class societies, as fundamentally based on forms of coercive tribute, combine with the approach of uneven and combined development (UCD)? UCD starts from what Löwy has called 'the viewpoint of totality'; that is, what in the modern capitalist context might be termed the international (Löwy 2006a, 31–32). This means that the UCD approach is based on the premise of intersocietal development, or the recognition that states and societies always develop in interaction with one another, from the earliest period of state formation up to the present day.[8] However, there is always an 'asynchronicity of development' (Allinson and Anievas 2009), meaning that the tempos and types of development in interacting societies are usually divergent. This gives rise to a second aspect, which is that of combination; or, in other words, the intersocietal adoption of technologies, ideas, cultures, institutions etc., resulting in their implantation within social settings very different to their origins, bringing together elements often understood as belonging to different levels of development.[9] We can thus understand the intersocietal development of human history as taking the form of a series of divergences and convergences among societies at different geographical scales, whether local (e.g. between the northern and southern regions of the Korean peninsula) regional (e.g. Korea and Japan) or continental (between 'East' and 'West'). So, in answer to the question posed above, the continuous struggle over surplus, which usually takes its spatial form as a conflict between central and local power, is always mediated by intersocietal relations (war, trade, cultural and intellectual exchange). New social combinations are constantly forming as a result of intersocietal contact, and thus constitute the terrain on which intra-class conflict over surplus takes place. In turn, this conflict over surplus drives the most fundamental form of divergence between pre-capitalist societies, between those dominated by a central tax collecting/ redistributing state and those in which power is decentralised among local lords, giving rise to such heterogeneous neighbours as Japan and Korea.

THE TRAJECTORY OF KOREAN HISTORY OVER THE *LONGUE DURÉE*

In the following I will show how the framework outlined in the previous section can be used to analyse the particular trajectory and characteristics of Korean history over the long term. To do this I will examine in chronological order some of the important turning points and processes in Korean history over the last two thousand years. However, having already argued that neither the trope of 'abnormal stagnation' nor that of 'European-style progress' have much explanatory value for Korean history, it is necessary to define what those particular characteristics of Korean history are. As I have indicated before, it is useful to understand the ways in which Korean (or in fact any) history is *divergent*, not just from such distant (not to say abstract) comparators as Europe, but also from Japan, and to an extent, China too. While Korea did not shift towards political fragmentation ('feudalism') in the way that Japan did in the centuries either side of 1000 CE, neither did its hereditary aristocracy give way to an appointed bureaucracy to the same extent as occurred in imperial China. In the phrase coined by James Palais, Korean dynasties instead established, over a number of centuries, an 'aristocratic/bureaucratic balance' (Palais 1984). This characteristic was itself closely related to a series of other features. First, Korean history between 668 and 1910 was dominated by three long-lasting dynasties—Silla, Koryŏ and Chosŏn—with only one short interregnum period (892–936), culminating in the exceptionally long-lasting Chosŏn dynasty (1392–1910). Second, aside from some brief, atypical periods, Korean society did not develop a dominant military culture or military class, as happened in Japan. Third, the social status structure was relatively rigid and did not allow for substantial movement between status groups, meaning that slavery survived for a long time and there was comparatively little interchange between the aristocracy proper (the *yangban*) and the secondary status groups.[10]

From Early State Formation to Silla Conquest

State formation on and around the Korean peninsula was intersocietal from the beginning.[11] In fact, it could not have been anything but, as Korean state formation was an example of the universal phenomenon of secondary state formation, taking place on the periphery of Chinese civilisation. This intersocietal interaction took the form of both hierarchical influence from China and peer polity interaction with neighbouring polities to the north and on the Japanese islands. By the late first millennium BCE, at the latest, there existed on the Korean peninsula and in the region to the north (what is now usually referred to in English as Manchuria), agricultural societies based on the farming of rice and other grains, with class differentiation and simple polities centred around chieftains. There is evidence that at times they coalesced into larger confederations (Old Chosŏn, Koguryŏ), but a decisive change came with the conquest of the northern part of the Korean peninsula (the Taedong and Yalu River basins) in 108 BCE by the Chinese Han Dynasty under Emperor Wu (r. 141–87 BCE). The Han empire then proceeded to create a commandery system in the region that would last for more than 400 years. This set up a sphere of interaction where the peoples and polities of the Korean peninsula, and by extension the Japanese archipelago, came into direct contact with Chinese civilisation. Within the main commandery, Lelang, which was centred on what is now Pyongyang in the DPRK, a new hybrid culture developed with the extensive importation of Chinese intellectual and material culture (Oh 2008). The Han commanderies also fought, traded and negotiated with the emergent polities surrounding them. To the north and east was Koguryŏ, often seen as a bona fide ancestor of 'Korea' (especially by the modern North Korean state), which repeatedly went to war with the commanderies and which eventually overwhelmed Lelang in the fourth century CE. To the south were the confederations of statelets known as the Three Han (Samhan) which traded with the commanderies, especially in iron. Rulers of early Korean polities were frequently enfeoffed by the leaders of the Han commanderies, giving them a form of legitimacy that came from the Chinese emperor. With the commanderies there arrived on the peninsula: the Chinese writing system, Chinese-style bureaucracy and official ranks, attire, architecture, philosophy, weaponry, arts and so on.

However, it was not just a matter of emergent local polities interacting (or *converging*) with a stronger and more advanced neighbouring society. As Michael Seth argues (2011, 46), it was the weakening of that stronger neighbour after the fall of the Han Dynasty (220 CE) that allowed the space for autonomous peripheral states to develop, just as the somewhat later decline of the Roman Empire did at the other end of the Eurasian continent. It was the space created by the decline of Chinese hegemony that allowed not only for the outright adoption of Chinese culture and forms of class rule but also their combination with indigenously generated forms to create new centralised monarchical states. This process culminated in the late fourth century CE with the beginning of Korea's Three Kingdoms period, dominated by

Koguryŏ in the north, Paekche in the southwest, Silla in the southeast, along-side the small confederation of Kaya in the central south. This led to a new phase of intersocietal development in which multiple Korean states interacted with multiple Chinese states and also with multiple emerging polities in the Japanese islands, the most prominent of which was Yamato in southern Honshu (Barnes 2007; Pai 2000).

In the period from the late fourth century onward, missionary Buddhism became an increasingly important vector of Chinese civilisation (and to a lesser extent Indian cultural influence) and it is very likely the case that Buddhism was key to the establishment on the Korean peninsula of such important technologies as the Chinese writing system and architecture (Seth 2011, 33). However, Buddhism, Confucianism and other cultural imports were not necessarily adopted wholesale or without adaptation in the Three Kingdoms, and this is where the issue of combination arises. Indeed, we do not have to look far to find combinations of pre-existing forms of rule and culture with newly arrived Chinese forms within the Three Kingdoms. Silla provides some of the best examples, partly because it was the latest developer among the Three Kingdoms,[12] but it was by no means unique. As Seth notes (2011, 38), even the institution of kingship itself 'had to contend with strong, local, tribal and aristocratic traditions' pushing Sillan kings to ostentatiously seek legitimacy in Buddhism by taking Buddhist names and lavishing money on the building of temples.

Two institutions in particular stand out as examples of earlier social forms that survived into the centralised monarchical Silla state and combined with the new social forms. The *Hwabaek* was a council of aristocrats that made important decisions on the basis of unanimity, alongside the monarch, even convening to elect the king himself. Such councils of ministers staffed by members of prominent aristocratic lineages would continue to be a feature of governance in Korea throughout the premodern period, resulting in a monarchy that was very rarely all-powerful. A second Sillan social institution was the *kolp'um* or 'bone rank' system that theoretically organised the whole of Silla society into a series of ascriptive ranks based on birth. At the top were two 'bone ranks': the 'sacred bone' from which kings and queens could be chosen and the 'true bone' who were the most exalted aristocrats, hailing from branches of the royal family and closely related clans. Below these were six further head ranks that encompassed the lower ranking aristocrats and the commoner class. Like Paekche and Koguryŏ, Silla also introduced a system of bureaucratic ranks based on the Chinese model that ran in parallel to the *kolp'um system,* creating a complex enmeshing of ascriptive and bureaucratic status within the aristocracy. We do not know much about the internal dynamics of the Sillan ruling class nor its preferred forms of surplus extraction, but we can speculate that the *kolp'um* system was in part a way of controlling both the ascription of privilege and the distribution of surplus, as a strategy in the struggle for surplus among non-producers. It also seems likely that it had a legacy for later Korean history, with its institutionalisation of clear, codified status distinctions and its emphasis on hereditary lineages over meritocratic bureaucracy (Seth 2011, 40). There is no doubt that the Three Kingdoms period also saw the development of new and more systematic forms of class rule and surplus extraction, most notably the introduction of formal taxation and the rapid expansion of slavery, spurred by near constant warfare between the kingdoms. While it is hard to know just how far state tax collection capacities developed, the discovery of Silla village census records indicates that, by the eighth or ninth century at least, the Silla state had introduced a complex bureaucratic system for classifying arable land and people in order to extract agricultural surplus and labour power (Lee 1984, 80).

The shifting alliances and inter-kingdom warfare of the fifth, sixth and seventh centuries also dragged in Japanese polities and eventually became a full-scale international war in the late seventh century when Silla allied with the Chinese Tang Dynasty to overcome its rivals. Once again the intersocietal stage was decisive in the process of Korean state consolidation as the intervention of the newly established Tang at the behest of Silla allowed the Korean kingdom to overcome its rivals in 668 and then expel the Chinese, creating by 676 the first state encompassing the majority of the Korean peninsula.

The Fall of Silla and Reconsolidation Under Koryŏ

Silla's conquest of the Korean peninsula south of the Taedong River in the late seventh century did not mean that an all-powerful centralised state had suddenly been established. Historically, as states such as Silla have expanded their territory and attempted to incorporate elements of 'foreign' ruling classes, it has become more difficult for them to control the distribution of surplus and, by extension, to prevent the emergence of alternative power centres. By the late eighth century, such centrifugal tendencies were already beginning to arise in Later Silla with the rise of a social group described in the sources as 'castle lords' (*sŏngju*). The situation worsened in the ninth century as resources flowed away from the central state, a process that was also occurring in Tang China and in Heian Japan at the same time. This led to the only significant interregnum period in Korea's premodern history after 676, with the breakdown of the kingdom into what became known as the Later Three Kingdoms (901–936). This was also a period of rebellion and banditry, the new rival kingdoms of Later Koguryŏ and Later Paekche both being founded with the help of bandit-rebels. The period saw a repeat of the warfare that had dogged the peninsula prior to 676 and ended with the collapse of Silla, and the defeat of Later Paekche by a general named Wang Kŏn. He founded the Koryŏ Dynasty, whose rule over the whole peninsula began in 936 and would last for over four centuries.

This cycle of consolidation and fragmentation is clearly a universal feature of premodern state societies and not in itself particularly remarkable.[13] What is significant then is the way in which this cycle can cause similar, sometimes neighbouring, societies to diverge over the medium term. It is thus worth examining how Wang Kŏn achieved a reconsolidation of the Korean polity within a relatively short space of time and avoided the long-term decline of central authority that was experienced in Japan during this period. Certainly, the proximity of the Korean peninsula to China allowed Koryŏ, and later Chosŏn, to absorb influences from Tang and Song administrative models relatively quickly. But the founder Wang Kŏn also pursued some more down to earth consolidation strategies, including marrying 29 wives from various warlord families and old Silla aristocratic clans. However, the reality was that during the first few decades of Koryŏ, while there was a unified overarching political authority, a strong centralised state did not yet exist and aristocratic clans and warlords still maintained their authority and walled towns in the countryside (Duncan 2000, 14). This changed gradually over the next couple of centuries as successive Koryŏ kings worked to consolidate the centralised state via various means. Some of the most important of these included: the superimposition of a bureaucratic administration over local areas; the collection of taxes from smaller aristocratic families; the establishment of a large army loyal to the royal family; the reorganisation of central government institutions on the Tang model; the purging of aristocrats who challenged royal power; and, the halting introduction of a meritocratic civil service examination system.

Two particularly notable victories were scored by the state in the 'struggle for surplus' during this period. The first was a move to reduce the slave holdings of aristocrats in the 950s, since slaves were a source of significant economic and political power. The second was perhaps the most important of all: the introduction of a prebend system called *chŏnsi-kwa* in which state officials were given incomes from non-inheritable grants of land; an by the state to bring much larger swathes of surplus under its direct control.[14] As in the earlier state formation/consolidation phase of the fourth to fifth centuries, it is not the case that Chinese 'technologies of rule' were adopted in an unmediated fashion; they were instead combined with local institutions and adapted to local circumstances, creating new hybrid social institutions. By the twelfth century, Koryŏ state consolidation had produced a strong central state, but it was by no means a perfect replica of a Chinese model. Instead, sovereignty in the countryside took a nested form, with a hierarchy of aristocratic power under the central royal power (Seth 2011, 84). Of course, these victories were neither complete, nor did they last all that long.[15]

The Koryŏ–Chosŏn Transition

The transition from the long-lived Koryŏ dynasty to the even longer-lasting Chosŏn dynasty took place in the late fourteenth century without any significant breakdown of the central state and with relatively minor bloodshed. However, over the preceding two centuries the state had been weakened by a series of major challenges to the Koryŏ polity. The first of these was a military takeover in the late twelfth century that put the Ch'oe family in the seat of power for 88 years, leaving the monarchy in place, but powerless. The second challenge came from outside the country, with the arrival of the Mongols in 1231. A period of bloody upheaval ensued, resulting in Koryŏ becoming a client state of the Mongol Yuan dynasty from 1270 until the late fourteenth century. Meanwhile, at a molecular level, other processes were at work with the emergence of what Duncan terms the 'central bureaucratic aristocracy' and the appearance of large landed estates owned by aristocratic clans. This meant the development of a new aristocracy whose power lay in gaining official appointments in the central government, while at the same time accumulating large private landholdings, often in other parts of the country to a clan's original ancestral seat. This then created a new form of compromise between state and aristocracy in which 'meritocratic principles and bureaucratic procedures were applied within a generally aristocratic framework' (Duncan 2000, 96). However, the source of aristocratic wealth remained basically the same during this period and into the early Chosŏn: landed estates worked by rent-paying tenants or by slaves. The central bureaucratic aristocracy did begin to become a drain on the state in the thirteenth and fourteenth centuries as they both increased the size of their estates and their level of control over the peasant population, thus depriving the state of revenues from taxes, tribute goods and corvée (Duncan 2000, 185).

This situation of a state weakened by Mongol domination and the draining of resources by a powerful bureaucratic aristocracy led to an existential crisis for the Koryŏ dynasty and a coup by the Koryŏ general Yi Sŏnggye in 1388. As well as putting himself on the throne and declaring a new dynasty in 1392, Yi and his supporters set about carrying out a programme of reform in order to reconsolidate state power and control over resources. The key moment in this process was the Rank Land Law (Kwajŏn Pŏp) of 1391 which attempted to re-establish a prebend system and return land outside of the capital region to state control. However, it did nothing about the private landholdings of the central aristocracy, and this class, now coalescing as the *yangban* class of the Chosŏn dynasty, continued to coexist with the central state in a precarious equilibrium. As John Duncan writes (2000, 213): 'The result was a perennial struggle between the Chosŏn state and its *yangban* officials for access to the country's resources'.

Another dimension of the transition from Koryŏ to Chosŏn was ideological, as the reformers who allied themselves with Yi Sŏnggye (later King T'aejo) were keen adherents of Neo-Confucianism, who believed in the re-ordering of both state and society along moral lines laid down by Confucius and by the founder of Neo-Confucian thought, Zhu Xi. In practice this meant combining abstract ideas about the hierarchical nature of social relations between people, with the reality of Korean social and cultural practices. As well as arguably aiding in the consolidation of the Korean state after the fourteenth century, over a few centuries this brought profound changes to Korean society, pushing Buddhism into the margins, diminishing the power of women within the family and changing the way in which clans and inheritance were organised.[16]

The 'Long Dynasty': Chosŏn's 500 Years

The Chosŏn dynasty was not only exceptionally long, it was also relatively peaceful. The Korean peninsula was left largely undisturbed by the successive Chinese dynasties of Ming and Qing, provided that Chosŏn accepted their suzerainty. At the same time, China was prepared to come to Chosŏn's aid when necessary, in order to protect its own flank, as it did in the 1590s when the Japanese under Toyotomi Hideyoshi embarked on two devastating invasions of Korea. The peninsula also remained relatively isolated from maritime trade routes and the encroachment of European merchants into East Asia, beginning in the seventeenth century. While this international setting goes some way to explain the longevity and relative stability of the dynasty, it was also the outcome of the preceding phases of state consolidation, and the particular compromise between state and aristocracy that emerged from the Koryŏ–Chosŏn transition. Of course, the struggle for surplus between state and aristocracy did not cease during the Chosŏn period, but it was contained within certain boundaries, largely through the establishment of what Palais called the 'aristocratic/bureaucratic balance'. This meant that the ruling *yangban* class was defined both by aristocratic status and landholding *and* by the ability of individuals to pass the civil examinations and become office holders. Thus the state was able to tie members of the elite to central institutions and closely align the fate of individual aristocratic clans with the state itself. According to Palais, this was closely related to the absorption and implementation of Confucian ideology, leading to an 'increased emphasis on knowledge, writing, and the civil arts through the use of the examination system for recruitment, and a decrease in inherited status' (Palais 1984, 430).

Although contained, the struggle over surplus clearly did continue during Chosŏn, and, as in the Koryŏ period, there was a long-term tendency for resources to drain away from central control and for private landholdings and slaveholdings to increase at the expense of central tax revenues. This struggle could take various forms in different periods and circumstances. For example, in the century after the Hideyoshi invasions of 1592–1598, the slave population became a locus of conflict between the state and the *yangban*.[17] On the one hand, the *yangban* wanted to increase, or at least maintain, their holdings of slaves, as they were one of their main sources of wealth. On the other, the government wished to control and reduce *yangban* slave holdings, as slaves did not pay tax or provide corvée and were thus a drain on state resources. To increase their holdings of slaves the *yangban* encouraged mixed slave-commoner marriages, while in response, the state enacted laws that would emancipate the children of such marriages (Palais 1996, 231–32). The state also attempted to gain closer control over the population and prevent the slave population from increasing by carrying out regular censuses and enforcing an identity tag system called *hop'ae* in the mid-seventeenth century (Seth 2011, 150).[18]

The more conventional push and pull between tax and rent also continued into the late Chosŏn period and, in fact, intensified. This mostly took the form of an increasing area of land that lay outside of taxation because *yangban* clans found ways to keep their landholdings off the tax registers, through bribery and official forms of tax exemption. Besides the landholdings of *yangban* clans, there also arose the problem of increasingly rich and powerful Confucian Academies (*sŏwon*) that had come to have a position analogous to the Buddhist church in the Koryŏ dynasty, or perhaps the Christian church in medieval Europe. With their own large holdings of land and slaves, they had, by the mid-nineteenth century, become another locus of surplus extraction and redistribution outside of the control of the state. Thus, as Palais notes (1991, 61), even in the mid-eighteenth century, 150 years after the devastation of the Hideyoshi invasions, the Chosŏn state had not been able to recover the tax base it had before the war. During the nineteenth century, the tax base continued to narrow and tax revenues decreased drastically over the course of the century, giving rise to a full-blown fiscal crisis by the 1870s–1880s, when the government was effectively insolvent (Pak and Pak 1988; Miller 2016, 85–86).

Much effort has been expended by Korean historians to locate progressive tendencies in the late Chosŏn period (1598–1910) in order to make the argument that Korea was moving decisively towards capitalism and modernity under its own steam. The evidence for this is weak, but this does not mean that the adjective 'stagnant' can be applied to this period of Korean history (Miller 2007, 23–29). Korean society continued to have its own dynamic, shaped by the struggle over surplus and its relations with its neighbours, that cannot be reduced to either side of the stagnation/progress binary. After the Hideyoshi invasions some new elements were added to this dynamic, most significantly a clear tendency towards commercialisation of aspects of the economy, which aided economic recovery but also added new elements of instability to the social system as a whole. However, even in the eighteenth and nineteenth centuries, after some four centuries in existence, the Chosŏn state retained a formidable capacity to extract and redistribute surplus, which meant that merchants relied on the state in a multitude of ways and commerce itself was firmly embedded in the tributary social system. This embedding of commerce and the stalemate achieved by the state in its struggle with the *yangban* aristocracy seem to be the two main factors that led early modern Japanese observers to label Korea as stagnant.

Premodern Korean history over the *long durée* was, therefore, a story of state formation and consolidation, punctuated by crises that were repeatedly resolved in favour of a stable central state with increasing powers of surplus extraction. This process, mediated constantly by Korea's intersocietal relations with its neighbours, led to a particular form of state-aristocracy compromise not seen in either premodern China or Japan, that has been termed the 'aristocratic/bureaucratic balance'.

CONCLUSION

In this chapter I have set out to argue for a different way of approaching Korean history over the *longue durée* that moves decisively away from the Eurocentric starting point implied by both sides of the stagnation/progress dichotomy. I have also attempted to show how this approach could work in practice when applied to some key events and processes over the course of 1,600 years of Korean history. In doing this I positioned myself explicitly against the theory of 'Asiatic' stagnation propounded in various forms by Japanese colonial historians and Korean Marxists alike, demonstrating how these approaches tended towards circularity of argument and were based largely on the notions of historical abnormality and lack, when compared to the European model. Moreover, I also rejected the idea of an inherent and inevitable progress in Korean history, as advocated by many postcolonial Korean historians. This model too is founded on Eurocentric, methodologically nationalist assumptions and suffers from a weak empirical basis. Instead, I argued for a reconceptualisation of Korean history—like all histories—as fundamentally constituted by unevenness and combination within a field of heterogeneous societies and polities, at different spatial scales, in constant relations with one another.

As shown above, this approach brings to the fore certain features of Korean history over the *longue durée*. First, over this long period the trend was consistently towards the consolidation of the central state, despite inter-dynastic crises and devastating wars and invasions. However, this does not mean that the Korean state settled once and for all the struggle over surplus. Instead it would be more accurate to say that the struggle raged on for the whole period over the collection of tax and rent and the ownership of land, over slaveholdings and over the provision of corvée labour. But through various means, most prominently the adoption of a Chinese-style bureaucracy and examination system with its accompanying Confucian ideology, successive Korean states were able to at least contain the struggle over surplus and in the process create the aristocratic/bureaucratic balance that characterised the Korean ruling class prior to the twentieth century. Along with this came a series of other features that set Korea apart from Japan, including, but no limited to, the non-development of a distinct military culture or military class; a relatively rigid ascriptive status hierarchy with a large slave population; and the embedding of commerce within tributary social relations. Nevertheless, this does not mean there is anything abnormal about Korean history, it is rather, a completely normal sub-unit of the wider picture of human history and no doubt many other histories can be found that display similar characteristics.

I have aimed to outline above the way in which the history of a particular society is a continuous pattern of divergence and convergence (or unevenness and combination) within a wider field of polities. In premodern societies like the one examined here this pattern was deeply intertwined with the question of coercive surplus extraction and distribution. On the one side, the struggle over surplus between state and elite was decisively shaped by intersocietal relations, including wars, transfers of ideas, institutional forms and technologies, tribute, trade and diplomacy. In other words, 'the international' was constitutive of the 'internal' social structure and the balance between central and local power in a particular society. On the other side, the changing shape of state-aristocracy (central-local) relations within a society produced unevenness at the intersocietal level, bringing about the divergence of neighbouring societies such as Korea and Japan over the long term.

NOTES

1. The key figure in establishing the backwardness of Korean history was Japanese economist Fukuda Tokuzō (1874–1930), who had studied under Karl Bücher and Lujo Brentano in Munich. See: Miller 2010, 4–5.

2. Perry Anderson (1974, 462–72) has identified the key features of the AMP as: (1) state ownership of land; (2) independent village communities; (3) servile social equality; (4) lack of a nobility; (5) state hydraulic works; (6) influence of geography and climate; and (7) stagnation.

3. For previous critiques in English of the South Korean historiography, see Palais (1998) Duncan (2000, 3–6) and Eckert (1991, 1–6).

4. In his *Passages from Antiquity to Feudalism*, Perry Anderson argues for a distinct 'nomadic mode of production' as well as slave, 'tribal-communal' and feudal

modes (218). His understanding of the concept of mode of production is also clearly set out in the conclusion to his *Lineages of the Absolutist State*.

5. For Samir Amin's original description of the tributary mode of production, see Amin (1976, 13–58). Eric Wolf's chapter on modes of production in *Europe and the People without History* (1982, 73–100) is one of the most concise and illuminating pieces on the concept. For Wolf, human societies have been dominated by three MOPs: kin-ordered, tributary and capitalist, although he deliberately refuses to see these three as part of an 'evolutionary sequence', preferring to talk of 'historical relations' between them.

6. As Marx wrote in *Capital*, Volume III: 'The surplus labour for the nominal owner of the land can only be extorted from them by other than economic pressure, whatever the form assumed may be' (quoted in Wolf 1982, 80).

7. See in particular Chapter 5 ('State Formation and the Struggle for Surplus') where Haldon examines a number of different tributary social formations.

8. Many would argue that the intersocietal character of human development goes back much earlier than this, but for the purpose of the argument here it is sufficient to note that it dates from at least the period of early state formation.

9. For a discussion of UCD in pre-capitalist societies, see Matin 2007, 428–29.

10. By secondary status groups here I mean those groups or social layers who were not members of the *yangban* aristocracy and could not participate in the higher examinations but were nonetheless more privileged than commoners and slaves and had formed long-lasting lineages with access to their own privileges. Examples include the *chungin* class of technical specialists, the local clerks called *hyangni*, the military class called *muban* and the officially sanctioned merchants.

11. Talking about early Korean state formation is immediately fraught with difficulties due to the fact that it is impossible at this time to define anything as being 'Korean' in the sense that we mean it today. However, here I will use the working definition of any emerging polity, whether existing on the Korean peninsula proper or to its north, that was clearly a historical antecedent of the first generally accepted 'Korean' states of the Three Kingdoms period (c. fourth century CE–668 CE).

12. Because Silla eventually conquered the other kingdoms subsequent historiography has been heavily slanted in its favour. Thus the traditional date for the founding of Silla is the earliest (57 BCE) even though it did not emerge as a state until centuries after Koguryŏ.

13. In an interesting section on Silla's rise and fall in global perspective, Michael Seth notes that 'The eighth century was a period of political centralization and outward trade and prosperity in most of Eurasia, while the late ninth was a period of political fragmentation and decline'. He goes on to note that Korea, while on the periphery, was obviously already integrated into the wider Eurasian or even Afro-Eurasian world (Seth 2011, 73).

14. Palais wrote of this system that it was 'an ambitious attempt by the central government to assert its control over the income of the ruling class, to increase its strength at the expense of the aristocrats of Korean society' (Palais 1982, 185).

15. Palais estimated (1982, 184) that prebendal land only made up one fifth of all arable land in the mid-Koryŏ period.

16. The classic work on this process of social change is Deuchler (1992).

17. There has been considerable debate over the character of slavery in premodern Korea. As was the case in many premodern societies, the term used for slave—nobi 奴婢—can cover a great variety of different modes of existence and degrees of unfreedom. This could range from people who lived and worked in the household of their *yangban* owner to others who resided far away from their owner, living and working independently on their land much like tenant farmers or serfs.

18. This brief discussion of the struggle over slaveholdings is indebted to an MA dissertation by Sangwon Shin (2015).

Chapter 5

Combination as 'Foreign Policy'

The Intersocietal Origins of the Ottoman Empire

Kerem Nişancıoğlu

The study of the origins of the Ottoman Empire is an inherently 'speculative and perilous' (Goffman 2002, 29) exercise, limited by a 'black hole' (Imber 1987) of historiography that is deprived of reliable first hand sources yet bursting with politically charged historiographical propagandising (Abou-El-Haj 1991, 23–25; Tezcan 2011, 83).[1] Written during the period of Ottoman imperial decline, the first-wave of modern Ottoman historiography tended to emphasise the political and institutional weaknesses of Turkic and Muslim people as part of a wider political project of imperial penetration into the Middle East. In 1916, Herbert Adams Gibbons argued that Ottoman administrative forms were appropriated from Byzantium, through the conquest and defections of Christians (Gibbons 1916; see also Diehl 1957 [1920]). In a study that would inform the orientalism of modernisation theory (see e.g. Huntington 1968b; Landau 1984; Lewis 2002; Zurcher 1993), Paul Wittek (2012) argued that it was the proselytising zeal of Muslim *ghazi* bands that was the motive force behind Ottoman expansion. The essence of the Ottoman Empire was therefore to be found in the religious-ideological identity of Islam. In the context of the Kemalist project of state building in the 1930s Fuat Köprülü sought to challenge Western approaches by rearticulating Ottoman history through the methodological straitjacket of nationalism (Köprülü 1992a; 1992b; 1999). He therefore emphasised the morphology of the Oğuz tribe, via the Seljuks, into the Ottoman Empire by tracing a lineage of political leadership that was ethnically Turkish in essence.

Historical materialist accounts were at the forefront of the second wave of Ottoman historiography, providing a much-needed corrective to the essentialism that pervaded the first-wave by placing an emphasis on social relations of production. Whether conceptualised as tributary (Banaji 2011; Haldon 1993), feudal (Avcıoğlu 1968, 15–16; Berktay 1987; 1990; Boratav 1983; Haldon

1991), or Asiatic (Divitçioğlu 1967, 34; Islamoğlu-Inan and Keyder 1976; 1977; 1987; Nalbantoğlu 1978, 65–66)[2] certain social relations were identi-fied as crucial to understanding the Ottoman Empire—a division between the ruling *askeri* class and the ruled peasant *reaya* class on the one hand; and an intra-ruling class division between a central patrimonial authority and provincial landed elites on the other. Surplus was appropriated through taxes that were paid by peasants to local landed elites, who either transferred them to the Ottoman patrimonial centre—the sultan and the *devşirme*—or kept them in return for military service, as institutionalised in the *tımar* system. The logic of Ottoman power was therefore rooted in a tributary relationship, wherein the Ottoman state obtained control over the means of production and the ruling class. Thus, built into historical materialist accounts was a social relational understanding of the functioning of Ottoman power.

However, historical materialist accounts generated their own peculiar—very much materialist—essentialisation and ossification of Ottoman history by replicating an image of the empire as static and incapable of change. They have therefore been unable to account for how social relations between the peasantry, landed elite and patrimonial ruler were reconfigured, especially from the eighteenth century onwards (Tansel 2015; Tezcan 2010). Such accounts were moreover unable to explain how and why the Ottoman Empire was constructed around these particular social relations, and were unable to provide an account for the origins of their particular configuration (Anievas and Nişancioğlu 2015).

When taken together these differing approaches show that there is an enduring problem of essentialisation and ossification in the way the Ottoman Empire has been theorised, whether in terms of Islam, Turkish ethnicity, Byzantine institutions or social relations of production. This chapter dem-onstrates that the source of this problem is rooted in a social ontology that derives some foundational essence of the Ottoman Empire *from within*, be it cultural, ethnic, institutional, or social. That is, each of the above approaches is guilty of a pervasive *internalism*, where the history of the empire is explained exclusively through its own internal features (Nişancioğlu 2014).

It seems, then, in order to free the study of the Ottoman Empire from the shackles of essentialism and ossification, we must break out of the inter-nalist straitjacket that has for too long informed Ottoman historiography. In this chapter I argue that the idea of uneven and combined development (UCD)[3] provides a particularly apposite framework through which we can move beyond internalism and in so doing de-essentialise theorisations of the Ottoman Empire. The 'uneven' of UCD demands that we cannot approach the question of how the Ottoman Empire came into being from an onto-logically singular perspective (i.e. as the single legacy or morphology of a particular society, say Muslim, Turkic, Seljuk or Byzantine). It must rather be understood as occurring within a developmentally differentiated social totality—an intersocietal world—which in turn necessitates a broader synchronic viewpoint—a world-historical perspective that incorporates studies of Anatolian, Inner Asian and Byzantine history is required. The 'combination' of UCD demands we incorporate, rather than overlook, points of interaction between these differentiated units and their combinatory consequences as constitutive pieces of the Ottoman puzzle.

In particular, I seek to show that the historically specific class configurations (between *peasantry, patrimonial authority* and *landed aristocracy*) and the logic of power (*state control over the means of production and the ruling class*) that made up the Ottoman Empire were constituted and determined, in large part, by international conditions. These relations between peasantry, patrimonial authority and landed aristocracy were not formed solely through the unfolding of an internal Ottoman dynamic, but were the products of an interactive—that is, an uneven and combined—form of development. More specifically still, I seek to show that the institutions through which these class relations were expressed— the *reaya-askeri* distinction, *tımar* land allocations and the central functions of the *devşirme* and sultan—were all products of combined development.

In the first section I will elucidate the unevenness of the Anatolian geopolitical milieu in the thirteenth and fourteenth centuries. This section demonstrates how a multiplicity of social formations was constitutive of Anatolian history in this period with a particular focus on the Inner Asian nomads, the Seljuk Empire and the Byzantine Empire. I argue that the ebb and flow of these social formations, and their attendant interactions, created a peculiar geopolitical condition rife with a multiplicity of social relations, identities and institutional forms. Then, in the second section I will turn to how these conditions intersected and interacted. I argue that it was out of the flux of the north-western Anatolian corner of Bithynia that the Ottoman emirate emerged and expanded into an empire. As such, it was deeply imbued with the traditions of this geopolitical context and came to draw on the heterogeneous heritages of these different influences in its period of state building. The genesis of the Ottoman state, from semi-nomadic tribe into sedentary empire, was in turn defined by a series of responses to this specifically intersocietal context, and that an Ottoman 'foreign policy' of combination—of combining the developmental achievements of these various actors—was constitutive of the Ottoman state as such.

UNEVENNESS IN ANATOLIA

Our starting point is therefore the social unevenness of the Anatolian milieu in the thirteenth and fourteenth centuries. This was a period in which the flow and ebb of Mongol invasions had opened the region to migrations of Turkic pastoral nomads from Inner Asia. These invasions precipitated the fall of Seljuk rule, while in the West the conquest of Constantinople by the Fourth Crusade eventually inspired the Byzantines to turn their imperial attention to reconsolidating their western territories. This left Anatolia, the lands in the middle of this geopolitical vacuum, in a highly fragmented state of flux, comprised of a multiplicity of nomadic, semi-nomadic and sedentary communities, dynasties and statelets. There was a large Christian Byzantine sedentary population that had remained in Asia Minor despite the breakdown in Byzantine rule. There were nomadic and semi-nomadic Turkic tribes, most typically wedded to the traditions of the Inner Asian steppe and Ilkhanid structures of rule. There were wandering Muslim literati of the former Seljuk administration searching for employment. In addition, there were sizable traces of Christian crusaders such as Franks and Catalans, and pockets of Jewish communities.

Inner Asian Nomadism

The source of much of this unevenness can be found in the geopolitics of the Eurasian steppe from the thirteenth century onwards. Marked by the persistent opposition and interaction between nomadic and settled peoples (Matin 2007) the steppe proved conducive to the establishment of vast nomadic empires, capable of waves of conquest that spread from China in the East to Byzantium in the West. The geopolitical conflicts between nomadic and sedentary groups would often create internecine conflicts over access to land or over spoils of raids. This meant that 'when one group triumphed over another, the latter would flee and push aside a third to secure for itself an area for grazing' (Chaliand 2006, 3). Waves of nomadic empire building would therefore tend to create 'chain reactions' of displacement, migration and resettlement that transmitted the peoples and traditions of nomadism throughout Inner Asia to its hinterlands.

Among the inheritors of such transmissions and combinations was the Ottoman Empire. We see this in a series of westward demographic shifts, brought about by three waves of Inner Asian nomadic migrations and empire building between the tenth and thirteenth century, that drove Turkic nomads into Anatolia. The first at the beginning of the tenth century witnessed large-scale migrations westwards that culminated in the advancement of the Seljuks across Asia Minor. The Seljuk victory over the Byzantines in the Battle of Manzikert in 1071 firmly established the dynasty in Asia, and opened the pastures of Anatolia to waves of Turkic nomadic migrations from the east (Cahen 2001, 14; Turan 1970, 233). With the second wave of migrations from 1230 to 1270, the Mongols established an administrative hold over central Asia and Asia minor, forcing existing populations to migrate westwards

(Lindner 1983, 15; Melville 2009, 53). It is in the context of this second wave of migrations that the arrival of the Ottomans in Bithynia must be placed. The Noghai, a Pontic nomadic community, were driven to Bithynia to escape the Mongolian expansion (Heywood 2000, 109–14; Kafadar 1995, 44–45). Through relations of war and alliance with Byzantine and Bulgarian princes, the Noghai became important actors in the region, developing knowledge of the new and abandoned lands on the Byzantine marches in the process (Zachariadou 1978, 262). Following Noghai's death, his followers settled in Bithynia, forming the embryonic Ottoman state. Indeed, Heywood argues that the very name 'Osman' evolved from the Pontic term for leader of a tribe – *Ataman* (Heywood 2000, 113).

Finally, a third wave intersected with the growth of the Ottoman Empire at the turn of the fifteenth century. Under the rule of Timur, the Ilkhanid Empire poured westwards, defeating the Ottoman Sultan Bayezid I in Ankara (1402) and establishing administrative control over much of Anatolia. The Ottomans were placed under Ilkhanid suzerainty, while many of the Anatolian nomadic leaders (*beys*) that had become vassals of the Ottomans switched allegiance to Timur who restored them to their original autonomy (Lindner 2009, 109). This instantiated a temporary reform of Ottoman state practices (İnalcık 2000, 17–21), in particular raising the significance of maintaining a centralised state that could withstand the fragmentary tendencies of nomadic empires. The significance of this for the emergence of the tributary mode of production will be elaborated in the final section.

These developments also precipitated the transmission of the Inner Asian traditions into Asia Minor, firstly by Inner Asian nomads, then the Seljuks and Mongol *Tümen* and then later by the Ottomans (Lindner 2009, 116). The development of the Khan's household armies, pioneered by Chenghis Khan's *cerig* army, was directly appropriated in the Ottoman case, with the recruitment of the *yeniceri* ('new *cerig*') standing army (Togan 1991, 196). Many Ilkhanid practices in land regulation and tax appropriation were directly copied by the Ottomans; in the case of extraordinary taxes (*avariz*), and taxes levied in kind for military purposes (*ulufa*), the Ottomans used exactly the same terms as the Ilkhanids (Shinder 1978, 509–510). Ottoman coins were modelled on Ilkhanid predecessors, adopting the monetary unit *akçe* (Lindner 2007, 96). Like the Mongols, the Ottoman conception of law making was defined in the secular terms of the supreme ruler's will. The secular Ottoman legal code, the *Kanun* was in many ways referential to the Mongolian *jasagh* (Togan 1991, 195). And like the Ilkhanids, this secular code co-existed with the *Şeriat* Islamic law (Shinder 1978, 510).

It was not just the institutional principles of nomadism that continued once the Ottomans became a more sedentary polity. The mobility of nomadism itself was a constitutive feature of Ottoman society well up until the eighteenth century. Indeed, nomads constituted 27 percent of Anatolian population as late as the 1520s (Kasaba 2009, 66–74). But moreover, the practice of *sürgün* ('obligatory transfer') required the migration of sedentary and nomadic communities in order to settle in newly conquered territories. This could be used either to coerce rebellious tribes, or to generate consent by offering improved living standards in newly annexed lands and frontiers. In short, the very mobility of nomadism constituted a crucial plank in the mediation of relations between patrimonial authority, landed nobility and the peasantry.

The early Ottoman 'state' was therefore deeply imbued with the character-istics of the nomadic mode of production, which is central to grasping how and why it was able to successfully conduct its own imperial formation. A key 'value' of nomadic state formation in this regard was the way in which it responded to incorporating the 'incremental complexity' of territorial expan-sion and conquest through an 'expanding range of solutions to issues of governance' (Di Cosmo 1999, 28). The peculiarity of Ottoman state building therefore lies in its distinctive solution to the growing complexity of social relations that came with its territorial expansion—that is, how these inher-ited nomadic tendencies were combined with and refracted through social relations whose origins came from spatial settings distinct from the Inner Asian norms. It is therefore necessary to trace the influence of these other influences—Seljuk-Islamic and European-Christian.

The Breakdown of the Seljuk Empire

The Seljuk state itself was built precisely through the nomadic 'laws of motion' elucidated above, involving a synthesis of sedentarised hierarchi-cal institutions with nomadic horizontal ones. As the Seljuks passed from nomadic confederation to sedentary tributary state 'new elements were added en route or absorbed in the new homeland' (Golden 1992, 207). At its core was an egalitarian structure of regional rulers—*maliks* or *emirs*—each of whom had a legitimate claim to the title of Sultan or Supreme Sovereign (Golden 1992, 220; İnalcık 1976, 10). (Geo)political competition both within the empire (among competing regional rulers) and without (primarily Mongolians and Byzantines, but also Christian crusades), necessitated the maintenance of a military structure that could withstand these centrifugal and centripetal forces (Cahen 1968, 35–36; Golden 1992, 207).

First, the Seljuks utilised conscription—*ghulam* (Bosworth 2010, 51). Through this system, slaves were levied from conquered lands, converted to Islam and transferred to the Seljuk palace to form a standing army which at its peak numbered 12,000 men (Turan 1970, 254). Secondly, in order to meet the double challenge of supporting *ghulam* and appeasing Turcoman nomadic marchers, the Seljuks granted *iqta*—non-inheritable pieces of land in which all ownership and governance was deferred to the Seljuk palace (Amitai 2010, 546). Smaller *iqta* were granted to *ghulam* commanders (Cahen 1968, 39) and conferred the right of tax collection in exchange for military service to the central authority (Findley 2004, 70–71). Larger *iqtas* were usually assigned to the most powerful Turcoman commanders—*emirs* or *maliks*—on the frontiers of the empire, thereby serving a triple purpose: to mobilise against external threats; to carry out increased expansion; and to mitigate against any provincial challenge by these commanders to central authority (Bosworth 2010; Turan 1970, 232). Thirdly, Seljuk rule depended heavily on *akhis*—urban confraternities organised around heterodox Islam and linked by solidarity and comradeship. These were fraternal organisations for the regulation of work, production and trade, and groups of social activists that could at times challenge and undermine ruling aristocracies, governments and the orthodoxy of the Caliph (Cahen 1968, 199–200; Lindner 2009, 106). They could also be deployed as supplementary military forces to defend towns in the event they came under attack (Cahen 1968, 337–41). In certain towns where no regional rulers lived, *akhis* would function as de facto governors, maintaining law and order, engaging in charitable exercises and providing local infrastructure such as hospices and communal shelter (Golden 1992, 356). In this context *akhi*-dominated cities appeared as proto-city-state republics, semi-independent of any religious authority or sovereign (Lowry 2003, 71–72). These were sufficiently powerful groups that maintained social cohesion in the aftermath of Seljuk collapse, and thus formed a vital basis of political and economic power that the Ottomans would have to come to terms with during their own period of expansion.

Finally, these practices were underpinned, legitimised and codified through the cultivation of Muslim scholar-administrators—either members of the *ulema* or more heterodox dervishes—to its imperial centre. In particular, the Seljuks were the first to give centres of Islamic scholarship—*medresses*—real importance; the scale and institutionalisation of them under the Seljuks was unprecedented (Cahen 1968, 43). Moreover, the *ulema* were able to acquire great wealth and institutionalise their power through *waqfs*, which were pious foundations, primarily established to benefit a religious institution such as a mosque, school or hospital (Cahen 1968, 178). Between *waqfs* and *medresses*, the Seljuks cultivated Islamic officials—*kadıs*—to administer state functions through the application of *Şeriat*. Seljuk state building also involved the provision of conquered towns with their own *kadı* (Cahen 1968, 152) who would legitimise Seljuk rule (and rulers), administer ordinary justice, occasionally perform some military and diplomatic tasks, act as judicial consultancy and supervision of trade, crafts and land titles (Ephrat 2002, 34–37; Rogers 1976, 71).

By the end of the thirteenth century the Seljuks proved incapable of sustaining the empire. Confronted by the geopolitical pressure of Mongol expansion and prone to internal divisions, the Seljuks eventually collapsed following the fatal defeat to the Golden Horde in the battle of Köse Dağı in 1243 (Lindner 1983, 12). Subsequently, the geopolitics of the Anatolian region became defined by the tumultuous relations between a multiplicity of statelets (*beyliks*) that emerged out of the ashes of Seljuk rule (Turan 1970, 251)—Germinyans, Karamans Mentese, Aydin, Saruhan, Karasi and Osman (Golden 1992, 354–55).

In addition to these *beyliks*, the collapse of Seljuk rule had left in its wake *akhis*, *kadıs* and dervishes who carried the institutional and cultural memory of Seljuk statecraft. With the expansion of the Ottoman Empire in Anatolia in the fourteenth century, these institutions would become assimilated into the Ottoman state, eventually becoming a part of the administrative backbone of the proto-Ottoman state. *Medresse* educated Islamic schoolmen and former *kadıs* migrated to Ottoman territories where their clerical capabilities were required to govern sedentary polities. *Akhis* remained in towns and villages throughout Anatolia, providing social and economic ties and administrative continuity between *beyliks* (Lindner 2009, 115). Dervishes would be patronised in order to consolidate and unify ideologically diverse and heterodox communities (Golden 1992, 359). These were agents of combined development that were central to transmitting and developing Islamic legal codes and institutional features to the Ottomans. The use of Arabic codes in early *waqf* entitlements (Lowry 2003, 79), the extensive presence of *akhi* taverns, hospitals and soup kitchens in Ottoman towns and the marriage of Osman with the daughter of a dervish (Golden 1992, 359) all point to a strong Seljuk influence in the early Ottoman state. Later, as sedentarisation became a necessity, the Ottomans would repeat the Seljuk practice of drawing on slave recruits—*kul*—from its conquered territories to furnish a standing army—Janissaries—and the state bureaucracy—*devşirme* (Shaw 1976, 27). This central administration was counter-posed with *tımar* land grants which would support frontier marchers and Janissaries in much the same way as Seljuk *iqtas* functioned. Thus, 'seemingly, within two generations of their emergence the Ottomans had taken on many of the administrative trappings of earlier Islamic dynasties via the medium of the Seljuks' (Lowry 2003, 86).

The Ebb of the Byzantine Empire

The flux of the Anatolian milieu was additionally complexified by developments that affected the other remaining imperial power in the region—the Byzantine Empire. Despite very different origins, rooted in the breakdown of Roman imperial power, the Byzantines shared many similarities with the

Seljuks with whom they competed over the territories of Anatolia. Central to Byzantine social reproduction was control over land and its taxation, in which the landlord-tenant relation was subsumed under a state that could exercise a high degree of control over the local aristocracy (Frankopan 2009, 113–15). Imperial authorities controlled provincial magnates, denying them any real autonomy—'born out of service to the sovereign' the position and reproduction of the aristocracy 'never ceased to be linked to him' (Cheynet 2006, 42). The state was also responsible for setting the levels of peasant taxation and protecting their status as formally free of any ties to local magnates (Harvey 2003, 46–47).

Consequently, imperial involution took hold as the central authority lost both its internal coherence and its control over provincial functionaries. The impulse for this breakdown was intersocietal. The combined effects of Frankish conquests, Bulgarian wars, demographic pressure from Slav, Bulgar and Turkic migrations, Mongol invasions and Seljuk incursions meant that by the late eleventh century, the Byzantine Empire had lost substantial amounts of political authority in Asia Minor and South Eastern Europe (Chrysostomides 2009, 6, 9–10, 21–22, 29). In this period, state control over its rural magnates weakened to the point that provincial armies were dismantled and internal court conflicts and civil wars became a persistent feature of imperial politics (Anderson 1996, 277). The weakening of central authority reached an apex in the Komneni era (1081–1185), when provincial magnates gained control of the state and institutionalised *pronoia* land benefices (Oikonomides 2002, 1042). These gave *pronoia* holders extensive autonomy in local provinces, with control over fiscal and military powers, in return for military service to the empire. Decentralisation became the norm as *pronoia* was extended so that holders could appoint non-state managers in place of state officials to administer new holdings (Lindner 1983, 12). When Constantinople was captured by the Fourth Crusade in 1202, a weakened Byzantine imperial centre resorted to multiplying and expanding *pronoia* in its remaining territories until eventually many of these landholdings became hereditary (Harvey 2003, 71; Oikonomides 2002, 1056). Moreover, numerous typically feudal practices were imported into the region by Frankish crusaders, further undermining central authority (Anderson 1996, 282). With these developments, 'free peasants were increasingly degraded into dependent tenants or *paroikoi*', whose enserfment caused growing social stratification and deterioration in their social wellbeing (Harvey 2003, 37). In Asia Minor this process was especially intense. The loss of Constantinople and the relocation of the imperial capital to Nicaea precipitated the subordination of Anatolian peasants to new *pronoia* landowners that had moved into the region from the west (Harvey 2003, 77).

The Nicaean period (1204–1261) also saw the emergence of *akritai* border guards. These were semi-independent auxiliary troops that were established as part of an extensive frontier defence system designed to protect Nicaea from Turkic nomadic marchers—*akıncıs* or *ghazis*. *Akritai* were exempt from taxation and entitled to full disposition of booty acquired through border raids (Lindner 1983, 11). Some were entitled to small non-hereditary *pronoia* landholdings, while all were supplemented by an annual wage intended to maintain loyalty to the imperial centre (Oikonomides 2002, 1044). But under the reign of Michael VIII Palaeologus (1259–1282) their independence was circumscribed as they were assimilated as campaign troops. This had a negative impact on their material position in Byzantine society, often resulting in interruptions in their pay and restrictions on land entitlements (Bartusis 1997, 304). The decline in material standing of *akritai* in Anatolia occurred largely because following the recapture of Constantinople in 1261, the Byzantine Empire's attention turned almost exclusively to maintaining and expanding its western territories. Michael VIII reordered the social organisation of Anatolia by neglecting *akritai* upkeep and re-garrisoning his armies in Europe from which he would conduct further military campaigns. Breaking these military ties created a lack of security in Anatolia, leading to military decay and economic breakdown (Imber 2009, 6–7; Vryonis 1975, 47).

The recession of Byzantine rule in Anatolia left in its wake a neglected military class and a discontented local population that had become distrustful and disobedient of Byzantine tax burdens (Anderson 1996, 292; Sugar 1993, 3). It was the Byzantine's failure to protect Bithynia and subsequent restlessness of its Anatolian subjects that opened numerous geopolitical possibilities for Turkic expansion into Byzantine territories. As Turkic nomads overwhelmed Byzantine landholdings through migration and predation, there was little or no resistance from local peasant populations (Anderson 1996, 292). In the context of widespread imperial collapse—both Byzantine and Seljuk—the loyalty of local populations came to be based less on imperial allegiance or ideology and more on mutual advantage (Goffman 2002, 33). Many Christian lords and *akritai* became socially closer to Turkic *akıncıs* than their Byzantine compatriots and switched allegiance to tribal groupings—such as the Ottomans—that offered better prospects of social and material security and gains (Bartusis 1997, 304). As the Ottoman Empire expanded westwards, Greek, Armenian, Slav and Albanian nobility became prominent members of the early Ottoman ruling class (Vryonis 1969, 269).

The symbiosis of Christian and Turkic communities demonstrates not only the efficacy of Inner Asian norms of empire building practiced by the Ottomans in this Christian setting, but also the fact that Christians were crucial to the construction of the Ottoman state. The importance of this frontier syncretism in Ottoman state formation was personified in the figures of Köse Mihal and Gazi Evrenos, two cofounders of the early Ottoman state alongside the eponymous Osman (Lowry 2003, 64). Both were originally

Christian. Mihal was a Byzantine frontier lord (Lowry 2003, 8) and Evrenos was most likely of Aragonese or Catalan origin, and had travelled to the Levant as part of a mercenary army conscripted to fight in Byzantine civil wars (Lowry 2003, 59).

The frontier syncretism between Turks and Christians extended beyond the mutual benefit of the raid. Diplomatic marriages also formed a crucial mechanism through which the Ottomans managed to maintain and hasten their imperial expansion into Christian territories. In 1343, Sultan Orhan married the daughter of a member of the Byzantine royal family to garner political leverage in inter-dynastic Byzantine feuds. Mehmed II's stepmother was the daughter of a Serbian prince. Suleyman the Magnificent's mother was the daughter of the Crimean Khan. Suleyman's wife, Hurrem, was originally from Ukraine (then part of Poland) and exercised considerable power in foreign policy (Kasaba 2009, 44–45). The Ottomans also made use of pre-existing administrators and rulers in territories that had heavily resisted Ottoman expansion. Following the Ottoman conquest of Constantinople, two nephews of Byzantine Emperor Constantine XI Palaiologos and potential heirs to his throne, were captured, linguistically and religiously assimilated, and then appointed to high positions in the Ottoman state. Mehsi Pasha became *Sancak Bey* (governor) of Gallipoli before being promoted to Grand Vizier. His brother, Murad Pasha was anointed *beylerbey* (district governor) of Rumelia (the Balkans). These weren't exceptions; a number of bureaucrats were drawn from indigenous Balkan populations through the practice of levying children from conquered Christian communities. Several of these were, moreover, members of already existing aristocracies whose lands had been conquered by the Ottomans (Lowry 2003, 116–17). Byzantine scribes were crucial to the development of the Ottoman state's clerical practices. And the overwhelming majority of the *devşirme* were recruited from Christian lands, forming a central plank of the Ottoman administrative and military system (Vryonis 1969, 272–276). Through these processes, the Ottomans were able to subsume 'members of the Byzanto-Balkan aristocracy into the Ottoman ruling class' (İnalcık 1954, 112–22; Lowry 2003, 115–30).

These were all agents of combined development—the swathes of former Christian warriors, princes, princesses, administrators, governors and peasants that were assimilated into the Ottoman state all brought with them their own political, economic and cultural traditions that were appended onto pre-existing Ottoman institutions. Local laws in conquered territories were often reproduced and sometimes appropriated into the Sultanic code (Sugar 1993, 6). By leaving existing agrarian relations intact, there emerged a significant degree of institutional continuity between the *pronoia* land grants and the *tımar* system that replaced it (Cahen 1968, 182–83; Imber 2009, 194; Vryonis 1969, 273).

THE OTTOMAN 'FOREIGN POLICY' OF COMBINATION

The preceding argument has sought to delineate three interrelated spatio-temporal vectors of uneven and combined development that coalesced in the conjuncture of fourteenth century Bithynia to create the conditions for the emergence of the Ottoman state. Having thus far identified these institutional, social, political and economic forms of other societies that were appropriated by the Ottomans, it is necessary to demonstrate why these were systematically and successfully brought together in the fourteenth and fifteenth centuries under the aegis of the Ottoman state. In doing so, this section demonstrates the centrality of intersocietal relations in the making of the *reaya-askeri* and centre-province relations that undergirded the Ottoman social formation.

As we have seen, with the breakdown of imperial authority among the Seljuks and Byzantines, and the persistent waves of nomadic pressure from Inner Asia, fourteenth-century Anatolia was characterised by multiple and overlapping forms of social relations and 'layers of authority' (Kafadar 1995, 125). In addition to the remnants of Seljuk and Byzantine rule, nomadic raiders and semi-nomadic *beyliks* combined with towns dominated by *akhi* organisations. These communities crisscrossed with wandering dervishes, displaced peasants, merchants and former members of the *ulema*. These different social groupings, communities and individuals lived in a 'precarious symbiosis' of syncretic interaction and understanding—'multi-ethnic, multi-religious, nomadic, and sedentary, conflict-ridden and peaceful all at the same time' (Barkey 2008, 41). This was a 'world of dizzying physical mobility' (Kafadar 1995, 61) in which information, customs, laws and social relations were persistently uprooted, transmitted and re-formed. Consequently, the success of any state building was heavily dependent on how far any of these particular groups were able to manage relations with each other. The success of the Ottomans must therefore be located in large part in how they negotiated precisely such a 'foreign policy' with the 'outside world'. This took place in two stages (İnalcık 1954)—first, through the assimilation, or 'caging'[4] of surrounding populations through a mixture of coercion and consent; secondly, by institutionalising the subordination of these surrounding communities through the development of the tributary mode of production.

In the first phase of Ottoman expansion, the conquest, raiding and pillaging of sedentary communities formed the basis of imperial expansion. Many towns and cities were completely or partially destroyed in the process of conquest, allowing Ottoman raiders to appropriate significant amounts of surplus through extortion and looting (Lindner 1983, 24; Vryonis 1969, 253–66). The effects of these conquests were exacerbated by the planned and unplanned migration of Turkic nomads into newly conquered territories, adding substantial demographic pressures on sedentary communities (İnalcık 1954,

122–24; Kiel 2009, 155–56). Both migration and predation caused significant displacement as pre-existing communities sought security in well-guarded towns and cities (Lindner 1983, 26; Vryonis Jr. 1975, 56–57). But coercion was not the only mechanism through which the Ottomans expanded. Consent was developed on the basis of inclusivity that was afforded by horizontal and egalitarian relations between marcher bands, typical of Inner Asian nomadic traditions. Sources from the early period of Ottoman expansion show that predation was relatively free of religious or ethnic connotations (Kafadar 1995, 86). Instead, secular and egalitarian terms such as *akıncı* and *yoldaş* ('comrade') were used to mobilise Muslim, Turkic and Christian marchers (Lowry 2003, 52).

On this basis the House of Osman proved adept at mobilising waves of conquest throughout Anatolia and South East Europe. As the leader of a post-Seljuk *ghazi* movement, Osman carried a reputation for conquest which attracted neighbouring *beyliks* and Turkmen tribes to his territories (İnalcık 1976, 15). Former Byzantine *akritai* clans also found the prospects of equality in decision making and distribution of booty a major attraction. Thus the 'togetherness' of different groups was ultimately based on the common interests of social reproduction—pastoral migrations, predation of sedentary communities and existential survival (Lindner 1983, 24). It was the material benefits of alliance, rather than any ethnic, lineal or religious identity that buttressed Ottoman growth.

Such consent generation through material reward extended beyond (semi-) nomadic bonds to encapsulate relations with sedentary societies. Byzantine institutional and economic weakness meant that many local Byzantine governors decided to join the Ottoman tribe as a better guarantee of security and income, safe in the knowledge that Osman would grant them continued control over their land. Indeed, by the mid-fifteenth century, the majority of Ottoman *tımar* holders were descendants of pre-Ottoman military classes or nobility, with over half of them of Christian descent (İnalcık 1954, 113–15). Local peasant populations also found that the Ottomans offered greater security and fiscal leniency in comparison to the dwindling Byzantine authority (Kafadar 1995, 131; Lowry 2003, 57). Subsequently, many turned to the tribe of Osman for justice and support against nomadic predation from other *beyliks* (Lindner 1983, 26; Lindner 2007, 79).

Similarly, the conquest of former Seljuk towns tended to leave *akhi* administrative structures, legal practices and economic practices intact, generating consent among Muslim urban communities (Lowry 2003, 53). So important were they in the early stages of Ottoman expansion that Orhan's succession from Osman was secured by creating *waqf* endowments for *akhis* and Sufi orders (Shaw 1976, 15). The Ottomans, rather than acting benevolently, were acutely aware of the material benefits of maintaining local populations for the purposes of political security and high economic productivity (Shinder 1978, 514). Undergirding the material benefits of accepting Ottoman rule was an ideology especially suited to the indeterminacy of frontier identities. Dervishes under Ottoman patronage converted people to Osman's tribe through an admixture of tribal mysticism and Islam. Osman himself cemented this important power base by marrying the daughter of a Sufi sheikh which allowed him to cultivate relations with, and prestige among, Sufi groups and *akhi* organisations (Barkey 2008, 51–52). The Ottomans thus acted as a hinge connecting post-Byzantine Christian lords, *akritai* and peasant populations, Turkmen tribes, post-Seljuk *beys* and *akhis*, and wandering members of the *ulema* and dervishes.

Why was it that Osman, and not any other *ghazi* leader, that emerged as this pivot of combination? For Rudi Linder (2009, 35), it was Osman's personal ability as a leader in negotiating ties between social groupings as diverse as Inner Asian nomads, former Seljuk *beys* and former Byzantine *akritai* and peasantry. For Halil İnalcık (1977, 267), it was the accident of geography, the proximity of the Ottomans to the Byzantine frontier. Even bracketing these contingent factors, it is clear that the development of the Ottoman dynasty in this period was determined by its ability to negotiate a set of international determinations—the condition of unevenness in Bithynia—through allurement and accommodation of different communities and the combination of various social forms. Osman, and more broadly the Ottomans, were agents of combined development *par excellence*.

Because imperial expansion was predicated on the social rewards of such combination, success bred success. Through the conquest of the Byzantine settlements of Bursa (1326), Iznik (1329) and Izmit (1331), Orhan became pre-eminent among the *beys* of the marches. The incorporation of the Karasi bands into Ottoman service provided the impulse for an extension of the raids into the Balkans prefiguring the capture of Thrace and Gallipoli. The Ottomans thus achieved a permanent foothold in Europe opening further possibilities for expansion in the region. By 1371 Serbian, Macedonian and Byzantine princes acknowledged Ottoman suzerainty. Simultaneously, the Ottomans consolidated in Anatolia, seizing Ankara and Konya and defeating the Karaman *beylik* in the process (İnalcık 2000, 21–24).

Such expansion led to a significant complexification of Ottoman politics as it sought to come to terms with how to maintain the unity of diverse groups under a single political unit. The Ottomans thus became subject to the 'contradictions of sociological amalgamation' (Allinson and Anievas 2010b) common to the nomadic mode of production. As the reach of Ottoman-led raids expanded they required forms of social and military organisation that could meet the challenge of siege warfare with sedentary communities, namely a reliable and constant levy of manpower and supplies (Hall 1991, 43; İnalcık

1977, 285). This meant moving away from the nomadic horse archer as the primary military unit, to the development of a reliable levy of troops—the Janissaries—that could engage in the protracted campaigning of siege warfare (Fodor 2009, 223). Politically and socially this meant that the old system of independent and equal warriors that partnered in raiding became increasingly obsolete (Di Cosmo 1999, 36; İnalcık 1992, 247). Resources required for the upkeep of infantry troops necessitated the concomitant employment of bureaucrats that were, unlike nomadic marchers, well versed in sedentary traditions of administering systems of taxation, tribute and law (Bromley 1994, 40). The Ottomans made use of former members of unemployed *ulema* who, following the collapse of the Seljuk Empire, were migrating through Anatolia in search of patronage. Administrators of former Byzantine territories were also incorporated to perform these functions so that by 1324–62 there were numerous Christians involved in the running of the Ottoman state, serving as judges, police, military officers and bureaucrats (Lowry 2003, 86–89).

As centralisation loosened bonds of power sharing between the Ottomans and *ghazi beys*, the empire became subject to the dangers of involution associated with the nomadic-sedentary dialectic (Di Cosmo 1999, 36; Lindner 1983, 32). Ottoman expansion afforded conquering *beys* land and sources of revenue in new territories, enabling them to establish themselves as autonomous centres of power (Shaw 1976, 23). In the face of growing centralisation, *beys* sought to retain the privileges associated with horizontalist norms, claiming autonomy of rule and surplus extraction within the frontier territories (Imber 2009, 129). Briefly in the 1370s (Kafadar 1995, 138), and again at the turn of the fifteenth century under geopolitical pressure from Ilkhanids (Hodgson 2009, 435), these centrifugal forces threatened to fragment the Ottoman polity. That the Ottomans were able to survive, and then reconsolidate and expand, was largely down to their ability to co-opt rebellious *beys* and, where necessary, coerce and subjugate them. Both methods were ultimately dependent on the emergence of a centralised administrative system and political unity that could conduct these tasks through coercion, and wealth appropriation and its redistribution (Kafadar 1995, 139). In short, combination was acting as both a compulsion and opportunity for the formation of a centralised state apparatus.

The development and crystallisation of such a state form constituted the second phase of Ottoman expansion. Under the reign of Murad I, the slave levy of Christian boys, the *devşirme,* became an institutionalised practice, reflecting the need for a central patrimonial army and administrative bureaucracy loyal to the sultan (Barkey 2008, 76). Recruited from among men with no ties to the Anatolian Turkic families, the *devşirme* was from the start an attempt to consolidate a centralised state as a counterweight to provincial forces (Kafadar 1995, 141).

As hierarchical state structures crystallised, the Ottoman centre increasingly laid claim to land, revenue, slaves and booty appropriated from the frontiers in the process of *ghaza* conquest (Lindner 1983, 32). Through the appointment of the first *kadı-asker* Murad I created a centralised treasury, which established land survey registers, and organised the distribution of revenue and collections of taxes through land allocations (*mukatah*) such as the *tımar* (Kafadar 1995, 146). Also under Murad I's reign, the Ottomans established a formal distinction between the *askeri* ruling class and *reaya* subject class, codifying legally and ideologically the appropriation of surplus through taxation rather than through raids (Di Cosmo 1999, 36). Taxation was systematised by developing extensive inventories of taxable resources on *tımar* lands. These formed official tax registers that set the rate of agrarian exploitation (Imber 2009, 196; İnalcık 1954, 103). Consequently, surplus appropriation that had previously been confined to localities of pre-existing *pronoia* or *iqta* was redirected to feed a burgeoning Ottoman imperial centre. Through the regulation of *tımars* the Ottomans were also able to cultivate social stratification between the old *beys* of the marches and the central administration, wherein the latter established control over the former. The institutionalisation of the *tımar* thus went hand in hand with the development of the Ottoman centre, as agrarian surplus generated by the *reaya* was siphoned off to the imperial centre. The establishment and consolidation of *tımars* against an expanded state was a function of the subordination of different sections of the Ottoman community—but in particular the ruling class and means of production—under the tributary mode of production.

The reigns of Sultans following Murad I demonstrated a concerted attempt to deepen the institutionalisation of tributary rule. Under the rule of Bayezid, provincial land and population surveys, a central treasury and a bureaucracy established the absolute authority of the sultan in the provinces. In particular, the slaves of the *kapıkullar* proliferated throughout the institutions of Ottoman power becoming the predominant holders of *tımars* (İnalcık 1976, 28). In 1453, following the conquest of Constantinople, Mehmet II attained the prestige and territorial basis through which he could consolidate the institutionalisation of the tributary mode. He increased the size and strength of the Janissaries by recruiting 5,000 new men and providing them with improved weaponry and wage increases. Meanwhile, old Turkic notables from the marches that had acquired private property in land were dispossessed. The land was reclassified as state land and distributed as *tımars* among Janissaries (Barkey 2008, 77–79). A similar dispossession of the *beys* took place in the sultan's household. The higher echelons of the Ottoman state—such as the Grand Vizier and *kadı-asker*—were henceforth drawn almost exclusively from the sultan's personal slaves instead of from the *beys* of the frontiers. In contrast to other Muslim empires, state law—*Kanun*—was established as a distinct body of law alongside *Şeriat* that maintained the preponderance and absolute authority of the sultan, allowing him to promulgate law without the intervention of the *ulema* (İnalcık 1976, 47–48). Finally, the practice of fratricide (wherein the new sultan executed his siblings during the process of succession) was institutionalised, thus limiting the potential for drawn out civil wars though which ruling-class conflict could destabilise the Ottoman centre (Kafadar 1995, 153).

The reign of Mehmet II thus witnessed the emergence of 'the idea ... that an *amir* was a natural necessity in human society, that he who was strongest had the obligation to extend his sway as far as possible in order to increase the area of social order and peace' (Hodgson 2009, 562). In short, this crystallised notions of Sultanism and patrimonial authority as such—the heirs of Osman were more than first among equals, and a higher entity standing above the differentiated communities that had gravitated around or been conquered by the Ottomans. Moreover, this emergent notion of Sultanism exhibited traits of the developmental combination that had created it. Thus, Mehmed II expressed his supremacy by linking himself to the khanate genealogy of Inner Asia, the heir of Islamic imperial traditions, and now also the inheritor of the Roman seat of power. By presenting himself at once as 'xan, gâzi and Caesar' (Golden 1992, 365), Mehmed II articulated patrimonial authority as the living embodiment of the processes of uneven and combined development that brought the Ottomans to imperial preponderance on a tributary basis.

CONCLUSION

This chapter has argued that developmental difference, multiplicity and thus intersocietal interactivity are necessary parts of understanding how the classical Ottoman Empire came into being. Specifically, the emergence of the basic social relations of the tributary mode were determined by relations of unevenness in Anatolia, brought about by nomadic migration, the collapse of the Seljuk Empire and the 'western turn' of the Byzantine Empire. It was the combined development of the institutional and social remnants of these disparate communities that the Ottomans had to negotiate in their process of state formation. This occurred in two steps: first, through the process of incorporating the multiplicity of political communities into a loosely unified confederation. Secondly, through the political response to the contradictory complexification of social relations brought about by this incorporation. The outcome of this combined development was the social stratification between *askeri* and *reaya*, on the one hand, and between members of the old and new ruling class, on the other, through the creation of a standing army, the emergence of a centralised bureaucracy and the elevation of the sultan as absolute and hereditary ruler. In short, uneven and combined development in fourteenth-century Anatolia gave rise to the forms and configurations of social stratification typical of the tributary mode, wherein the Ottoman state obtained control over the means of production and the ruling class.

This chapter also offers an alternative to the essentialist characterisation of the Ottoman Empire in the Orientalist terms of Islam or nationalist conceptions of Turkic ethnicity. This chapter has shown that early Ottoman history was only loosely attached to religion and ethnicity in terms of political identity or ideology. The period of Ottoman expansion (and indeed beyond) was instead marked by extensive collaboration with (as well as conquest of) Christian and non-Turkic communities, in line with nomadic structures of religious inclusivity. The very absence of a central and coherent authority, or an embedded culture, in the Anatolian milieu meant that religious identities were heterodox, fleeting and malleable. From the very beginning of the empire, all sections of Ottoman society—patrimonial authority, landed nobility and peasantry—were composed of actors from a multiplicity and indeed hybridity of ethnic backgrounds. And, in line with the nature of uneven and combined development typical of the tributary mode, it was largely *after* 1517, with the conquest of Egypt and Syria, and later Baghdad, that the demography of the empire became predominantly Muslim. With this change came new pressures of ruling-class reproduction and legitimation which entailed the subsequent move away from social heterogeneity towards a more prominent use of Muslim state practices and ideology (Barkey 2008, 102; Lowry 2003, 96, 113). This increased the influence of the *ulema*, strengthened the claims of the sultan as head of the Caliphate and gave rise to the emerging European perception of the Ottomans as a specifically Muslim threat. As Simon Bromley argues, the Islamic composition of the Ottoman Empire was not a fixed essence, but 'a contingent feature of the necessary intermediation in tributary forms of rule and appropriation' (Bromley 1994, 40). That this 'necessary intermediation' was, again, determined by international relations suggests that the internalist essentialism of Orientalist and nationalist approaches is historically untenable and thus theoretically partial. But moreover that the framework of uneven and combined development can provide an explanation for the apparent contingency of the Ottomans' turn to Islam further demonstrates its analytical power in comparison to essentialised and static approaches to world history.

NOTES

1. I would like to thank the following for their comments and suggestions on different versions of this chapter: Alexander Anievas, Kamran Matin and Justin Rosenberg. All mistakes are my own.

2. I would like to thank Yavuz Tuyuoğlu for alerting me to the significance of these debates. Although I do not deal with the details of the mode of production debate here, a more in-depth survey is offered in Anievas and Nişancioğlu (2015).

3. For recent key interventions in debates around uneven and combined development, see Anievas (2012); Matin (2013a, 2013b); Rosenberg (2006); Rosenberg (2013b).

4. For a discussion of 'caging', see Anievas and Nişancioğlu (2015) and van der Pijl (2007).

Chapter 6

Revisiting the Transformation of the Nineteenth Century and the 'Eastern Question'

Uneven and Combined Development and the Ottoman Steppe

Jamie Allinson

The history of the nineteenth-century Ottoman Empire provides particularly fertile ground for scholars examining the historical sociology of global change. The vision of the empire presents a series of paradoxes emblematic of the period of the 'Great Transformation' as a whole: simultaneously a crucial player in the European Great Power system, and Islamic Empire; object of pseudo-colonial management in the guise of the 'Eastern Question'; ultimate source of, or nostalgic contrast to, the hecatombs of the contemporary Middle East. It is surely no accident that the last years of the Sublime Porte during the nineteenth century have come to be loaded with such discursive valence—for the empire formed a particular variety of 'inside outside', straddling and constituting the 'seam of the encounter' between Europe as its imagined exterior.

Late Ottoman historiography has thus come to inform a part of the debate around the theory of 'uneven and combined development' (UCD), with which this volume is concerned. This interest derives from the particular place occupied by the Ottoman Empire within the process of uneven and combined development, understood as the multilinear interactions of different patterns of social relations at a global level such that the distinct character of social relations in a given society feeds back into the interaction itself.[1] The history of the Ottoman reforms from above concentrates broader experiences mapped in the nineteenth century by Barry Buzan and George Lawson (in this volume) among others: the way in which the confluence of economic transformation, rationalised state administration and progressive modernity became the index of Great Power status. In this transition from a multi-actor and multi-civilisation world to one of states, the nineteenth-century Ottoman experiences play a crucial role. The key debates in Ottoman historiography, around the two axes of 'decline versus expansion' and 'internalism/ externalism', have become intertwined with crucial debates in the enterprise of uneven and combined development as international relations (IR) theory: the question of the transhistorical status of UCD, and associated with that, the potential pitfalls of Eurocentrism. The interaction of the Ottoman Empire with a European states system, and the wholesale reforms undertaken by the Ottomans in the nineteenth century have been used to underpin the argument that UCD functions best as a transhistorical concept shorn of Eurocentric trappings that undermine accounts of extra-European agency.[2]

In this chapter, I intervene in this debate. I take up the case, not of the Ottoman Empire's Anatolian heartland but of the sub-Damascene steppe lands that would, after the First World War, become Transjordan. I maintain that, although critiques that point out the significance of Ottoman agency and the centrality of diffusion, hybridity and geopolitical pressure from the 'non-West' in the making of European modernity are certainly correct and well-taken, these points of critique are compatible with a view of UCD as both invested with a Marxian content in the form of modes of production and dependent for its full activation on the transition to one such mode—capitalism. Following Robbie Shilliam (2004), I argue that this transition, the process of 'primitive accumulation', gives substance to processes of uneven and combined development.

UCD therefore finds common ground with a certain version of the postcolonial endeavour, studying, in Partha Chatterjee's (2013) words, 'primitive accumulation under different historical conditions'. In particular I argue that the predominant mode of production in the Ottoman Empire was tributary: in this aspect the empire did not differ from pre-capitalist Europe *except* in that the typical crisis dynamic of the tributary mode, between centralisation and decentralisation, were settled in different ways. European feudalism and the 'fractured tributary mode' characteristic of the relations between pastoral nomads and sedentary agriculturalists in the Arab steppe were thus points on a continuum rather than opposite poles. The nineteenth-century reforms, although certainly reflecting tendencies internal to the Ottoman social formation, were nonetheless aimed at the extension of Ottoman 'infrastructural' power into the steppe representing an attempt to bring about mimetic primitive accumulation. This statement does not imply an absence of agency however: I seek to demonstrate how the conflict between centralising state and tribute-taking formations in the empire's Arab provinces provided the basis for a particular kind of combined development with consequences for the later politics of the region. In so doing, I attempt to engage with, and take on board, the arguments of critics who have pointed to the lack of extra-European agency in UCD.

This chapter proceeds in the following steps. In the first section I review the linked questions of the transhistorical status of UCD and the risk of Eurocentrism, and how these relate to research on the historical sociology of the external relations of the late Ottoman Empire. I then present my own theoretical position, viewing the nineteenth-century reforms of the empire as the response of a fundamentally tributary social formation to the 'whip of external necessity'. The subsequent historical narrative of this response seeks to demonstrate how local agency and the 'whip of external necessity' interacted in the conflict between the extension of state power and the tribute-claiming Bedouin of the Ottoman steppe.

THE OTTOMAN NINETEENTH CENTURY AND UNEVEN AND COMBINED DEVELOPMENT

The series of fiscal, agrarian and governmental reforms undertaken by the Ottoman Empire in the nineteenth century have long formed a fulcrum for historical accounts of the Middle East (see, e.g., Islamoglu-Inan 1987; Gerber 1987; Khoury and Kostiner 1990; Bromley 1994; Inalcik 1994). In recent years, the key debates in Ottoman historiography centering around the two axes of 'declinism' and 'internalism/externalism' have become intertwined with lines of division in the enterprise of uneven and combined development as IR theory (Nişancioğlu 2014) and with criticisms of UCD as running the risk of Eurocentrism (cf. Hobson 2011; Tansel 2015). The role of the Ottoman Empire in the emergence and operation of the European states system, and the nature of the programme of attempted social transformation by the nineteenth-century Porte, have been given as examples of how UCD is applicable across historical epochs, and capable on that basis of explicating non-European agency in the making of global capitalism.

The interweaving of these debates is visible in the presentation of UCD as an answer to perennial questions in late Ottoman historiography. The first of these debates runs between the once orthodox position that the Ottoman Empire fell into secular decline at some point after the sixteenth century (Lewis 1987; Bromley 1994; Inalcik 1994) versus the challenge that there was no such secular trend, or at least not a predetermined one (Keyder and Islamoglu-Inan 1987; Gran 1987; Sunkar 1987). The second aspect of the debate concerns whether the main forces in the decline (or transformation) of the empire were external or internal to it. As Kerem Nişancioğlu argues (2014), UCD does indeed present a possible route out of this impasse by taking as its point of departure the sociological unity of these two forms of explanation. However, in presenting a theoretical framework in which the 'external whip of necessity' plays such a large role in producing the Ottoman reform process, does one not risk obscuring the historical agency of Ottoman actors (Tansel 2015)?

The objection that the idea of the 'whip of external necessity', as well as being a highly ill-chosen metaphor, obscures the agency of non-European actors, is a powerful one. In Trotsky's usage, it refers to the means by which pre-capitalist ruling classes were impelled to adopt social forms characteristic of the capitalist powers that posed a geopolitical threat to them (Trotsky 1997, 2). In both its content (the compulsion coming from the 'West' towards non-Western ruling classes) and its textual context (the discussion of 'back-wardness') the concept of the 'whip of external necessity' therefore seems at ever-present risk of collapsing into Eurocentrism. In the following pages, I attempt to demonstrate that this objection can be overcome, by providing an account that demonstrates non-European agency within a process that was nonetheless fundamentally directed towards mimetic primitive accumu-lation—a process that therefore cannot be understood without the threat of 'external necessity' as consciously articulated by the Ottoman rulers them-selves. This argument does not require a conception of European uniqueness: as pointed out above the tributary nature of the empire did not differ from pre-capitalist Europe *except* in that the typical crisis dynamic of the tributary mode between centralisation and decentralisation were settled in different ways. European feudalism and the 'fractured tributary mode' characteristic of the relations between pastoral nomads and sedentary agriculturalists in the Arab steppe were thus points on a continuum rather than opposite poles.

In making this argument, I rely upon a conception of the late Ottoman periphery as dominated by the 'fractured tributary state'. Tributary relations are those in which the direct producers control the means of production but do not appropriate the surplus themselves. Therefore, by contrast with the capi-talist state form, the relations between the (usually agrarian) direct producer and the exploiter are 'political' rather than 'economic' in that they are based on '"non-economic compulsion"—contrasted by Marx with the (notionally) free bargaining between capitalist and wage-worker in a capitalist economy' (Hilton 1990, 5). The agrarian direct producers of the tributary mode thus have the means to reproduce themselves but render some portion of the sur-plus to a ruling class that exercises 'actual or potential violence, that is … physical force and ideology' to appropriate this surplus (Haldon 1993, 77). The transition from this form to one in which direct producers are market and wage-dependent constitutes the primitive accumulation process. In the work of both Marx and later Marxists, primitive accumulation has come to take on two distinct meanings: the former sense in which the term is used in this chap-ter and, in a distinct but related usage, the 'letters of blood and fire' in which the history of capital is written, the historical accumulation through plunder, empire and slavery by which England (and other European powers) acquired the means of capitalist take-off.[3] The programme of reform undertaken by the Sublime Porte was mimetic in this sense—not that it was any less 'real' than the experience of England or France but in *conscious emulation* of the separation of the direct producers from the means of production and with the aim of increasing the empire's readiness to defend itself against the threat from the West.

The advantage of the above framework lies in seeing ('Western') feudalism and ('Eastern') tribute-paying societies not as different modes of production rendering the respective geographical areas dynamic or stagnant but rather in placing these empirically observable relations along a continuum generated by the dynamic of the tributary mode itself. Such a conception allows us to escape the supposedly *sui generis* nature of European society contrasted with a stereotypical vision of a stagnant Eastern despotism into which Europeans expanded. I follow Samir Amin (1976, 14) and John Haldon (1993, 64) in accepting that European feudalism was a variant of tributary social relations. Whether surplus is appropriated by (feudal) rent or (tributary) tax is not a fundamental difference but a variation in the 'control exercised by the ruling class, or the state or state class over the community' and 'while this certainly affects the rate of exploitation, it does not affect the actual nature of the mode of surplus appropriation' (Haldon 1993, 65). The degree of fragmentation of centralisation of power is a historical result—not foreordained in advance—of the contest between the central and peripheral parts of the exploiting state class. The basis of these contests lies in the two central divisions of the tributary mode. One is the horizontal one between direct producer and the appropriator of the surplus: the appropriation 'resisted more or less strongly and in many different ways, ranging from labour service inadequately performed to open rebellion … [that is] the conflict of classes, central to Marxist theory' (Hilton 1990, 5). The tributary mode's unity of economic and extra-economic coercion, however, means that a second, vertical division, lies not between units competing via the market but between central and local control of the coercive power by which surplus is extracted. This explains the constant tension in tributary systems between a central node of 'despotic power' and its functionaries who seek to transform their local control over the tribute into longer-lasting claims to exploitation. Topography and geography may help such a result come about (deserts, mountains and other impassable terrain can give an advantage to the local exploiters) but do not determine it. The attempted centralisation of Ottoman power, the 'parcellized sovereignty' (Anderson 1974, 397, 407) of feudal Europe, the *han* of the Japanese samurai and so on represent historical outcomes of this struggle.

This framework also allows us to understand the basic social relations of the Ottoman Arab steppe as those of an extreme example of the fragmented tributary mode. The core of these social relations was, on the one hand, the practice of *khuwwa*, the taking of tribute by pastoral nomads (for whom the term 'bedouin' is retained here, although its meaning is contested) from settled cultivators *(fellahin)* and, on the other, *musha',* collective agricultural tenure. *Khuwwa* was levied on those cultivators (and travellers) who fell within the tribe's effective zone of control, the *dirah*. It was these relations that the Ottomans attempted, in response to what Trotsky called the 'whip of external necessity', to transform into tax-paying private property (i.e. mimetic primitive accumulation), which produced the unintended outcome of a combined social formation.

The practice of *musha'*, although not universal and co-existing beside practices interpreted by later scholars as simple private property (Fischbach 2000), necessarily involved some communal control over production. In *musha'* villages the individual household cultivated its lands as a private unit but the quality and quantity of that land was periodically redistributed through the community—which is to say the heads of households—to ensure a rough equality across time. The cultivators in *musha'* villages at least did not hold absolute alienable rights over their land, this being subject to a moral economy negotiated at the level of the community as a whole and producing a surplus accruing eventually to the sheikh, the state or the local bedouin. Certainly there were wide variations in this system in the amount and method of partition (Fischbach 2000, 39) and in the spread of the system itself. Often tribal relationships passed across the distinction between pastoral nomadism and settled agriculture. However, it was *fellahin* who paid tribute to bedouin, not the other way around. The nomadic tribal unit was both more mobile and more attuned to military conflict than most settled communities. In a social formation based on coercive surplus extraction, the bedouin therefore possessed a strategic advantage over settled cultivators, which they used to obtain surplus in the form of *khuwwa*.

The taking of *khuwwa* by nomads from settled communities (as well as anyone seeking to pass through their territory) thus reflects the form of surplus extraction in a fractured tributary system. A technologically advanced standing army, of the sort that the Ottomans later brought to bear, may be able to defeat mobile warriors (although even then only in certain areas). However, a smaller settled community of cultivators, unprotected by hills or rivers, would be no match for the mobility of the nomads. The greater the range of the nomads, based on the hardiness of their type of livestock, the greater the strategic advantage they derived, an advantage secured by the predominance of the camel (Hamarneh 1985). The relationship was reversed only when a settled community was wealthy and established enough to send a permanent military force against the bedouin (Marx 1993, 349). Thus, sedentary cultivation was most advanced in those communities protected by mountainous landscapes from bedouin raids, or the Jordan river (Rogan 2002, 24, 27).

The pre-capitalist social relations were thus tributary but fragmented and were reflected in two social practices—*musha'* and *khuwwa*—the transcendence of which would represent a process of primitive accumulation initiated by Ottoman and later British authorities. However, the result of this process was not the replication of an ideal-type of capitalist social relations but rather, as Trotsky outlined for Russia, a combined social formation whose trajectory to certain alignments can be traced back through these social processes. The remainder of this chapter provides the empirical substance of this process, beginning with the story of the attempted Ottoman reforms due to what Trotsky called the 'whip of external necessity'.

OTTOMAN MIMETIC REFORM AND THE 'WHIP OF EXTERNAL NECESSITY'

The integration of the Ottoman Empire as a 'zone of dependent support' into a 'single capitalist world' (Migdal 1994, 10), which was to transform the coercive social symbiosis of settled and nomadic communities around the Jordan river, was embodied in the body of reforms and extension of the empire's central coercive power in the later nineteenth century (Quataert 1994, 762). This body of measures, collectively discussed under the heading of the 'Tanzimat', represented a similar process to that of the Russian emancipation of the serfs or the Japanese Meiji Restoration (cf. Allinson and Anievas 2010a): attempts by tributary ruling classes to catch up and compete with the capitalist states. This was the 'whip of external necessity' produced by unevenness leading to the attempt to 'turn foe in tutor', which then led to combination.

As noted above, recent scholarship on Ottoman economic history has conscientiously questioned the idea that the empire's economy stagnated in the nineteenth century (Quataert 1994, 843) and furnished us with evidence of the development of a native Ottoman bourgeoisie. Although these qualifications are important and caution against any notion of the empire as a purely passive recipient of imported European techniques, it is difficult to view the reform of the Ottoman land code and administrative re-organisations of the Tanzimat as anything other than an instance of how '[i]nternational relations intertwine with "internal relations" to bring about 'new, unique and historically concrete combinations' (Gramsci 1971, 182). In this section I seek to demonstrate how the feedback loop of uneven and combined development worked on the Ottoman Empire. I show how the competitive advantage of European states produced by the uneven development of capitalist social relations manifested itself in the disintegration of the outer provinces, fiscal crisis and consequently the compulsion to emulate capitalist social relations.

The Ottoman Empire under Sulayman the Magnificent was not merely a successful tributary state in a world of tributary states: it was the pre-eminent power west of the Himalayas, its revenue double that of the bloated Habsburg domains (Anderson 1974, 365). Yet by the late nineteenth century a gap—perceptible to and evident in the conceptions and actions of Ottoman rulers themselves—had opened up between the empire and Western European states (Issawi 1980, 1). The 'internal' aspects of this gap, such as the tendency of Ottoman tribute-taking structures to become local tax-farming rackets throughout the eighteenth and nineteenth centuries, cannot be separated from its 'external' aspects, such as the imposition of unequal trade concessions and the secession of outer provinces under European protection or control (Issawi 1980, 1–3). As a result, the empire was engaged in near constant defensive warfare of some kind, being at war for fully 53 of the years between 1800 and 1918 (Quataert 1994, 789). This feedback loop between geopolitical and social relations provides us with the beginning of the social trajectories along which the future Jordanian state would travel: a process of attempted transformation engendered by the collapse of Ottoman manufacture in the face of Western European competition, the decreasing relative level of income gained through the tributary system and the loss of the empire's most productive territories. The attempt to extend—or rather to invent—the Ottoman state as an 'infrastructural' state, the buttress of an autopoietic system of capitalist property relations was thus a conscious response to this crisis.

Where is the historical substance for this claim? A strong case has been made that the Ottoman Empire itself was a significant factor in the rise of capitalist social relations in Europe (Nişancioğlu 2014; see also Anievas and Nişancioğlu 2015). Yet an empirically visible change in Ottoman fortunes is closely correlated with the shift in trade away from the cross-Anatolian routes to the trans-Atlantic and Indian Ocean transport of specie and commodities (Issawi 1980, 2). It was in the second quarter of the nineteenth century that the 'influx of European goods began in earnest—hand manufactures made in labour-intensive Western workshops as well as the more familiar machine-made cotton yarn and cloth' (Quataert 1994, 762). The Anglo-Ottoman trade convention, signed in 1838 in partial recompense for British aid in the campaign against Muhammad Ali, prohibited the granting of state monopolies and provided a model for the favourable treatment of merchants (Keyder 1987, 29). The empire was 'peripheralised', becoming increasingly dependent on agricultural tribute (Keyder and Islamoglu-Inan 1987, 60–62). Thus the empire was losing out in a process of 'coercive comparison' (Barker 2006, 78) with those states in which capitalist social relations of production prevailed. As a result, the central state sought desperately to remove or marginalise 'its domestic rivals—urban guilds, tribes and provincial notables—while maintaining its place in the new world order' (Quataert 1994, 762).

The success of this attempt was mixed. The military superiority of Western capitalist powers such as Britain and France over the Ottoman Empire both reflected and fed back into the crisis of the tributary system. As Eugene Rogan writes, using Michael Mann's concept of 'infrastructural power':

> [T]he penetration of society which infrastructural power allowed for an even greater share of production to be collected in taxes, which was essential for the maintenance of large-standing armies. While such changes were more characteristic of the nation-states of Western Europe, even multi-national Empires such as Russia and Austria had developed the infrastructural power to finance the modern armies which menaced Ottoman domains. (Rogan 2002, 2)

Throughout the nineteenth century the empire lost its most productive agricultural provinces either directly to European imperialism or to local secessionist movements aspiring to emulate the French revolutionary model. The earliest and most instructive example can be found in the Napoleonic invasion of Egypt in 1798 (Mitchell 1988, 17). The French occupation spurred the rise to power of Muhammad Ali, a local military commander, whose leadership combined the centrifugal tendency of tributary extraction with the aspiration to build a new mimetic order. Ali seized the Syrian provinces from Ottoman control, only to be frustrated by the Western powers (Rogan 2002, 2). Algeria was lost to French invasion a few years afterwards.

Worse was yet to come, as the most productive European provinces were lost from the 1820s onwards. These provided the bulk of Ottoman revenues and their loss was 'devastating' to the empire's economy (Quataert 1994, 768). The empire was losing the provinces most productive of the agricultural tribute upon which the entire structure was based, and therefore losing further the capacity to govern other provinces. The case can be overstated: revenue actually increased from 1809 to 1885. However, the increase did not keep pace with the rate of increase in expenditure, leading to the crippling effective loss of fiscal sovereignty in 1881 (Issawi 1980, 361). This cycle of budgetary crisis stimulated the Ottoman drive to extend taxable cultivation (Rogan 2002, 45). This would inevitably bring a clash with the system of *khuwwa*, the central relationship of the fragmented tributary relations of production that prevailed in the lands that became Jordan. The process of Ottoman reform, instigated to 'turn the foe into tutor', was embodied in the Gulhane Rescript of 1839, the revised land code of 1858 and the expeditions to re-assert authority over the steppe and desert of southern Syria.

The Rescript and the Land Code were two faces of the same coin—or rather they represented the unfolding of unified tributary power into the division of economic and extra-economic coercion characteristic of those societies that had trounced the Ottoman Empire in geopolitical competition. The

Gulhane Rescript established the general prospectus of change that would be carried out in the 1858 Land Code (Mundy and Smith 2007, 14). The 1839 Rescript established the principle of individual liability, equality before the law and security of private property (Anderson 1974, 389). The Land Code introduced a version of such principles into the economic base of the empire, which would also require the extension of effective governance into those areas beset by fragmented tribute-taking authorities such as the *khuwwa*-taking nomads.

Interpretations of the Land Code vary as to whether it was a success, derived from a process of agrarian change or served to impose it and whether it actually altered practices on the land (Mundy and Smith 2007, 3–4). However, the code introduced different principles of registration and taxation introduced to increase revenue along the lines of the successful capitalist states that were in conflict with the *khuwwa* system. The code thus sought to promote the process of mimetic primitive accumulation. The code established the right of individuals as legal owners of previously collective usufruct lands provided they could demonstrate their registration in a '*tapu*' deed (Rogan 2002, 13). The individual rather than the community thereby became responsible for the payment of taxation (Rogan 2002, 13). Designed to maximise revenue through taxing every piece of cultivable land (Issawi 1988, 286), the code established a means under which uncultivated land reverted to state control. This implied, of course, that productively cultivated land and its fruits, after tax, were the alienable property of the registered owner. This is a different conception of property to that of *musha'*, evidence of continuity with the pre-Land Code period notwithstanding (Fischbach 2000, 35), and one that would lead to inevitable conflict with the *khuwwa* system: the premise of the Land Code being the separation of economic extraction and coercive power. Donald Quataert's (1994, 857) apt characterisation of the Land Code as bearing a 'capitalist trunk and a mercantilist foot', which reflects 'the transitional nature of the state itself', indicates the utility of considering this period as the starting point of a combined social formation.

BREAKING TRIBUTARY POWER

The Ottomans thus adopted a twofold strategy to promote taxable cultivation by breaking the unity of economic and extra-economic coercion. Although the Ottoman administrators may not have expressed themselves in such terms, their twofold approach to the problem perfectly reflected this requirement. On the one hand, the Ottomans sought to inflict exemplary defeats on the bedouin tribes; on the other, to induce settlement by stipulating that land registration (under the terms of the 1858 code) would be permitted only to those who actually cultivated their lands, and by introducing communities—mainly Circassians and Christians—who would not pay *khuwwa*. The settlement and registration of land by these communities led bedouin tribes such as the Bani Sakhr to register their own *dira* (Fischbach 2000, 46).

For the Ottomans to assert control over the steppe meant a change of both personnel and policy, one that was only reached some years into the Tanzimat reforms. As part of the reforms, the Porte appointed the efficient Mehmet Rasid Pasha to the position of *wali* (provincial governor) in Damascus (Rogan 2002, 48). Rasid's remit was to extend the reorganised governance of the Ottoman state in its sub-Syrian hinterland, and he set about this work with vigour. Damascus sent military expeditions south to break the power of the Bani Sakhr and 'Adwan tribes (Rogan 2002, 51). That military power, of course, formed the precondition for the extraction of *khuwwa*. Rasid Pasha reversed the strategic imbalance that had hitherto guaranteed extractive rights to the pastoral nomadic tribes. In the campaigns against the 'Adwan, the Ottoman forces were aided by their adversaries' attachment to recently created areas of cultivation and short-range livestock pastures, undermining the advantage of easy flight into the Eastern desert (Hamarneh 1985, 62).

The Pasha moved his forces gradually southwards, from the most extensively settled and cultivated zones (which submitted to central authority more easily) down into the Balqa' valley (Rogan 2002, 49). The expeditionary force was more sizeable and technologically advanced than previous Ottoman attempts, comprising three infantry battalions, nine cavalry squadrons and several artillery pieces (Rogan 2002, 49). We can judge the impressiveness of the force by the reaction of the people of Salt, who soon submitted to the Pasha, and rendered 3 million piastres in tax arrears to him (Rogan 2002, 50). Having established a base in the only town of the Balqa', Rasid thrust at the 'Adwan encampment, killing 50 of their number, driving them from their tents and livestock and capturing their paramount chieftains (Rogan 2002, 52). This marked a serious blow not just for the 'Adwan and their allies but for the practice of *khuwwa* as a whole.

The *khuwwa* takers could not simply tolerate this turn of events. The Bani Sakhr reversed their traditional rivalry with the 'Adwan—demonstrating perhaps the consciousness of a systemic threat to their practices of surplus extraction—and allied with them to raid Ramtha in 1869, reasserting their rights to *khuwwa* under Rasid's nose in the cultivated district of the Hawran (Rogan 2002, 51). Rasid could no more accede to this bedouin provocation than the Bani Sakhr could willingly give up their extractive rights: two systems of surplus extraction were in conflict. Weakness on the Pasha's part could have endangered the entire project of the new Ottoman power in the steppe (Rogan 2002, 51). Accompanied by the British and French consuls, Rasid's 4,000 Ottoman soldiers bested the Bani Sakhr and obtained their submission and 225,000 piastres to pay for the expedition: '[i]f the first Balqa' expedition introduced direct Ottoman rule to the district, the second campaign confirmed that the Ottomans were in Jordan [sic] to stay' (Rogan 2002, 51–52).

Rasid Pasha's campaigns were not the end of *khuwwa*, however. The topographical division between Southern Hawran and Northern Hijaz revealed itself in the limits to Ottoman power. Sharply conscious of the threat posed by the increase of British interests in Egypt, culminating in the 1882 occupation of the country, the Ottomans engaged in a number of schemes to establish an administrative centre in Ma'an ruling over the sparsely populated steppe surrounding the Haj route (Rogan 2002, 54). The choice of Ma'an reflected the intertwining of geopolitical and sociological factors that characterised the Ottoman modernisation project as a whole, which was 'motivated by economic and strategic concerns: the sedentarisation of the tribes, the extension of cultivation, linkage with the Arabian Peninsula and, after 1882, from potential British incursions' (Rogan 2002, 54).

Yet the Ottomans found themselves still circumscribed by the limits of a despotic rather than infrastructural power. Ma'an was too remote and its inhabitants too used to making their own bargains with the local bedouin, to be governed, let alone become a centre of governance (Rogan 2002, 34). The Damascene pashas had somewhat more success when they shifted focus to Karak. However, they were only able to establish themselves thanks to a rift between the local Bani Sakhr and the Al-Majali, the ruling clan of Karak. Even then the Ottomans entered Karak in 1893 only after a week-long siege and an agreement to make the Majalis governors of the new Karak district (Rogan 2002, 55). The frailty of central Ottoman power was demonstrated by the Karak revolt of 1910. The further south and east the Ottomans proceeded, the more frustrated their schemes tended to become.

The scope of Ottoman re-engagement was therefore geographically circumscribed as its predecessors had been. Nonetheless, the Ottoman efforts in the Balqa' and northward districts were no mere repetition of the temporary raids of the pre-Tanzimat era—tentative jabs of the tributary state into its hinterland. Rather the pashas sought to make productive tax-paying cultivable land out of the steppe and desert. This meant abolishing *khuwwa* relations (implying the military operations described above) and installing communities that could bear tax-paying market relations. The second track of Ottoman policy in doing so was to settle or resettle such communities in the more fertile areas of the territory: a common policy across the empire (Quataert 1994, 849).

The Ottomans settled Circassian refugees from the Balkans and the Caucasus in the Balqa' valley, heartland of the Bani Sakhr, in two waves; between 1878 and 1884 and again between 1901 and 1906 (Rogan 2002,

73). The authorities granted them land, tax-free, to settle and farm around Amman. The Ottoman motive was to use these sturdy farmer-fighters to put an end to *khuwwa* relations. The Circassians, culturally remote incomers to the region, would have no truck with paying tribute to bedouin—on whose *dirah*, moreover, they had settled—resulting in frequent clashes and occasional alliances between the two (Rogan 2002, 75–76). They also introduced cut roads and wheeled transport. Such settlements had a knock-on effect, leading the *khuwwa*-taking tribes to register their land in the Balqa' within the terms of the 1858 Land Law (Fischbach 2000, 46). The settlement of Christians, fleeing an inter-clan dispute in Kerak, produced a similar effect around Madaba (Rogan 2002, 82). These Christians engaged in permanent agriculture and paid taxes but not *khuwwa*. Against the protests of Sattam al-Fayiz, the paramount chief of the Bani Sakhr whose men had mounted raids for *khuwwa* against the Madaba Christians, the Ottomans awarded the lands to the Christians. The award further alerted 'the powerful tribes of the region that they risked losing lands held by customary rights unless these were registered with the government land offices, put under cultivation and taxes regularly paid' (Rogan 2002, 81).

The preceding survey of the origins and process of Ottoman reform, undertaken to render that tributary empire fit to fend off the 'whip of external necessity', indicates the beginning of the trajectory of Jordan as a combined social formation. The Ottomans sought to imitate the dual separation of direct producer from means of production (or at the very least, conferring legal title to those means) and of economic and non-economic coercion: in other words, primitive accumulation as a means to 'catch up'. What were the important results of this process for these later developments?

The following aspects, which were later deepened by the British Mandate, can be identified as providing the social basis on which certain alignments were chosen and implemented: a topographical division in the campaigns against *khuwwa*-taking; a relatively more egalitarian landholding structure in parts of the territory; and the emergence of division between *khuwwa* takers, or former *khuwwa* takers, and the actual cultivators of lands they registered. These are all aspects of the transformation of one form of surplus extraction into another but without the decisive replacement of the older form. What emerged from this process was a combined social formation, rather than any purely 'capitalist' or 'tributary' one: a formation in which the vertical unity of the tribute-taking pastoral nomads was preserved, but based upon sharecropping by landless labourers attracted to the newly registered lands.

One must first note the geographical, or rather topographical, division. Land registration in the Tapu registers under the terms of the 1858 Land Code was only fully carried out in 'Ajlun. In the Balqa' the Bani Sakhr and others participated in the competitive registration detailed above. Further south the

Ottomans did not intervene strongly, although a market in land does seem to have existed in some districts (Rogan 2002, 92). Elements of the tribe as an economic unit were preserved—by social distinction of the kind described above or by the persistent geographical division above and below the valley of Wadi Mujib at the lower end of the Dead Sea. *Khuwwa* continued to be taken in these areas and the sharecropping arrangements on Bani Sakhr 'plantation villages' retained elements of coercive subordination (Rogan 2002, 89). In the areas under full Ottoman control the taxes on the newly registered lands, although regularised and set at a maximum (Quataert 1994, 846), were still collected by tax farming. The Ottomans tried repeatedly to abolish tax farms but lacked the infrastructure to replace them (Quataert 1994, 854).

The renewed attempt at tax collections undertaken in the later nineteenth and early twentieth century provoked a series of revolts, the most serious of which occurred at Karak in 1910 (Hamarneh 1985, 87). These revolts might be said to have reflected the 'moral economy' consciousness of direct cultivators under a tributary system: they would pay tribute either to the central state or to nomadic incursion but not to both (Rogan 2002, 185). A reasonable inference from the Karak revolt 'is that the effective boundary of direct Ottoman rule in Syria in 1910 was the massive canyon of Wadi Mujib, which divided the districts of Salt and Karak' (Rogan 2002, 215). This distinction took on even greater relevance under the British Mandate after the First World War as officials sought to govern both a 'tribal zone', characterised by what the colonial administrators saw as a warlike backwardness, and an area potentially at risk of infection by excessively modern doctrines of equality and anti-colonialism.

Within these distinct zones further aspects of the transformation of the agrarian political economy distinguished the lands that would become Jordan. The first of these was the confirmation of a relatively egalitarian balance of landholding. This was not an inevitable outcome but it did affect the later trajectory of the state in its relations with the populist Arab nationalism of the 1950s. In the areas registered and subject to the Tapu land registers according to the Land Code of 1858, the resulting distribution was fairly egalitarian: a marked contrast to other future Arab states such as Egypt, Iraq and Syria, in which the late nineteenth century saw a marked polarisation between landlord and cultivator (Issawi 1982, 138). Land was for the most part 'owned ... by the cultivators who lived on it' (Fischbach 2000, 55). There were some large landholdings, certainly, such as the 'entire village' in the northern Jordan Valley 'owned by a man from Tiberias and the Beni Sakher shaykh who settled there with his clan' with '[t]he tribesmen ... reduced to sharecroppers' (Hamarneh 1985, 89). Thus *effendis* and absentee landlords were present but not dominant (Fischbach 2000, 54–55). *Musha'* lands were not for the most part forcibly partitioned but voluntarily divided into fractions (Rogan 2002,

54). Norms of partition and cultivation varied, particularly between hill and plains villages (Mundy and Smith 2007, 236). This distribution can only be described as relatively egalitarian, however. It was common for one group (*shuyukh*, or some such term) to gain at the expense of the *fellahin* (Fischbach 2000, 52). Nonetheless, this inequality in land did not extend to the domination of the countryside by *effendis*, the resentment of which formed the social context for nationalist officers' movements in Egypt, Iraq and Syria (Be'eri 1970, 456). Again this process was reinforced in the mandate period.

BEGINNINGS OF A COMBINED SOCIAL FORMATION

Perhaps the most significant feature of the late Ottoman period for the emergence of the Jordanian combined social formation was the change in social relations of production among the pastoral nomadic tribes. The Ottoman re-extension of the state produced a tendency—only that—for the fractured tributary relationships of the previous period to be replaced by something closer to capitalist social relations but with a crucial distinction that the horizontal ties of the tribe remained. This partial move from *khuwwa* to waged or semi-waged exploitation on the land was embodied in the so-called 'plantation villages' that emerged in particular among the Bani Sakhr and ʿAdwan. The plantation village was an agricultural settlement registered in the name of the tribe but worked by sharecropping tenants, often *fellahin* fleeing Palestine or Egypt (Rogan 2002, 90).

These developments represented something of the 'combining of separate steps' as the 'material content' of uneven and combined development (Trotsky 1997, 27). The ʿAdwan and the Bani Sakhr were the predominant tribes in the central areas east of the Jordan river. A few decades previously both had practiced pastoral nomadism and *khuwwa*-taking fairly extensively. The ʿAdwan, as mentioned previously, had taken up settled agriculture to a greater degree than the Bani Sakhr but their domains, even in 1880, were reported to hold countless droves of camels covering the plains (Hamarneh 1985, 61). The Bani Sakhr were 'fully nomadic camel herding bedouin' at the beginning of the nineteenth century (Lewis 1987, 124). Their *dirah* (territory) stretched mainly from summer grounds in the Eastern Balqaʾ in the central area of Jordan roughly from Amman to Karak, to winter grounds in the Wadi Sirhan around the 'right angle' in the post-mandate Saudi-Jordanian border (Lewis 1987, 124). They lived by camel herding, *khuwwa* from Salt and Karak and from the passage of the *haj* through their territories—the pilgrims with camels and guides—and were paid by the Ottomans to give *haj* caravans safe passage (Lewis 1987, 124). As discussed below, although the 1858 Land Code allowed the Bani Sakhr and their paramount chiefs to become significant landowners, they were not fully settled cultivators even in the twentieth century. The plantation village was part of the solution to this conundrum. By the 1930s many of the Bani Sakhr (and other tribes such as the Huwaytat) migrated with camels for part of the year while also controlling cultivated land (Bocco and Tell 1994, 123). They were no longer deep desert camel herders but neither were they settled yeomen. Even as late as 1952 the Department of Lands and Surveys found that of 2,404 Bani Sakhr households, 1,935 (81 percent) lived in goat-hair tents, 352 in stone houses, 87 in wooden or other houses and 30 in caves (Lewis 1987, 140).

These tribute-exacting pastoral nomadic confederacies adapted to the mimetic modernisation drive of the Ottomans by means of sharecropping plantations. The ʿAdwan and the Bani Sakhr did register lands but partitioned them: in the case of the Bani Sakhr in a geographical division of *musha'* land into southern, northern and central sections. The area east of the Balqa' valley, extending into the Wadi Sirhan, was left as common *dirah* pasture, allowing the tribe's members to continue their pastoral nomadic lifestyle (Hamarneh 1985, 61). The settled lands were mostly farmed by Palestinian or Egyptian sharecroppers. Title was assigned to named shaykhs in a fairly consensual process involving heads of household within the tribe—by contrast, the relationship with the *fellahin* sharecroppers was based on the sharecropper providing a fifth or more of the crop as rent, usually increasing as time passed (Lewis 1987, 130). A British traveller in 1876 reported that:

> [The bedouins] send across the Jordan, or to the few villages in the Gilead hills, and hire Christians to till their lands for them. Some Moslems [sic] go out for this purpose.... These laborers are called fellahin. We should call them small farmers, or more properly, peasants. The farmer, at the beginning of the season, or when the contract is made is given four, five, or six dollars as the case may be. He receives also a pair of shoes, and has seed furnished him. But, besides these things, he receives nothing. He must provide his own men, cattle and implements. He must pay his own help and do all the work from ploughing to threshing. (Joseph Merrill in Hamarneh 1985, 90)

This form seems to have spread quite rapidly. By 1883 there were nine tax-paying bedouin villages in the Salt district, traditionally the domain of the ʿAdwan, and by 1908 there were 19 such villages around Madaba in the orbit of the Bani Sakhr (Rogan 1994, 45). There were reported to be 19 villages around the district of Jiza in the 1880s and 25 in the 1890s; by the formation of the state of Jordan most of the land between Amman and Madaba and some beyond the Hijaz railway seems to have been cultivated (Lewis 1987, 131). This phenomenon is important because it established a pattern that was later reinforced and transformed by the military subsidy of the British Mandate: the decline of tribute taking but its replacement by another form of surplus extraction that did not lead to the breakdown of the pastoral nomadic tribe seen, for example, in Iraq.

The mimetic reforms of the Ottomans generated contradictory dynamics, however. The extension of cultivated land and the suppression of *khuwwa* had begun to tell against bedouin livelihoods. Rogan delineates the effects of the Ottoman reform period thus:

> The documentary evidence supports a working hypothesis that the poorer, more sedentarized tribes, whose members drew a greater share of their subsistence from agriculture, tended to communal tenure of tribal properties. Their shaykhs were less likely to hold vast, individual tracts of land because the tribesmen could ill afford such concentration.... It is only among the wealthier, more powerful tribes that the sheikhs accumulated vast individual holdings. The tribesmen of the Bani Sakhr, with their great herds, drew ample subsistence from pastoralism and preserved their disdain for agricultural pursuits. This freed their shaykhs to register vast tracts of land without dissent from the rank-and-file, whose livelihood was not adversely affected so long as they enjoyed access to good pasturelands. (Rogan 2002, 188)

These dynamics seemed to return with the period of disorder in the post-First World War era and could have led to the primitive accumulation of rural landed property and impoverished labour seen elsewhere, but this was only a potential outcome: the make-up of the Jordanian combined social formation owed much of its origin to the way in which the strategic relationship of surplus extraction was transformed in the late Ottoman period.

CONCLUSION

What does the preceding discussion tell us about the nineteenth century and the position of 'the Great Transformation in the Historical Sociology of IR'? To be sure, the tributary social relations prevalent in the Ottoman Empire possessed their own dynamic—outlined in this chapter as the unity of economic and extra-economic coercion. As such, it was prone to crises of centralisation and decentralisation, and to the fraying and fracturing of the system in areas beyond the penetrative reach of the central authority. These did not result in different social relations of production but, rather, in a fragmented version of tributary relations. The sub-Syrian steppe was dominated by relations of this kind and most especially by the payment of tribute in the form of *khuwwa* by settled cultivators and weaker pastoralists to the large and powerful pastoral nomadic tribes.

The tributary system was not a static one, but uneven and combined development offers us an insight into how the 'whip of external necessity' brought about an attempt at mimetic modernisation by the Ottoman Empire—a strategy with significant legacies for later states. These were primarily in the geographically distinct distributions of social relations on the land, the relatively egalitarian distribution of that land among cultivators and the replacement in some areas of relations of tribute not directly by wage labour and profit but by a form of sharecropping that allowed pastoral nomadism to continue. It was this form of social relations—the replacement of *khuwwa* by an alternative that was neither capital accumulation nor wage labour that comprised the heart of a combined social formation in Transjordan.

What might this extensive discussion of one historical experience, in the somewhat liminal lands of the sub-Damascene steppe add to debates on UCD? This chapter has attempted to demonstrate that the above outcome derived *both* from a conscious attempt to emulate primitive accumulation, carried out by the rulers of the Ottoman Empire, and from the resistance to—in some cases, adoption of—that programme by tributary power-holders. In so doing, this chapter will hopefully have contributed a historically-grounded instance of the emergence of a combined social formation through 'primitive accumulation under different historical conditions' (Chatterjee 2013).

NOTES

1. For a more extended discussion of the concept based on this definition, see Allinson (2016). For related but distinct uses of UCD, see Matin (2013c), Anievas (2014a) and Anievas and Nişancioğlu (2015).
2. The key interventions in this debate are Nişancioğlu (2014) and Tansel (2015).
3. The clearest statement of the former interpretation is in Marx (1987, 97–98). The latter is found in the famous passage in Marx (1990, 873–76). The two forms of the concept are merged in Federici (2004) and Harvey (2003).

Chapter 7

Asian Sources of British Imperial Power

The Role of the Mysorean Rocket in the Opium War

Luke Cooper

One of the main controversies raised in the lively discussions over the theory of uneven and combined development in international relations (IR) (Allinson and Anievas 2009; Davidson 2009; Matin 2007; Rosenberg 2006; 2010) has concerned its allegedly Eurocentric (Bhambra 2011; Sabaratnam 2011) or *non*-Eurocentric nature (Anievas and Nişancioğlu 2013; 2015; Hobson 2011; Matin 2013a; Matin 2013c; Nişancioğlu 2014). Like the wider debate, the latter argument has focused on the relationship of the concept to temporal change (Allinson and Anievas 2009; Davidson 2009; Rosenberg 2006; 2010). However, while the broader conceptual argument has concerned whether the theory applies in equal measure to capitalist and pre-capitalist intersocietal relations, the postcolonial critique of uneven and combined development accuses it of failing to break with a *stadial* conception of history (Bhambra 2011; Sabaratnam 2011). As Gurminder Bhambra puts it, 'We were all seen to be headed in the same direction and Europe, or the West, simply provides the model of where it is that the rest of the world would arrive' (Bhambra 2011, 12).[1] In Leon Trotsky's original incarnation, the theory does appear to retain such a teleological view rooted in an implicit notion of the 'historical priority' (Nişancioğlu 2014, 328) of a select few culturally advanced Western states. For whereas the contemporary literature largely, with some exceptions (Davidson 2006; 2009), has viewed uneven and combined development as a spatially *universal* dynamic, insofar as its effects are felt in *all* modern societies, Trotsky, in contrast, argued that it was primarily applicable to societies of a 'second, third or tenth cultural class' (Trotsky 1967, 23).

While such culturalist formulations add considerable grist to the mill of the postcolonial critique of uneven and combined development, they might be dismissed as reflecting the values of the time were it not for the manner in which Trotsky put the claim on methodological grounds. 'The theory of the repetition of historic cycles', he wrote, crediting the Enlightenment philosopher Giambattista Vico (1984) with its invention, 'rests upon an observation of the orbits of old pre-capitalist cultures [in which] ... a certain repetition of cultural stages in ever new settlements was ... bound up with the provincial and episodic character of that whole process' (Trotsky 1967, 22). Despite Trotsky conceiving of the concept of uneven and combined development as a challenge to this 'repetitious' view of history, this critique of Vico clearly remains partial. For he appears to endorse his view of pre-capitalist societies as 'provincial and episodic', and thus subject to the repetitious evolution of endogenous stages, but argues that capitalism intensifies relations between countries and, in so doing, creates the possibility of multilinear, i.e. non-*stadial,* patterns of development. Although Trotsky's view on whether combined development applied to pre-modern social forms was often ambiguous (Barker 2006), he clearly implies that 'skipping stages' emerges only once capitalism had transformed the pace and scale of interaction between societies globally. As such, his break with a *stadial* conception of development, and with it the unilinear view of history, arguably remained incomplete.

These remarks of Trotsky need not, however, confirm the postcolonial critique of uneven and combined development. Of these two processes, unevenness and combination, the second arguably presupposes a multilinear view of history. Most historical materialists critical of Trotsky's theory still see unevenness as a quality of all human social development (e.g. Smith 2006). But recognising this alone is insufficient to properly capture the multilinearity of societal change. The peculiar development trajectories characteristic of a multilinear view of history occur in part due to the interchanges between multiple societies, i.e. their existence 'in combination' with one another, and this in turn gives rise to 'the international' as a social phenomenon (Rosenberg 2006; 2010). The interaction this multiplicity entails results in experimentations in development, the outcomes of which cannot be known in advance (Cooper 2013).

If these assumptions can be drawn from the theoretical underpinning of uneven and combined development, then perhaps Trotsky's teleological digression should be seen as conflicting with the deeper conceptual insight he brought to historical materialism. A revision of Trotsky's theory can therefore move away from the Eurocentric teleology that Bhambra rightly holds to be problematic (Bhambra 2011). In its non-Eurocentric conception, the theory offers a dynamic and shifting picture of the world as emulation, competition, alliance forging and cultural and social interchange which, in all its forms, serve to reproduce change rather than stasis in the 'combined' global order. In short, this view of combined development implies that there are no schematic stages or preconceived norms (Sabaratnam 2011), but multiple, co-existing levels of social development in a world of intersocietal interactions.

As this outline suggests, my own use of uneven and combined development (Cooper 2013; 2015) is based on a more 'open' version of Trotsky's idea, which avoids *a priori* claims about the nature of the intersocietal interaction found in a specific historical conjuncture. This casts the researcher as an explorer of the concrete relations and causes found within any specific moment of historical development. But I also maintain following Rosenberg (2006; 2010) that whether we are concerned with analysing the conjuncture or entire historical epochs, they should be visualised in their societal multiplicity, i.e. involving social dynamics that are particular to, and reflective of, the interactive coexistence of many societies. While this has too often been overlooked by accounts rooted in the theoretical vocabulary of 'society' in the singular (Rosenberg 2006), these intersocietal processes have arguably provided a central impetus to social change and political transformation across the *long durée* of human history.

The Opium War provides a suitable testing ground for these theoretical coordinates. While it was undoubtedly a watershed moment for East-West relations (Arrighi, Ahmad and Shih 1999, 233), the scale of Britain's victory has fostered misleading conclusions on the long-term state of development in the Qing Empire. The war has tended to be read in Eurocentric terms as the totemic representation of the decline of Asia and the culmination of hundreds of years of European ascendency. While the British *did* decisively defeat the Qing, the claim that China had experienced many centuries of decline is wrong but still widespread. For instance, one popular history has described the war as an example of 'the Medieval Era fighting the Industrial Age' (Hanes and Sanello 2002, 65; see also Adas 1990, 186–87; Crossley 1991, 117–18; Rawlinson 1967, 110). Others have been more circumspect, but still argue that by the time of the conflict China's armaments were 'outdated by one or two centuries' (Headrick 1981, 90).

In this chapter, I demonstrate the empirical problems with this assessment. Focusing on the special role played by Britain's mimicking of the Indian Kingdom of Mysore's rocket technology, I draw out the knowledge transfers which underpinned Britain's victory. But British development was not only socially combined with Asia, the impetus to modernise also arose from the hostile nature of the world order—that is, the geopolitically combined eighteenth-century international system. Recognising the way that this drove Britain's colonial ascent allows for a more nuanced account of British imperialism, which stresses the period from 1780 to 1840 as a decisive one for the emergence of the polity's hegemony over Asia. Importantly, these empirical realities demonstrate how Britain encountered a 'whip of external necessity' (i.e. competitive geopolitical pressures) in which the direction of the causality proceeded, at least in part, from the Asian to the European and from the non-capitalist to the capitalist. As such, the implications of the analysis go beyond simply recognising the role of Asia as a 'shaper' of Britain's development, because they point to the causal significance of interaction with the non-capitalist world for the historical formation of capitalism as a genuinely global system.

BRITAIN, CHINA AND POST-MUGHAL ASIA AT THE TURN OF THE NINETEENTH CENTURY

Conceptualising the interconnected nature of European and Asian development is central if existing explanations of the Qing's defeat to Britain are to be challenged. By superimposing two *temporal* eras, the 'medieval' and 'industrial' (Hanes and Sanello 2002, 65) onto the *space* of the Orient and Occident respectively, Eurocentric accounts assume the regions had an endogenous development that could be legitimately 'tested' by success or failure of their leadings states in war. In other words, it is taken for granted that 'any given trajectory of development is the product of ... immanent [internal] dynamics' (Nişancioğlu 2014, 328). This problematic view is present in many mainstream accounts of the Opium War (Hanes and Sanello 2002, 65; see also Adas 1990, 186–87; Crossley 1991, 117–18; Rawlinson 1967, 110). It underpins analyses despite the fact that nearly all scholars now recognise the social and technological achievements of the Chinese empire, which was, for most of its lifetime, more advanced than the European polities (Amin 2011; Elvin 1973; 2002; Goldstone 2008; Hobson 2004; Mielants 2008; Needham 1987). But many researchers who argue this still tend to locate the Middle Kingdom's decline in the face of a 'rising Europe' at around the sixteenth century. As Giovanni Arrighi put it (2009, 43): 'The century long eclipse that China and the surrounding region suffered from the end of the Opium Wars to the end of the Second World War can be traced to a fundamental asymmetry in East-West relations during the preceding five hundred years'.

    John M. Hobson (2004) and Kenneth Pomeranz (2000) have, however, challenged this position by advancing the claim that Britain did not surpass Chinese levels of development until circa 1800 or even later.[2] These writers choose to eschew theorisation of the class and social structure underpinning the British and Chinese cases, preferring instead to analyse empirical indices of development comparatively. But their arguments challenge the social relations-based approach in its various manifestations (Arrighi, Ahmad and Shih 1999; Anderson 1974; Brenner 1976; Sweezy 1954; Wood 2002; Wallerstein 1974) by implying that *capitalist* England only surpassed the levels of material wealth found in the polities of South and East Asia when it had transformed into *industrial-capitalist* Britain.

By the turn of the nineteenth century, processes of state and class formation in Britain, nonetheless, contrasted sharply with those found in the Qing polity. Contrary to the Eurocentric theories of the 'Asiatic mode of production' (Bailey and Llobera 1981) or 'Oriental despotism' (Wittfogel 1957), markets were always a component part of the imperial Chinese tributary system. Private wealth holders who lacked a position within the state were, however, a secondary strata—in both class and political terms—to the scholarly officialdom (Abu-Lughod 1989, 340; Anderson 1974, 462–550; Myers and Wang 2002; Needham 1969, 197; Rowe 2002). In contrast, European geopolitics since the sixteenth century had witnessed a 'sequence of ever more powerful states that ... identified with capitalism' (Arrighi 2009, 29). The British mercantilist state that militarily challenged Qing moves to curtail its merchants' lucrative trade in opium, was only the latest to see securing the interests of its traders through colonial means as a central pillar of its overseas policy (Arrighi 2009, 29). A British merchant petition to parliament calling for military action, forming part of the drive for war with the Qing, summarised this disposition thus: 'trade with China can no longer be conducted with security to *life and property*, or with credit or advantage to the *British nation*' (quoted in Hanes and Sanello 2002, 79, emphasis added).

This symbiotic relationship between the nation-state and capital contrasted sharply with the economic and political features of the dynastic land empire ruled by the Qing. Under the Qing, markets expanded and commercialisation was rapid, but the form this took was of *extensive*, Smithian growth based on land-reclamation and proto-industry (Pomeranz 2000, 211–85). Capacity for further extensive growth of this kind was reaching its limits by the close of the eighteenth century (Pomeranz 2000). While the polity was wealthy its rentier social structure inhibited investment in the industrial sectors key to the transformation underway in Britain: 'Landlord rents, usury and official taxes supported upper class parasitism, leisure and luxury consumption including much personal service. Most important, government lacked the strength, the ideas and the impulse to shatter tradition and lead toward economic development' (Fairbank 1978, 19).

Bureaucratic obstruction, rather than a lack of means, was thus arguably central to the Qing failing to escape the Smithian growth cul-de-sac (Wallerstein 2002, 53–56). In short, what Ramon Myers and Yeh-chien Wang call the '[Qing] reticular market economy', because of its combination of command/state, customary and market elements, 'was not hospitable to either Western-style capitalists or capitalism' (Myers and Wang 2002, 645). Britain therefore had both the Western capitalists with an incentive, and a strong capitalist state with the capability, to intervene militarily in Asia to ultimately impose capitalism in a highly exploitative form, based on the extraction of rentier-colonial rights for its merchant classes.

This brief comparative analysis of the distinctive political economies of the two polities draws out the significance of state formation for the development of particular typologies of ruling class power. In neither the Qing Empire nor the British realm was the class structure formed endogenously, however. Both had been socio-economically *combined* through the development of an international trading economy from the sixteenth century onwards (Hobson 2011, 162; Myers and Wang 2002, 587, 627–28). Geopolitical relationships also shaped the domestic processes of class and state formation in the two societies. The European order was chiefly characterised by intense armed conflict between imperial-dynastic states across the eighteenth century, notably the rivalry between the House of Bourbon and House of Hanover, which saw their respective French and British realms almost permanently in conflict. Internal stability and social order required the external use of armed force to secure the commercial and colonial interests necessary for domestic prosperity (O'Brien 2010, 29). It was thus a mercantilist order in which 'war and preparation for war' (Tilly 1993, 14) were essential ingredients of economic growth. Military success opened up new markets for exports and raw materials, catalysed domestic demand and with it private sector investment and, ultimately, created an impetus for institutional change favourable to an intensive economic model (Hudson 2014, 56–57; O'Brien 2010, 29). Trotsky saw in such geopolitical circumstances the creation of a 'whip of external necessity' (Trotsky 1967, 23) owing to the way it placed states in a competitive interrelation, impelling them to undertake institutional and economic modernisation to succeed. In the eighteenth-century context, this fostered a political economy based on commercial-colonialism. European geopolitical conflicts driven by mercantilist economics thus implied a relationship between state and merchant different to the one seen in the Qing. As R. Bin Wong explains:

> Both Chinese and other traders in Asia expected little from their governments and in return did little for them. This lack of connection between merchant and government was fundamentally altered by the European merchant empire. Irrespective of the particular institutional mechanisms deployed by a particular European country's merchants, all held a fundamental belief that state and merchant shared a common interest in exploiting economic opportunities. (Wong 2002, 458)

However, while the Qing was clearly not a mercantile state of the type seen in Europe, it would be Eurocentric to consider a competitive geopolitical environment per se to be a quality of European politics alone. Indeed, the Qing oversaw a rapid military expansion into the Asian interior in the eighteenth century that militarily defeated its major local rivals. Partly in recognition of Qing power, Britain did not make military moves in East Asia until it was in a much stronger global position, with its initial focus on the Indian subcontinent reflecting the opportunities afforded to the realm by the de facto collapse of Mughal rule and the long history of commercial success European maritime empires enjoyed in the Indian Ocean. As a result, the Indian subcontinent was a central theatre in both the Seven Years' War (Danley and Speelman 2012) and the American War of Independence (Stoker, Hagan and McMaster 2011), not only for the French and British colonial forces, but also for the subcontinent's post-Mughal statelets.

In terms of the latter, arguably the most important was the Kingdom of Mysore. A long-standing tributary state of the Mughal Empire it emerged as a de facto independent polity out of the Carnatic Wars (1744–1763). However, in doing so, it also illustrated the complex web of sovereign claims which the European colonial powers were seeking to manipulate. Haidar Ali, a military officer who rose to power in the polity and assumed executive control in 1761, did not seek to replace the Kingdom's *raja,* even when the incumbent holder of the position died in 1766 (Habib 2002, xx). Instead, Haidar drew his political legitimacy from the dying Mughal political system. By obtaining the title of 'Haidar Ali Khan and the office of the *faujdar* of Sira' from Basalat Jang, a claimant to the office of the Viceroy of the Deccan, Ali was able to use the notional framework of Mughal sovereignty to establish himself as the political superior of the Mysorean *raja* (Habib 2002, xx). Haidar's exposure to Western military technique during the Carnatic Wars convinced him of the need to rapidly modernise the polity and he undertook fiscal reforms that allowed him to fund a large standing army (Habib 2002, xx–xxi).[3] While he was careful to ground these new relations of class and state in Mughal precedents, the centralisation of power these reforms entailed implied a highly modern approach to state formation. In the series of wars Haidar fought against the British East Indian Company[4] during the second half of the eighteenth century his enemy's main advantage lay in the war-readiness of their army personnel.[5] But the very nature of war making meant that the Company's bid for hegemony in the subcontinent was far from irresistible—indeed, victory often looked far from certain amid several setbacks.

This contingency of outcome to Britain's geopolitical conflicts in Asia can also be seen in the contrasting fortunes of Qing and British power into the 1780s. While Britain had emerged strongly from the Seven Years' War, the American Revolutionary War dealt a serious blow to its imperial standing (Hobsbawm 1996, 24–25). The settlers' victory was aided by Mysore's initially successful war on the British East India Company, which was sponsored by the primary ally of the dissident American states, France (Reeve 2011, 91–92)—a fact that affirms the highly 'combined' nature of the late eighteenth-century world order. In 1783, Britain's political and social elite was thus lamenting the polity's loss of influence and openly discussed a new period of British imperial decline. One commentary captured this mood with a series of dark prophesies for the future state of Britain's global power: 'The stagnation of external commerce, the consequent destruction of our naval force, the decay of our manufactures, the consequent depopulation of the country [due to emigration to the new world] the transplanting of our manufactures into other countries, [and] the diminution of our resources [territorially and economically]' (anon 1783, 20).

This anonymous author's bout of colonial melancholy was summed up with the phrase: 'the sun of Great Britain must set never to rise no more' (anon 1783, 20). Others similarly spoke of how the country was 'in the most critical situation she had ever experienced' and warned of economic ruination if parliament were to launch further hostilities (Day 1783, 3–4). These fears proved unfounded as Britain retained an 'economy strong enough and a state aggressive enough to capture the markets of its competitors' (Hobsbawm 1996, 33). However, the dependency of the economic model on warfare made expansion highly risk-prone with the polity's eventual triumph in the Napoleonic wars by no means guaranteed. In other words, it would be wrong to view Britain's unparalleled nineteenth-century hegemony as an almost inevitable outcome of its industrialisation, because the latter was in large part driven forward by geopolitics, and thus subject to reversals and setbacks experienced on this terrain, as well as the opportunities for commercial expansion military victory promised.

In several respects, Britain's position contrasted sharply with that of the Qing state in the last two decades of the eighteenth century. Whereas for Britain the territorial losses of the 1780s fostered fear of the polity's decline, Qing complacency reflected the success of their military expansion into their western interior. The 'Ten Great Campaigns' established Qing rule over Xinjiang, consolidated control of the Dalai Lama in Tibet as a tributary polity and, in doing so, decisively defeated the rival Zunghar state in Mongolia (Perdue 1996, 757–59; 2010a). Military conquest was followed by rapid colonial settlement, which boosted agricultural output, encouraged inter-regional trade and commerce, and was also accompanied by state-developmental mining and irrigation projects (Perdue 2010a, 324–408). Success was, however, not entirely uniform and long prior to the Opium War, the Qing failed in its campaign to subordinate Myanmar (1765–1770), which had the effect of forcing it to accept greater independence of other South East Asian polities, notably Siam (Dai 2004). Settler colonialism fostered prosperity, but the dependency of the Qing economy on this form of economic development left it vulnerable to stagnation once territorial expansion ran up against its limits. As this transpired towards the close of the century, it brought instability in its wake as 'subjects routinely engaged in processes of aggressive mutual struggle over issues of food, land, water rights, market access, rents, wages, women, gravesites, status, and countless other scarce resources' (Rowe 2002, 555). These domestic difficulties meant the Qing considered internal disorder, not external security, their main security concern (Jones and Kuhn 1978, 143–44; Thompson 1999, 173).

The 'great divergence' Pomeranz (2000) locates at the close of the eighteenth century reflected these economic problems. The Qing's state-dominated market economy could generate *extensive* growth through military expansion, but was unable to break out into an intensive pattern of growth. Importantly, both the British and Qing states were shaped by their distinctive experiences of the increasingly integrated world order. Indeed, as I shall show, Britain's wars with Mysore actually contributed to its victory in the Opium War.

THE OPIUM WAR: NARRATIVE AND REALITY

The one-sided nature of the Opium War's key battles certainly underlines the mismatch in capability between the two sides. According to Peter Perdue (2010b), a British government report from 1847 put their combat fatalities in the war at 69 with 451 wounded and also estimated that Chinese deaths were in the region of 18,000 to 20,000. But the issue remains whether it is correct to put this down to the technological inferiority of the Qing forces alone or if other factors, such as the lack of organisational competency of their military, have to be considered. This is not the place to definitively answer this question, but one must simply emphasise that the former has often been exaggerated and the latter underemphasised. Ironically, Qing success in expanding westwards (Perdue 2010a) disadvantaged them for their eventual conflict with Britain. Not only did it give rise to problems that typify 'imperial overstretch' (Kennedy 1989)—i.e. how to reconcile central control with social fragmentation and manage inevitable conflicts between settlers and locals over scarce resources (Perdue 2010a, 563)—but it also meant that the Qing lacked military threats that could have incentivised state modernisation efforts. After their victory in the Sino-Nepalese War of 1788–1792, the Qing became focused on internal economic and social problems, not foreign wars (Crossley 2010, 58–64). Britain's trade in opium was draining silver stock and creating price instability, but the Qing were divided on how they should respond—with one wing of the Court reluctant to take interventionist measures seen as unnecessarily costly (Crossley 2010, 63–64). Indeed, the opium trade only came to be seen by the Qing as a major issue of *external* security once addiction had become rife among imperial soldiers (Perdue 2010b).

Whereas Britain ran up an eye-watering state debt of 270 percent of its national income after the Napoleonic wars (O'Brien 2006, 1), the Qing were more cautious and lacked the financial instruments, as well as geopolitical imperatives, to undertake such a fiscal-military revolution. Some scholars have speculated that, ironically, the Qing 'would have been much more interested in articles of trade, such as weaponry, that the British had to offer' at an earlier stage had a Mongolian state continued to trouble its north-western frontier in the eighteenth century (Perdue 2010a, 564). Or, similarly, if the Ming loyalist, Zheng Chengong, who briefly occupied Taiwan after the fall of the dynasty, had succeeded in developing a south-eastern empire (Wong 2002, 460). In any case, the British state occupied strikingly more conflictual geopolitical circumstances. In short, unlike Britain, the conditions the Qing encountered between 1792 and the 1830s lacked a 'whip of external necessity' (Trotsky 1967, 23) and, as such, were a significant factor for their defeat in the Opium War.

Those who stress the technological superiority of the British forces often point to the role played in the conflict by British East Indian Company's warship, the *Nemesis* (Hanes and Sanello 2002, 65; see also, Adas 1990, 186–87; Crossley 1991, 117–18; Rawlinson 1967, 110). This was the first steam powered, iron-clad warship to sail around the Cape of Good Hope, which has been described as 'an exemplar of state-of-the-art technology' (Hanes and Sanello 2002, 115) that, in itself, 'cast further doubt on the already much contested image of China as a powerful and advanced civilization' (Adas 1990, 186). Undoubtedly, the ship constituted a real technical achievement that was a major factor in British victory. A key advantage the *Nemesis* enjoyed over equivalent Chinese vessels was its shallow draught that 'allowed the ship to thread its way up the winding channels' of rivers, making possible the successful British offensive on Canton (Janin 1999, 114). Nonetheless, the prevalent assessment, which sees this as the military culmination of many centuries of British technological prowess, is mistaken. Joseph Needham has demonstrated how the genuine advances in European nautical technology built on antecedent Chinese inventions (Needham 1971, 693–95). The Qing junks used in the war were also comparable in quality to the European trading ships of the late eighteenth and early nineteenth century (Hobson 2004, 58; Temple 2007, 186–98). Indeed, it was common for European traders based in eastern markets to source their ships from Asian shipbuilders in this period to reduce costs, which does not suggest they were significantly inferior (Mantienne 2003, 531–32).

British sources also imply a more technologically even contest than is often imagined in the literature. For example, the colonial force commandeered, and made active use of, two Qing war junks during the course of the conflict, which does not suggest they were grossly inferior to their own naval forces

(Bernard 1844b, 33). The same officer's account discusses how the Qing had also sought to adapt the most advanced European military vessels and armaments in response to the British threat. Intriguingly the officer describes this, in terms that anticipated Trotsky's famous geopolitical formulation, as an 'impulse of necessity':

> A large building-yard was discovered, with an immense quantity of timber collected in it; and there was a good-sized frigate-junk, of about three hundred tons, in course of building, in a regular drydock, something after the European model; they had evidently made a great step in advance in the art of shipbuilding: indeed, the longer the war lasted, the more the Chinese found themselves led on, by the 'impulse of necessity,' to attempt great changes, and, in many respects, improvements, not only in their vessels, but in their warlike weapons, and other matters relating to the art of defence. (Bernard 1844b, 134)

As this suggests, British superiority was real, but the Qing did undertake to catch up in the 1830s. Having enjoyed a half-century of *external* peace the Qing state was badly prepared for the war. Consequently, Britain overcame an enemy that was poorly trained, with underfed troops reluctant to fight and organised in a deteriorating Manchu banner system—it was these organisational problems that may have been decisive (Thompson 1999, 173). While technology played a role in the Qing defeat, British technical superiority emerged over decades, not centuries as has often been imagined. Moreover, key British technologies can be directly traced to Asian inventions, undermining the Eurocentric view of industrial modernity more broadly. Indeed, the focus on the *Nemesis* has led many scholars to overlook the role played by a technology that was equally important for the British victory, the Congreve rocket. Far from an invention endogenously generated by British industry, the device was based on a weapon the realm's colonial forces encountered in the Mysorean wars.

THE MYSOREAN-CUM-CONGREVE ROCKET

While the *Nemesis* entered into Chinese popular memory as the 'devil ship' (Cotterell 2011, 111), this was in no small part due to the vessel being armed with the Congreve rocket. At the Second Battle of Chuenpee, the rocket had a devastating impact on the Qing forces. Bernard described its terrifying impact on the enemy in these terms:

> One of the most formidable engines of destruction which any vessel, particularly a steamer can make use of is the congreve rocket, a most terrible weapon

when judiciously applied, especially where there are combustible materials to act upon. The very first rocket fired from the Nemesis was seen to enter the large *junk* against which it was directed, near that of the admiral, and almost the instant afterwards it blew up with a terrific explosion, launching into eternity every soul on board and pouring forth its blaze like the mighty rush of fire from a volcano. The instantaneous destruction of the huge body seemed appalling to both sides engaged. The smoke, and flame, and thunder of the explosion, with the broken fragments falling round, and even portions of disserved bodies scattering as they fell, were enough to strike with awe, if not with fear, the stoutest heart that looked upon it. (Bernard 1844a, 271)

Remarkably, the picture painted in this extract is highly reminiscent of another British officer's description of an attack on East Indian Company forces by Indian rocketeers during the Siege of Seringapatam (1799) in the Fourth Mysorean War:

The rockets and musketry from 20,000 of the enemy were incessant. No hail could be thicker. Every illumination of blue lights was accompanied by a shower of rockets, some of which entered the head of the column, passing through to the rear, causing death, wounds, and dreadful lacerations from the long bamboos of twenty or thirty feet, which are invariably attached to them. (Bayly 1896, 82)

It was, of course, no coincidence that the Mysorean and Congreve rockets had a comparable impact on the enemy, as a direct lineage can be traced from the latter to the former. Haidar Ali's rapid and successful upgrading of the state's military power included a battalion of rocketeers as part of a well-equipped standing army (Habib 2002, xxii). His eldest son, Tipu Sultan, took a special interest in the technological aspects to the modernising efforts of the regime. Succeeding his father in 1782 he saw the Second Mysorean War through to its conclusion on favourable terms. Having partly overseen the famous victory at the Battle of Pollilur in 1780, where the Mysorean rocket played a decisive role, Tipu expanded the Rocket Corps to some 5,000 soldiers (Narasimha 1999, 123). These developments all took place as a result of the particular constellation of the geopolitically combined development between Europe and the Indian subcontinent. In other words, for *both* the Mysorean and British realms technological change was driven by a 'whip of external necessity'. Tipu Sultan's technological breakthrough in rocket technology was, therefore, no accident of history, but reflected the sociological transformations elicited by the process of Mysorean state formation, itself arising from the impetus for social change generated by the threat the colonial activity of European powers posed to the independence of Mysore.

Rockets had a long history on the battlefields of Asia, having originally been developed in China under the Song dynasty (Needham 1987, 487–95). But the distinctiveness of the Mysorean design lay in its use of cast iron, rather than the wood and bamboo tubing found in the original Chinese weapon (Needham 1987, 488; Riper 2007, 14). Notably, this use of iron reflected the superior quality and efficiency of Indian production of the metal in the eighteenth century (Dharampal 1971, 20–24; Hobson 2004, 211). While iron made the rockets heavier, it also allowed for greater explosive to be added (Riper 2007, 14). The longest potential range of the rockets was considerable, reaching up to 2.4 km—a distance without any precedent or equivalent in the eighteenth century (Jaim and Jaim 2011, 134; Narasimha 1985, 6; Narasimha 1999, 123). The chemical mix of the gunpowder heightened this fear factor, with the sulphur producing 'odorous fumes and smoke of poisonous and corrosive sulphur oxides in the battle field, causing discomfort not only to soldiers but also to the horses and cattle carrying ammunition and other logistic supports'—an effect analogous to 'modern-day tear gas' (Jaim and Jaim 2011, 134). The release of carbon dioxide and carbon monoxide from the charcoal in the gunpowder also gave rise to streaks of blue light (Jaim and Jaim 2011, 134), adding further to the visual drama their use entailed, and prompting one British officer to describe them as both beautiful and terrifying (Bayly 1896, 85). Even once they had hit their target, the rockets remained in a state of high velocity until their fuel was exhausted (Bayly 1896, 82). While this suggests the rocket was not an easily controlled or precise weapon, it appears to have added to its effectiveness with British soldiers reporting chaos and anxiety in their rank and file: 'The shrieks of our men from these unusual weapons was terrific; thighs, legs, and arms left fleshless with bones protruding in a shattered state from every part of the body were the sad effects of these diabolic engines of destruction' (Bayly 1896, 82–83).

These observations describe a deluge of what were, essentially, swords attached to firecrackers spinning uncontrollably, and also indicate the respect for the capability of their enemy that British army personnel maintained even as they defeated the Mysoreans. The description of the scene is nonetheless similar to the famous victory of the Mysorean forces at the Battle of Pollilur in 1780 where rocket fire blew up two wagons of ammunition held by the British army, which saw some 4,000 troops of the British East Indian Company compelled to surrender (Munro 1789, 146, 154; Wilks 1869, 457–58). Importantly, the first-hand accounts of the British victory in 1799 indicate the relative parity in military capability which still existed between the two sides during their final battle (Bayly 1896, 82). Indeed, British military sources put the Mysorean defeat down to tactical mistakes made by Tipu, rather than any significant—let alone overwhelming—superiority enjoyed by the British side (Brittlebank 2003, 200). While others have suggested betrayals on the part of senior Mysorean military officials may have played a role (Hasan 1971, 309-10), there is no suggestion that the final conflict was anything other than closely fought and evenly matched.

Despite the scale of their earlier defeat in 1780, the British did not make moves to develop Indian rocket technology until after the defeat of Tipu and the Mysoreans in 1799:

> After the capture of Seringapatam and the death of ... [Tipu Sultan], the British shipped hundreds of rockets home to the Royal Arsenal as spoils of war. The point of the shipment was less to equip British troops with Indian rockets than to 'reverse engineer' them: take them apart, study how they were made, and learn how to build rockets that were as good or better. (Riper 2007, 15)

The technology transfer of the rocket to the Woolwich Arsenal illustrates the overall significance of Britain's achievement in 1799. Victory over Mysore opened the way to the taming of the Indian subcontinent. It also allowed the colonialists to appropriate this technology without having to reinvent the core design principles. That such a 'skipping of stages' took place exemplified how—at least in rocketry and the related iron production techniques— British equivalent capabilities were not significantly more advanced than their defeated foe at the turn of the nineteenth century. However, by applying the organisational principles of industrialisation to the rocket's refinement, the British were able to improve further on the original Mysorean design. William Congreve Jr., whose father had overseen the modernisation of the Royal Arsenal, took on the task of adapting the Indian weapon for British purposes. Inventing the 'Congreve rocket' in 1805 he downplayed, though did not wholly deny, the debt he owed to the original Mysorean device (Congreve 1827, 15). Congreve's playing down of the Indian influence is indicative of a nationalism that finds its echo in contemporary accounts of the irresistible rise of British colonial power. Thinking of Britain's wars in Asia, whether on the subcontinent or with the Qing, as a clash between contending stages of civilisation—one advanced, the other medieval—reflects the distorted, colonial way that modern Europeans have tended to imagine their own colonial histories.

CONCLUSION

The potential of the theory of uneven and combined development lies in its ability to offer a way of thinking about the past that emphasises the multiple and diverse linkages present in any historical process. These lineages of social and political transformation cannot be reduced to the mere transfer and adaptation of technological accomplishments from one society to another.

In this sense, the tale of the Mysorean rocket represents much more than a piece of 'object history'. For it illustrates the dynamic interrelation between geopolitical compulsions ('the whip of external necessity') and the industrial transformations of the late eighteenth and nineteenth centuries. To not only survive but also advance in an international order characterised by military conflict over commercial opportunities, the British developed a highly adaptive model of state formation with organisational structures that valued innovation and improvement. It was not alone in doing so, either in Europe or globally. Both the Qing (less successfully) and Mysorean Kingdom (initially, very successfully) sought to learn from and adapt to the wider international setting. British hegemony emerged from a combination of good fortune and the sheer number of military conflicts—each one replete with lessons and experiences—that they became involved in.

At a time in the discipline of international relations when many scholars are, quite correctly, revisiting the nineteenth century and emphasising its importance as a period of extraordinary transformation (Buzan and Lawson 2015; Lacher and Germann 2012), the theory of uneven and combined development provides the framework to visualise this process in genuinely global terms. The non-Eurocentric insight it offers scholars is also matched by its causal potential, which stresses the role of geopolitically combined development, and specifically the highly militarised and conflictual nature of the world-system, as central to generating the epochal shift in human development industrial society entailed. Not only does the nature of these conflicts indicate the contingency one must recognise in the ascent of British imperialism, but it also serves as a reminder—one more benign accounts of the global transformation may find uncomfortable—that the modern world-system was very much built on the foundation of colonial violence. The huge advance in material wealth achieved by Europe and North America in the nineteenth century cannot therefore be separated from the colonial practices pursued by the British hegemon in Asia across the eighteenth and nineteenth centuries. And this violent interaction between the non-capitalist world and the capitalist was an essential quality of the new industrial world order.

NOTES

1. Or, as Marx put it in a preface to *Capital*, 'The country that is more developed industrially only shows, to the less developed, the image of its own future' (Marx 1974, 19).

2. Hobson argues that in terms of gross national product China only fell behind 'as late as 1870', even though it fell behind in per capita terms at the turn of the eighteenth century (Hobson 2004, 77).

3. Indeed, in another sign of the sociological and political influence of Mysore on the British imperial project, the system of direct taxation of peasant income by salaried state officers he pioneered, which circumvented traditional local elites, would be imitated in the British East India Company's *ryotwari* system (Habib 2002, xxi).

4. Through its royal grants and charters, which gave domestic political legitimacy to its colonial activity, the British East India Company was effectively acting as an *agent* of the British state ('the Crown') in these wars (see Cohn 1996).

5. Between the Treaty of Paris (1783) and the Opium War (1839), Britain was involved in numerous military conflicts. These included the Second (1780–1784), Third (1789–1792) and Fourth (1798–1799) Anglo-Mysore Wars; the War of the First Coalition (1793–1797); the War of the Second Coalition (1799–1802), Second Anglo-Maratha War (1802–1805); the War of the Third Coalition (1803–1805); the War of the Fourth Coalition (1806–1807); the Anglo-Russian War (1807–1812); the War of the Fifth Coalition (1809); The War of the Sixth Coalition (1812–1814); the War of the Seventh Coalition (1815); the Anglo-Nepalese War (1814–1816); the Third Anglo-Maratha War (1817–1818) and the First Anglo-Burmese War (1824–1826).

Chapter 8

Rejecting the 'Staples' Thesis and Recentring Migration

A Comparative Analysis of 'Late Development' in Canada and Argentina

Jessica Evans

Within the field of comparative development, a distinct problematic has persisted through attempts to account for the significant historical divergence in late developmental trajectories between Europe's so-called 'settler colonies'[1] of the 'New World' and other colonial formations throughout Africa, Latin America and Asia (Armstrong 1985; Fogarty 1985; Solberg 1987; Watkins 1963). Within these discussions, settler colonies were singled out as a distinct form of colonialism, capable of superior developmental successes as compared with other forms of colonialism. While a range of attempted theorisations have been posited to explain these divergences, the one which became dominant within the field of comparative development studies was the staples theory of economic development. Yet, while the staples theory of economic development could point to some factors distinguishing late transformations in settler versus non-settler colonies, a significant lacuna has persisted within the body of literature inasmuch as it has been unable to account for the divergent paths of development within settler spaces themselves which emerged throughout the twentieth century. It is with this problematic that the present chapter is concerned.

Emerging out of Canadian political economy, the staples theory of economic development suggested that settler colonies, as with other colonial formations, developed within the context of a dependent integration within the world market predicated on commodity export production. However, unique to settler spaces was the additional factor of a high resource and land base relative to those of capital and labour[2] (Watkins 1963, 143–44). As a consequence, dependent development took place in the absence of demographic pressures on scarce resources, as was the case in much of the rest of the colonised world. Indeed, the development of settler colonies, because of these 'favourable' ratios of natural resources to demographic pressures, required a massive injection of both European populations and capital into the settler space. Given this lack of demographic pressures, staples arguments relegated explanatory primacy to the role of the particular resources available within the developing economy and the export commodity that served to launch settler colonies into the world market (Innis 1995; Watkins 1963, 143–44). This rather singular focus on the commodity itself, however, has meant that the pivotal role of massive immigration has received rather cursory examination, having been treated as a relatively neutral market input (Palmer 1983, 133).

A focus on the character of the export commodity itself, I argue, has been unable to account for how two settler spaces developing on the basis of the same export commodity and with remarkably similar resource and land endowments could exhibit such divergent developmental outcomes. This shortcoming has been most apparent when contrasting Argentine and Canadian developmental trajectories predicated on wheat export production, which though proximate throughout the nineteenth century, diverged significantly throughout the twentieth century. In this chapter I wish to draw attention to the inadequacy of treating migration as a neutral input and highlight the qualitative differences that attended different migrant populations with regards to their material strategies of social reproduction. I argue that massive immigration served as a potent mechanism of 'combined development' which contributed significantly to the variable developmental outcomes experienced in Argentina and Canada. Indeed, the critical factor in explaining divergent developmental outcomes in Argentina and Canada is to be found in the ways that different migrant populations' strategies of reproduction interacted with those conditioned by the prevailing social property relations in the colony, resulting in different processes of class formation and inducing different incentives to revolutionise the production process. In the next section, the staples literature on economic development in settler colonies is reviewed. I then turn to a brief outline of the theoretical framework I develop in order to analyse the role of migration within these two cases of late development, drawing specifically on Political Marxism and Trotsky's concept of uneven and combined development (UCD). Following this, I provide a brief historical sketch of Argentine and Canadian economic development, highlighting the shortcomings of staples theory in explaining divergent paths of development throughout the twentieth century. In the final two substantive sections, I examine the differential impact that large-scale European immigration had on processes of class formation and economic development in each case.

In developing the argument of this chapter, I hope to be able to contribute to three distinct bodies of literature. First, this argument presents an intervention in the comparative development literature concerning so-called staples producing settler colonies. Second, I hope to intervene in the literature on labour migration by inserting a qualitative dimension which suggests that the interests and agencies of migrants themselves exerted (trans)formative impacts on the recipient space. Far from being a ready, transportable and flexible labour force, migrants' contribution to labour markets depended critically on the sets of social property relations conditioning their strategies of reproduction both at home and abroad. Finally, through the deployment of UCD, this chapter contributes to the further development of this analytical concept within the field of historical sociology and international relations in its specification of migration as a concrete mechanism of combination.

STAPLES AND DEVELOPMENT WITHIN SETTLER COLONIES

The staples thesis of late development in the 'new countries' of European settlement might be seen as developing first, and primarily, within the tradition of Canadian political economy through the work of Harold Innis. At the core of the staples thesis is a Ricardian political economy which explains production and development as the result of technological and geographical determinations, and the extension of commercial trade networks as a means of accumulating capital and thus stimulating industrialisation (McNally 1981, 163). These endogenous conditions of technology and geography, however, are further situated in an international problematic which sees domestic development as being stimulated through the integration of peripheral economies into the world market on the basis of staples (raw commodity) export to Europe (Schmidt 1981, 70). Thus, staples theory brings together elements of a technologically deterministic understanding of development with those of an internationally situated theory of dependent development.

For the economic historian Harold Innis, Canada's economic development on the basis of staples industries was effected through the increase in mercantile networks and infrastructure required for domestic staples production to meet foreign (largely British) demand for raw commodities. However, Innis insisted that the mere fact of staples production for export was not enough to ensure economic development, as different commodities contained within their very nature different capacities to stimulate these kinds of large-scale infrastructural projects. It was on this point, Innis argued, that the staple itself contained within it certain geographical and technological limits and possibilities for stimulating economic linkages. In Canada, early fish and fur exports were unable to stimulate economic linkages conducive to large-scale development. The introduction of timber trade, however, would demand far more extensive and intensive transport infrastructure, and it was this that would lay the foundation, finally, for agricultural and mineral staples production which launched Canada firmly onto the world market as an independent producer of commodity goods (Innis 1995, 3–20).

At the core of the staples approach, then, are two sets of determinations. In the first instance, there are the unequal terms of trade which exist between the hinterland and metropole and which affect the integration of the hinterland into the global economy. In the second instance, however, there are the geographical, physical and technological characteristics of the commodity, or staple, itself, which are said to determine the social and technical organisation of production in the economy (McNally 1981, 163; Schmidt 1981, 70). The development of capitalism within settler colonies was therefore explained through the accumulation of merchant capital, generated by the technological and geographical requirements of particular staples' production. In so much as this was the case, no distinction between the character of the production and trade of fur, timber, wheat, minerals etc. was required. Each of these stages in Canada's trade relations with foreign markets, were for Innis characterised as capitalist, to lesser or greater degrees. Ultimately, however, Innis's work remained rooted firmly at the level of description. It was only later, with the work of Mel Watkins (among others) that a fuller elaboration of the staples premises as a theory of economic growth occurred (McNally 1981, 162; Schmidt 1981, 70; Watkins 1963, 141).

The premises of Innis's staples account of development, according to Watkins, could become a theory of capital formation only upon a fuller theorisation of the possibilities for backward, forward and final demand linkages, which evolved out of staples industries. These linkages could include inducements to invest in industries using the outputs and inputs of the export industry as well as for consumer goods in the export sector. While all of these factors placed explanatory primacy on demand determinants, Watkins moved beyond Innis in his attempt to theorise supply side determinants, or the conditions under which such inducements to investment might be expected to take place (Watkins 1963, 145).

In identifying these so-called supply side determinants, Watkins highlighted the role played by domestic entrepreneurs in identifying and exploiting market opportunities to invest in expanding industry linkages. The propensity of a given economy to produce these 'entrepreneurial types' was in turn argued to be contingent upon the prevailing social values and institutions of the society in question. Now, what is crucial to highlight at this point is that the staples thesis fundamentally viewed the social and technical aspects of society emerging from the very character of the staple resource, which was being exploited for export production (Watkins 1963, 146). Thus, a tautological explanation resulted, where the ability to exploit a staple for economic diversification and industrialisation was itself contingent upon the nature of that staple and, hence, the geographical predispositions of a given social formation were ultimately and inescapably determinant. Consequently, there has been effectively no room for a consideration of social relations (notably, class), except as they were defined in the sphere of circulation. As a consequence, the consideration of migration in staples theory has been reduced simply to its characterisation as the neutral and necessary inputs of factors of production (labour) into a technologically and geographically determined production process.

While the revival of Canadian political economy in the 1970s would bring about efforts to update classical staples theory through, among other things, the addition of concepts of class, these attempts nevertheless remained stunted in so much as their ability to actually shift staples theory away from its overly technicist and deterministic framework (McNally 1981, 166–68). For the most part, these efforts remained bound to a conception of class which was defined by social positions within the sphere of circulation. In other cases, dominant classes were defined through their relationship with the metropole, while subordinate classes were defined by their productive relationship with the dominant class (Schmidt 1981, 77). In either case, these conceptualisations of class within the revived staples framework completely foreclosed a notion of class as formed through processes of social and productive struggle. That staples theory has been incapable of conceptualising class as a dynamic social force, formulated through historical processes of struggle is not surprising given the essentially teleological notion of development as a technological process that lies at its core.

SOCIAL PROPERTY RELATIONS AND UNEVEN AND COMBINED DEVELOPMENT

In proposing a recentring of migration within the comparative development scholarship of settler colonialism, I argue for an understanding of the dynamic means through which class forces are produced, and how these come to impact the particular characteristics of the production process. To do this, I develop an alternative analytical framework which draws upon two theoretical bodies within Marxist historical sociology; those of 'Political Marxism' or the social property relations approach (SPR); and, Trotsky's concept of UCD. Below, I provide a brief review of the basic premises of each framework before moving on to lay out my specific application of these two in the context of class formation and economic development in Canada and Argentina.

The central contribution of the SPR approach to historical sociology is its specification of the particular historical processes involved which give the capitalist mode of production its foundational dynamics and drives towards competitive accumulation. Within this approach, articulated first in the pioneering historical work of Robert Brenner on the transition to capitalism in the English countryside, social property relations of reproduction are re-centred as the pivotal axis around which the compulsion towards competitive accumulation and, hence, technological and industrial innovation is generated. Thus, rather than characterising capitalism as a mode of production emerging from either increases in trade or technological innovation, it is the ways in which different actors reproduce themselves, contingent upon property relations, which explains capitalism's historical specificity (Brenner 1982, 16).

According to Brenner, the origins of the capitalist mode of production are to be found in the English countryside and are the unintended result of pre-capitalist actors' rules and strategies of reproduction. Within a structure of pre-capitalist property relations, neither exploiters nor producers were dependent upon the market and hence were free from the need to produce competitively for exchange. The direct producers within the feudal mode of production held direct access to their means of reproduction through individually or communally held land, while exploiters reproduced themselves through the appropriation of part of the product of these direct producers through varying forms of extra-economic coercion. Under such a system of property relations peasants had no compulsion to sell their labour power or land, while exploiters could only increase wealth through a redistribution of income away from peasants, namely coercion, a tactic which required economic surpluses to be unproductively invested in military and political apparatuses (Brenner 1982, 17).

Through the enclosure movements, the separation of direct producers from their means of subsistence had the effect of transforming these strategies of class reproduction in such a way that both exploiters and producers became dependent on the market. Where direct producers no longer held access to land and other means of (re)production, exploiters could no longer extract surplus directly from peasant producers through political mechanisms of coercion and taxation but instead came to rely on the extraction of surplus through the labour process. Because the surplus value of such extraction was only realisable in the form of exchange value, however, producers became dependent on the market (and hence the 'economic') for their reproduction. Direct producers, on the other hand, 'freed' from their means of subsistence would for their part become compelled to sell their labour power on the market in exchange for a wage. A condition which underpinned this emergent market economy was the loosening of political mechanisms of coercion and exclusion and the introduction of limited, nominal freedom among many (though by no means all) actors in the form of 'citizenship'. For our purposes here, what the SPR approach draws our attention to is the ways in which specific property relations condition the parameters within which actors reproduce themselves, which opens up or closes off particular production strategies at the macro-level (Brenner 1982).

Now, it is important to note that I have not dwelled on Brenner's account of the particular historical conditions which led to the transition from feudal to capitalist social property relations in England. This is a deliberate omission, as for our purposes, the historical dynamics of the transition which took place in England cannot be assumed to have been reproduced in every subsequent transition to capitalism. Rather, understanding capitalist transformations outside of England require that we situate these later transitions within the international system and developing global capitalist market. For once capitalism took root in England it would later come to develop in such a manner which exerted pressure on the production and accumulation strategies of other states and these competitive pressures would, in many cases, require that other states adapt and transform their own strategies of accumulation and production—in short, their entire structure of social relations. Importantly, we should not assume that such actors deliberately sought to undertake a transition to capitalism. Yet the sum total of these pressures of competitive accumulation would eventually lead to the generation of distinct, amalgam forms of capitalist social relations. To understand these processes, I suggest we should look to Trotsky's concept of UCD.

At the core of UCD is the notion that capitalism needs to be thought of as an integrated totality which simultaneously incorporates and divides the world through the generation of uneven and divergent forms of capitalist development (Ashman 2009, 30–31). In its arguably fullest articulation, UCD was developed through the work of Leon Trotsky as both an explanatory device as well as a concept enabling the development of revolutionary praxis. Unevenness, Trotsky proposed, was one of the most general laws of the historical process and this was owing to the unevenness of socio-historical development arising from the variability across time and space of ecologically given conditions (Allinson and Anievas 2009, 50). From this general law of unevenness, Trotsky argued that a second general law was generated—that of combined development—which denotes the process by which different 'stages' of the developmental journey are combined in an amalgam of the archaic and modern (Davidson 2009, 11–13).

As a first cut, UCD was a means of explaining the sudden and convulsive ruptures which were taking place in 'backward' countries such as Russia—where social development no longer assumed a gradual character but proceeded at a terribly rapid, conflictual and often unstable tempo (Davidson 2009, 13). What Trotsky identified in Russia and other 'backward' social formations was not simply a repetition of the developmental transitions that had preceded in Western Europe but something entirely unique, and the uniqueness of these developmental processes was owing to the specific character of UCD within the capitalist mode of production. It was only under capitalism that unevenness became a qualitatively poignant analytic. The sharpness through which unevenness expressed itself arose from the universalising logic of capital expressed through competitive pressures, which necessitated sudden and explosive transformations through a process of interiorising external capitalist relations and technological developments within the extant social structures of a given formation (Allinson and Anievas 2009, 52). This process of transformation carried with it the possibility of skipping whole stages of development hitherto assumed in the transition to capitalism, though it could also and alternatively serve to reinforce the existing class structures and modes of accumulation.

Combined development, then, is the critical component of UCD and this is the process wherein the early transitions to capitalism developed on the basis of a transformation of social relations which then came to exert pressure on other regions of the world. This pressure took the form of the competitive logic of accumulation which compelled a process of catch-up in the so-called backward regions of the world through a transformation of their own social relations.

Yet, despite this process of catch-up being driven by a singular logic of capitalist accumulation, the actual course of catch-up and the transformations which would result could never replicate those which took place in the earlier transitions (Davidson 2009, 11–15). This, for Trotsky, was because the logics of the capitalist mode of production must confront the logics of accumulation and reproduction which exist in and are unique to the geographical and historical context in which these interactions took place (Davidson 2009, 14). These unique interactions resulted in specific processes of class formation and struggle which conditioned the transformation of the logics of reproduction and accumulation. For our purposes here, UCD is an important concept that allows us to comprehend differential processes and patterns of class formation within the capitalist mode of production, and underlying this is the pivotal notion that there is no singular or objective form that class structures must take. Class, instead, is understood as being constituted through an ongoing and relational process.[3]

The core argument of this chapter is that the late-capitalist transformations in European settler colonies must be understood within the larger, integrated context of world capitalist development. But to assert this in abstract terms, pointing to the general transformative pressures that developed from the expansionary and compulsive logic of capitalist accumulation in the core of the world economy tells us little as to how specifically these compulsive pressures were transmitted to the settler colonies and with what effects for divergent and particular transformations. Indeed, without a specification as to the precise mechanisms which exerted these abstract competitive pressures, analysis runs the risk of falling into a trap of either technological determinism and, hence, a forces of production mode of argumentation, or to see late development as being the result of a functional, abstract capital-logic. This latter tendency, I argue, cannot adequately account for the necessary element of active and dynamic human agency, of class struggle, which operates within material and historically given conditions but which nevertheless shapes the particular transformations which occur. To this end, I suggest that migration, a factor which was a substantial element in settler-colonial development, must be drawn into the analysis. The nineteenth-century Atlantic migrations, I argue, were a specific mechanism through which settler colonies were drawn into the remit of the world market, and which carried with it the 'advantage of backwardness' in so much as there was an underlying assumption that migration would effectively allow settler spaces to 'skip' the long process of primitive accumulation and proletarianisation, through the importation of a ready-made wage-dependent population. The particular combinations of migrants within the extant property relations in the colony, however, were significant in generating historically and geographically specific class forms and strategies, which shaped the parameters and possibilities for late-capitalist transformation.

DEVELOPMENT AND DIVERGENCE IN CANADA AND ARGENTINA: CHALLENGING THE STAPLES THESIS

In proposing a re-assessment of Argentine and Canadian late-capitalist transformations through the lens of migration, I am seeking to answer a core set of questions. Firstly, what were the existing political and class structures and the prevalent logics of accumulation and reproduction within Argentina and Canada during the 1860s[4] when efforts at late development began in earnest? Secondly, who were the migrants and what were the material conditions underpinning their emigration from Europe? What were the logics of accumulation and reproduction with which they were engaged? Finally, what types of struggles were (or were not) produced through the combination of migrants with extant class forces and how did these condition the possibilities for the transformation of accumulation strategies in each respective setting? This latter question speaks to the conditions established for technological innovation, and whether accumulation proceeded according to the production of absolute or relative surplus value.

Canada and Argentina were both countries that formed part of the first wave of transatlantic expansion during the sixteenth century. While both spaces were colonised by different European powers (Canada being colonised by Britain and France, Argentina being colonised by Spain), both were the recipients of quasi-feudal social arrangements (Schedvin 1990, 536). Development had been slow in both places, owing to a number of factors including the extensive campaigns of genocide and war waged against the indigenous populations and the failure to discover a solid export commodity until the late nineteenth century, at which point formal independence from the metropole was also achieved (Solberg 1987, 1–3).

In the late nineteenth century, a boom in the global market for wheat helped to catapult both Canada and Argentina into the global market and accelerate development. The global wheat boom, in turn, led to a massive increase in immigration in order to make profitable the 'barren' grasslands of the prairies and pampas. From the 1880s until the beginning of the twentieth century, Canada and Argentina were seen to be following proximate paths of development, with Argentina eventually outperforming Canada in world wheat sales, though the two remained competitive and proximate in their internal levels of economic development (Solberg 1985, 53).

Contrary to the expectations of the time, however, from 1910 onward Canada began to outperform Argentina with regard to both the quantity and quality of its wheat exports. From the post-First World War period and on, Canadian agriculture began to expand production through mechanisation, while Argentina experienced agricultural decline and eventual stagnation (Adelman 1994, 3–15, 263; Solberg 1987, 2). It is on this point that the staples thesis is inadequate. The staples thesis would suggest that cereal staples contain within them a certain production function which determines the technical character of production and which then determines the range of possible forward, backward and final demand linkages which can develop from staple production. Yet Canada and Argentina developed on the basis of the very same staple, wheat, but where Canadian wheat production led to the eventual diversification and industrialisation of the economy, Argentine wheat production resulted in agricultural decline and a protracted, late, industrial development process. How, then, do we account for these differences, given the strikingly similar starting points and conditions of development up until the First World War?

Jeremy Adelman has noted that one of the critical issues with staples theory is that it tends to assume that the forces of production will automatically adjust to market forces. In this sense, technology is seen as something which is exogenous, in so much as the chosen technique for production is attributed as a quality of the commodity itself. If this were the case, however, the development of wheat, irrespective of whether it was in the pampas or the prairies, would have resulted in similar processes of mechanisation (Adelman 1992, 272–73). Yet, Argentina continued to develop its land through the perpetuation of strategies of absolute surplus production whereas Canada, through mechanisation, transitioned to a strategy of relative surplus production, a hallmark of industrialised capitalism. According to Adelman, the choice of technology (the creative power) cannot be attributed to the commodity itself—this is precisely that type of commodity fetishism which Marx argued distorts the true nature and relations of production under capitalism (Marx 1976, 164–65). Rather, the precise technique of production, the technological as well as social and material organisation of production, is fundamentally determined by the kinds of social relations within which production itself takes place. This is to say that production is a social rather than technical relation.

Looking at Argentina and Canada throughout the late nineteenth and early twentieth centuries, the most marked differences one finds are precisely those to do with social relations. More specifically, Canada and Argentina differed significantly with regard to the forms of property relations that prevailed within the colony, constituting an initial condition of unevenness, as well as within the countries of origin for the majority of their immigrant populations. Thus, social property relations within Canada and Argentina produced different class forces and strategies of accumulation and reproduction. At the same time, the immigrants who would come to establish agricultural production in each space, came from different parts of Europe, themselves characterised by uneven social property regimes, so that their motivation for emigrating in the first place had been circumscribed by very different conditions of reproduction and accumulation. Migrants, therefore, were not simply neutral market inputs extended to the colonies as a means of drawing them into the remit of the expanding capitalist market. Rather, their very reasons for emigrating owing in part to their own country's property regime, and how such intentions were reinforced or reconfigured by the parameters of reproduction that prevailed within the colony, bore important consequences on the range of available strategies for wheat production within Argentina and Canada, respectively.

In Canada, the enclosure of the prairies, following a series of lengthy wars aimed at clearing the grasslands of their indigenous inhabitants, proceeded in large part through a state-led settlement project. In a rich, comparative historical analysis of wheat development on the prairies and pampas, Jeremy Adelman (1994) has argued that the influence of the United States' Homestead Act functioned as an almost unquestioned model for Canadian settlement policy which took shape in the Dominion Lands Act of 1872. Under the Lands Act, settlement was to be promoted through the establishment of small family owned and operated farms, where deeds to the land were to be obtained through at least three years on the land (with at minimum six months of each year working the land through cultivation) as well as a $10 administration fee. While the state also engaged in land sales directly to settlers, it was largely through homesteading that settlement was achieved on the prairies. To be sure, the private market for land through large companies such as the Canadian Pacific Railway or the Hudson's Bay Company operated in conjunction with homesteading. However, private sales ultimately contributed little to the early settlement of Canada's grasslands. Competition with state distributed land, virtually free of charge except for an administration fee, meant that private companies could not sell land at a profitable rate. As a result, the enclosures of the prairies were enacted dominantly through a deliberate public settlement scheme (Adelman 1994, 23).

The publicly led rather than private settlement of land had a number of consequences on the shape of social property relations resulting and the course that agricultural production would take. In the first place, the public monopoly on land sales established a ceiling on the price of land which served as a check against private sales and the formation of a class of large land owners. Because private land sales could not operate competitively outside of the publicly established price of land, settlement and ownership remained open to immigrant settlers of varied means, so that prairie land ownership was fragmented and diversified rather than concentrated. The combination of public land transfers and their attendant requirements for cultivation, along with the small-scale and diversified ownership of land on the prairies created the conditions under which small-scale, owner operated agricultural production predominated. The family farm became the seat of prairie wheat development and this, in turn, bore consequences for subsequent patterns of class formation and technological innovation (Adelman 1994, 24–49).

Because the distribution of land on the prairies militated against the development of a landed elite, the Lands Act created mutually reinforcing tendencies for existing class structures and nascent wheat development. The predominant interests reflected at the national political level were those of urban merchants situated in Toronto and Montreal who were dependent on the maintenance of market protection from US and British competition. This protected economy, however, could only be supported through the earnings made on raw commodity exports, and consequently the political and economic elite in Canada were significantly bound to the fortunes of wheat production (Solberg 1987, 55–58). As a result, the Macdonald conservative government received considerable elite support in its efforts to advance and implement a National Policy (1876) on development which hinged on a high tariff, massive immigration and public support for a national railway. The National Policy, for our purposes, had two main consequences for prairie wheat development. First, elite support for the National Policy meant that the Canadian government was able to pursue immigration recruitment through a series of active policies and strategies, and additionally was permitted to control and direct the internal movement of incoming migrants. Second, it raised the costs of wheat production as the costs of Canadian produced farm implements were higher than imports. These factors served to significantly distinguish prairie wheat development from that on the pampas. As we shall see, in Argentina a landed elite blocked the development of any form of national development strategy such that both the tariff and active immigrant settlement were prevented.

The Lands Act and the homesteading process created a class of farmers who were obliged to engage in commercial enterprise by virtue of owning their means of production in land. Agricultural wheat production was the most attractive option for these farmers as wheat cultivation was uniquely well suited to small plots of land and was relatively easy and quick in its rates of turnover so as to allow farmers to meet homesteading requirements for land ownership. While farmers tended to labour on their own farms or hire themselves out to nearby farms for most of the year, the harvest season entailed a dramatic rise in the demand for wage labourers. The high seasonality of labour demand, thus denoted a requirement for a mobile and flexible labour force. Yet, the ability to attract wage labourers to the prairies was stunted by two key factors. On the one hand, so long as public land remained available through the Lands Act, immigrants were far more inclined to settle land as farmers than to establish themselves as waged labourers (Adelman 1994, 40–45; Solberg 1987, 58). However, this in itself cannot fully explain the reticence of immigrants to Canada to sell their labour power on the market. Indeed, as the choice plots of public land began to dwindle, immigrants would continue to choose homesteading over labouring, obtaining both credit and land through the private market (Adelman 1994, 40–45). I suggest, then, that it is necessary that we look to the motivations of the migrants themselves, owing in large part to the conditions of reproduction within which they were situated in their country of origin.

The National Policy's promotion of an active and selective state-led immigration recruitment project resulted in the application of highly selective, racist criteria for targeting immigrants. In general, the Canadian state limited its active recruitment to the so-called 'preferred races' of Anglo-Saxon and Nordic origin, while making qualified exceptions for impoverished eastern and central European peoples (Avery 1979, 18–23). The origins of the Canadian settler population was significant in that all areas under active recruitment had themselves undergone a transition from feudalism to capitalism wherein market dependence and the sale of labour power had become general means of survival, while ownership over ones means of (re)production was increasingly difficult to retain in the home country (Eltis 1983, 257). On the one hand, then, the choice of recruitment sought to replace an indigenous population with one which had ostensibly been converted to so-called liberal values of rational, individual thrift and private labour. At the same time, however, emigration appealed to those actually migrating precisely as a means of (re)gaining possession over land and, hence over their own social reproduction, without having to submit to the vagaries of the labour market. Thus a conflict existed in the objectives of those promoting and those seeking emigration such that migrants sought to begin a life in the New World as a means of providing a bridge over the class divide, allowing labourers to become owners of capital.

The above assertions are borne out by Adelman's research which found that despite initially trying to promote emigration among the 'best of the Anglo-Saxon agricultural classes', emigration was difficult to induce so long as potential migrants' conditions of reproduction could be ensured through ownership in property at home. Indeed, Canada's Commissioner of Immigration William McCreary, suggested during the early years of active immigration policy that rapid settlement would be achieved only through the movement of those without capital in their home country, who could then see in Canada the prospects of improving one's lot through homesteading (Adelman 1994, 150). Emigrating from a space in which a transition to market dependence had already been achieved, Anglo-Saxon settlers saw their fortunes at home as that of the subservient waged labourer. Seeking escape from such conditions, Canada was a space in which the emigrant could ostensibly leap the gulf between owners of capital and sellers of labour through the production of staples for the world market.

It is on this point that the peculiarities of Canadian class formation on the prairies became significant for the course of development in wheat production. While the staples thesis would have it that mass immigration served to both settle the land and supply the necessary labour for wheat production, it was precisely the difficulty in obtaining an adequate supply of wage labour which induced rapid technological advances in the production of prairie wheat. Returning to the concept of UCD, let us recall that the Canadian economy was being developed on the basis of a subordinate integration into global commodity markets as an exporter of raw materials. One of the key means through which this integration was effected was precisely through massive immigration from the core of the global economy which provided the necessary 'human material' for production. In part, the strategy of mass European immigration was to import a 'ready-made' labour force. Indeed, because the mass of immigrants were the working-classes of England, Scotland, Whales and Ireland, it was often assumed that they would be ready, willing and able to perform these same roles in Canada as needed. Yet, the ways in which these migrants interacted with the configuration of social property relations in Canada itself actually militated against the establishment of a permanent rural proletariat.

So long as the agricultural frontier was expanding, the availability of land meant that settlers would first and foremost seek to become capital owners and small farm operators through both homesteading and, later, through access to credit markets and private land sales (Adelman 1994, 40–45; Schmidt 1981, 80–82). Farm owners faced significant challenges in turning over a profit as a result of the effects of tariffs on farming inputs which raised the production costs of wheat. Such wheat could not remain competitive on the world market where competitors produced without a national tariff. While the costs of production could be lowered through an alteration of the wages paid to farm labour, the dearth of waged labour on the prairies meant that farmers themselves provided the bulk of labour in wheat production, hiring themselves out to neighbouring farms when circumstances required (Adelman 1992, 279–80; Solberg 1987, 98). Given that these labourers were not a landless proletariat, but rather owners of the means of production, and thus their fortunes were tied to the productivity of wheat and its sale on world markets (which itself was constrained by the costs of production under the tariff), farmers-labourers organised so as to place an upwardly buoyant pressure on the wage rate. In the long run, in order for production to take place successfully, the only option remaining to make wheat competitive was to revolutionise the production process through a rise in the organic composition of capital and a transition to relative surplus value production (Schmidt 1987, 80–86). Thus the technological innovation of wheat production on the prairies was born out of the particular interaction of migrants and settler social property relations, which led to the formative role of market-based, competitive imperatives.

The enclosure of the Argentine pampas proceeded in a completely different manner from that of the Canadian prairies and as a consequence, produced very different social property configurations. Rather than a dominant merchant elite, Argentina was subject to the interests of a landed, ranching elite at the time of confederation, a fact of considerable importance within the context of the 1863 Constitution that had decentralised political powers to the provinces (Solberg 1987, 14–17). The provinces, however, were financially vulnerable after having waged bloody and costly campaigns of genocide throughout the pampas in order to eliminate the indigenous populations (Adelman 1992, 274). This financial vulnerability resulted in the provinces having to sell off huge swaths of land to the existing landed elite. Land ownership and its attendant political influence was thus concentrated in a minority ranching elite whose interests were opposed to state-led agrarian and industrial development policy (Solberg 1987, 16).

The interests of the landed classes were bound to a practice of extensive land exploitation. This meant that the competitive imperatives associated with wage intensive production did not apply to the primary reproductive strategies of the dominant Argentine classes. Rather, the much more intensive cereals production was given secondary status to that of ranching. The predominance of the cattle industry resulted in land being the key source of capital investment for the agrarian elite owing to the speculative and productive profits to be reaped (Solberg 1987, 10). Because of this, the settlement of the pampas was seen as not only superfluous, but also threatening to the landed classes of Argentina who actively stymied state efforts to successfully implement a homesteading policy of family-farm production. Indeed, following a financial crisis in 1890, the state was forced to sell off its remaining tracts of land to the estancia owners of the pampas, thus finally closing off the option of settlement and development through homesteading (Adelman 1992, 274). At the same time, free and open access to world markets for the export of cattle products caused the Argentine elite to organise political pressure against the erection of a developmental tariff for the generation of new industries (Solberg 1987, 14–17, 28).

To be clear, cereal exports would come to predominate in the Argentine economy. Yet the landed elite would continue to reproduce themselves first and foremost through ranching and speculative land profits. This class-based reproduction and its consequences in the social organisation of land ownership meant that wheat production occurred on the basis of a leasehold or tenancy form of production in contradistinction to Canada's owner production of wheat on the prairies (Adelman 1992, 278–80).

The predominance of tenant-production on the pampas functioned as a disincentive for the mechanisation and intensification of wheat production in at least two key manners. First, the resilience of the *estancieros* to fracture their landownership meant that they favoured a circular rather than permanent migration scheme. Land tenancy, with its short contracts of three to four years, was well suited to these temporary forms of migration (Adelman 1992, 278). Simultaneously, tenant farmers themselves had little incentive to revolutionise wheat production through capital investment, as short-term contracts favoured quick turnovers and returns in the short-run over the long-term intensification of production. Thus, it appears that the social property relations particular to Argentina were significant in effectively mitigating or staving off the competitive pressures of world market production in the short-run. However, as Solberg has noted (1987, 28), looking to the effects of elite machinations on farming patterns is itself inadequate. Indeed, had there been more permanent migration, or the wish for such settlement, immigrants would have been far more likely to organise and lobby for their own interests in the form of agrarian development policy, tariff protections etc. It is on this point that the strategies of reproduction within which immigrants themselves were embedded were critical to the course of Argentine development. Again, the developmental outcome of Argentine wheat production was the result of the particular combination of extant social property relations and migrants— the so-called neutral technology that was being imported in order to 'leap stages' of development was precisely a labouring class that was to arrive readily docile and complacent. Yet, as we shall see, the Italian populations that dominated immigration to Argentina in the late nineteenth and early twentieth centuries did not automatically produce that quintessential permanent class of wage-earners such that profit could only be earned through a rising organic composition of capital.

Immigration to Argentina was dominated by Italians, largely from the more rural southern regions which persisted in a feudal social structure until into the nineteenth century. However, Italians were only settled upon as the inevitable though 'lesser stock' of European immigrants (Adelman 1994, 110–11). Initially Argentine officials saw their new country as being the European outpost of Latin America, a bastion of 'white European civilisation and industrialisation'. As a consequence, early government efforts to recruit immigrants to Argentina were targeted at Anglo-Saxon and Northern European countries, which sought to entice potential settlement through offers of land via a family-farming scheme (Nugent 1992, 96; Solberg 1987, 30). Ultimately, however, such immigration did not occur. On the one hand, Anglo-Saxon and Northern Europeans appeared to prefer immigration to Canada and the United States (Nugent 1992, 44). At the same time, however, the means of incentivising immigration available to the Argentine government were radically curtailed by landowners' stymying efforts to promote family-farm settlement through their progressive monopolisation of the land market. As a result, immigration incentives were limited to subsidised passages which had little appeal to the Anglo-Saxon emigrants seeking an escape from wage labour and the chance to set up their own plot of land to farm and make their private fortune on (Adelman 1994, 113–14; Solberg 1987, 30).

Italian immigration to Argentina became predominant for a number of reasons. On the side of endogenous conditions favouring Italian immigration, the labour needs of immigrants were necessarily short term. A highly flexible, mobile and circular migrant population was desirable in the context of the monopolised land ownership in the pampas. As a result, the needs to be fulfilled by immigrants were either seasonal harvest labour or short-term land tenancy, over a period of three to four years. Conveniently, the harvest season in Italy was opposite that of Argentina and hence it was possible for Italian emigrants to partake in circular labour migration while still maintaining their own livelihoods at home. Additionally, the distance between Italy and Argentina was far more conducive to short term and return travels, than would be that between the Northern European countries and Argentina (Adelman 1994, 112–15).

As indicated above, however, it is not adequate to simply look to the endogenous conditions surrounding immigration, as any number of other potential countries could have provided for the labouring needs of Argentina and with varied consequences. That Italian immigration was dominant in Argentina was significant owing to the particular strategies and practices which motivated emigration in the first place, and conditioned Italians' interaction with the Argentine economy on the pampas.

In contrast to the emigration taking place from Northern Europe where the social relations of feudalism had been dismantled and where the institution of market dependence had taken place, southern Italy throughout the nineteenth century remained firmly rooted in feudal institutions and social practices. As J.S. MacDonald has argued (1963), the conditions of feudal property arrangements in the Italian South favoured a strategy of emigration in response to peasant landlessness and poverty. Land customs which saw the fragmentation of ownership through inheritance and dowry practices resulted in the creation of land plots so small they were unviable for agricultural production and therefore had to be sold off to large estate owners. Peasants as a result became sharecroppers and were responsible for all capital provisions on the land. Consequently, very little capital was invested and agriculture yielded uncertain and minimal profits. Permanent waged labour had not yet become a convention of reproduction as peasants still had access to their means of reproduction, though mediated through sharecropping contracts or feudal land relations. Temporary migration was thus undertaken as a means of acquiring capital abroad to reinvest in the land at home (Macdonald 1963, 69).

As a result of the endogenous property relations and the strategies of Italian immigrants on the pampas, then, labour was available in abundance and at a high elasticity given its circular nature. Such conditions meant that the pressing incentive to mechanise production in order to reduce wages (as occurred in the labour scarce prairies of Canada) did not apply to the Argentine pampas. Additionally, for short-term land tenants, profits were to be made through a rapid turnover in wheat production to be sold on the global market. Their strategy was one of maximising profits while meeting the financial obligations of landowners, within the short period of their tenancy contract. Hence, those Italian immigrants who engaged in tenancy rather than seasonal labour had a vested interest in keeping the barriers to trade low and were themselves little inclined to invest long-term capital in revolutionising the production process (Solberg 1987, 4). All of this meant that wheat production on the pampas proceeded through a process where profits were reaped through the limited form of extensive agricultural production, which required vast (though finite) quantities of both land and labour. Clear disincentives to the mechanisation of agriculture were exerted on both migrants and landowners such that both the closing of the frontier and the end to extensive land exploitation as well as the onset of war in 1914 and the disruption of immigration served to send wheat production into a crisis from which it would take decades to recover (Nugent 1992, 118).

CONCLUSION

As argued above, the staples thesis of economic development has been inadequate in explaining the causes of differential development within settler spaces, and this is owing to the essential commodity fetishism which lies at its core, and its understanding of production as a technical rather than social relation. Both Argentina and Canada were integrated into global capitalist markets on the basis of export wheat production, and yet the ways in which wheat did or did not stimulate endogenous processes of industrial growth were markedly different, with Canada 'taking off' in the twentieth century and Argentina falling behind. As a result, a focus on the commodity being produced in itself is inadequate.

A significant element in the development of both spaces (and this holds for settler colonies generally) was that global market integration and capitalist transitions were initiated through massive immigration intended to make profitable the 'barren' grasslands of the prairies and pampas. In effect immigration was to function as an imported capitalist technique—the institution of waged labour—as overseas immigration by its very nature meant that new arrivals were dispossessed of their means of production. However, how immigration actually functioned in each setting was dramatically different, such that the establishment of a rural proletariat was far from certain. Yet, the staples thesis completely ignores this fact treating immigration as a neutral input to the production of wheat; that immigration provided the labouring needs of wheat appears an unquestioned truth.

The differences I have suggested above for how immigrants as a supposed technology of production interacted with the extant social arrangements in both Canada and Argentina, however, provided for completely different strategies of reproduction of both immigrants and owners of capital such that pressures to engage in a transition from absolute to relative surplus value production in wheat were present in Canada but not in Argentina. Migration, in this sense, functioned as a mechanism of UCD. Combined in so much as it was intended to draw into the global market both spaces through the ostensible importation of a ready-made proletariat. Uneven in that the interaction of dispossessed immigrants within each settler space was conditioned by varying social property relations and therefore produced radically different consequences for the paths of wheat production and broader patterns of national development which ensued. At the heart of this analysis as contrasted to the staples thesis, is the fundamental assertion that production is a social rather than technical relation and, as such, the materially grounded agencies and interactions of the human beings involved are of absolute significance in explaining divergences in the developmental fortunes of Canada and Argentina.

NOTES

1. Here I am referring to the so-called 'white settler colonies' which were characterised by the dispossession and marginalisation of indigenous populations, the mass importation of European populations to 'settle' the land and a high ratio of land relative to population. Included in this category would be Argentina, Australia, Canada, Chile, New Zealand, the United States and Uruguay (Willebald and Berola 2013).

2. That settler spaces were 'void of demographic pressures' is itself a matter of social and political economic determination rather than geographical fortune, as the staples thesis would posit. While the mass genocidal displacement of indigenous peoples' physical and cultural presence was a historical precondition of these spaces, this does not confirm the idea of terra nullius inasmuch as there remained significant indigenous presence. That these populations continued to be externalised, rather than absorbed, into the nascent development of a capitalist political economy (as labour or otherwise) is an issue beyond the scope of this present chapter, but which I address more fully elsewhere.

3. It should be noted that the contemporary application of UCD to international relations takes its starting point from the work of Justin Rosenberg, whose work also constitutes a point of division amongst scholars using the concept. Precisely, this division concerns the historical specificity of UCD versus its potential transhistorical application. Drawing upon Trotsky's initial formulation, Rosenberg has attempted to develop the idea of UCD to explain the very fact of the 'international' system itself (as opposed to Trotsky's more limited concern with explaining variable capitalist development). This move has required a conceptual stretching of unevenness and combination beyond the remit of the capitalist mode of production, a move which has been met with a considerable degree of resistance.

In their contribution to the inaugural debate on UCD within the *Cambridge Review of International Affairs*, Jamie Allinson and Alexander Anievas take up the problem of general abstractions within Rosenberg's deployment of UCD (Allinson and Anievas 2009). While agreeing with Rosenberg that there is a latent, if mundane, way in which we can read UCD transhistorically, the authors argue firmly that its causal significance is only fully activated under the conditions of capitalist competition. For the authors, UCD can be used as a transhistoric general abstraction only if it is used to create historically specific, concrete categories for analysis. In contrast to this, Rosenberg has used UCD as a transhistoric abstraction which is both that which explains and from which all other explanations derive. This method of abstraction is argued to be fully at odds with the methodologies of Marxist sociological theory. Instead, the authors argue that as per Marx's methodology, a general abstraction should be utilised as the basis from which to posit a presupposition, which can then account for a concrete general condition whose historical form is nonetheless explained by further categories and concepts. In this more nuanced sense, UCD can be posited as a transhistoric general abstraction only if it is situated in a mode of production analysis, which gives us the historical material with which to make sense of its particular operation within a given historical juncture (Allinson and Anievas 2009).

I take seriously Allinson and Anievas's argument that UCD can only attain explanatory capacities within a mode of production theory. To this end, I propose that the SPR approach of Brenner *et al.* is a promising means of situating UCD within concrete tendencies owing to the material configuration of social relations. The strength of the SPR approach is that it provides for an understanding of the specificity of a mode of production in terms of its laws of motion or rules of reproduction, contingent upon a particular, historically specific arrangement of social property relations. This, however, is not the same as asserting a totalising and universalising schematic of social relations absent of agency. Specifically, as concerns the capitalist mode of production, I suggest that the SPR approach allows us to understand capitalist expansion not only as the expansion of impersonal laws of accumulation and reproduction, but rather as the expansion of particular configurations of social relations. Though these social relations produce their own logics of accumulation and reproduction, the fact of their connectivity with human subjectivity and agency renders them malleable (within particular historical parameters) rather than absolute. By understanding the relationship between different historical and geographical configurations of social property relations, subjectivities and agencies, it is possible to comprehend how the interaction (or combination) of different (uneven) social property regimes will produce novel forms of political, class and labour organisation such that capitalist modernity is never manifest in a singular and universal form, but is always variable in its concretely combined character.

4. It is important to note here that I am dealing with the period starting from confederation in each case. As such, existing indigenous social property relations had already been largely displaced and in each space, owing to the nature of such displacements, a new configuration of social property relations had been erected by early settlers. In beginning from the point of confederation, I am examining the period in which a distinctly 'national' development project was undertaken in contrast to the explicitly dependent settler development that had taken place prior to this point. This process of national development involved what is critical for my analysis here—an attempt to develop a national labour market through mass immigration.

Chapter 9

Navigating Uneven and Combined Development

Britain's Africa Policy in Historical Perspective

William Brown

The early years of the twenty-first century saw a renewed focus on Africa within Britain's foreign policy. Although not a major feature of Prime Minister Tony Blair's initial years in office, a series of events and trends—from increasing emphasis on development cooperation and global poverty reduction to intervention in Sierra Leone—pushed Africa up the policy agenda. The continent was declared a major focus of Blair's second administration culminating in the Commission for Africa and the G8 summit at Gleneagles in July 2005. Policy priorities shifted somewhat in the aftermath of the financial crisis and with the advent of Conservative-led governments from 2010. Yet even so, by 2015 Africa was still a key focus of a much-enlarged UK development cooperation effort—Africa being the largest regional recipient of UK aid—and declared 'at the heart' of UK foreign policy on development and security issues (Duddridge 2015).

The renewed focus on Africa, from Blair onwards, brought forth a host of historical parallels. For some, Blair's liberalism and desire to transform and 'heal' Africa, resurrected Victorian liberal ideals of progress in the 'dark continent' (Brown 2006; Williams and Young 2009; Duffield and Hewitt 2009). For others, the ideational importance of Africa continued the deeply embedded British conceptions of Africa as an 'empty space' where Britain could 'do good' (Gallagher 2013). For others still, the focus on Africa and the increasing challenge to Western influence posed by Chinese engagement with the continent presaged a 'new scramble for Africa' (Carmody 2011). Indeed, Africa's very rise up the policy agenda, coming after a period of relative neglect in the 1980s and early 1990s in which Africa was of marginal concern to UK governments (Ireton 2014), was itself redolent of a shift in British policy that occurred in the late nineteenth century. Africa had moved from a landmass whose significance 'lay in the transitory importance of its shores to the enterprises flowing past them' to taking centre stage in a rapid expansion of colonial control (Robinson, Gallagher and Denny 2015, 14).

However, if we look at the aims and prospects of recent British policy towards Africa, we find that such parallels do not by themselves grasp the dynamic and changing nature of interaction between Britain and Africa. Indeed, the legacies of the past weigh heavily on the present as revitalised aims for liberal transformation in Africa come up against the legacies of past interaction. This chapter explores the historical evolution of Britain's policy towards Africa using ideas drawn from the theory of uneven and combined development. I argue that we can understand shifts in British policy towards Africa as attempts to navigate problems thrown up by the developmentally highly uneven nature of the relationship and the contradictory developmental outcomes of combined development. As such, it posits the key location for understanding changes in British policy as the point of interaction *between* Britain and Africa. In doing so the chapter also draws on the ideas of Ronald Robinson in locating the vicissitudes of British imperial policy as reactive and interactive manoeuvres with non-European political actors (Robinson 1972, 1986).

The chapter has two main aims. First, and most substantively, it seeks to outline an evolving dynamic in relations between Britain and Africa whereby the legacies of past processes of combined development shape and constrain current and future policy choices. Second, at a broader level, by locating the point of analysis on relations between British and African actors it seeks to investigate ways of developing less Eurocentric accounts, creating space for understanding the impact of non-European agency, even while the focus remains on British, and wider Western, policy. It seeks to do this by using both the more general depiction of international relations provided by uneven and combined development and the more specific 'excentric' analysis of imperialism developed by Robinson.

The chapter is organised around three key phases in British Africa policy: the advent of colonial rule; the evolution of colonial development policy prior to independence; and the resurgence of liberal transformatory aims within British policy this century. The chapter briefly sets out some of the theoretical and conceptual issues on which it draws in analysing these three periods before taking each in turn.

UNEVENNESS AND 'EXCENTRIC' IMPERIALISM

This chapter draws on Justin Rosenberg's work on uneven and combined development to frame an account of the evolution of, and challenges facing, British Africa policy.[1] It does this in two main ways . First, it uses uneven and combined development to characterise evolutions in British policy as attempts to navigate a highly uneven and interactive relationship with Africa. Uneven and combined development posits international relations in general as social processes of interaction between unevenly developed societies.[2] The world is and always has been composed of multiple societies that are unevenly developed across a range of economic, social, cultural, technological and political dimensions; they all have to engage with the 'outside world' in some way and have institutions and processes relating to managing diplomacy in its 'broadest sense' (Rosenberg 2006, 320). The development of any one society over time therefore is inherently a process of combination—a dialectical, dynamic and intersocietally interactive unfolding of multiple causal factors. However, the advent and expansion of industrial capitalism accelerated and intensified these processes of interaction making 'development' as a whole a world-wide, combined and in many respects increasingly uneven, process. Seen through this lens, British policy towards Africa, from the nineteenth century onwards, represents an extremely uneven case of intersocietal interaction, driven initially by the expansion of British and wider (uneven) European capitalist industrialisation. However, both in the early period of colonisation and more recently, this unevenness played out in ways that have often limited the successful realisation of British policy aims.

The second use of uneven and combined development is to explain why British Africa policy aims have often been frustrated. The theory argues that rather than producing a homogeneous international system, intersocietal interaction produces successive novel, hybrid and heterogeneous developmental outcomes and forms of state among 'catch-up' or 'later developing' countries. This insight is of key importance in understanding the evolution of British policy in Africa over time. At various points—in the pre-colonisation period, the early years of colonisation, in the late colonial promotion of 'development' and more recently—liberal transformatory aims have animated British policy towards Africa. Yet at each point, the heterogeneous outcomes of combined development have frustrated liberal ambitions. British policy as a result shows phases of advancing and then stepping back from the pursuit of liberal change in Africa. As with other historical and contemporary policy examples, where universal liberal principles collide with a highly differentiated world,[3] processes of uneven and combined development in Africa have presented to British policy makers an evolving set of dilemmas.

Recognition of the importance of European development and expansion has been a mainstay of both orthodox and more radical accounts of the European role in Africa in the colonial and post-colonial eras. However, in those accounts not only is the direction of interaction almost entirely one-way traffic—European or Western expansion into or impositions on Africa—but the role of unevenness is cashed in largely in terms of European technological, economic and military advantage over Africa. The Africanist historian Frederick Cooper noted this very point:

Scholars have been too quick to leap from the unevenness of power, which reached an extreme in the nineteenth century, to an assumption that capitalism, Europe, or colonialism was necessarily an overwhelming force in the world.... Scholars have trouble conceptualizing asymmetrical relationships, which nonetheless do not imply total power of one side over the other. To explore such relationships is to see the limits of power as well as its extent and above all to look at how people on the weaker end of the connection pushed back.... (Cooper 2014, 9)

Acknowledging the role of 'people on the weaker end' is a crucial step if we are to move away from more Eurocentric accounts and to explain the production of the varied and divergent outcomes from interaction. One of the promises of the theory of uneven and combined development is that it provides more scope for doing just this (Hobson 2011; Anievas and Nişancioğlu 2015).

It was a critique of orthodox and radical theories of imperialism, and their failure to acknowledge the role of non-European actors in accounts of imperialism, that characterised Ronald Robinson's work (1972, 1986).[4] In it, and in his work with John Gallagher (Gallagher and Robinson 1953; Robinson, Gallagher and Denny 2015), Robinson sought to give an 'excentric' account of British Africa policy, one which located the causal dynamic at the point of interaction between an expansionist Britain and the non-European societies it came into contact with. According to Robinson (1986, 271), 'when imperialism is looked at as an inter-continental process, its true metropolis appears neither at the centre nor the periphery, but in their changing relativities'.

Perhaps most interestingly for our purposes, Robinson developed an account in which a key role is played by the variation (perhaps read 'unevenness') that existed among the non-European societies which Britain encountered; the varied reactions of those societies to European expansion; and the different economic and political outcomes that resulted from such interactions. These elements are most clearly seen in Robinson's account of the period of British colonisation of Africa in the late nineteenth century and the following section draws heavily on that account. As we will see, these varied processes laid the basis for later challenges facing Britain's Africa policy. However, as Robinson himself did in later work, the chapter will bring forward key insights of this account of colonisation into the post-colonial period as well.

SCRAMBLING OR 'FUMBLING TO ADJUST'?

Britain's accelerating industrial development and international expansion in the mid- to late nineteenth century meant that its interaction with Africa was characterised among other things by two important trends: increasing intensity and increasing unevenness. The combination of both resulted in a massive expansion of British territorial possessions in Africa. However, the route by which that outcome was arrived at was neither straightforward nor dictated by trends in Britain alone. 'The most striking fact about British history in the nineteenth century', Gallagher and Robinson noted, 'is that it is the history of an expanding society' with industrialisation causing an extended and intensified impact overseas (Gallagher and Robinson 1953, 5).

However, in marked contrast to the mercantilist era, while British power was deployed to enforce the *pax Britannica,* 'liberation' rather than acquisition was the goal, and free trade rather than monopoly was the means to achieve it (Robinson, Gallagher and Denny 2015, 4). For the mid-century Victorians, empire assumed a moral purpose, not to rule the world but to redeem it (Ferguson 2003). And it was thought that commerce, perhaps accompanied by the other C's—Christianity and civilisation—would by itself liberate other peoples from their 'backward' and 'despotic' societies (Pakenham 1991). In contrast to some other accounts of the Scramble for Africa, Robinson and Gallagher argued that the eventual acquisition of territory at the end of the century was not driven by a sharp change in British policy per se. Rather, policy was relatively consistent across the century, seeking to encourage and protect British commercial expansion and political influence by whatever means were needed but with a preference for avoiding territorial expansion (Gallagher and Robinson 1953, 13). As Robinson later framed it (1986, 281): 'By informal means if possible, by formal means if necessary, imperialism integrated new regions into international capitalist economy, providing local *pax* and strategic protection'.

Indeed, the focus of British expansion was often not within the formal empire. Just prior to the Scramble, over half of British investment and two thirds of exports went to areas not under British political control (Robinson, Gallagher and Denny 2015, 8). In Latin America, for example, integration into British-dominated international trade meant that the need for political and military intervention by Britain was limited. Nevertheless, continued industrial expansion 'made new demands upon British policy' as new and varied underdeveloped areas came within the British orbit (Gallagher and Robinson 1953, 7–8). The unevenness of the world Britain was encountering also meant that a whole range of strategies were deployed, from commercial treaty (the main form by which Britain gave formal recognition to other polities), to anti-slavery treaties signed with African leaders, to protectorates and outright colonisation, creating a patchwork liberal empire of formal and informal relationships (Gallagher and Robinson 1953, 11).

Colonisation, furthermore, only occurred where it was seen as both necessary and possible by British policy makers. 'Not all regions will reach the same level of economic integration at any one time', Gallagher and Robinson wrote (1953, 6), 'neither will all regions need the same type of political control at any one time'. This unevenness among non-European societies, and the ways in which they reacted to British expansion, therefore had a key role in shaping the strategies Britain deployed. Formal political control was sought only when informal influence was not sufficient to secure economic or geopolitical aims, but also only where it was politically or military feasible. Often these two conditions did not obtain. In Latin America and areas of British settlement, it was often regarded as unnecessary. In parts of Asia—China and the Ottoman Empire—greater political control might have been seen as desirable, given the barriers to British and European commerce that remained stubbornly in place, but there were severe limits to achieving it (Gallagher and Robinson 1953). In Africa, meanwhile, political takeover did eventually come to be seen as necessary (Robinson, Gallagher and Denny 2015; Robinson 1986).

Three key points are worth noting at this point. First, although takeover came to be seen as 'necessary' in Africa, from a British point of view, it was possible only in a restricted sense—through the construction of very particular forms of political rule centred on a limited commitment of resources and military force combined with a creation and strengthening of what were represented as 'traditional' African political structures (see following section). This bequeathed deeply problematic legacies for those societies once independence was won, and indeed for later British policy makers.

Second, the 'need' for colonisation manifested itself in very different ways in different parts of Africa, at least from the British perspective. Unevenness within Africa, and the fluidity of the wider geopolitical pressures on Britain, meant that the establishment of colonies should not be seen as a mono-causal process. The British entry into Africa, in this view, arose from disparate situations, all 'products of different historical evolutions, some arising from national growth or decay, others from European expansion.... All of them were changing at different levels at different speeds' (Robinson, Gallagher and Denny 2015, 466).

Third and more generally, we should note that this understanding of colonisation makes a decisive move away from Eurocentric accounts and establishes a critical role for the societies and peoples 'a the weaker end of the connection' (Cooper 2014, 9). It was precisely those non-European agents who the British at the time regarded as 'without history' (Wolf 1982), and the varied patterns of resistance and accommodation they pursued, who shaped whether, where, when and how the British resorted to formal imperialism. Colonisation and British policy choices were shaped by indigenous politics as well as European: 'From beginning to end imperialism was a product of interaction between European and extra-European politics' (Robinson 1972, 119).

The unevenness of 'extra-European politics' that confronted the British in the late nineteenth century was itself, of course, the product of multiple prior processes of combined development too complex to trace here. Nevertheless, two factors are worth highlighting briefly for their role in subsequent British expansion in Africa: the impact of the slave trade and African reactions to earlier phases of European expansion.

The collaborative informal imperialism that Britain pursued for much of the nineteenth century in Africa was itself not new but rather had been at the core of the slave trade which 'combined European initiative with African collaboration'—Europeans financing and organising the trade and Africans dominating the capture and delivery of slaves prior to transportation (Wolf 1982, 204). Leaving the unimaginable human impact to one side, the political effects were also important though collaboration had highly divergent political impacts on African polities (Wolf 1982; Anievas and Nişancioğlu 2015). Some, such as Benin, were for a time able to strengthen and consolidate their existing structures. In others, such as Asante, Oyo and Dahomey, the trade helped to fuel state formation itself, giving rise to new and increasingly powerful polities. In other regions, notably the Congo, the increasing reach of slaving into the interior ultimately weakened existing political structures to the point of collapse. The supply from Europe of firearms, as well as other elite goods, added to the dynamic processes of change, radically altering the balance of power in many regions, and allowing the emergence of new combined forms of state (Wolf 1982; Anievas and Nişancioğlu 2015).

Despite Britain abolishing the slave trade in 1807, 2 million slaves were transported from Africa between 1810 and 1870 (Wolf 1982, 196). The British expectation had been that 'legitimate commerce' would naturally eclipse slave-based production. 'The actual course of events', Bernard Waites notes (1999, 109), 'was very different'. Indeed, not only did slavery continue but the very products of legitimate trade, such as palm oil, came to the market on the backs of slave labour (Waites 1999). In trying to curtail what Britain had earlier done so much to bring about, and address the slavery that Livingstone referred to as 'an open sore of the world' (Pakenham 1991, 1), Britain was drawn into ever deeper involvement in African politics.

The second factor to note is what Pablo Idahosa and Bob Shenton (2004) have called the national developmental responses in Africa to the 'wave of European modernity'. In places as diverse as Tunisia and Madagascar, existing elites initiated processes of reform, state building and development designed to fend off increasing European influence. In Asante, ruling elites actively sought to draw on European expertise and training in consolidating the state and implement a policy of 'peace, trade and open roads' with the Europeans (Idahosa and Shenton 2004, 78–79). And in Ethiopia, attempts at modernisation and military reorganisation were able to hold off colonisation, despite military defeats by the British, until the arrival of Italian fascism in the 1930s (Idahosa and Shenton 2004; Makki 2011). The key importance of these efforts was not that they were successful—most were not. Rather, it was that they were emblematic of the manoeuvring, resistance and accommodation to European expansion seen across Africa.

Two further cases were of crucial importance to the unfolding of the Scramble for Africa—Egypt and South Africa. Of overriding importance to British concerns in the late nineteenth century was India, the economic gains from which kept Britain abreast of its increasingly powerful rivals in Europe and America (Wolf 1982, 312). Yet, for most of the nineteenth century, Britain sought to ensure the safety of routes to India, via the Cape in South Africa and later Suez in Egypt, through informal influence or, in the case of Cape Colony, limited territorial acquisition. But in both cases, the strategy came unstuck, leading not only to occupation of both areas but successive occupations in the upper Nile Valley in Sudan and Uganda, and in southern Africa in Rhodesia and Nyasaland (Robinson, Gallagher and Denny 2015).

Following Napoleon's defeat and removal from Egypt, Mehemet Ali oversaw a centralisation of government finance, modernisation of the military and Egyptian territorial expansion and national economic regulation (Idahosa and Shenton 2004; Gallagher and Robinson 1953). Increasing integration with Europe followed, notably through investment in the Suez Canal and extensive lending from European banks. Bankrupt by 1876, political revolt in Egypt aimed at limiting European influence and threatened both the canal and European bank loans and led eventually to British occupation in 1882 (Gallagher and Robinson 1953, 14). Though designed as a temporary expedition, so difficult was the task of recreating a collaborative political settlement that the British remained in Egypt until 1956.

In South Africa, British occupation had been limited to the Cape Colony, seeking to have enough presence there to secure the coast and exert influence over the Boers to limit their political ambitions and prevent them from provoking a revolt among the Africans expelled or subjugated by the Boers' march into the interior. Already antagonistic and unstable, these informal and semi-formal arrangements—with Boer republics and African polities—were ultimately destroyed by the huge expansion of economic interaction occasioned by the development of the Kimberley diamond mines. This altered 'all the conditions of South African politics' according to one British official (quoted in Robinson, Gallagher and Denny 2015, 58) showing how intensified economic interactions could 'tear down, as well as build up a system of colonial collaboration' ultimately leading to the Boer War (Robinson 1972, 125).

There were important consequences of both the Egyptian occupation and the ever deeper immersion in South African politics. After Egypt, Britain ceded ground to European rivals in West Africa and to Germany in East

Africa but in the official mind at least it created a pressing need to secure the upper Nile Valley. The difficulties of doing this informally—given the Mahdi rebellion in Sudan and the absence of viable collaborative arrangements in East Africa—prompted further colonial expansion (Pakenham 1991). Following a very different dynamic, the economic expansion of South Africa led to Rhodes's expeditions northwards, overcoming the resistance of the Ndebele and establishing new British protectorates, later to become colonies, in southern Africa.

Even in West Africa, attempts to rule through informal means ultimately came up against the difficulties posed by African polities creaking under pressure of an intensifying European presence. In Gold Coast, collaboration with Asante eventually broke down as other European powers pressed their interests with the until then powerful Asante elite, leading to the (failed) assertion of a British protectorate in 1891 and final colonisation in 1901 (Warner 1999; 2001). In Lagos, the frustration of British attempts to remove rulers engaged in slavery led ultimately to annexation. In both cases, the move towards colonisation in one location had further consequences leading to 'an inexorable British advance inland' (Havenden and Meredith 1993, 52–60).

Thus while the 'Scramble for Africa' is often presented as a relatively coherent and uniform process of colonisation it was in fact an uneven and differentiated set of events even just within the British case (German, French, Portuguese and Belgian expansion each had their own dynamics). While occasioned by the intensification of increasingly uneven interactions between Britain and a variety of African polities, British policy showed itself to be a reactive and evolving response to the varied situations across Africa. The perceived need for imperialist relations to take the form of colonial empire rested on the absence or collapse of viable collaborators (Robinson 1986, 271–73; 1972). Yet, too often the Europeans forced indigenous elites to play for too high stakes, cutting them off from traditional bases of support and forcing Europeans to change tack. 'More often than not', Robinson concluded, 'it was this non-European component of European expansion that necessitated the extension of colonial empires' (1972, 130).

From an earlier belief in the power of the informal 'empire of liberty' to transform the world, the realities of the late nineteenth century expansion into the diverse polities of Africa presented a far more difficult prospect to the British. The reality of expansion 'shocked' policy makers into a realisation that 'the growth of communities into harmonious commercial and political partnership with Britain was not after all a law of nature' (Robinson, Gallagher and Denny 2015, 469). The unplanned acquisition of a succession of African colonies was the result. And yet, as Frederick Cooper notes (2014, 10), 'Empires … had to make their power felt in particular contexts. Conquest was usually the easier part of empire building: administering an empire—let

alone transforming societies—was the hard part'. By the start of the twentieth century, the difficulties of ruling and developing the regions now under
British control posed a new set of dilemmas.

DEVELOPMENT AND CONTROL

If the British acquisition of an African empire can be seen as the outcome of
its attempts to manage the increasing intensity and unevenness of the emerging economic and political relations it now had with African societies, its
approach to governing and developing the colonies it now possessed was no
less easy to navigate. A key constraint on policy was the continuing influence
of the Victorian unwillingness to commit large amounts of men and money
overseas. As a result, Victorian ambitions of liberal transformation were
curtailed and the British 'became less concerned to liberate social energies
abroad and concentrated on preserving authority' (Robinson, Gallagher and
Denny 2015, 470; Mamdani 1996). Even if resources had been available, the
Indian mutiny had left an 'indelible mark' on the Victorians, demonstrating
that Westernisation was a 'dangerous and explosive business' (Robinson,
Gallagher and Denny 2015, 10). One colonial governor in West Africa argued
against more ambitious aims of transformation: 'If we allow the tribal authority to be ignored or broken, it will mean that we, who numerically form a
small minority in the country, shall be obliged to deal with a rabble.... There
could only be one end to such a policy, and that would be eventual conflict
with the rabble' (Sir P. Girouard quoted in Lugard 1965, 216). Pacification,
and pacification on the cheap at that, became the overriding goal (Idahosa and
Shenton 2004; Robinson 1972).

The key collaborative mechanism utilised to achieve this end was what
became known as 'indirect rule' codified in Lord Lugard's *The Dual Mandate
in British Tropical Africa* (1965). Colonial states operating along these lines
can be seen as a particular combination of different forms of rule. Mahmood
Mamdani (1996, 19) described them as 'bifurcated' states: 'The colonial
state was a double sided affair. Its one side, the state that governed a racially
defined citizenry, was bounded by the rule of law and an associated regime of
rights. Its other side, the state that ruled over subjects, was a regime of extra-
economic coercion and administratively driven justice'. That is, one side of
the state, concentrated on urban areas, approximated the impersonal, 'civil'
political form of rule of modern capitalist states based on law, albeit racially
defined; the other side consisted of various forms of customary and personal
rule, non- or only partial separation of labour from the land, extra-economic
coercion and exploitation, and concentrated in rural areas. They were two
arms of a single polity within an over-arching colonial authority.

Moreover, each side of these bifurcated states was itself a form of combined development. The rural side of the state was based on supposed African 'customary rule'. Yet, according to Mamdani (1996), customary rule was neither an authentic expression of Africanness, nor an entirely European invention. It was the product of the colonial imagination and the articulation of colonial power with pre-colonial societies which were in any case in a state of flux. Imperialists gave recognition to 'native' traditions 'to build up a tribal authority with recognised legal standing' (Lugard 1965, 217) and accentuated and refashioned existing communities and polities. In many places this preserved or enhanced rather than transformed the 'tribal' or ethnic basis of what Europeans saw as the essential basis of African societies, strengthening 'ethnic compartmentalisation' and reinforcing the authority (and authoritarianism) of rural elites (Robinson 1972, 136; also see Mamdani 1996; Havinden and Meredith 1993, 75).

In the urban centres of power, while a racialised form of 'civil rule' was constructed, fiscal pressures meant that it was a state shaped by their particular colonial conditions. The principle that colonies should be self-financed from revenue or self-financed commercial loans was a tenacious one in British policy (Ireton 2013, 5–6). Though direct taxation was at times used, either in kind, in labour, or money, indirect taxation of imports and exports was the chief means of raising finance for infrastructural development and to pay administrative costs of colonies. It was both cheap to collect and avoided more extensive intrusions into the newly tribalised rural populations (Idahosa and Shenton 2004, 82). Where direct taxation was used, collection was often farmed out to the chiefs and headmen who utilised their mediating role to enrich themselves as well as fund the colonial administration (Idahosa and Shenton 2004, 82; Robinson 1986). Cooper (2002) labelled the states that grew out of these constraints 'gatekeeper states' sitting astride the 'gate' through which imports and exports flowed in order to raise finance by the least troublesome means they could. They too can therefore also be seen as products of combination: neither African nor European 'they emerged out of a peculiar Euro-African history' (Cooper 2002, 160).

In some respects, indirect rule, itself a form of collaboration, allowed the British to re-establish control in place of the systems that had broken down prior to the Scramble. Rural authorities served as intermediaries between the urban centres of authority and the mass of the population in the countryside. This made 'playing' African politics easier for the British because government patronage—honours, contracts and social services—was easier to dispense (Robinson 1972). Also, in order to sustain their own administrations, colonial authorities began to develop infrastructure in places such as Nigeria and Ghana if for no other reason than to facilitate the flow of trade which could be taxed (Havinden and Meredith 1993, 101–3).

Nevertheless, pressures grew to do more than simply sustain colonial administration on the cheap. By the early twentieth century, there were already policy differences emerging. So-called 'social imperialists' saw in colonial expansion a means of serving British interests as well as providing moral and social improvement to indigenous populations while remaining conservative with regard to initiatives aimed at capitalist development in rural areas (Gallagher 2013). On the other hand, 'imperial reformers', led most notably by Joseph Chamberlain, were more ambitious (Gallagher 2013, 38). 'We are landlords of a great estate', Chamberlain proclaimed, 'it is the duty of a landlord to develop his estate' (quoted in Havinden and Meredith 1993, 88). The idea that British rule would benefit Africans had been around for some time but, as Gallagher points out, the idea that it would be the state actively driving this, whether through Chamberlain's imperial assistance or Lugard's indirect rule, was a new idea (Gallagher 2013, 49).[5]

However, shifts in British policy to more fully address the idea of development of the colonies were typically slow and reactive. In 1924 and again in 1926, concessions on loans for capital projects were made available to colonies in Africa and in 1929 parliament passed the Colonial Development Act providing funding for capital projects in those colonies without 'responsible government'—mainly the West Indies and Africa (Ireton 2013, 7; Morgan 1980). However, even here motives were mixed. Gladstonian principles of avoiding long-term financial commitments still prevailed and British interests to stimulate British employment through increased trade were key factors in passing the Act.

Between the wars, British policy never fully resolved the tension inherent in Lugard's dual mandate, pulled as it was between the need to organise the empire for home benefit at a time of high unemployment and the increasing focus on trusteeship that flowed from the Paris Peace conference (Havinden and Meredith 1993, 138). Hopes were raised in the colonies of development and social spending that could only be delivered through injections of public money while back in London the Treasury maintained a commitment to self-financing 'empire on the cheap' (Havinden and Meredith 1993, 138). Though imperial preference was increased between the wars, other initiatives to promote trade within the empire (for example, through the empire marketing board) were half-hearted (Havinden and Meredith 1993).

By the mid- to late 1930s, a number of factors began to push Britain to reconsider its policy. First, demands increased from Nazi Germany for the return of its colonies mandated to Britain after the First World War. The demand was rejected but it increased pressure on Britain to show that it was living up to its commitments on 'trusteeship' in all its colonies (Morgan 1980). Second, the failure of Britain, along with the rest of the League of Nations, to take any meaningful action against Mussolini's invasion of

Ethiopia seriously undermined British standing in the colonies and helped to fuel nascent nationalist movements (Havinden and Meredith 1993, 194–7). Third, the colonies themselves were struggling to maintain their finances. Having allowed colonies to borrow, the depression meant most struggled to increase exports sufficiently to generate the surpluses necessary to service their debts (Havinden and Meredith 1993, 179). Finally, and perhaps most dramatically, labour riots in the West Indies and labour unrest in some African colonies prompted a resurgence of debate about the social and economic conditions within the colonies (Havinden and Meredith 1993, 194–7). Numerous publications, including several on the anti-colonial political left, drew attention to the poor economic and social conditions in the colonies and the government itself commissioned Lord Hailey of the Royal Institute of International Affairs to address the absence of basic statistical information in his *An African Survey* published in 1938 (Morgan 1980). In presenting his report in 1938, Hailey said of the commitment to trusteeship, 'I sometimes wish that we could place our hands on our hearts a little less, and set them to explore our pockets a little more' (quoted in Morgan 1980, 28).

One outcome was the 1940 Colonial Development and Welfare Act providing a much-enhanced fund for colonial development and for research into the colonies. The shift from the 1929 Act was notable, with a much more explicit focus on colonial development (Ireton 2013, 7–8). There was also a new commitment to work towards self-government within the British Empire. Nevertheless, funds under the CDW Act remained small in comparison to the developmental needs of the colonies (Ireton 2013, 17). Moreover, post-war conditions were so dire in Britain that there were severe limits on the level of public investment in the colonies and a need to address the severe shortages in Britain, somewhat blunting the commitment to 'new standards of trusteeship'.

Perhaps more fundamental was the continued drag on ambition that arose from concerns with maintaining British authority. Development threatened to weaken the 'traditional' authorities on which British rule rested. As Robinson put it: 'The less the pro-consuls demanded of their mediators in the way of reform, the safer they were; and the more they tried to develop societies into modern, secular shapes, the harder it became to solve collaborative equations' (Robinson 1986, 280). Consequently, even with a greater commitment to development from London, many governors dragged their feet. In places, colonial authorities 'followed policies that were directly and indirectly inimical to the development of colonial capitalism … where development seemed to lead away from a peasant-based society, local officials were far more cautious' (Havinden and Meredith 1993, 158). Policy ought to 'preserve the social organisations we have inherited and modify them only gradually … within the limits set by the tolerable pace of social change' as Arthur Creech

Jones put it (quoted in Havinden and Meredith 1993, 312–13). The growth of a waged urban working class was 'universally feared' (Idahosa and Shenton 2004, 84).

Complicating matters further, development also threatened to build up the proto-nationalist forces in the colonies. Increases in social expenditure led to expanding administrations and, particularly at the local level, a growing cadre of educated Africans. This not only generated conflict with the chiefs, who feared the loss of their pivotal position between colonisers and rural population, it also brought colonial administrators up against the newly emerging African 'political class' who used staffing and financing of local government as resources for nationalist party-building (Dorman 2015; Gabay 2015; Idahosa and Shenton 2004; see also Allen 1995). Further moves to strengthen the position of 'moderate Africans' by devolving power, and developing electoral representation, merely increased these trends. The result, as Cooper noted, was that the developmental colonialism of the 1950s had decreasing room for manoeuvre (Cooper 2002, 53). The Mau Mau rebellion and growing opposition in Gold Coast and Nigeria further raised the costs of maintaining a developmentalist empire.

Speaking in 1940, Lord Hailey had presciently claimed 'History will look back on this period as being the most critical stage of African development; errors made now … may well create situations which the future can rectify only at the cost of great effort and much human distress' (quoted in Havinden and Meredith 1993, 204–5). And indeed, the legacies of Britain's often faltering attempts to manage its relations with Africa left long legacies for both the states that eventually emerged independent in the 1960s and 1970s and for later British policy makers.[6]

THE LATE REPRISE OF LIBERAL TRANSFORMATION

For much of the period after independence, Britain's relationship with Africa was characterised by 'disengagement, withdrawal and damage limitation' (Porteus 2008, 7). Conflict in Southern Rhodesia and South Africa, where the majority of Britain's commercial and strategic interests were focussed, was the main priority in African diplomacy (Porteus 2008, 8). By the 1990s, even the Cold War-driven concerns in southern Africa had faded and commercial ties with other regions had further eroded Africa's importance to Britain as well as to other European countries. The limited but important powers that independence brought had been well deployed by African governments to try to limit external influence over domestic politics. Conservative governments had proven keen to leave the manifest developmental and peace-keeping and humanitarian challenges to multilateral organisations and the European

Commission and after 1979 aid budgets were under severe pressure (Ireton 2013). And yet, by the turn of the century, Africa was not only rising up the policy agenda in Britain, absorbing ever more prime ministerial attention, but was also the focus of a revitalisation of a British policy agenda aimed at liberal transformation.

The reasons why Africa should have become such an important issue under the Labour governments after 1997 are varied. Labour's pledge to create a new international development department and to have an ethical dimension to foreign policy, together with the increasing influence of large development-oriented NGOs, were key factors. A series of political and military crises in Nigeria, Zimbabwe and Sierra Leone added to the focus on Africa. Internationally, moves to address African states' unsustainable debt burden, and a greater emphasis on poverty reduction as a shared international goal, laid the foundation for a fuller engagement with 'Africa' as a policy issue (Gallagher 2013; Porteus 2008). Concerns about security, especially after 9/11, and migration, added to a perception that the pre-existing 'hands-off' approach to Africa policy could not last.

Britain's re-engagement with developmental challenges in Africa coincided with a widespread rethink among donors about how to promote development and the role of overseas aid.[7] Fundamentally, this was a debate about how to achieve economic growth in Africa through liberal political and economic change. This emerging post-Cold War policy discourse suited Labour's values, rooted as it was in the positive developmental role of human rights, democracy and better governance (Gallagher 2013, 6). It added a more political dimension to development discourses while also softening some of the harsher edges of the extant 'neoliberal' focus on economic liberalisation (Carothers and De Gramont 2013). Moreover, the new policy consensus chimed with the political orientation of the prime minister who famously drew Africa into the centre of foreign policy in the wake of the attack on the World Trade Centre, proclaiming in his 2001 Labour Party Conference speech that 'The state of Africa is a scar on the conscience of the world. But if the world as a community focussed on it, we could heal it' (Blair 2001).

Blair's own approach to Africa was morally driven in a way that was strongly redolent of the early twentieth-century imperial reformers (Gallagher 2013). Inderjeet Parmar (2005, 222–23) has traced the links between Blair's liberal internationalism and turn of the twentieth century imperial visions. The influence on Blair of 'New Liberal' social reformers such as J. MacMurray and T.H. Green, and Christian socialists such as R.H. Tawney, shaped his view of politics and history as a moral striving for societal improvement. This tradition also influenced Blair's international vision and especially his favourable view of 'imperialist' humanitarian actions abroad (Parmar 2005, 225). Julia Gallagher too notes how under New Labour, Africa policy was 'set aside' from other policy areas, an imagined space, untrammelled by the complexities of domestic politics, where Britain could 'do good' (Gallagher 2013, 4). The terrorist attacks on New York gave a compelling strategic argument to add to this moral focus on Africa's 'problems' (Porteus 2008, 42).

Like Victorian visions of an expansive realm of liberty and prosperity, New Labour's approach was one of liberal transformation in Africa. As with those earlier periods, it required available collaborators on the African side. The result was a kind of 'liberal bargain' (Brown 2006), an exchange of aid, debt relief and policy changes on trade and other issues by the developed world, on the one hand, for radical liberal reform of the way in which African states govern and pursue economic development, on the other. It was neatly summed up by Blair in his 2001 Labour Party conference speech: 'On our side: provide more aid, untied to trade; write off debt; help with good governance ... access to our markets ... on the African side: true democracy, no more excuses for dictatorship, abuses of human rights; no tolerance of bad governance ... Proper commercial, legal and financial systems' (Blair 2001).

Such a bargain tied in closely with the prevailing donor approach to development aid which insisted that having the right political, legal and policy conditions for aid was an essential prerequisite for aid to be effective (Kelsall *et al.* 2013). Importantly, it also dovetailed with, and helped to reinforce, African initiatives led by South Africa and Nigeria, pushing in the same direction (Landsberg 2011). Most notably the formation of the African Union in 2001 and the launch of the New Economic Partnership for African Development (OAU 2001)—in which Blair had a significant hand too— seemed to provide the requisite partners on the African side of the bargain.

The high-water-mark of Blair's pursuit of this deal came in 2005 with the publication of the Commission for Africa report, *Our Common Interest*, and the G8 summit at Gleneagles. Despite its subsequent lack of impact, the report was closer to a comprehensive statement of British policy towards Africa than anything else produced in recent decades (Porteus 2008, 62). Its vision for change in Africa set out the need for

> the right economic, social and legal framework which will encourage economic growth and allow poor people to participate in it ... establish[ing] an economic environment that encourages investment ... security, setting sound economic policies under the law, collecting taxes and delivering adequate public services like health and education ... legal systems to protect basic property rights, human rights, and respect for contracts. (Commission for Africa 2005, 24)

Even the G8, rather more in the real political world than the Commission, were cajoled into pledging enough by way of aid increases and debt relief to suggest the West was interested in furthering the liberal deal (G8 2005).[8]

Any aid relationship is in some respects both an expression of, and an attempt to deal with, unevenness (Brown 2009). However, when the policies around aid move from more limited aims of ameliorating the effects of under-development through social and welfare spending, to far more ambitious aims of social transformation, the unevenness of the relationship becomes far more problematic. On the one hand, is a disjunction between what are perceived to be the ideal—liberal—conditions for growth and development and the historical realities of the forms of state and society that exist. On the other, is a disjunction between a 'one-size fits all' policy prescription of donors and the varying social, political and developmental trajectories among societies on the receiving end of aid. New Labour's Africa policy was beset by both of these problems.

Taking the first disjuncture at face value, the kind of change that Britain sought to achieve in Africa was massively ambitious. Richard Sandbrook argued (2005, 1120) that the Commission for Africa was calling for 'nothing less than a Great Transformation' in African societies. 'In reality', he concluded (2005, 1123), 'the triumph of economic and political liberalism in many countries represents, not mere reform, but revolutionary change'. The problem for British policy was that to a large extent Africa was conceived within it as a 'blank sheet' onto which, for the first time, Britain was inscribing a grand design, ignoring much previous history (Porteus 2008, 133; also see Gallagher 2013). Policy makers wished to draw a new picture of British Africa policy as if on a clean sheet of paper: 'Floating free of difficult historical implication, British officials fashion their relationship with Africa as if virtually from scratch' (Gallagher 2013, 118). This construction of policy involved a highly simplified view of the 'Other' (often idealised as an undifferentiated African poor) which could not admit to conflicts of interests, messy and complex relationships and the need to address distributional conflicts (Gallagher 2013, 22).[9]

What was lacking, some noted (Lockwood 2005), were the tools with which to bridge this gap between aims and reality. Just as in asymmetrical relationships of the colonial period (Cooper 2014), so too in aid relationships, politics at the 'non-European end' matter a great deal. And while in the colonial period, Britain could seek to influence internal politics by intervening directly in collaboration (Robinson 1972), post-independence, the international posed a much greater obstacle. If what was driving policy was the aim of 'social transformation at a distance' (Williams and Young 2009) then it was a distance not just of geography but of political independence, and histories of combined development too (see Brown 2006; 2013). The limited tools of British leverage (Porteus 2008) and the limitations imposed by Blair's ideational construction of Africa (Gallagher 2013) both served to temper the reality of policy.

As with other liberal interventions (Anievas 2014b), the second disjuncture between uniform policy prescriptions and the diversity of political realities on the ground, merely exacerbated the problem. Donor policy from the mid-1990s had increasingly centred on a kind of 'one-size fits all' programme for governance reform through which to lay the necessary basis for development to take off (Kelsall *et al.* 2013). As Thomas Carothers and Diane De Gramont noted (2013, 27), 'The aid landscape was soon populated by projects attempting full-scale transfer of Western models, navigated by visiting Western experts with little knowledge of local contexts'. Britain's new Africa policy suffered similarly. Even the lengthy Commission for Africa report, while acknowledging unevenness and the need to pay constant regard to Africa's diversity—'every country has a mix of social and economic realities that differ from other countries' it noted (Commission for Africa 2005, 126)—it nevertheless addressed issues of governance through broad generalisations. Nowhere did it show the detailed, nuanced understanding necessary if external leverage was to have any political purchase (Porteus 2008, 76–77; Kelsall *et al.* 2013).

As Tom Porteus argues (2008, 134), fifty years earlier Britain had abandoned an empire that it knew relatively well after concluding it lacked the resources to maintain much less transform it; now it was embarking on an ambitious and costly programme of transformation with far less knowledge and expertise. Furthermore, policy was run by the Department for International Development (DfID) specialising in development policy rather than diplomacy and, one might add, one which had grown in size and importance somewhat at the expense of the Foreign Office and its country knowledge and diplomatic tools. While DfID shared other donors' view as to what the problems were in Africa, it relied on finding examples that worked and 'scaling them up', ignoring the diversity of conditions on the ground and difficult questions about whether generalised developmental approaches were appropriate to different African contexts (Porteus 2008, 132–33).

The Conservative-led governments in power from 2010 might have been expected to enact a revision of British policy towards Africa, particularly in a context of austerity. The response, however, was mixed. On the one hand, the coalition government of 2010–15 sustained Britain's financial commitment to overseas development, reaching the symbolic ODA commitment of 0.7% of GDP in 2013. Prime Minister Cameron also continued the liberal commitment to good governance as the basis for development. In several speeches going back to 2005, Cameron committed to a 'golden thread that links property rights, free markets, free trade, the rule of law, honest government, sound finances, economic progress and social advance' (Cameron 2005).[10] However, while this formulation re-states the disjuncture of previous Labour policy between desirable conditions and a diverse reality, and did little to identify any means by which it could be resolved, it was accompanied by more pragmatic shifts in policy.

Both in the Conservative-led coalition and the majority Tory government that followed in 2015, three shifts in particular were important. The first, in partial recognition of the difficulties of persuading countries to liberalise, was a concentration of bilateral aid on countries seen to be providing some of the necessary 'golden' conditions for development (DfID 2011). A second shift, driven by poor economic conditions in Britain and burgeoning commercial relations between Africa and China, was to alter the balance between 'doing good abroad' and British self-interest. Whereas Labour had denied any real tension between these two, the Conservative-led governments made a more overt priority of British trade development and investment interests. Finally, there was a continuation of longer-standing trends (Woods 2005) in using overseas development aid in security-related ways. The emphasis on the need for stable government in Africa served both development and security agendas and meant that development funding and security-driven projects around failed states overlapped with each other.

In recognition of the difficulties of seeking to promote 'social transformation at a distance' development policy analysis also took a more pragmatic turn. Donor policy had sought to promote 'ideal' (liberal) conditions for development through political and economic reform. The patent difficulties of achieving this in the context of diverse African politics which had their own dynamic and purpose, prompted some to argue that donors needed greater understanding of the complexities involved (Barder 2012b). Others argued that 'good enough' and 'second best' conditions for development— which might include clientelist corrupt practices and even human rights abuses—might have to be tolerated (Kelsall *et al.* 2013). Whether this signalled a wider repetition of the colonial era retreat from liberal aims in favour of support for more authoritarian forms of rule remains to be seen.

CONCLUSION

The ironies of history weigh heavily on British Africa policy. The resurgence of 'missionary zeal' (Parmar 2005) in British dealings with Africa was one thing; the fact that it was conducted with such apparent neglect of its historical antecedents was quite another. As this chapter has shown, contemporary British policy towards Africa is hedged on all sides by its past efforts to manage its long-standing, deep and highly uneven relationship with Africa. The policy trajectory that we see is therefore not simply a contemporary reprise of an earlier liberal imperialism. While Britain's long-term preferences remained broadly consistent—for liberal transformation of Africa and integration into the world economy—the policy changes in pursuit of that aim have been more dynamic. The alternations in policy—from informal relations to colonisation; a transformative civilising mission to securing authority; developing the 'great estate' to curtailing the extent and pace of reform—all reveal an imperial power forced to tack in the face of the complex patterns of developmental unevenness it had helped to bring about.

This chapter has used the theory of uneven and combined development to reveal this dynamic and dialectical evolution. It has shown how British policy choices continually have had to confront the complexities of previous phases of combined development which themselves have been heterogeneous. Greater historical awareness of these processes might enable greater clarity in the evaluation of contemporary policy choices. The disjuncture between aims and realities, and the diversity of different political and economic circumstances within Africa, were themselves products of processes of uneven and combined development established through the interaction of British liberal imperialism and African politics a century before.

The analysis presented here has also explored in a tentative way the potential synergies between the general framework for understanding international relations provided by uneven and combined development and the more focussed substantive analysis of colonialism and theorising about imperialism of Ronald Robinson. In both, the intent has been to begin to shift the emphasis of explanation away from a narrative driven entirely from European interest and calculation and to create space within which to see the importance of those 'on the weaker end of the connection'. For, as Cooper (2014) notes, the 'African problems' Britain and other Western actors now seek to address are not simply African, they are the co-productions of a deeply intertwined history.

NOTES

1. Some key sources in this expanding literature are: Rosenberg 1996, 2005, 2006, 2007, 2013a, 2013b.

2. This is a commonplace but often overlooked and 'surprisingly consequential' fact, Rosenberg notes. It is one that is recognised—empirically if not theoretically— by writers such as Eric Wolf who wrote, 'Human populations construct their cultures in interaction with one another, and not in isolation' (Wolf 1982, xv).

3. For example, see Anievas' (2014b) examination of Wilsonian diplomacy.

4. I do not explore aspects of what has been termed the Robinson-Gallagher debate in this chapter (for example see Louis 1976; Porter and Holland 1988). There is also a short but interesting evaluation of Robinson's work in Brewer's *Marxist Theories of Imperialism* (1990) where he states 'I see little or nothing in [his work] that is incompatible with Marxism (if that matters)' (1990, 258).

5. These influences, with an emphasis on how states could actively 'do good', were also absorbed by the early Labour Party. As we will see, New Labour's return to Africa in this guise was a resurrection of these older ideas (Gallagher 2013, 39).

6. As Robinson noted, 'All the national movements that won independence were more or less functions of neotraditional politics organised in the form of modern political parties', they worked well as an opposition to colonial rule, much less well as developmental agent for the country as a whole (Robinson 1972, 138).

7. The creation of DfID in 1997 saw the first UK white paper on development in 22 years, followed by the International Development Act of 2002 and further White Papers in 2000 and 2006 (Ireton 2013, 49–52).

8. Trade concessions were a continual sticking point and in the event only Britain stuck to its aid pledges.

9. There were things that went with this, including a denial of any fundamental conflict between British self-interest and African welfare. Some key politicians, including International Development Secretary, Claire Short, denied the relevance of empire to the contemporary period (Gallagher 2013, 82).

10. In 2012 Cameron repeated the point: 'You only get real long-term development through aid if there is also a golden thread of stable government, lack of corruption, human rights, the rule of law, transparent information' (Cameron 2012; also see Barder 2012a).

Chapter 10

The Impact of the 'Global Transformation' on Uneven and Combined Development

Barry Buzan and George Lawson

This chapter focuses on the ways in which the nineteenth-century 'global transformation' impacted on uneven and combined development (UCD).[1] The first section sets out our general understanding of UCD. The second section argues that the intensification of UCD by the global transformation led to a highly centred, core-periphery global order during the nineteenth century and much of the twentieth century. This was expressed first as a *Western-colonial* international society lasting up to 1945, and subsequently by a *Western-global* international society. The third section sketches briefly how since 1945, and more obviously since the early part of the twenty-first century, world politics is increasingly characterised by a decentred international order, still intensely combined, but also demonstrating a marked diffusion in the distribution of power, status and wealth. The result is a less uneven, but more intensely combined world order.

In general terms, this chapter supports two of the main contributions made by this book. First, as with the volume as a whole, our account rejects an emphasis on, let alone any autonomy of, either 'inside-out' or 'outside-in' explanations. All the sites where modernity took root were particular combinations of local and global dynamics—as discussed below, British industrialisation was fuelled by the de-industrialisation of India, while imperialism 'over there' fed into state-formation 'at home'. The relational sensibility that underpins this chapter—and this book—sees social sites such as 'foreign' and the 'domestic', 'East' and 'West', and 'metropole' and 'colony' as neither analytically separable, nor empirically discrete (also see Go and Lawson 2016).

Second, like many other contributors to this volume, we enlist uneven and combined development in order to generate a non-Eurocentric account of macro-historical change. We examine the intersocietal interactions, especially trade, technology transfers, imperial extraction and exchanges of ideas, which generated the global transformation. And we stress the 'entangled histories' and 'multiple vectors' that combined to vault Western states into a position of pre-eminence during the nineteenth century (De Vries 2013, 46). Such an account stands in contrast to Eurocentric approaches, which see the emergence of modernity as conditioned by forces both internal and unique to Europe (Jones 1981; Landes 1998; North *et al.* 2009). In our view, modernity was not self-generated through the unfolding of particularly European economic practices (such as double entry bookkeeping), institutions (such as representative governance) or symbolic schemas (such as the Enlightenment). Rather, modernity was forged through the co-constitution of the local and transnational, and its core vectors were intersocietal, from capitalist expansion to imperialism. From the sixteenth to the nineteenth centuries, a relatively thin international system sustained forms of interaction that were crucial to the development of global modernity (Anievas and Nişancioğlu 2015). From the nineteenth century onwards, global interactions became more unbalanced as a major mode of power gap opened up between the European (and later American and Japanese) 'leading-edge' and most other polities.[2] These dynamics allowed a small number of mostly Western states to project their power around the world. But this power projection did not produce a world of homogeneous social orders. Rather, as we explore below, it led to diverse amalgams of old and new, and indigenous and foreign (Anievas and Nişancioğlu 2015, 48-53). Core and periphery were intensely locked together even as their entwining fuelled a stark unevenness in terms of power differentials and in terms of how social orders were constituted. Modernity was a global process both in origins and outcomes.

In one important way, however, we depart from most other contributions to this book: our use of UCD is analytical-heuristic rather than causal-explanatory. Using UCD as a framing device allows us to construct a relatively straightforward account of macro-historical periodisation: during the early phases of the global transformation, development became both much more uneven and much more combined; in recent years, there has been a (partial) reduction of the former and a (powerful) intensification of the latter. We are not concerned with deploying specific causal dynamics associated with UCD theory. Rather, we see global modernity as generated by the *interplay* between three macro-dynamics: industrialisation (and associated processes of de-industrialisation), rational statehood (and imperialism) and ideologies of progress (liberalism, socialism, nationalism and 'scientific' racism). It is the configuration generated by the intersection of these three macro-dynamics that produced the global transformation, not any specific causal wager associated with UCD. For our purposes, UCD is most usefully seen as an analytical shorthand rather than as a theoretical schema containing a set of auxiliary causal claims.

UNEVEN AND COMBINED DEVELOPMENT

Like Justin Rosenberg (2010; 2013a), we understand 'unevenness' to be a basic fact of historical development, even if degrees of unevenness vary considerably across international orders. There are three drivers that lie behind the universality of uneven development: first, the diversity of geographical endowments; second, the physical separation of political units; and third, the differential impact of 'combination', whether this takes the form of the spread of ideas, the transfer of technologies, trading networks, security alliances, or practices of subjugation and emulation. 'Combination', by which we mean the ways in which social orders trade, coerce, emulate, borrow and steal from each other, is also intrinsic to any international order and, like unevenness, can vary greatly in degree. Before the nineteenth century, degrees of combination varied mainly with geography, which facilitated deep connections in some environments (most notably where there were available sea and river routes), but obstructed it in others (particularly in the case of land barriers). Available technologies, most notably the quality of ships and knowledge of navigation, and up to a point the construction of roads, also made a major difference to degrees of combination. By contrast, degrees of combination since the nineteenth century have been heavily determined by industrial technologies. Under the impact of steamships, railways, highways, aircraft, spacecraft and electronic means of communication from the telegraph to the internet, the importance of geography falls away, and combination intensifies rapidly, and probably permanently. Combination therefore increases directly with the third element of UCD: 'development'. Combination is both a homogenising force, as seen in pressures to conform with, or measure up to, standards of 'modernisation', 'Westernisation' or 'civilisation', but also one that promotes differentiation, as in the multiple responses around the world to these pressures.

In this perspective, UCD stands as an alternative to Kenneth Waltz's (1979, 76) formulation of homogenisation into like units through 'socialization and competition'. Both Waltz and Rosenberg see socialisation and competition as consequences of combination. But they disagree about their effects, with Waltz favouring homogenisation into 'like units', and Rosenberg stressing that the particular timing and circumstances of socialisation and competition produce variable outcomes. The extreme conditions created by macro-historical transformations such as the one that took place during the long nineteenth century expose the logic of the latter with great clarity. Major transformations of this kind have a distinct point or points of origin in which a particular configuration emerges and is sustained. This configuration is produced and reproduced through intersocietal interactions. Ian Morris (2010, chapter 2), for example, charts how in an earlier macro-transformation, settled agrarian communities spread from the hilly flanks of Mesopotamia northwest into Europe, and from other originating cores, as in China, to wider zones. Further changes spread outwards from this leading-edge (or edges). The pace of spread varied according to the mediating effects of social and physical environments. Agriculture was slow to spread to less productive soils and climates, and some modes of social order were more receptive to it than others. If unevenness was—and is—a basic fact of historical development, different peoples and places encounter macro-transformative pressures at different times and under different circumstances (Rosenberg 2010; 2013a).

The spread of a new 'mode of power' thus produces diverse outcomes.[3] Each social order that encounters the new configuration has its own way of adapting to it. The 'whip of external necessity' (Trotsky 1997, 27) produced by a new mode of power is often coercive, occurring through force of arms. But intersocietal dynamics also take the form of imitation. Some social orders do not take on the new configuration at all, either because of internal resistance to the changes it requires, or because of attempts by leading-edge polities to maintain inequalities between them by denying access to elements of the transformation. Others succeed in developing indigenous versions of the new configuration. 'Late' developers are not carbon copies of the original adopters, but develop their own distinctive characteristics. In this sense, the interactions between different social orders produce not convergence, but (often unstable) amalgams of new and old. For example, during the nineteenth century, German industrialisation was not a replica of British development, but took distinct form, even as it borrowed from the British experience. Likewise, Soviet and, more recently, Chinese development also maintained their own 'characteristics', combining new technologies and productive forces alongside inherited social formations. Through the analytic of UCD, it becomes clear that development is multilinear rather than linear, proceeds in fits and starts rather than through smooth gradations and contains many variations in terms of outcomes. One indicator of the ways in which polities adapted in diverse ways to the nineteenth-century global transformation is the variety of ideologies that have emerged to define different assemblages of economy, politics and culture in the modern world: liberalism, social democracy, conservatism, socialism, communism, fascism, patrimonialism and more. These 'contradictory fusions' aver that historical development is jumbled, and often compressed (Rosenberg 2010).

Because global transformations are generated through multiple revolutions from new political formations to the advent of new technologies, they amplify the link between development and combination. Such transformations typically generate increases in productivity and population, plus increases in the complexity of social orders and physical technologies, consequently producing a denser, more deeply connected international order. The expanded scale, complexity and technological capacities of agrarian polities meant that they had more intense relationships with both their neighbours and peoples further away than their hunter-gatherer predecessors. Those relationships were military, political, economic and cultural, or some mixture of these. In this way, the scale and intensity of combination within the international sphere increased, meaning that every society became less self-contained and more exposed to developments elsewhere. As social orders became larger in scale and more complex in terms of their internal organisation, differences between them were accentuated and interactions between them intensified. Late developers cannot escape the influence of earlier adopters, but neither do they reproduce them. The mutual constitution of unevenness and combination is thus intensified by development, producing larger, more complex and more diverse social orders bound together in denser, more interdependent ways.

CENTRED GLOBALISM

During the nineteenth century, a 'global transformation' intensified the meaning of development, and therefore the logic of UCD, to an unprecedented degree, resulting in the formation of a highly centred core-periphery international order. As discussed above, we see the global transformation as constituted by a concatenation of three interlinked processes: industrialisation, the rational state and ideologies of progress. Once this concatenation had formed, it constituted a new mode of power with massive transformative potential. Some of the roots of this mode of power went back centuries. But it was only in the nineteenth century that the whole package coalesced in a small group of polities from where both its effect (a revolutionary configuration in the mode of power) and its challenge (how other societies responded to this configuration) became the principal dynamic through which international relations was conceived and practiced. In this context, development not only took on a new form and meaning, but also became highly dynamic, driven by seemingly endless cycles of technological innovation.

Because the global transformation initially took root only within a relatively small number of polities,[4] and because its new, complex and highly dynamic mode of power was extremely difficult to copy, global unevenness was intensified to an unprecedented extent. During the nineteenth century, the development gap between societies opened more widely than ever before. Global modernity encountered peoples living in a variety of political, economic and cultural formations, from hunter-gatherer bands to city-states and empires. In size, these social orders varied from groups of a few dozen to empires consisting of tens of millions of people. This variety meant that the power gap between core and periphery, and the challenge posed by the global transformation to those in the periphery, prompted quite different experiences of modernity. A relatively even distribution of global power among several, mostly lightly connected, agrarian empires was replaced by a radically uneven global distribution of power in favour of a handful of mostly Western polities. Some peoples and polities were able to resist or adapt to the global transformation's multiple assault; others were consumed by it. At one end of the spectrum were the many indigenous peoples in settler colonies who were all but obliterated; at the other were those like the Japanese who adapted the modern mode of power to indigenous social formations.

The Japanese case is particularly interesting because for a century it was the only major example of a non-Western people acquiring the revolutions of modernity quickly, and using them to overcome the power gap established by the global transformation. With the Anglo-Japanese alliance of 1902, Japan formally joined the ranks of the great powers, and its development went on to outpace many European laggards. In effect, Japan was the first mover in what we now think of as the 'rise of the rest' that began in earnest during the 1970s. Why Japan was able to do this so early is as difficult a question as why modernity first took root in northwest Europe. Jamie C. Allinson and Alexander Anievas (2010a, 479–85) offer useful explanations in terms of a conjuncture of: an unusual Japanese class structure (especially the fluid position of the samurai); fortuitous timing (having a first encounter with the West in the 1850s rather than the 1880s); being less attractive than China and India in terms of extractable resources; and being able to turn the multiple challenges of global modernity into the stimulation of a developmental state rather than a retreat into feudalism. Japan also had some other notable advantages. Unlike China, it was able to provide a cultural bridge between 'modern' and 'archaic' by retaining its emperor and its Shinto religion. When the Qing dynasty collapsed in 1911, China's political continuity was broken and the country fragmented into decades of warlordism and civil war. And again unlike China, Japan was able to appropriate nationalism as a unifying idea to help it through the turbulence of modernisation. Because the Qing were Manchu, they could not use nationalism without threatening their ruling position in relation to the Han majority. Japan, of course, also had the advantage of warning time. A decade before it was forced to respond to Commodore Perry's black ships, it could observe closely what was happening to China during the Opium Wars.

The extremely rapid emergence of a modernising core, including both Western powers and Japan, during the nineteenth century meant that never before had unevenness been felt on this scale, with this intensity, or in a context of such close, inescapable interdependence. Those convinced of their cultural superiority and with access to advanced weapons, industrial production, medicine and new forms of bureaucratic organisation gained a pronounced advantage over those with limited access to these sources of power. After around 1800, these dynamics fostered a substantial power gap between a small number of Western polities and other societies around the world (Buzan and Lawson 2015, chapter 1). In principle, this power gap could be closed: those with access to the configuration that sustained the global transformation could move from periphery to core. In practice, this move was made exceptionally difficult not only by the depth of the transformative package, but also by practices of imperialism and other forms of interventionism that reinforced the advantages of the established core. Japan was the exception that proved the rule. The result was a shift from a 'polycentric world with no dominant centre' to a core-periphery international order in which the leading edge was located in the West (Pomeranz 2000, 4). This hierarchical international order lasted from the early nineteenth century until the early years of the twenty-first century.

The first phase of this centred global order took the form of a *Western-colonial international society*, and this form remained dominant until 1945. Western-colonial international society was global in scale, but extremely unequal. Its core comprised most European states, their now independent former settler colonies in North America, and from the late nineteenth century Japan. Its periphery was a mixture of colonies, largely absorbed into the sovereignty of their metropoles (most of Africa, South Asia and Southeast Asia), the decolonised polities of Latin America, and a handful of classical agrarian powers still strong enough to avoid colonisation, but weak enough to be treated as unequal (China, Iran, Egypt, the Ottoman Empire). Although there was a trickle of erosions of inequality between core and periphery before 1945, Western-colonial international society broadly endured until the end of the Second World War.

Western-colonial international society was the starkest possible expression of the uneven and combined character of global modernity. Because imperialism was the outward expression of the new mode of power, it exemplified the unevenness between the haves and have-nots of the global transformation. At the same time, imperialism was one of the principal means through which polities and peoples were combined on a global scale. During the long nineteenth century, European powers sought to exert control, both directly and indirectly, over most of the globe. If the bulk of European imperialism took place during the 'Scramble for Africa', which saw European powers assume direct control of large parts of Africa, the extension of imperialism went well beyond the 'Scramble'. Between 1810 and 1870, the United States carried out 71 territorial annexations and military interventions (Go 2011, 39). The United States first became a continental empire, seizing territory from Native Americans, the Spanish and Mexicans. It then built an overseas empire, extending its authority over Cuba, Nicaragua, the Dominican Republic, Haiti,

Hawaii, Puerto Rico, Guam, the Philippines, Samoa and the Virgin Islands. Other settler states also became colonial powers in their own right, including Australia and New Zealand in the Pacific. Japan, the only non-Western state to fully incorporate the revolutions of modernity during the nineteenth century, constructed an empire in East Asia. Russian expansionism accelerated during this period, both southwards to Uzbekistan, Kazakhstan and Turkmenistan, and eastwards to Sakhalin and Vladivostok. Imperialism, therefore, was a central vector within the uneven and combined character of global modernity and an equally central tool of the core-periphery international order that arose from it. Politically, militarily, economically and demographically, a relatively small group of mostly Western polities created a colonial international order that privileged their treasuries, their strategic interests and their people. They subordinated the rest of the world while, at the same time, coercively extending to planetary scale the configuration that underpinned global modernity.

A central feature of Western-colonial order was the uneven extension of industrialisation, production and finance, which generated a core-periphery order in which the ebbs and flows of metropolitan markets, commodity speculations and price fluctuations controlled the survival chances of millions of people around the world. The global transformation produced a single, highly combined, world economy for the first time. This global economy was enabled by improved technologies of transportation and communication, technologies that also made war and politics global, producing an integrated, yet hierarchical, global order. Accelerating market integration amplified both unevenness and combination (Bayly 2004, 2). On the one hand, commodities increasingly flowed from the periphery into the core: by 1900, Britain was importing 60% of its total calories and the average distance travelled by the fruit, vegetables and animals it imported was 1,800 miles (Schwartz 2000, 105). At the outbreak of the First World War, Britain imported 87% of its food and a similar proportion of its raw materials (Ruggie 1982, 401fn69). On the other hand, capital and manufactured goods flowed from the core into the periphery. These two-directional flows, however unequally constituted, could increase both trade and growth. West African trade, for example, centred on palm oil, groundnuts, timber and cocoa, increased by a factor of 4 between 1897 and 1913 (Frieden 2006, 74). In Latin America, economies grew at four times the rate of Asian polities and at six times the rate of Central and Eastern European states between 1870 and 1913 (Frieden 2006, 73). In some sectors, peripheral states led the world: by 1900, Brazil produced 80% of the world's coffee exports; by 1913, Chile provided half of the world's copper and Malaya produced half of the world's tin (Frieden 2006, 73–5).

During the initial phase of the global transformation, therefore, the development gap between polities opened more widely than ever before and, at the same time (and for the same reasons), the planet was bound together more tightly than in previous eras. This dynamic vaulted a few Western states into a period of unprecedented, if temporary, dominance over other parts of the world (Hobsbawm 1962, 15, 44). On the basis of the new mode of power, the West became hegemonic over many aspects of international relations, projecting new forms of organisation and new ideas that destabilised existing social orders, both at home and abroad. During the nineteenth century, the West broke open and overwhelmed the remaining bastions of the classical world (the Ottoman Empire, China and Japan), and overcame the environmental barriers both of disease (that had restricted Europeans to coastal enclaves in Africa) and distance (through the advent of railways, steamships and the telegraph). As Eric Hobsbawm (1962, 365) notes, 'nothing, it seemed, could stand in the way of a few western gunboats or regiments bringing with them trade and bibles'. This configuration enabled new organisational forms to emerge such as the nation state, the modern firm, intergovernmental organisations (IGOs) and, more broadly, proto-global civil society in the guise of transnational social movements ranging from anti-slavery campaigners to advocates of free trade. For better or worse, and often both together, the long nineteenth century saw the transformation of the daily condition of people nearly everywhere on the planet. The nineteenth century was, therefore, the beginning of what we might call 'the Western era', setting loose revolutions in terms of both material capabilities and symbolic schemas.

Rosenberg (2013a) argues that the Great War of 1914-18 was the culmination of the uneven and combined development of global modernity, and the industrialisation of violence that had been unfolding for more than eight decades. There is some truth in this claim. But the highly unequal Western-colonial order nonetheless endured throughout the interwar period, after which it gave way to *Western-global international society*. By adopting the term *Western-global*, we take a position on how to understand contemporary international society and how to deal with the legacy of its colonial origins. The idea that there is a global international society rests on the view that it emerged from the expansion of Western international society to planetary scale, with decolonisation producing states that were homogenous, if only in the sense of being sovereign equals. The price of independence, or for those not colonised the price of being accepted as equals by the West, was the adoption of Western political forms and the acceptance of the primary institutions of Western international society: the market, the legalised hegemony of great power management, positive international law and suchlike. 'Modernisation theory' held out the prospect of the 'Third World' becoming more like the 'First World' (Rostow 1960), while polities around the world were categorised as 'developed' and 'developing', or 'advanced' and 'emerging'. In each of these classifications, the Western mode of economic, political and cultural organisation was taken to be both natural and pre-eminent. In significant respects, therefore, the post-1945 era saw the maintenance of a hegemonic, core-periphery structure in which a Western core was surrounded by regional international societies that existed in varying degrees of differentiation from, and subordination to, that core.

This second phase of centred globalism was defined by the delegitimation of racism and colonialism, the abandonment of divided sovereignty in favour of sovereign equality, and the dismantling of empires. Yet many features of Western-colonial order remained, from the discourse and politics of development, aid, intervention and migration, to structural inequalities in the world economy. During this period, the mode of power that underpinned the global transformation remained predominantly sited in a small number of mostly Western states plus Japan, and later South Korea, Taiwan and Singapore, thus perpetuating a core-periphery order, albeit with a reduced degree of formal imperialism. The end of the Cold War even strengthened the position of the Western core by valorising economic strands of liberalism (reconstituted as 'neo-liberalism') as the prototypical feature of modernity (Lawson 2010).

Such dynamics, along with rapid technological changes, helped to foster increasing levels of combination. Yet while the shift from Western-colonial to Western-global international society still reflected a centred global order, this period also saw the beginning of a decline in levels of unevenness. The shift from divided sovereignty to formal sovereign equality reduced differences in political and legal (and racial) status, and this shift was reinforced by a proliferation of IGOs. In some ways, these IGOs perpetuated the core-periphery inequality of status by legitimising what Gerry Simpson (2004) calls the 'legalised hegemony' of the great powers. But, in general, they supported sovereign equality, and the great power principle saw a non-Western state (China) take up a permanent seat on the United Nations Security Council. Several other states, most notably the Asian Tigers, developed rapidly. So too, from the 1980s onwards, did China, thereby greatly expanding the core of the modern global economy. The military gap narrowed in a number of ways, particularly with the widespread diffusion of light infantry weapons (making territorial occupations extremely expensive), and the much narrower diffusion of nuclear weapons to some developing countries (Buzan and Lawson 2015, chapter 8).

These first two phases of the global transformation brought to an end the long period in which human history was mainly local and contact between distant polities mostly fairly light. From the nineteenth century on, human history became increasingly global, contact among far-flung peoples intense and development both more uneven and more combined. Driving these changes was the global transformation from predominantly agrarian to primarily industrial societies, and from absolutist orders to rational states, along with the emergence of novel symbolic schemas sustained by ideologies of progress.

DECENTRED GLOBALISM

The revolutions of modernity are still spreading and intensifying—'globalisation' refers to their outward expansion (Giddens 1990, 45–54). As modernity continues to spread and intensify, Western dominance is being increasingly challenged. In the early twenty-first century, we are living in the beginning of the end of this highly unequal phase of the revolutions of modernity: *centred* globalism is giving way to *decentred* globalism. Decentred refers to the ways in which the configuration that marks the global transformation is no longer concentrated in a small group of polities, but is increasingly dispersed. Globalism marks both a basic continuity and an intensification of earlier phases of the global transformation in which the configuration of modernity assumed planetary scale. In the contemporary world, power and development are increasingly less unevenly concentrated and more combined than in previous periods of global modernity. Those polities that were once on the receiving end of the global transformation are employing its mode of power to reassert their position in international society.

Slowly and unevenly, but at an accelerating pace, the massive inequality across the planet that was established during the nineteenth century is being eroded. The mechanism behind this closing of the power gap is the same one that created it in the first place: the revolutions of modernity. Politically, legally and demographically, the gap has narrowed significantly; economically and militarily it has narrowed less, but still appreciably (Buzan and Lawson 2015, chapter 7). This is both changing the composition of the core (making it larger, more diverse and less white/Western) and changing its relationship to the periphery (as the core and semi-periphery get bigger, and the periphery smaller). The revolutions of modernity began by producing an unprecedented degree of inequality in a context of highly uneven and combined development. Development remains highly combined and that is likely to increase rather than decrease. It is still uneven, but in many key respects that unevenness is diminishing. Some parts of the former periphery have either caught up with and joined the old core, or are on their way to doing so. However, as noted above, combination is both a homogenising and differentiating force. So, while the diffusion of modernity reduces unevenness in some respects (most obviously power, status and wealth), it sustains it in others. For example, while there has been a narrowing of ideological bandwidth compared to the twentieth century—virtually all states around the world are now organised around capitalist logics—this homogenisation comes with what looks like a quite stable diversity of political forms, from 'liberal democratic' (e.g. United States, United Kingdom), through 'social democratic' (e.g. Germany, Japan) and 'competitive authoritarian' (e.g. Russia, Malaysia) to 'state bureaucratic' (e.g. China, Saudi Arabia) (Buzan and Lawson 2014a).

The diffusion of modernity is only homogenising up to a point. Thereafter, it is diversified by distinct cultural and political formations. The economic crisis that began in 2008 may well come to be seen as the tipping point at which the extreme unevenness and centredness of the period of Western domination began decisively to give way to a less uneven, more decentred global order (Buzan and Lawson 2014b). The distribution of power, status and wealth in the contemporary world is becoming less uneven and more diffuse *among* states (though not necessarily or even probably *within* them). In general, this means that the West will lose its privileged position in international society. This is already visible in the emergence of new sites of global governance (e.g. the G20), economic formations (e.g. the BRICs) and security institutions (e.g. the Shanghai Cooperation Organisation). The diffusion of power is being accompanied by a diffusion of legitimacy, making it difficult for the United States to hold onto its sole superpower status.

The age of superpowers was a particular consequence of the highly uneven distribution of power created by the Western-colonial phase of global modernity and sustained by its Western-global phase. During these two periods, polities like Britain and the United States amassed sufficient relative power to be world dominating. That level of capability is no longer possible. With many states becoming wealthy and powerful, no single polity will be able to accumulate sufficient relative power to dominate international society. Decentred globalism will remain highly combined but will also be increasingly less uneven in terms of power, status and wealth. It is both the successor to the Western-dominated era of the nineteenth and twentieth centuries and, in a way, marks the restoration of the classical order in which the distribution of power was fairly even. The difference between the contemporary era and that before the nineteenth century is that, whereas much of the world before the nineteenth century was only lightly combined, the contemporary era is one of intense—and intensifying—combination.

CONCLUSION

To sum up, our argument is that the global transformation strengthened the impact of UCD in two ways. First, the global transformation opened up a very large and difficult to close gap between those in possession of the modern mode of power and those without access to it. Second, the global transformation hugely increased degrees of combination. The new mode of power largely swept away the geographical-environmental determinants of unevenness and combination, and replaced them with a redefined version of development. By producing massive increases in both unevenness and combination, the global transformation generated an international order characterised by centred globalism. In the early years of the twenty-first century, a more decentred global order is emerging in which unevenness is diminishing but levels of combination are intensifying. This is not to say that unevenness will disappear—it was both produced by the global transformation and also productive of it in that a much smaller 'core' appropriated the vast resources of the 'periphery'. But in the contemporary world, the Western-led order enabled by the early unevenness and combination of global modernity is beginning to erode. In its place is emerging a more decentred and more globalised order, one that comes clearly into view when viewed through the analytic of uneven and combined development.

NOTES

1. In this chapter, 'global transformation' is used synonymously with 'global modernity'. For a full discussion of these terms, see Buzan and Lawson (2015, 1–10).

2. By 'leading-edge', we mean those polities in which the configuration of the modern 'mode of power' first assembled. We discuss the concept of the 'mode of power' below.

3. By 'mode of power', we mean the material and ideational relations that are generative of both actors and the ways in which power is exercised. As noted above, during the global transformation, three dynamics (industrialisation, rational statehood and 'ideologies of progress') combined to generate a new basis for how power was constituted, organised and expressed—we refer to this as a shift in the 'mode of power'. *Contra* most IR approaches, changes in the mode of power are more significant than changes in the distribution of power, affecting not just outcomes, but the basis for how interactions take place and are understood.

4. As already suggested, this is not to say that the sources of the global transformation were endogenous to these polities. To the contrary, global modernity was forged from intersocietal, often coercive, interactions between 'core' and 'periphery'. To take one illustration, Indian textiles were either banned from Britain or levied with high tariffs, while British manufacturing products were forcibly imported into India without duty. Between 1814 and 1828, British cloth exports to India rose from 800,000 yards to over 40 million yards, while during the same period, Indian cloth exports to Britain halved (Goody 1996, 131).

Chapter 11

The Ethiopian Revolution

A World-Historical Perspective

Fouad Makki

In the last quarter of the twentieth century, two distinct but interconnected revolutions profoundly transformed state and society in late imperial Ethiopia. A social revolution in 1974 overthrew the imperial dynasty and abolished the tributary order that had sustained an age-old agrarian aristocracy. The political charge released by this popular upheaval detonated the rigid connections between class and ethnic hierarchies that was a conspicuous feature of the imperial formation, unleashing a series of ethno-nationalist insurgences that culminated in a second political revolution in 1991 that replaced the unitary state with a Federal Republic. While each of these revolutions had its own specific temporality and social character, they were arguably intertwined with each other through a series of social and national conflicts that intervened between them. This gave the entire period a certain unified character so that it is possible to see the successive revolutions as two moments of an overarching revolutionary transition from an *ancien régime* empire to a modern republic. Once the enormous turmoil generated by these revolutions had subsided, the stabilised social order that issued from them differed greatly from the expectation of its makers. Radicals by conviction and hostile to the order of capital, the revolutionary actors that instituted the second republic found themselves the unwitting agents, and later committed architects, of a political and social order conducive to the spread of capitalist commodity relations.

What accounts for this disjuncture between subjective intentions and objective outcomes? And what does it tell us about the character of the revolutions and the epochal consciousness of the revolutionary actors? How might we make sense of the sharp turn in ideological and political commitments without invoking a metaphysics of modernity impervious to human agency, or a ruse of reason set in store by the cunning of history? Rather than invoking, by way of explanation, a zeitgeist of modernity or the workings of some specious iron laws of history, my intention in this chapter is to suggest an interpretive and explanatory socio-historical account by situating the Ethiopian revolutions in a world-historical context of material and cultural connections. This international premise departs sharply from the analytic frameworks that most previous studies have brought to bear on the subject. For the most part, these were beholden to a national unit of analysis and neo-Orientalist representations of Ethiopia as an insular and ancient kingdom, home to the legendary Queen of Sheba and the Prester John, a biblical land ensconced in a mountain fortress 'forgetful of the world, by which it was forgotten' (Gibbon 1776 [1907]). This orientation was reinforced by Ethiopia's sovereign status at the height of European colonialism in Africa, and subsequent nationalist scholarship internalised and exalted this presumed insularity as a sign of historical antiquity and civilisational integrity. Twentieth century Ethiopia was thus largely conceived as an entity whose connections with world history had no more than an incidental bearing on its otherwise wholly internal dynamic of continuity and change.

This national circumscription of the effective force field of social change is paralleled by recent analytic trends that tend to reduce the complex spatiotemporal configuration of revolutions to sharply delimited 'events'. In one sense, it is of course undeniable that 'Revolution is a term with a precise political meaning: the political overthrow from below of one state order, and its replacement by another. Nothing is to be gained by diluting it across time, or extending it over every department of social space' (Anderson 1984, 12). But this does not mean 'events' and 'structures' are mutually exclusive and juxtaposed to each other; they actually co-determine and presuppose each other. Complex social phenomena such as revolutions are concatenations of events generated by a 'conjuncture of structures' in which structure 'is both the medium and outcome' of social practice (Sewell 2005, 127, 121).

Analytically, these observations imply a critique of methodological nationalism and modes of social inquiry that take the national state, or a set of delimited events, as the natural boundaries of analysis. They suggest instead a relational conception of social change in which the international is an integral dimension of social reality that 'arises specifically from the co-existence within it of more than one society' (Rosenberg 2006, 308).[1] From this vantage point, the international is not a contingent facet of discreet national entities, but a constitutive and causally consequential dimension of them. A central dynamic of the international over the past few centuries has been the expansion of capitalism and the momentous political and subjective transformations it brought in its train. The unparalleled force of modern industry made capitalism a universal dissolvent of the pre-existing social world, subverting and disregarding inherited beliefs and boundaries and compelling societies the world over to respond and adapt to its imperatives at the risk of political extinction (Marx and Engels 2002).

This profoundly transformative historical system emerged between the sixteenth and twentieth centuries in the process of European colonial expansion overseas, a process that forcibly conjoined separate world regions into an unequally integrated world-system that made the advent of a world market possible. With the European partitioning of Africa at the end of the nineteenth century, the whole world was entangled in the material and ideological dynamics unleashed by this colonial form of capitalist modernity. The new world-system, with Europe situated at its centre, was structured by a multi-dimensional polarisation, and as the relations between its core and peripheries changed, so did the terms in which its constitutive hierarchies were conceived. Over the centuries, these relations were framed in terms of a series of antithetical oppositions: civilised/primitive, modern/traditional, advanced/backward, and First World/Third World. By the mid-twentieth century, with the disintegration of the European colonial empires, they were once again recast and the mastery over nature that was central to the Western scientific ethos became the new key to the legitimation of global inequalities. Drawing on Enlightenment ideals that better knowledge could help forge a better society, science and technology offered a seemingly more plausible basis for the continued assertion of Western hegemony. The notion of 'development' acquired global significance in this context, providing a powerful framework through which relative inequality and the promise of a future beyond it could be imagined. Unlike the ideology of the civilising mission, 'development' was also a project nationalist and anti-colonial leaders could embrace (Cooper and Packard 1997, 1–44).

Once global inequalities were reframed in this way, structural comparisons between different kinds of societies could be hierarchically ordered to produce a scale of progress in which the present of the West represented the future of the rest (Osborne 1991, 17; Ferguson 2005). This unilinear vision of modernisation was reinforced by the restless dynamics of the capitalist world market. Capitalist industrialisation involves a continual transformation of nature and an accelerating restructuring of the social world that gives rise to a sense of historical movement as unidirectional. And it is within this homogeneous conception of historical time, and the temporal ideologies of progress and modernisation it gives rise to, that the idea of development emerged as a widely accepted framework for bringing global hierarchy and interdependence into a stable relationship. Capitalist development has of course never been a purely national or linear process as the paradigm of modernisation implied. While societies across the world invariably came into contact with the dynamics of capitalism and its systemic pressures, they were not thereby transformed into mere mirror images of its industrial core. The expanded reproduction of capitalism inevitably encountered distinct social and cultural configurations that were differentially integrated into its evolving dynamics. The concrete historical forms these took across the uneven social terrain of the international varied greatly and built on the pre-existing social and cultural forms in non-linear and contradictory ways. This interactive and differentiated process of capitalist development effectively foreclosed the formation of a homogenised global modernity or purely autarkic forms of national development.

The political and social implications of this contradictory unity of world capitalist development were the subject of a politically charged controversy within Russian Marxism from the turn of the twentieth century. Situated on the eastern edge of an industrialising West, the Russian intelligentsia was preoccupied with the problematic of 'backwardness', and it was in an attempt to understand the resulting peculiarities of Tsarist Russia's belated industrialisation that Leon Trotsky first developed his theses on uneven and combined development. Proceeding from the observation that capitalism was a world-historical formation in which societal interdependence, rather than independence, was a key determinant of social change, Trotsky argued that under pressure from a militarily and economically more advanced West, societies situated on its expanding frontier would be compelled to respond by embarking on projects of catching-up. In so doing, they could take advantage of a 'privilege of historic backwardness' generated by historical unevenness, adapting the latest technical advances and thereby 'skip a whole series of intermediate stages' of development. This, however, did not mean they could simply reproduce the developmental trajectories of the industrial pioneers. The fact that industrialisation had occurred somewhere necessarily changed the conditions of its emergence elsewhere, so that a mere repetition of developmental forms was ruled out. While societies like Russia could make use of existing advances in science and technology, these were typically grafted onto non-capitalist social forms so that the overall pattern of their development necessarily took a combined form: 'From the universal law of unevenness thus derives another law which, for the lack of a better name, we may call the law of combined development—by which we mean a drawing together of the different stages of the journey, a combining of separate steps, an amalgam of archaic with more contemporary forms' (Trotsky 1960, 4–5). Instead of a linear succession of predetermined stages within discrete boundaries, capitalist development was a relational and differentiated process that precluded the serial reproduction of independent processes of industrialisation. This interactive dynamic implied, moreover, that no single composite or normative model of development would emerge, since many different social articulations were possible. This made capitalist development not only interactive but also multilinear (Makki 2015).

Uneven and combined dynamics are of course not confined to the economic and political spheres alone. They also operate at the level of culture and forms of historical consciousness.[2] Given that an organic evolution of societies was precluded by the intersocietal dynamics of social change, uneven and combined development generated contradictory tensions that made late developing societies acutely vulnerable to periodic social and political convulsions. These contradictions acquired explosive dimensions from modern forms of historical consciousness, including a profound sensibility of relative 'backwardness' that was generated by material and cultural unevenness in the context of capitalist expansion. Reinhart Koselleck has argued that this epochal form of historical consciousness was informed by:

> the nonsimultaneity of diverse but, in a chronological sense, simultaneous histories. With the opening up of the world, the most different but coexisting cultural levels were brought into view spatially and, by way of synchronic comparison, were diachronically classified. World history became for the first time empirically redeemable; however, it was only interpretable to the extent that the most differentiated levels of development, decelerations and accelerations of temporal courses in various countries, social strata, classes, or areas were at the same time necessarily reduced to a common denominator. (Koselleck 2002, 166)

The meta-narrative of world history this apprehension of modernity made possible had a profound impact on the imagination of people across the world, and world history since the onset of the French and Industrial revolutions came to be seen as the unfolding of a single inexorable process of rationalisation and secularisation. Social change was consequently understood as a contradictory process of adaptation to these forces of modernity. And it was in relation to the underlying empty, homogeneous conception of historical temporality, and the sense of historical movement as linear and progressive, that modern social actors became preoccupied with their place in 'an unequal world and the shape of their pasts and futures' (Donham 1992; 1999). Nation-states – the paradigmatic institutional forms of modernity – were henceforth viewed as situated ahead or behind each other along a single axis of historical time, and it was within the terms of this hierarchy of modernity that vernacular modernisms, 'attempts to reorder local society by the application of strategies that have produced wealth, power, or knowledge elsewhere in the world', can be properly located:

> Without uneven development, without increasing capitalist competition and commodification across world markets, without the unidirectional and universally present pressures created by technological advance, and perhaps most of all, without capitalist media, it would be impossible to understand why intellectual vanguards the world over have posed the problem of 'backwardness'. (Donham 1999, xviii)

The social stratum most haunted by this consciousness of relative 'backward-ness' was the bilingual intelligentsia of the peripheral societies. Intellectuals were central to both nationalism and revolution not least because uneven and combined development augmented their strategic political position relative to that of the other main social classes. The turn to radicalism was in part gener-ated by the impossibility of repeating the developmental pattern of the core countries within the terms of the classical modernisation paradigm. There was no way to simply evade the handicaps that Western industrialisation imposed on late developing societies. Social progress and catching-up would have to be a conscious revolutionary project against the wider structures of power that reproduced the condition of 'backwardness'. Revolution was thus conceived as a 'way to jump "ahead" by 'cutting history off at the pass' (Anderson 1991, 156–57; Donham 1999, 2). While not devoid of normative commitments to justice and equality, revolutions became essentially instru-ments for mobilising subaltern populations and constructing a more interven-tionist state capable of hastening the project of modernity.

The particular alliance of social forces that comprised these revolutionary movements, and the ideological orientation of its leading strata, varied greatly from one revolutionary context to another. But for all this heterogeneity and the hybrid ideological registers in which the politics of catching-up was articulated, a central impetus informing the consciousness of revolutionary actors was a deeply felt sensibility of 'comparative backwardness'.[3] In this respect, these revolutions can in part be understood as conscious efforts to meet the challenges posed by the uneven and combined dynamics of capitalist world development. To define the chain of revolutionary transformations in the global periphery in this way is to obviously emphasise only one of their dimensions, and is by no means intended to minimise their emancipatory impulse. Nor does such a characterisation exhaust the complex social integu-ments, discursive registers and cultural meanings of each revolution. To imply otherwise would be to impose a reductively static and abstract category on what are in fact dynamic processes of change, and greater appreciation of local circumstances and forms of consciousness is required in any specific historical analysis. But to neglect their imbrication with and conditioning by the uneven and combined dialectics of capitalist modernity, and the contra-dictory developmental and political syndromes it typically generates, is to commit no less a violence of abstraction.

This political dialectic of the revolution against backwardness was refracted in distinctive ways in different countries, and my intention in this chapter is to examine the momentous revolutions in Ethiopia within its sug-gestive analytic framework. The revolutions in Ethiopia afford a fascinatingly intricate illustration of a more general process not least because the *ancien régime* remained sovereign in the age of high colonialism in Africa.

As a result, the Ethiopian social formation did not experience the sorts of transformations commonly associated with colonial capitalism elsewhere. But for all the idiosyncratic survival of its articulated political and cultural institutions, it could not escape the geopolitical and economic pressures of the international order, and particular social groups within it have at different times felt the imperative to respond to these challenges. As the following sections illustrate, the key turning points in the political and historical trajectory of twentieth century Ethiopia were decisively shaped by these uneven and combined dynamics of the international.

IMPERIAL ETHIOPIA AND THE TRIBUTARY ORDER

The backdrop for the distinctive trajectory of the Ethiopian state lay in the anterior evolution of the Abyssinian social formation. From at least the twelfth century, we know that social stratification in the agrarian polity was articulated around rights derived from persons on the land. Peasants were in principle free with secure access to land known as *rist* that was reckoned on a kinship basis. Superimposed on this communal form of tenure were *gult* (tributary) rights asserted by a class of lords, the *bala-gult* (those with rights to tribute), in the form of a portion of the peasant produce and various kinds of labour services. This social property complex had important consequences for the developmental dynamics of the Abyssinian polity (Donham 1986; Tadesse 1972). Since the class of agrarian lords did not necessarily own the land tilled by the peasants, they exercised no control over the production process and could do little to augment production and the agricultural surplus. Peasants likewise had little incentive to enhance productivity since all surplus was subject to predatory appropriation by the lords (Wolde-Aregay 1984).

The long-term structural effect of this social property relationship was a sharply reduced potential for technological innovation or productive advance more generally. With no social impetus for intensive gains in productivity, and unable to overturn the customary rights of the peasants, warrior lords found extensive territorial expansion to be the best means of increasing the social surplus. This expansionary territorial dynamic required coercive apparatuses to suppress the peasantry and to counter competing warrior lords. And it was in this process of constructing ever-larger machineries of coercion that tributary states were formed or torn down.[4] The fundamental rationale for the expansion of the Abyssinian state lay in this particular social property configuration, and it was the sinews of imperial expansion that at the end of the nineteenth century enabled Menelik II to transform the Abyssinian kingdom into the Ethiopian Empire and to defeat Italy, the aspirant colonial power, at the Battle of Adwa in 1896.

The new empire incorporated a population and territory more than double that of historic Abyssinia and was able to respond to the challenges posed by the new international constellation of forces from a position of relative political autonomy. But formal sovereignty was no decisive measure of the empire-state's insulation from international geopolitical and economic pressures. However much its social and political form appeared to defy historical time, insofar as it could not survive without the world market and international strategic alliances, it necessarily encountered the limits of relative autonomy and was forced to respond to the dynamics of the international order. Ethiopia's rulers thus felt compelled to transform the tributary order through a project of modernisation from above. This reform project went through two distinct phases before the accumulating contradictions it generated exploded in a profound social revolution in 1974. In the first of these periods, from roughly the turn of the century to the Italian occupation in 1935, adaptation to international pressures and prevailing norms took the form of a selective appropriation of ostensibly modern institutional forms on a structurally non-modern tributary state. Late nineteenth-century territorial expansion was essentially a straightforward extension from adjacent geographical bases, and in the absence of an elaborate bureaucratic administration to accompany it, the new imperial power basically reproduced relations of personal delegation. But once the avenue for lateral expansion was closed off by the presence of adjacent European colonial states, augmentation of the social surplus could only take place through intensive appropriation rather than extensive absorption of new territories and regional peasantries. The resulting system of surplus extraction reduced the peasantry to a status akin to serfdom (Tibebu 1995; Crummey 2000). And without any significant remaking of the tributary order, the institutional and social grounds for a more enduring centralisation were fundamentally absent (Donham 1986, 37–44; Markakis 1974, 106–7).

It was this weakly integrated political structure that collapsed abruptly in the face of Mussolini's aggression in 1935. The occupation over the next five years reconfigured various aspects of the imperial system through policies designed to undermine the legitimacy of the emperor (Donham 1994, 36–37). By weakening the regional nobility, the Italians inadvertently created propitious conditions for the emergence of a more centralised absolutist monarchy in the post-restoration period (Rahmato 1988; Zewde 1984). In the subsequent three decades, Haile Selassie appropriated various administrative functions that were the mainstay of the regional nobility through the creation of a central treasury, an integrated court system, a centralised bureaucracy and a professional army (Zewde 1991, 91). Graduates from the expanding system of higher education were recruited into these new institutions of the state, and by the early 1970s some twenty thousand secondary school graduates had joined the civil service and standing army.

As their traditional privileges were eroded, the nobility turned to the greater powers of the central state to protect their interests. Their integration into the state apparatus, and the diminishing institutional basis of their autonomy, meant that they no longer required private retinues to enforce tributary relations, and resources once used to enlarge the number of followers could now be directed towards commerce or real estate. But only a handful of the regional nobility were interested in pursuing a new vocation as merchants or capitalist farmers.[5] So unlike absolutist state formation in post-Renaissance Europe, where the expansion of commerce and commodity relations provided the technical and economic basis for the consolidation of dynastic states, royal absolutism in Ethiopia was enabled by international, particularly United States, material and technical assistance. As Fred Halliday and Maxine Molyneux rightly observe, it was this exogenous determinant 'that enabled the archaic regimes to prolong their suspension in the historical time of pre-capitalist monarchy, then wrenched them forward into the historical time of social revolution in the post-colonial world' (Halliday and Molyneaux 1981, 20).

These pre-emptive reforms from above were not just economic or political but entailed cultural transformations as well, and the elaboration of a state sponsored 'official nationalism' was in this respect a crucial accompaniment to dynastic centralisation. At the turn of the twentieth century, the Ethiopian Empire had evolved with a largely Orthodox Christian cultural ensemble at its core and numerous ethno-religious communities on its peripheries. By right of conquest and the assertion of divine right, the emperor ruled subjects in a hierarchy that reinforced cultural and social difference. Faith and dynasty were considered adequate foundations of imperial power and the monarchy was largely indifferent to the principle of nationality. At the core of this imperial complex were the ethno-religious community of the Habesha (Abyssinians), an Orthodox Christian community with their own Church and sacred script. This sense of a wider religious community and identity was consolidated in the relational space formed by the regional expansion of Islam from the tenth century onwards, becoming in time a source of terrestrial identity as much as it was a force of spiritual salvation.

This cultural nexus experienced a steady if uneven transformation during the post-1941 process of dynastic centralisation, the establishment of an administrative language-of-state, the extension of modern schools and the formation of a mass media. It was during this period that the identity of the imperial state became permeated by the regional culture of the politically dominant Shewa Amhara. Amhara culture supplied the state's language, its myths of origin, and its most ubiquitous symbols. The boundaries of what it meant to be Ethiopian came to be shaped by this culture, and much like the official nationalisms of the Russian and Magyar nobilities before it, the Ethiopian dynasty sought to naturalise itself through a 'willed merger of nation and dynastic empire' (Anderson 1991, 86, 110). The term *zega* that eventually came to designate the category of citizenship had historically referred to an uprooted person and thus a subject. Its subsequent interpellation as a hybrid subject/citizen category was emblematic of the essentially conservative and preemptive nature of the state-sponsored nationalism that emerged under the international impetus of post-war decolonisation and the spreading norm of the nation-state (Mengestie 2004).

All these changes inaugurated a major reconfiguration of the markers of imperial identity from a primarily ethno-religious to an increasingly ethno-linguistic one. Its first casualty was logically enough the cultural ensemble of the Habesha itself, which now fractured along Amhara and Tigrinya ethno-linguistic lines. Language and ethnicity increasingly came to condition access to high office, which presumed a relatively fluent command of Amharic (Markakis 1984, 4). If nationality and ethnicity had hitherto been of little concern to the imperial regime, dynastic centralisation and official national-ism had made the choice of administrative language, and the cultural identity of the state, a profoundly contested political issue. But this was a relatively late phenomenon in imperial Ethiopia. Prior to this period, the *lisane negus*, the king's language, meant little to subaltern social strata. Material backward-ness, the absence of a developed apparatus for the dissemination of 'national' culture, and limited social and geographical mobility all reinforced separate social and cultural spaces and insured that the inhabitants of the empire retained their primary adhesion to local face-to-face communities and an imagined religious community (cf. Levine 1965). It was only in the transition to modern forms of power that language acquired political efficacy, and the one social group most directly impacted by it was the intelligentsia, a stratum produced by the process of monarchical modernisation and fated by history to administer its denouement.

THE INTELLIGENTSIA AS MODERNIST VANGUARD

Throughout the twentieth century, the Ethiopian intelligentsia was haunted by the spectre of capitalist modernity. Its leading figures wrestled with its significance and searched for a specifically Ethiopian path to modernity (Zewde 2002; 2014). Before the 1960s, they were mainly aligned with the modernising monarchy to promote administrative and educational reforms. But by the turn of the 1960s, as the project of a gradual path of reform from above entered into crisis, the political centre of gravity within the intelligen-tsia shifted to the left, and its active members began to envisage a revolution-ary transformation of Ethiopian society. The monarchy was hence the very symbol of backwardness, a feudal relic and a dead weight on society.

The opening of the Haile Selassie I University in 1960, and the gradual expansion of the state bureaucracy, enhanced the social weight of the intelligentsia. And as the institutional scope of their activities increased, their symbolic power took on a new meaning, further amplified by the awe the written word commanded in a largely illiterate society. The newspapers they published and the radio programs they ran provided powerful mediums for the propagation of new ideas. During the 1930s, they looked to Japan as a model of a non-Western emperor system that had successfully 'modernised'. They were instrumental in drafting the 1931 Constitution along the lines of the Meiji Constitution, and helped promote administrative reforms that strengthened the centralising dynasty at the expense of the regional nobility. But some leading figures of the intelligentsia, haunted by awareness of the Ethiopia's position in the hierarchy of power and wealth, began to question the significance of political sovereignty itself. Afawarq Gebre Iyassus, who had collaborated with the Italian occupation, was later to confess that, 'I did what I did because I believed that if Italy took over Ethiopia, civilized it and made it prosperous, the day will then come when the Ethiopians, having become civilized, strong and prosperous, will free themselves from Italy, just as the United States did with England' (Zewde 2002, 56).

With the advent of decolonisation in Africa and Asia and the post-war boom in the world economy, this sensibility of being behind became even more acute, and was a decisive element in the political motivations informing a failed coup attempt in 1960. As Brigadier General Mengistu Neway—the leader of the aborted coup—explained, 'I ruminated over why the Ethiopian armed forces were so easily broken by the forces of the enemy [the Italians in 1935] and I realized that it was fundamentally because of our backwardness' (Greenfield 1965, 199). This feeling was also echoed in the statement the Crown Prince was forced to read over the radio: 'The Ethiopian people have a history of more than 3,000 years, but in that long history no progress was made in agriculture, commerce or industry…. While the newly formed independent nations of Africa are making progress, Ethiopia is lagging behind, and this fact is now realized' (Balsvik 1985). By the end of the decade, a more radicalised intelligentsia had emerged as the most vocal opponents of the *ancien régime* outside the armed nationalist rebellion in Eritrea. Ascribing the ease with which the failed coup was put down to the strategic failure of its sponsors to mobilise popular sectors behind it, they turned to a new form of radical politics that combined opposition to the imperial order with an ethical concern for the poor. They saw themselves as the vanguard of a coming revolution conceived as a vehicle for hastening the project of modernisation and catching-up. And if a model of such a revolution was needed, world history had already supplied it: 'the Bolshevik revolutionary model has been decisive for all twentieth century revolutions because it made them imaginable in societies still more backward than all the Russias. It opened the possibility of, so to speak, cutting history off at the pass' (Anderson 1991, 156–57). What the radical intellectuals found particularly attractive about Marxism-Leninism was not so much the abstract promise of universal emancipation and individual self-actualisation, but the demonstrable example of the Russian and Chinese revolutions as models of an alternative and accelerated path to modernity (Donham 1999, 122–30). This broadly diffused conception of revolutionary politics was a manifestation of the manner in which Marxism-Leninism was appropriated in conditions of late-twentieth-century Ethiopia (Woldegiorgis 1989, 10–11). Largely untouched by any direct experience with capitalist factories and farms, or a wider liberal public sphere and representative form of government, their Marxism was essentially academic, incubated in the space of the university. Armed with an ostensibly scientific theory of history, they set out to radically uproot the old order and forcefully hasten the forward march of history – whatever its costs. This developmentalist orientation downplayed basic questions of democracy, civil liberties and political pluralism as expendable luxuries Ethiopia could ill afford. The country had to first go through a phase of socialist primitive accumulation which required great sacrifice and effort. For this archetype of the revolutionary vanguard:

> To be a socialist therefore is to recognize the inevitable and to speed it up with the help of a scientific outlook and a disciplined admiration for the leaders and prophets of socialism who marked out the future road. To be a socialist is to help remove obstacles from the road of inevitable progress, that is, to fight for the defeat of backwardness in institutions, backwardness in humans, and humans who are backward.... This is the frame in which the view that 'freedom is recognition of necessity' made perfect sense. Ethics becomes but a recognition of and service towards the inevitable progress. Any other attitude to morality is utopian sentimentalism and/or a legacy of pre-scientific thought and hence, of course, 'petty-bourgeois'. (Shanin 1990, 72)

Denied any legal or institutional space for independent political expression and organisation, the radical intellectuals took their concerns to the streets, at first discreetly, but by the late 1960s, more openly and audaciously, heralding the emergence of a new kind of political activism.

REVOLUTION FROM BELOW AND THE FIRST REPUBLIC

By the early 1970s, the post-restoration project of modernisation was running out of steam, and the more the monarchy attempted to reform the state, the more it encountered a structural contradiction. Modernisation required a degree of mobilisation without putting at risk the legitimacy of the monarchy itself. This set critical limits to dynastic modernisation from above, and after almost three decades of reform, the mass of the rural population remained mired in abject poverty, while unemployment and social marginalisation made daily life for the plebeian sectors in the towns exceedingly difficult and challenging. Economically, there was little discernible dynamic of commercialisation and the rate of agricultural output steadily declined between 1957 and 1973 (Clapham 1988, 187). Politically, the aristocracy that dominated the upper house of the nominal parliament repeatedly blocked the modest proposals for land reform. The unilateral dismantling of the federal arrangement with Eritrea in 1962, which was to prove fatal for the empire, reflected the deeply conservative mindset of the nobility that viewed even limited forms of representative government and civil liberties as anathema (Retta 2000).

The accumulating contradictions of this imperial amalgam started to surface in the early 1970s. The most consequential catalyst of the rising political unrest was the mass famine of 1973, which was to claim an estimated one hundred thousand lives. The absence of any discernable response to avert the famine, the impact of the 1973 international oil crisis, and opposition to proposed higher education reforms fired-up pent up tensions among students, taxi drivers, rank-and-file soldiers and civil servants that erupted in a series of spontaneous demonstrations, mutinies and strikes. The scope of the mass mobilisations took the imperial regime by surprise. Besieged on all sides, and with the army neutralised by a clandestine committee of junior officers known as the Derg, the emperor made one concession after another, emboldening the popular mobilisations. In the months preceding the fall of the monarchy, the Derg removed the concentric circles of power around the throne before unceremoniously deposing the isolate emperor on the 12th of September 1974 (Halliday and Molyneaux 1981; Lefort 1983; Tiruneh 1993). The growing opposition to the regime was encapsulated in the language of a revolt against *huala-qerent* or 'backwardness'. As Colonel Mengistu, who emerged victorious in the faction fights within the ruling Derg, later recalled: 'It seemed as though "fire" was coming out of the mouths of the speakers when they were making speeches about the backwardness of Ethiopia, the history, the suffering of its people and the progress made in other countries' (Donham 1999, 19).

Shortly after the Derg seized state power, however, its repressive policies split and polarised the radical opposition along the twin axis of class and nationality. Simplifying somewhat, it can be argued that those intellectuals most assimilated into the core imperial culture tended to emphasise the class character of the state and to give priority to cross-cultural class alliances;

while those coming from the peripheries of the empire put equivalent emphasis on the cultural identity of the empire-state as an essential feature of the prevailing pattern of social inequalities. Both positions were articulated in a discourse of Marxism-Leninism, and several of the leading figures of the student movement had debated over these issues in exile before returning to Ethiopia to face each other as bitter rivals.

Socially, the most consequential measure enacted by the new Republic was the land reform of 1975. The reform granted peasants use-rights of up to ten hectares per household and banned the selling, mortgaging, exchanging or leasing of land, and the hiring of wage labour. Tenancy and related forms of subordination were done away with and the few large commercial farms were turned into collective or state farms. Long-entrenched common-places concerning the place of the poor in the social order were undermined and peasant households experienced a relative expansion in income in the immediate post-reform years. In the regions incorporated into the empire at the end of the nineteenth century, the land reform was also experienced as a form of cultural emancipation, transforming the oppressive ethnic hierarchies that accompanied the spread of imperial rule and the tributary order. The reform created a relatively homogeneous tenure system with small variations in the quality and size of individual allotments. But if the peasantry largely welcomed the land redistribution as an end in itself, it could only be a transitional arrangement for the post-revolutionary state. Redistribution was viewed as a necessary but insufficient condition for removing the structural fetters on productivity, which required mechanised state farms or producer cooperatives as the productive socialist analogues of capitalist agriculture. The threat to smallholder tenure was consequently never far and following the Great Famine of 1984 the regime embarked on large-scale projects of resettlement and villagisation, as peasant households from the turbulent north were resettled in regimented villages in the south (Berriso 2002, 117). This high modernist scheme proved basically counterproductive. By the end of the decade, production levels had declined to levels below those of the early 1970s, and given the failure to realise anything approaching the expected level of producer cooperatives, the state turned to coercive means to extract surplus from rural households.

The forced march to modernisation was combined with the ruthless suppression of all manifestations of politicised ethnicity, and the young officers that seized state power refused to hand it back to the people constituted as a sovereign body. The state became the embodiment of the 'nation-to-be', substituting bureaucracy for democracy and passive obedience for active citizenship. And by alienating the peasantry and the ethnic intelligentsias, it set in motion the conditions for various peasant-based armed ethno-nationalist movements. A peasantry burdened by state exactions and an intelligentsia alienated by military rule and the project of official nationalism, joined forces to launch a sustained assault on the state. In May 1991, in a dramatic reversal of the pattern a century earlier when forces from the imperial core conquered and subjugated the peripheries, a coalition of nationalists from the peripheries now marched triumphantly on the centre. As Eritrea became a sovereign state following a United Nations supervised referendum, a Federal Republic based on ethnic administrative units was established in Ethiopia over the debris of the post-1974 unitary state (Tareke 2009; Young 2006).

REVOLUTION FROM THE PERIPHERY
AND THE SECOND REPUBLIC

The 1974 Revolution had transpired in an international conjuncture marked by a rising political ferment—from Vietnam to Cuba, from the Algerian revolution to the radicalisation of post-1967 Arab nationalism, from anti-colonial struggles in Portuguese Africa to the anti-apartheid movement in South Africa, and from May 68 in Paris to the revolutions in Iran and Nicaragua a decade later. This conjuncture was formative for the radical intelligentsia in Ethiopia and found political expression in a proliferating revolutionary and radical nationalist discourse. But by the time the second republic was established in 1991, the international situation had altered completely. The Cold War was over as Perestroika and Glasnost paved the way for the collapse of the Berlin Wall and the implosion of the Soviet Union, while post-Mao China was in the process of embracing the capitalist world market. In the rest of the world, the long recessionary wave in the global economy that started in the mid-seventies was accompanied by a neoliberal offensive fixated on the deregulation of the market, the privatisation of public assets, and the rolling back of social gains secured during the immediate post-war and post-colonial decades. In Ethiopia, the negative example of the post-revolutionary state further tarnished the political appeal of socialism, effectively alienating broad sectors of the intelligentsia from it.

It was in this altered international context that Eritrean nationalist forces assumed complete control over Eritrea while a coalition of nationalist forces, under the hegemony of the Tigray People's Liberation Front (TPLF), seized power in Addis Ababa. The latter proceeded to transform the unitary republic into a federal state along the lines of the then unraveling Soviet Union. This restructuring went some ways in reconfiguring the empire-state, generating among other things a reactive Amhara nationalism that like its Russian and Turkish precursors was the last to emerge in the empire. If the new regime—whose social and political base was in the northern region of Tigray—was to stabilise the volatile political situation and secure its legitimacy, it needed to make various political concessions. These concessions made possible a relative political opening within a largely restricted public sphere. And given the changed international ideological context, the TPLF rapidly discarded its pro-Albanian Marxist-Leninist discourse in favor of an articulated ideology of developmentalism which now came into its own – without ambiguity or circumlocution – as the expression of a radical nationalist 'revolution against backwardness'. Opposition to the new order would hereafter be dismissed simply as 'anti-developmentalist'.

This political reorientation led to the elaboration of a new strategy of accumulation mediated by market mechanisms and a regulated opening to the world market. It subsequently brought to the fore the crucial question of the land tenure system inherited from the 1974 Revolution, to which the new rulers were initially committed. But under pressure from the Bretton Woods institutions and demands for the restitution of property rights by returning émigres and newly emergent local capital, they started to backtrack from their previously pro-smallholder stance. While formally upholding the land law, they allowed local land markets to emerge and used market imperatives to bear on smallholder farming with the aim of generating an expanded social surplus for an industrialisation drive. Peasant households were progressively subjected to a criteria of market efficiency in a strategy that gave primary consideration to the mobilisation of land and labour for enhanced capital accumulation.

The transformation of agrarian social relations was facilitated by the 1975 land reform law that by vesting all land in the state had juridically expropriated the peasantry and endowed state authorities with plenipotentiary powers to reallocate land in the 'public interest'. With the turn to the market, this state monopoly of land was deployed to facilitate a spatially differentiated tenure rearrangement. In the densely populated highland core, the remaking of agrarian social relations primarily relied on the integration of smallholder farmers into the market through various mechanisms; while in the sparsely populated lowland peripheries, an archipelago of large-scale mechanised farming is emerging facilitated by the enclosure of the commons and the eviction of villagers from their ancestral land. In one of the great ironies of history, the radical nationalists that had fought to dismantle the core-periphery hierarchies of the *ancien régime* empire were now overseeing its reconstitution in new capitalist form. While so far limited in its reach, the expropriations are nonetheless creating the condition for a real subsumption of land and labour to capital, and might constitute the initial testing grounds for a much more extended process of dispossession in the highlands, making apposite for Ethiopia today Marx's nineteenth century warning to German producers: *De te fabula narrator* – Of you this story is told! (Marx 1976 [1867]).

THE DIALECTICS OF 'BACKWARDNESS' AND 'PROGRESS'

Viewed in terms of their long-term structural outcome, the successive revolutions in Ethiopia had effectively cleared the path for the expansion of capitalist commodity relations. The decisive factor in this outcome was the epochal shift in the international situation at the turn of the 1990s, a historical conjuncture marked by the implosion of the Soviet Union and the end of the Cold War. The speed with which revolutionary actors adapted to this changed international environment is partly explained by the epochal consciousness of relative 'backwardness' that was a basic element of radical nationalist ideology. This recasting of political commitments did not entail a total disavowal of the earlier Marxist-Leninist orientation. While much of the rhetoric of Leninism was discarded, the organisational forms it gave rise to—a centralised vanguard party and mass associations under its control—were redeployed for consolidating the new state power and for promoting a manifold business empire under the control of the party. Instead of nationalising the commanding heights of the economy as was the case with the 1974 revolution, this new market-based strategy was augmented by a corporatist type state exercising control over national labour federations and peasant associations.

What does this outcome suggest about the social and political character of the combined 'long revolution' in Ethiopia? Can it be conceived as a 'bourgeois revolution'? From the world-historical perspective adopted in this essay, such a characterisation is not entirely implausible. But it is not without its own analytic limitations and conundrums. For if a 'bourgeois revolution' presupposes a corresponding bourgeois class subject and world view to bring it into being, then the revolutions in Ethiopia were categorically not bourgeois. But if we put the emphasis on its objective outcome – the establishment of a political and legal framework for the development of capitalist social relations– it arguably constitutes a bourgeois revolution even if only by proxy and in a highly mediated sense. But rather than a peculiarity of the Ethiopian revolution, this non-correspondence between social subject and historical tasks appears to be a general feature of bourgeois revolutions, virtually none of which represented a straightforward contest between a rising bourgeoisie and a declining aristocracy:

> none of the great turbulences of the transition to modernity has ever conformed to the simple schema of a struggle between a feudal aristocracy and industrial capital of the sort presupposed in the traditional Marxist vocabulary. The porous pattern of feudalism above, the unpredictable presence of exploited classes from below, the mixed disposition of the bourgeoisie within, the competitive pressure of rival states without, were bound to defeat this expectation. In that sense, one could say that it was in the nature of 'bourgeois revolutions' to be denatured: these transformations could never have been the linear project of a single class subject. Here the exception was the rule – every one was a bastard birth. (Anderson 1992 [1975], 112–13).

This disjuncture between social agents and structural outcomes is arguably a feature of the uneven and combined dynamics of capitalist world development whereby international geopolitical pressures can press different social agents to the task of removing the structural obstacles to the expansion of capitalist commodity relations. One of the ways this occurs is through revolutionary projects of 'catching-up' which are framed by a linear conception of historical development and the temporal ideologies of modernisation and progress (Ferguson 2005, 161–81). From this perspective, unevenness is read under the exclusive sign of backwardness, and revolutions become a means of catching-up and accelerating the transition to modernity. This worldview has provided a seemingly secure ground from which particular modernist futures could be imagined in different societies across the world and an instrumental relationship of means to ends could be justified.

Today, in the second decade of the new millennium, when virtually all the revolutionary projects of the twentieth century have been defeated or reversed, a critical reevaluation of such 'revolutions against backwardness' has become a necessity. And any consequential critique will have to come to terms with two central themes that were constitutive of them: the ideology of Progress and a normative model of the future derived from an abstracted history of the West. The notion of progress that was integral to these revolutions was subjected to a particularly illuminating critique by Walter Benjamin in the context of the bloody conflagrations of the Second World War and the descent of European civilisation into barbarism. Criticising the conventional conception of history as progress and as automatic and continuous improvement, Benjamin reconceived capitalist development as a steady accumulation of disasters that 'keeps piling wreckage upon wreckage'. Revolutions, rather than accelerating history, would thus have to constitute a redemptive 'interruption' of it, a pulling of the fire alarm before the heedless lurch of human civilisation into the abyss (Benjamin 1969, 263; Löwy 2006).

If the critique of a blind faith in the telos of modernity is one essential point of departure for emancipatory struggles today, the other is the centrality accorded a model of the future derived from an abstracted history of the West with all its Eurocentric assumptions of unidirectional change. Writing in a conjuncture marked by anti-colonial struggles, and in terms that have lost none of their force of conviction, Frantz Fanon gave powerful expression to this emergent sense of anti-Eurocentrism:

> Humanity is waiting for something other from us than such an imitation, which would be almost an obscene caricature. If we want to turn Africa into a new Europe and America into a new Europe, then let us leave the destiny of our countries to Europeans. They will know how to do it better than the most gifted from among us. But if we want humanity to advance a step further, if we want

to bring it up to a different level than that which Europe has shown it, then we must invent and we must make discoveries.... For Europe, for ourselves and for humanity, comrades, we must turn over a new leaf, we must work out new concepts, and try to set afoot a new man. (Fanon 1963, 315–16).

These critiques by Benjamin and Fanon occupy different analytic registers and are not without their internal tensions. But they provide a necessary antidote to all naïve ideologies of progress as well as positivist and evolutionary conceptions of history derived from Eurocentric assumptions. Together, they suggest a political orientation that is in some sense Janus faced, with one face turned towards the condition of relative 'backwardness' and the terrible reality of absolute scarcity; and the other towards the seemingly endless 'progress' of capitalist commodification and over-accumulation, and the social and ecological threat generated by its recurrent dynamic of creative destruction. Separated by a huge gulf in wealth and power, these contrasting conditions might appear unconnected. But they are in fact outcomes of the same historical process of capitalist world development. The condition of the one was largely the creation of the other, and any meaningful internationalism today requires a dialectical conjoining of the 'revolution against backwardness' with a 'revolution against progress'.

NOTES

1. For recent studies of revolutionary change informed by the idea of uneven and combined development, see Matin (2013c) and Anievas and Nişancioğlu (2015, 174–214).

2. In a critical survey of Western Marxism, Perry Anderson has argued that the 'law of uneven and combined development governs the tempo and distribution of theory too: it can transform laggard into leading countries, benefiting from the advantages of latecomers, in a comparatively short period' (Anderson 1976: 102). In a recent illuminating study, Robbie Shilliam (2009) has examined the 'international dimension of knowledge production' and the specific problematic of 'comparative backwardness' in shaping the thought world of German intellectuals, including Kant, Hegel, Weber and Morgenthau.

3. In many respects, this was a dynamic akin to that of feudal Europe. See for instance the characterisation of feudalism in the seminal essay by Robert Brenner (1985).

4. By the time of the 1974 Revolution, the enclaves of commercial agriculture amounted to just 2.3 percent (320,000 hectares) of the total area under cultivation, contributing no more than seven percent of the gross value of agricultural production. (Rahmato, 2008: 83)

Chapter 12

Uneven and Combined Development in the Sociocultural Evolution of World-Systems

Christopher Chase-Dunn and Marilyn Grell-Brisk

The comparative world-systems perspective advances the idea of semiperipheral development as a set of processes that have been important in sociocultural evolution since the first emergence of interpolity interaction networks (world-systems).[1] Whole world-systems are conceived as systemic interaction networks based on intensive exchange, cooperation and conflict. Very small world-systems are compared with larger continental and global ones. The notion of core/periphery relations is a fundamental concept in this theoretical approach. Uneven development and co-evolution are conspicuous features of the emergence of complexity and hierarchy within and between human polities. Polities that were in the middle of core/periphery structures were more likely to be the locus of the implementation of new technologies and new forms of organisation that facilitated conquest and empire formation and that expanded and intensified exchange networks. Sociocultural evolution then can only be explained if polities are seen to have been in important interaction with each other since the Palaeolithic Age (Rosenberg 2010). This idea was inspired by Leon Trotsky's concept of 'uneven and combined development' (Trotsky 1932).

Semiperipheral marcher states and semiperipheral capitalist city-states have been important agents of sociocultural transformation in world history since the Bronze Age. Studies of the growth of cities and of the territorial sizes of polities confirm the importance of semiperipheral development as a cause of scale changes in human sociocultural evolution. And the contemporary global system continues to show signs of this phenomenon. In this chapter we advance the idea that polities that have held intermediate positions in core/periphery structures (the semiperiphery) have often been the locus of the implementation of new technologies and forms of organisation that have facilitated conquest, empire formation and the expansion and intensification of exchange networks.

Core, periphery and semiperiphery are relational concepts that depend on the nature of interpolity interactions and the nature of the polities that are interacting. The semiperiphery is in between the core and the periphery, but the specific meaning of that 'in between-ness' depends on the structure of the larger system and the nature of the polities that are its parts. Christopher Chase-Dunn and Thomas Hall (1997) made an important distinction between core/periphery differentiation and core/periphery hierarchy. Core/periphery differentiation exists when polities with different levels of population density are systemically interacting with one another (making war, alliances or trade). Core/periphery hierarchy exists when some polities dominate and/or exploit other polities. Chase-Dunn and Hall do not assume that all world-systems (networks of systemic interpolity interaction) are organised as core/periphery structures. Rather they see core/periphery hierarchies as having emerged and evolved as capabilities for domination and exploitation of distant peoples have been developed. The inclusion of prehistorical small-scale polities in the scope of comparison allows for the study of the emergence and development of interpolity differentiation and hierarchy. The distinction between differentiation and hierarchy is important because it allows for the analysis of known cases in which less population dense polities (e.g. the Mongols) have exploited higher density ones (e.g. China), and for the study of possible cases of semiperipheral development in situations in which core/periphery differentiation, but not core/periphery hierarchy were present (see below). The nature of the semiperiphery thus depends on the nature of the interpolity system. In practice we can use population density differences (settlement sizes) and differences in modes of production (foraging, farming, pastoralism, etc.) to identify polities that are likely to have been semiperipheral to other polities.

Semiperipheral development has taken different forms. A kind of semiperipheral development occurred in prehistoric California in two small world-systems composed of sedentary and hunter-gatherer polities. And there were semiperipheral marcher chiefdoms in the Pacific that conquered other polities and formed island-wide paramount chiefdoms (Kirsch 1994). Semiperipheral and peripheral marcher states were the most frequent agents of the formation of large empires in world history (Inoue *et al.* 2016). Semiperipheral capitalist city-states encouraged the production of surpluses for exchange and commercialising since the Bronze Age. Europe was a semiperipheral promontory of Afroeurasia that rose to global hegemony because the weakness of its tributary empires allowed the emergence of capitalist states (Chase-Dunn and Hall 1997, 90–3). All the modern hegemons (Netherlands, United Kingdom and the United States) were formerly semiperipheral states before their rise to hegemony (Chase-Dunn and Hall 1997; Anievas and Nişancioğlu 2013). And the contemporary global system continues to demonstrate signs of semiperipheral development both in terms of upward mobility and transformation.

The concept of uneven and combined development in the writings of Leon Trotsky has played a significant role in the formation of the idea of semiperipheral development.

In his studies of the 1905 Russian Revolution (*Results and Prospects* and *Our Revolution* which he wrote in 1906 and 1907, respectively), Trotsky contended that Russia could not reproduce the kind of capitalism that had emerged in Western Europe. Rather, Russian development would need to be constructed in the context of the already existing Europe-centred world economy. Trotsky explained this by proposing his twin laws of uneven and combined development: 'Unevenness, the most general law of the historic process, reveals itself most sharply and complexly in the destiny of backward countries.... From the universal law of unevenness thus derives ... the law of combined development—by which we mean a drawing together of the different stages of the journey, a combining of separate steps, an amalgam of archaic with more contemporary forms' (Trotsky 1932, 5–6). For Trotsky, development was uneven because history had already established that different countries grew economically at different rates and development was combined because backward countries, like Russia, would simply import, implement and execute the most advanced aspects of technology and organisation from Western Europe. However, this was not done 'slavishly' as 'a backward country does not take things in the same order' (Trotsky 1932, 4). Countries could move decades ahead of the developmental process by simply taking advantage of the knowledge and experience of the more advanced and developed countries, the result being an interlacing of backward and advanced processes of development—combined development.

Trotsky's twin laws have been a source of inspiration for the formulation of new ideas and concepts across disciplines such as the economic historian, Alexander Gerschenkron's (1962) idea of the advantages of backwardness as a boon for rapid industrialisation, cultural anthropologist Elman Service's (1971) concept of adaptivity as a spur to adaptive evolutionary change and historian Carroll Quigley's (1979) notion of a semiperiphery that mixes cultures to gestate new combinations that lead to competitive success. More recently, world historian and ethnographer Philippe Beaujard (2005) has contended that core, peripheral and semiperipheral polities co-evolve with one another despite interpolity exploitation and domination. Trotsky's twin laws have also been developed into a transhistorical and non-Eurocentric theory of international relations (Matin 2013a, 2013b) and an explanation of the emergence of hegemons (Anievas and Nişancioğlu 2013). For Justin Rosenberg (2010), archaeological evidence shows that transitions to agricultural societies were uneven in time and space depending upon environmental differences. And so uneven and combined development preceded the international but was important in the emergence of geopolitics. The case for uneven and combined development informing a theory of international relations based on historical sociology is advanced by Rosenberg (2010) and by Kamran Matin (2007). For instance, Matin (2007, 432) contends that 'the high mobility, predatory and war-attuned nature of nomadism were of the utmost importance in shaping the outcome and forms of the interrelation between the nomads and sedentary societies'. He applies this idea to pre-modern Iran. According to Matin, the use of a nomadic institution called the *uymaq* (a political-administrative unit consolidated in Iran under Tamerlane), produced the underdevelopment of private property. This was in part because of pre-modern Iran's relations with nomadic peoples and the resulting form taken by the Persian sultanates. All these scholars inform the central idea of this chapter, which is that much of socio-historical systemic transformation occurred in, and was fuelled by, peoples and polities who were in semiperipheral, and sometimes peripheral, locations within the world-systems in which they lived.

The semiperiphery lies between the core and the periphery. Given its position in the core/periphery hierarchy, the semiperiphery includes regions that mix both core and peripheral forms of organisation. Semiperipheries may also be spatially located between two or more competing core regions. And they may be regions where mediating activities link core and peripheral polities. They may also include regions in which institutional features are intermediate in form between those found in the core and periphery (Chase-Dunn and Hall 1997, chapter 5). So many semiperipheral polities are likely to be engaging in some form of combined development. The intermediate position between 'core' and 'periphery' explains why semiperipheral polities are most capable of reaping what Trotsky termed the 'privileges of backwardness'. This implies that the roots of those processes of developmental 'catch up and overtake' that Trotsky associated with combined forms of development stem mainly from the structural specificities of each world-system.

But it is important to note that engaging in transformational activities in the semiperiphery is not a guarantee of advancing into another phase or stage of development or of upward mobility into the core. Conceptualising the semiperiphery as being a stage in development ignores the relational and hierarchical aspects of interpolity relations in a larger world-system. The possibility of moving up into the core or down into the periphery is dependent not just on the activities being engaged in, but also on the relations that are operating in the world-system of which the semiperipheral polity is a part (Babones 2005).

World-systems have taken rather different forms depending on the predominant modes of accumulation (kin-based, state-based, capitalist). Furthermore, upward mobility into the core and transformational activity are not necessarily the same. It is possible for a semiperipheral polity to change the logic of social action within a world-system (as semiperipheral capitalist city-states did for thousands of years) without moving into the core.

Before proceeding with our argument that the semiperiphery should be seen as a wellspring of sociocultural evolution, we should first define, and therefore reimagine, the spatial boundaries of world-systems. Immanuel Wallerstein conceived of the semiperiphery as an essential and permanent element of the modern world-system (Wallerstein 1974; 1976). He sees the world-system as trimodal, with multicultural economies and a structurally unequal division of labour in the production of necessary goods for everyday life. An anthropological framework of comparison that considers both the prehistory and the history of world-systems is possible by defining whole systems as interpolity interaction networks in which the interactions (trade, warfare, communications, etc.) are important for the reproduction of the internal structures of the composite units and cause changes that occur in these local structures (Chase-Dunn and Hall 1997). Examinations of small-scale world-systems show that Wallerstein's notion of 'reciprocal minisystems' in which polities interact within a single homogenous cultural context (Wallerstein 1984) are actually rather rare. Most small-scale systems are multicultural and so spatially bounding them must focus on interactions such as alliance formation, warfare and trade that often occur between polities that have different languages and cultures.

Human polities have evolved from bands to tribes to chiefdoms to states, to empires and then to the modern interstate system of republics and hegemonic leadership. In *Rise and Demise*, Chase-Dunn and Hall (1997) contended that there have been three predominant modes of accumulation since the Stone Age: kin-based, tributary and capitalist (Wolf 1982). The qualitative transformations involved in the emergence of state-based and then capitalist logics of integration have often involved initiatives taken by actors from semiperipheral locations. Some types of semiperipheral development lead to upward mobility of the polities that implement innovations, while others do not do that but they do contribute to transforming the institutional structure of the whole system.

Hub theory scholars contend the innovations are most likely to occur in the core where information crossroads promote the recombination of ideas (e.g. Hawley 1950; McNeill and McNeil 2013; Christian 2004). Others claim that the semiperiphery, or even the periphery (Lattimore 1980), are important loci of new organisational, ideological and technological developments. Our position is that the most important thing for uneven and combined development is not where innovations occur but in what places they are implemented. Semiperipheral polities have a greater incentive and less disincentive to devote resources to new forms of organisation and technology than do most core polities. This is what Trotsky referred to as the 'penalties of priority' whereby earlier developed and dominant states suffer from a certain conservatism in adopting new technological and organisational innovations.

COMBINED DEVELOPMENT IN PREHISTORIC CALIFORNIA

The sedentary foragers of indigenous late prehistoric California provide two interesting examples of semiperipheral development in kin-based world-systems. Indigenous California has been the focus of intensive ethnographic studies mapping cultural, linguistic and material characteristics of native Californians (Kroeber 1976; Voegelin 1942), and of systematic studies by archaeologists (Jones and Klar 2007). In *The Wintu and Their Neighbors,* Chase-Dunn and Mann (1998) presented a study of late prehistoric Northern California as a system of interaction networks that linked small-scale polities (tribelets) across major linguistic divides. That study revealed that the Northern California systemic interaction networks were formed by warfare, trade and intermarriage ties that extended for many kilometres around the Sacramento River Valley and that linked Northern and Central California into a single prestige goods network based on the exchange of clam-shell disk beads. Chase-Dunn and Lerro (2014) note that the Northern California core/periphery hierarchy was very slight, but that there was an important degree of core/periphery differentiation constituted as interaction between valley-dwellers (Wintu) with larger villages and hill-dwellers (Yana) with smaller villages.

Northern California displayed an interestingly different version of what some anthropologists (Schneider 1977; Peregrine 1992) have called prestige goods systems. In most prestige goods systems, a local elite used its monopoly on the importation of prestige goods to reward and control local subalterns. You could not get married if Uncle Joe did not provide you with a special kind of pot or other ritually necessary exotic item. In Northern California local headmen were the ones who carried out inter-village exchange. This interpolity exchange was mainly organised as gift-giving among village heads who were competing with one another to establish and maintain reputations of generosity. This was not a commodified trading system, but this gift-giving was an important institutional substitute for raiding during periods of scarcity. These exchange networks were facilitated by the use of 'protomoney' in the form of clam disk shell beads, a storable symbol of value that allowed village headmen to accumulate wealth that could be exchanged for food or other goods. This kind of prestige goods system was not very hierarchical, but the facilitation of exchange networks across tribelet boundaries reduced the impetus to raiding, creating the conditions for greater population density and a relatively pacific structure of interpolity interaction. So, where is the semiperipheral development in this? It turns out that the Pomo, who lived adjacent to Clear Lake in Central California, were the main manufacturers of clam disk shell beads. They obtained clam shells by trading with the Coast Miwok that lived at Bodega Bay and they devoted a large amount of family labour time to producing round beads with a hole in them for stringing into the 'protomoney' that was used in the large down-the-line trade network linking Central and Northern California, including the Wintu and their neighbours (Vayda 1967). But were the Pomo 'semiperipheral' in any important sense?

First we shall describe a similar, but also somewhat different, instance of this kind of interpolity economic specialisation that existed in late prehistoric Southern California. The Chumash were sedentary foragers who lived along the Southern California coast in what is now Santa Barbara and Ventura Counties. They built and used a distinctive plank canoe (*tomol*) that allowed them to fish offshore and to develop a trade network that linked those living on the Northern Channel Islands with the villages on the mainland. The large coastal villages were also connected by trade in food items with smaller inland villages in the mountains and valleys adjacent to the coast. As population increased on the Northern Channel Islands the islanders increasingly special-ised in the production of olivella shell beads that came to function as proto-money in a rather large down-the-trade network that linked the Chumash with the Yokuts in the San Joaquin Valley and the Gabrieleno (Tongva) peoples in what became Los Angeles and Orange Counties. The island Chumash came to devote a rather substantial portion of their labour time to the production of shell bead money, which gave them something to exchange for food from the mainland (Arnold 2004). The natural resources of the islands were somewhat depleted by population pressure, which encouraged the islanders to specialise in the production of shell beads in order to have something to exchange for food from the mainland. Was this semiperipheral development?

As with Northern California, there is no evidence of interpolity exploita-tion or domination between island and coastal villages. Neither the Pomo nor the island Chumash lived in a core/periphery hierarchy in which some polities were exploiting and/or dominating other polities. But they did live in a situation of core/periphery differentiation—in which systemic interaction was occurring among polities with different degrees of population density. Studies of village sizes in late prehistoric California show that both the Pomo and the island Chumash had villages that were smaller than the village sizes that existed in adjacent polities. In Southern California the biggest vil-lages, and the biggest concentration of villages, were on the mainland coast. In Northern California the biggest villages were those of the Patwin in the southern Sacramento River Valley (King 1978, 60). The island Chumash example also suggests another aspect of semiperipherality. Some natural locations contain more resources that are useable to humans than do others. One cause of uneven social development is simply the uneven geography of natural capital. Core polities are those that occupy the best locations and non-core polities occupy less fecund sites. The island Chumash had less access to land-based resources such as deer and acorns, than did the mainland

Chumash and so their villages were smaller. And the Pomo had less access to riverine resources (anadromous fish runs) than did the Patwin who lived along the Sacramento River. If these were cases of semiperipheral development, the specialised activities of the protomoney manufacturers facilitated the emergence and intensification of the interpolity gift exchange network. This activity allowed a larger population to live on the islands and facilitated a regional world-system that had relatively more peaceful exchange and relatively less warfare.

SEMIPERIPHERAL DEVELOPMENT: UPWARD MOBILITY AND/OR TRANSFORMATION

Arnold Toynbee (1946) contended that the ecologically marginal locations that semiperipheral polities occupy are a motivating factor in their implementation of risky new technologies and strategies that often cause social change. Owen Lattimore (1980) also argued that non-core polities were often the source of important investments in new organisational and technological innovations. Innovations are often developed within core polities, at central nodes in transportation and communications networks, but semiperipheral polities are more likely to implement these than core polities are because they are less risk averse. Again, this is reminiscent of Trotsky's concept of 'penalties of priority' that afflict older sclerotic core polities.

Geographical unevenness is also important in Patrick Kirch's (1984) model of island settlement and the rise of semiperipheral marcher chiefdoms in the Pacific. The first arrivals to an island occupied the best locations with fresh water and good soil, usually on the windward side that received the most rainfall. Later arrivals populated the less desirable locations and so the conical clan system of closeness to the ancestors came to match the ecological unevenness of the island locations. The oldest, most senior, lineages occupied the best locations. But it was usually a junior chief from the leeward side of the island that conquered the rest to form an island-wide paramountcy, changing the scale of political organisation and facilitating greater organisational complexity—both upward mobility and transformation.

Semiperipheral capitalist city-states, on the other hand, long performed transformation without much upward mobility. These were states out on the edge of core regions that specialised in interpolity trade. Most often they were maritime enterprises (Dilmun, the Phoenician city-states, Melaka) but sometimes they organised trade over land (the Old Assyrian city-state). These trading states expanded exchange networks and incentivised the production of tradable surpluses since the Bronze Age, but they did not take power in the core until a concentration of them in one region, Europe, coincided with the relative weakness of tributary empires. As was the case in late prehistoric California, the capitalist city-states did not move into the core for a very long time, but they did make it possible for larger, more complex and hierarchical world-systems to emerge by expanding and intensifying exchange networks.

MARCHER LORDS

Semiperipheral marcher states—semiperipheral polities that conquer older core polities and form larger empire states—are both upwardly mobile and transformative. Examples include the Qin dynasty, the Neo-Assyrians, the Persians, the Macedonians, the Romans, the Inka and the Aztecs (Inoue *et al* 2016). The Akkadian empire is one of the oldest empires produced by a conquest of states. Prior to its unification by Sargon of Akkaʿ, the Sumerian city-states had existed for well over seven centuries. These ci y-states interacted through a complex economic network with a definitive core-periphery hierarchy. The core had a written language, theocratic government and irrigated agriculture. The periphery consisted of pastoralists, horticulturalists and specialised quarrying and manufacturing villages. An exchange network is known to have existed among the core and peripheral polities with both 'backwash and spread effects' (Myrdal 1963, 152). If the network dynamic between the core cities and the rest of Sumer was mostly a prestige good network with the older core dominating most resources, as Friedman and Rowlands have claimed (1977), a spread effect would be understandable. However, metalworking throughout the Bronze and Iron Ages has been attributed to mountain societies. Additionally, some amount of manufacturing occurred in the remote villages near large soapstone deposits. Both co-evolution and 'the development of underdevelopment' (Frank 1967) were occurring in the Mesopotamian system before the rise of the Akkadian Empire.

Sargon the Great, the eventual conqueror and unifier of the Sumerian city-states, was a cupbearer to the king of Kish, one of the core Sumerian city-states. Sargon was a servant belonging to a class of Semitic-speaking non-Sumerian immigrants who had long been present in the Mesopotamian heartland of cities. Sargon was able to unify all of Sumer through a military campaign creating a very large empire-state. He was described as a 'marcher lord' and a pioneer of hegemonic empire (Mann 1986). In chapter 5 of *The Sources of Social Power*, Michael Mann argues that the Akkadians were successful in their war effort and at unification of the city-states because they combined the Sumerian core-type military strategy (the use of heavy infantry) with a pastoralist military technology (composite bows). While the idea that Sargon used a combination of core and peripheral organisational and military technologies to conquer Sumer has been supported (e.g. Diakonoff 1991;

Mann 1986), other scholars have proposed other factors such as class and ethnic rebellion as having been important to the Akkadian rise (Yoffee 1993).

Typically, polities and interpolity systems cycle through centralisation (by conquest or incorporation) and decentralisation resulting from the decline of centralised power. When a polity within a region sustains a significant increase in size from the largest previous polity size in the region, it is called an 'upsweep' (Inoue *et al.* 2010). The Institute for Research on World-Systems Polities and Settlements (SetPol) Research Working Group at the University of California Riverside has quantitatively identified most of the major upsweeps in the territorial sizes of polities since the early Bronze Age in the world regions in which evidence is available about the changes in the territorial sizes of the largest polities. The SetPol Research Working Group identified twenty-one such upsweeps in five world regions since the early Bronze Age.

We examined these to determine whether or not they were the result of semiperipheral marcher conquests (Inoue *et al.* 2016). We found that over half of the polity upsweeps were produced by marcher states from the semi-periphery (10) or from the periphery (3). This means that the hypothesis of semiperipheral development does not explain everything about the events in which polity sizes significantly increased in geographical scale, but also that the phenomenon of semiperipheral development cannot be ignored in any explanation of the long-term trend in the rise of polity sizes.

The semiperipheral capitalist city-states promoted trade and commodification for millennia, increasingly linking Afroeurasia into a connected multi-core world economy. The relative weakness of tributary empires in the West in the context of a commodified institutional matrix allowed a strong regional trade matrix of autonomous city-states to emerge, and then the emergence of larger states that were under the control of capitalists. The rise of the West was another instance of uneven and combined development that occurred on a promontory of Eurasia.

And the spiral of development within the modern Europe-centred system continued to display uneven and combined development. Alexander Anievas and Kerem Nişancioğlu (2015) have argued that the developmental trajectory of European capitalism was significantly affected by the thirteenth- to fourteenth-century *Pax Mongolica*. In particular, Europe benefited significantly from what Trotsky called 'the privilege of historic backwardness'. Anievas and Nişancioğlu (2015, 87) write, 'Arising late on the periphery of this world-system, European development had the most to gain from the new intersocietal links being forged, particularly through the diffusion of new technologies and "resource portfolios" spreading from East to West'. And all of those capitalist nation states that were forereachers of the emerging capitalist world-system (the United Provinces of the Netherlands in the seventeenth century, the United Kingdom of Great Britain in the nineteenth century and the United States in the twentieth century) were all formerly semiperipheral powers who led in the deepening and expansion of capitalist economic development. The twentieth-century peasant wars and revolutions that challenged the core of the capitalist world-system attained their greatest power in semiperipheral Russia and China.

CONTEMPORARY SEMIPERIPHERAL DEVELOPMENT

In the contemporary global system, the semiperiphery continues to push the boundaries in terms of both upward mobility and innovative systemic change. The economic and political development of the semiperipheral BRICS (Brazil, Russia, India, China and South Africa) represent global challenges to the centrality of the United States, Europe and Japan. Contemporary semiperipheral polities are contributing to social change by implementing organisational and ideological forms that facilitate their own upward mobility and that transform, to some extent, the logics of social reproduction and development. The form of state capitalism that has emerged in China contributes a new note to the complex music of the varieties of capitalism in the global system. Giovanni Arrighi (2007) contended that the form of Chinese diaspora capitalism emerging in East Asia represents a somewhat progressive improvement over the financialised, bellicose and work-destroying Western version. Whether or not the Chinese version of foreign investment and resource extraction turns out to be better or worse than that of the West is still being played out in Africa, Southeast Asia and Latin America (Bergesen 2013; Grell-Brisk 2015).

Core–periphery interactions continue to evolve with the development of increasingly sophisticated digital and military technologies from the core, and organisations and institutions like ALBA (Bolivarian Alliance for the Peoples of Our America), the New Development Bank and the Asian Infrastructure Investment Bank (AIIB) from the Asian and Latin American semiperiphery. The increasing economic and political power of the semiperipheral challengers drives a certain amount of reorganisation of the global political economy. Many see US hegemony as being in slow decline and the emergence of the multipolar world that the BRICS say that they want (e.g. Chase-Dunn *et al.* 2011).

It is indisputable that deindustrialisation and financialisation have been major trends in core polities since the 1970s. This is most evident in the United States, where financialisation has been pushed to its limits and has been widely viewed as the main cause of the global economic recession of 2008. To a lesser extent there has also been a move towards financialisation among the semiperipheral polities. Some of the BRICs are becoming wise to the diminishing advantages of rapid export-oriented industrialisation. One could go so far as to state that the BRICS are in fact engaging in combined development. With its continued focus on economic growth and development through manufacturing while concurrently engaging in high finance (as with the AIIB), China is a good example of a semiperipheral country that is confronting the new twists of globalisation flexibly, combining elements in new ways. For instance, China could be seen as engaging in a form of combined development in the management of its economy. The Chinese approach has been termed anything from 'capitalism with Chinese characteristics' (Yasheng Huang 2008) to 'state-controlled capitalism', 'socialist market economy' and 'Chinese capitalism'. All these phrases suggest that China has combined and applied the different elements of the economies of advanced countries to its own socio-historical and political condition.

It has been noted by some scholars that the contemporary semiperipheral polities are not hot-beds of progressive revolution or even evolution. The 'pink tide' reaction against neoliberalism in Latin America led by President Hugo Chavez of Venezuela spread to most Latin American countries, but not to other regions of the world (Chase-Dunn *et al.* 2015). Many semiperipheral countries are under the control of reactionary elements and others are just trying to move up the food chain of global capitalism. Patrick Bond's (2013) article in the journal *Links* goes as far as to call the BRICS sub-imperialist powers that peddle and reaffirm neoliberal policies, and that help maintain the modern capitalist world-system and its institutional power structures. Bond points to, among many things, the numerous corporations such as DeBeers, Gencor (later BHP Billiton) and Liberty Life Insurance that benefited from South Africa's financial deregulation and the transition from 'racial to class apartheid' in the 1990s. Bond also reminds us about Ruy Mauro Marini (1972) who developed the concept of sub-imperialism in the 1970s. Marini saw Brazil to be the most prominent example of sub-imperialism. He contended that Brazil's expansionist policy in Latin America and Africa was driven by a quest for new markets, an effort to gain control over sources of raw materials and was intended to prevent potential competitors from having access to such resources.

Bond claims that South Africa has pursued these same kinds of sub-imperial policies, as have most of the other BRICS. In fact, according to Bond, the 2013 BRICS summit held in South Africa declared support for corporate land grabs, worsened Africa's retail-driven de-industrialisation, and revived the New Partnership for Africa's Development (NEPAD) programme—the embodiment of neoliberal policies in Africa, and of course, the BRICS bank.

Bond is not alone in his view that these semiperipheral polities are mainly engaged in propping up the existing power structure. William I. Robinson

(2015) decries the state-centric view of now globalised capitalism. He notes that the rise of China has been mainly due to foreign investment in manufacturing that uses cheap Chinese labour, and he stresses the extent to which China is an integrated part of global capitalist accumulation and an important player in what he calls an emergent transnational state. Ho-Fung Hung (2015a) and S.S. Karatasli and Sefika Kumral (2015) claim that China has pursued economic and political policies that primarily maintain the global status quo. In a recent *New York Times* article, Hung (2015b) contends that the China-backed AIIB has become a multilateral organisation that can only serve to buttress the prevailing global economic structures. Although China provided the initial financial support for the AIIB, in order to garner the support of most of the allies of the United States China had to forgo veto power over the actions of the new bank (Wei and Davis 2015). Hung points out that US hegemony at its height exerted huge power over the bilateral and multilateral institutions it helped to found after the Second World War. Hung also notes that the AIIB's capacity for influence and power in the global economy is limited given its multilateral nature and that it is unlikely to provide China with the means to supplant the United States as a global leader.

Still, the extent to which China and/or the other BRICS countries are shoring up the current core–periphery hierarchy is a point of contention. Bond sees the BRICS as mainly reproducing the hierarchical structures of the system because he has another world in mind—an egalitarian, cooperative and sustainable world society. Upward mobility in the system does not necessarily challenge the basic logic of the system or reduce its injustices. Bond is right about that. But this approach ignores the changes compelled by the rise of the BRICS. A shift of economic power away from Europe and North America towards the semiperiphery changes the equation with regard to global racial stratification. It makes global culture even more multicultural than it has previously been. It probably does not lower the magnitude of global inequality, because inequality within the BRICS countries has been increasing.

The idea that China could replace the United States as a global hegemon has been suggested by some scholars (e.g. Frank 1998; 2014; Arrighi 2007b), but few now really believe this. The rise of BRICS portends a more multipolar, less US-centric system. That is a big change from what has existed since the Second World War. Despite arguments that the AIIB will not help in China's rise to hegemonic power, the bank could serve as a serious alternative to the International Monetary Fund (IMF) and the World Bank for development funding and foreign aid in the Global South. China has been praised by many African governments as being more attuned to the needs of the Global South. Writing for the *Financial Times* in 2008, the President of Senegal, Abdoulaye Wade, explained, 'China's approach to our needs is simply better adapted than the slow and sometimes patronising post-colonial approach of European investors.... Economic relations are based more on mutual need.... [And] China, which has fought its own battles to modernise, has a much greater sense of the personal urgency of development in Africa than many western nations' (Wade 2008). The AIIB is in direct competition with the World Bank. The semiperipheral and peripheral polities are creating new anti-systemic and reformist institutions that facilitate a certain amount of disengagement with the old core. The BRICS New Development Bank (NDB) is intercontinental. The Development Bank of Latin America, the Community of Latin American and Caribbean States (CELAC), the Bolivarian Alliance for the Peoples of Our America (ALBA), the African Development Bank and a myriad of other new institutions have been organised in the Global South to counter the prevailing global structures of power. The most influential of these are those from the semiperiphery such as the NDB and the AIIB. The discourse about the need for an alternative to the US dollar in the global economy continues to persist. The dollar alternative issue may become more feasible if AIIB and NDB grow in size and influence despite the arguments made by Hung (2015a) and Bond (2013a; 2013b).

Many people in the Global South, especially the urban poor, have been under siege from the Washington Consensus and the neoliberal structural adjustment programmes of the IMF. The imposed structural adjustment programmes have been very unpopular and have not resulted in improved lives for the vast majority of people. This has resulted in populist reactions in many semiperipheral and peripheral states. The World Social Forum emerged in 2001 as a popular response to neoliberal policies. The semiperiphery, where so many of the impacts of neoliberal policies have been felt, has nurtured this kind of anti-systemic thinking. With its history of uneven and combined development and empowering transnational social movements, the semiperiphery has the potential to reshape the trajectory of global system.

NOTE

1. Thanks to Dmytro Khutkyy for helpful criticisms and suggestions on an earlier version.

Chapter 13

Navigating Non-Eurocentrism and Trotskyist Integrity in the New Trotskyist IR of World History

John M. Hobson

This chapter will hone in on the problems of Eurocentrism and *potential* ahistoricism that infect parts of the New Trotskyist International Relations (NTIR); an exciting approach (or more precisely a variety of approaches), which has emerged in the last decade within the discipline of IR.[1] These range from the orthodox approaches advanced by the likes of Neil Davidson (2009) and Sam Ashman (2010) to the more unorthodox approaches advanced by the likes of Justin Rosenberg (2006; 2007; 2008; 2010), Kamran Matin (2007; 2012; 2013a; 2013c), Alexander Anievas (2014a), Kerem Nişancıoğlu (2014) as well as Anievas and Nişancıoğlu (2014; 2015), Robbie Shilliam (2009a, 2009b) and Cemal Burak Tansel (2015). Probably the key pioneer of this unorthodox approach is Justin Rosenberg. The immediate difference between the orthodox and unorthodox approaches concerns the scope or depth of the historical terrain that is broached. The former tends to focus on the period of British industrialisation and its aftermath, whereas the latter works on a much deeper world-historical terrain that goes back *before* the period of Western European industrialisation and, at least in Rosenberg's work (2010; and this volume), reaches all the way back to Ancient Sumer (3,500 BCE). Rosenberg is currently working on a book-length treatment of this project, the findings of which are likely to be really exciting as this could well open up a genuinely original take on both IR and world history.

However, my twin-primary concern in this chapter is not simply to inter-rogate the scope of the historical terrain analysed but to consider the issue of Eurocentrism/non-Eurocentrism, on the one hand, and whether non-Eurocentric Trotskyism retains or breaks with Trotsky's original conception of uneven and combined development, on the other; something that for the sake of convenience I will refer to as 'Trotskyist integrity'. I ask the latter question precisely because many orthodox Trotskyists might well assume that applying uneven and combined development (UCD) to the pre-industrial era to effect a non-Eurocentric break with Eurocentric Trotskyism inherently breaks with Trotskyist integrity (e.g. Ashman 2010; Davidson 2009). But a primary upshot of my reading of the key non-Eurocentric works is that it is perfectly possible to apply UCD to the pre-industrial era in a non-Eurocentric manner while *retaining* Trotskyist integrity, for pre-industrial whips of external necessity took largely different forms to that which prevailed after British industrialisation.

To be more specific, there are several key claims that I advance in this chapter. First, those neo-Trotskyists in IR who contend that UCD is unique to the post-industrial era tend to fall into the trap of Eurocentrism. This is in essence because they treat the 'original' transition to capitalism in Europe as a wholly *intra*-European phenomenon—or put differently, as a 'virginal birth' or 'European miracle' (see Hobson 2011). By contrast, those who depict the existence of UCD as *preceding* industrialisation are capable of avoiding Eurocentrism in that they factor in non-Western influences in the rise of capitalism in Europe or equally when explaining the political development of non-Western countries—specifically Iran in Matin's work (2007; 2013c). This leads onto a second core claim which derives from an initial conundrum: the question as to whether one has to negate Trotskyist integrity in order to transcend Trotskyist Eurocentrism. For the orthodox approach insists that UCD is unique to the post-industrialisation era such that this process did not properly exist prior to then (and while I recognise that the orthodox Trotskyist approach deployed by Neil Davidson (2003) highlights an earlier instantiation of UCD this is confined to the specific case of Scotland in the late-seventeenth and eighteenth centuries and, therefore, the role of UCD in the context of the non-Western world remains out of bounds).[2]

Trotsky essentially argued that the capitalist mode of production is responsible for ushering in the full logic of UCD. By contrast, the non-Eurocentric approach, which narrates the existence of UCD in the pre-industrial era, necessarily undermines the unique relationship that UCD has with the capitalist mode of production that Trotsky largely imbied it with, leading to the question as to whether it has broken with Trotskyist integrity in advancing its non-Eurocentrism. But, as alluded to already, because this logic takes slightly different forms in the pre-industrial era then this poses no major problem in terms of retaining Trotskyist integrity. Either way, though, the core ramification is that the perceived gap which is thought to exist between these two wings of Trotskyism is much narrower than is commonly presupposed, thereby suggesting that the quest for a non-Eurocentric Trotskyism is nowhere near as fraught with the theoretical dangers that orthodox Trotskyists imagine.

The chapter proceeds through four sections. In the first section I outline the essential Eurocentric properties of the orthodox neo-Trotskyist approach to IR. The second section then considers the efforts of Alexander Anievas to advance a non-Eurocentric approach in his seminal prize-winning 2014 book, while the third section does the same for the equally seminal work that Anievas and Nişancioğlu have jointly undertaken on the rise of the West. The fourth section examines the pioneering efforts of Kamran Matin to break with Eurocentrism, focussing specifically on his 2013 book on Iran. In each of these sections I shall argue that when non-Eurocentrism is achieved it is done in such a way as to retain Trotskyist integrity. And finally, in the Conclusion I claim that while the presence of UCD can certainly be accounted for in the pre-industrial era, nevertheless, in agreement with Matin, Anievas and Nişancioğlu, it takes on largely different forms to that of the modern era.

PROBLEMATISING THE HISTORICAL TEMPORALITY OF UCD AND THE PROBLEM OF EUROCENTRISM

Within the neo-Trotskyist approaches that have emerged in the last decade in IR an internecine debate quickly followed concerning the issue of the temporality of UCD. This was largely prompted by concerns with Rosenberg's seminal effort to extrapolate the concept of UCD back in time, well before the Western industrial-temporal watershed. To this end the more orthodox Trotskyists, following Trotsky (1967) in this matter, insist that UCD only cuts in across the international system once capitalism has emerged in Western Europe.[3] Neil Davidson, for example, asserts that '[t]he immense difference between industrial capitalism and previous modes of production meant that, from the moment the former was introduced, combination became possible in a way that it had not been hitherto' (Davidson 2009, 18). Similarly, Sam Ashman insists that UCD should be used sparingly and should be applied only within the temporal confines of the last few hundred years of world history in which industrial capitalism has predominated. As she puts it:

> [a] danger with Rosenberg's analysis of uneven and combined development as a transhistoric phenomenon is that it loses sight of the 'great transformation' brought about by capitalist relations and political forms.... [UCD] is not a theory of the initial or first transition to capitalism, but of 'late' capitalist development—that is, of development which occurs in the context, and perhaps also as a consequence, of capitalism's pre-existence elsewhere. Once capital exists in one small corner of north-western Europe, development for all others is immediately transformed. (Ashman 2010, 184, 194)

However, Ashman's point that UCD does not apply to the 'original' birth of capitalism, which she assumes occurred spontaneously in Britain, constitutes the problem that comprises the tip of a very large, submerged Eurocentric iceberg. Because I have discussed all this elsewhere (Hobson 2011), I will move quickly here in making my point.

The orthodox Trotskyist point that the phenomenon of UCD is unique to the post-industrial moment represents an 'ultra-historicist' reading that buys into what I call the Eurocentric 'big bang theory' of world politics (BBT). This is a two-step narrative of world politics wherein the first step Europe makes itself is through the *Eurocentric logic of immanence* as a result of its own *exceptional* qualities. That is, Europe is viewed as *sui generis* such that it is not merely self-constituting but that it is capable of self-generated or independent auto-development. Given its exceptionalism so it is presumed that the breakthrough to capitalist industrialisation was an historical inevitability and that this outcome was always immanent within Europe's social structure; that it was pre-ordained or foretold. In such a way, the transition to capitalism within Western Europe is portrayed in effect as a 'European miracle' or as a miraculous virgin birth. Moreover, according to Karl Marx, Europe's self-generating dynamic is considered to be exceptional on the grounds that no such autonomous development into modernity was possible in the (unexceptional) East, where the Asiatic mode of production ensured that economic development is strangled at birth, owing to the economically repressive Oriental despotic nature of Eastern states (Hobson 2012, 52–58; see also O'Leary 1989; Turner 1978; Said 1978/2003). Interestingly, my critique of this Eurocentric problematique of development dovetails with that of Rosenberg's (2010) when he argues that the problem with traditional social theory is that it falls into the trap of ontological singularity (i.e., methodological nationalism) and fails to recognise the 'international' origins of domestic social change/development (even if he largely shies away from deploying the term 'Eurocentric'). All in all, in Eurocentrism no external non-Western influences are considered to play a part in the rise of Europe.

The second step of the BBT flows on ineluctably, for having made itself in the absence of any external help or pressures, and having risen to the top of the world distribution of power, Europe subsequently projects its global political will-to-power through formal imperialism in the first instance and informal imperialist globalisation in the second in order to remake the world—so far as is possible—in its own image. So to summarise the metaphor: with the 'big bang of modernity' having spontaneously exploded within Europe, the new social and political Western structure of power expands or diffuses outwards to remake the earthly universe. Key here is the orthodox Trotskyist emphasis on the emergence of UCD following British industrialisation, whereby all non-Western societies are forced to catch up with the West primarily so that they can militarily defend themselves from the impact of

Western neo-imperial rapaciousness; an argument that is central to Trotsky's explanation (1967) of Tsarist industrialisation after 1861.

Regardless as to whether this marks a 'realist moment' or not (a problem which opens up a separate debate),[4] the key point is that because the global logic of UCD *follows* Western European industrialisation we are left with an approach that reconvenes the familiar properties of the standard Eurocentric explanation of the rise of the West. That is, the complete absence of non-Western influences in the rise of the West—and hence the impossibility of Europe's ability to combine with non-Western developmental initiatives—means logically that the West broke through spontaneously into modernity as a result of its own exceptional properties (see Hobson 2011; Bhambra 2011). Or, put differently, precisely because the intersocietal logic that underpins Trotsky's concept of UCD is absent in the account of the rise of the West so the breakthrough can be explained through the standard endogenous intra-European ontology that is the hallmark of Eurocentrism. Thus, when Ashman (2010, 189) concludes that only 'once capitalism is established [spontaneously] in one part of the world [i.e., north-western Europe], it affects and changes the form of transition to capitalist development elsewhere' so, in refusing to apply the concept of UCD to the so-called 'original transition' to capitalism, Europe is deemed *ipso facto* to be *sui generis*, developing according to the Eurocentric logic of immanence that presupposes the assumption of European exceptionalism. In this way, I argue that orthodox neo-Trotskyism, as does its liberal counterpart, narrates not so much the rise of the West but the Eurocentric *Ruse of the West*.

However, an unorthodox neo-Trotskyist approach has also emerged that seeks in various ways, either implicitly (as in Rosenberg) or explicitly (as in Matin, Anievas and Nişancioğlu), to break with this Eurocentric problematique, above all, by bringing the logic of UCD squarely into the explanation of the original transition. In essence, some of the scholars working within this approach might well appear to be breaking the original Trotskyist Gordian Knot that ties UCD with the *post*-industrialisation phase by advancing the idea that UCD not only *preceded*, but was constitutive of, the rise of modern European industrial capitalism. This, I believe, is a fundamental requirement of a properly non-Eurocentric approach, Trotskyist or otherwise. In what follows I shall consider the most prominent recent publications of those neo-Trotskyist writers who have sought to break with Eurocentrism, beginning with a reading of Anievas's 2014 book before proceeding onto the work that Anievas and Nişancioğlu (2013; 2015) have done in terms of applying UCD to the rise of the West, closing with a reading of Matin's 2013 book on Iran. So to reiterate the key questions posed earlier: how effective are these interventions in breaking with Eurocentrism on the one hand and to what extent do they retain Trotskyist integrity on the other?

ALEXANDER ANIEVAS'S *CAPITAL, THE STATE, AND WAR*: A NON-EUROCENTRIC BRIDGE TOO FAR?

Anievas's seminal and indeed excellent book, *Capital, the State, and War*, parries with the problem of Eurocentrism in world politics. However, it is important to note at the outset a certain temporal disjuncture that this book creates with respect to the argument that I made above. For this book considers the 1914–1945 era and therefore does not seek to extrapolate the concept of UCD back before the moment of British industrialisation (whereas the writings that I examine in the subsequent two sections all go back before 1700). I mention this because this book offers a potential break with Eurocentrism even though it focuses on the post-1850 era, thereby in turn suggesting that a non-Eurocentric Trotskyism does not have to go back in time before industrialisation.

One of the themes of the book is to restore what Anievas calls 'the lost history and theory of IR':

> [f]oregrounding the ineluctably intertwined and co-constitutive nature of impe-
> rial rivalries, social revolutions, and anti-colonial struggles evident to policy-
> makers during the decades of crisis but subsequently lost in academic analyses,
> the study seeks to demonstrate how standard interpretations and assumptions
> about the period have been incomplete and often mistaken. (Anievas 2014a, 2)

This involves the inclusion of processes that are specific both to Marxism and to non-Eurocentrism. While I want to argue that retrieving such a lost history contains many important cues for a non-Eurocentric approach, ultimately delivering on this promised theoretical mission constitutes a bridge too far in this book. For what is missing is a sufficient account of non-Western *agency*, given that the European theatre of action and European agency constitute the central analytical gaze.

Chapter 3, which looks at the uneven and combined developmental origins of the First World War, opens with a promising insight with regards to non-Eurocentrism. There he sets out to examine three spatial vectors; first, a *West-East* plane of unevenness which looks at the successive phases of industrialisation mainly within Europe but also beyond; second, a *transatlantic vector* that links North America with Europe in general and the British Empire in particular; and third, a *North–South vector/constellation* interlinking and differentiating the multi-ethnic empires from Central and Eastern Europe to the Asia Pacific (especially India and China) into a dynamic of asymmetrical interdependency with the capital-industrial powers. He then proceeds to consider the role of the Ottoman Empire in the causes of the First World War, focussing specifically on the issue of Ottoman decline. His argument is that in the face of superior Western economic and military power the Ottoman Empire was unable to respond in an effective way such that its subsequent disintegration phase led to the problem of 'blocked development'. The Ottoman Empire then became immersed in the Balkans War; something which constituted a direct prelude to August 1914. But for Anievas, the real significance of the retreat of the declining Ottoman Empire is that it created a vacuum into which various European powers flowed; in particular, the outward expansion of the aggressive Magyar nobility of the Hungarian half of Austria-Hungary, which now came to be a crucial player in Central Eastern Europe and, moreover, following the 1878 Berlin Conference, Austria-Hungary came to govern over the provinces inhabited by Croatians, Serbians and Muslims. As Anievas put it:

> A further consequence of the Habsburg's eastward drive was the conclusion of the Dual Alliance of 1879 contributing to closer Franco-Russian relations. Though originally conceived as a defensive strategy by Bismarck, the alliance over time turned into yet another factor undermining international order. (Anievas 2014a, 93)

The Hungarian nobility's aggressive policy of Magyarisation poisoned Austria-Hungary's relations with its southern neighbours which also fed into the causes of the First World War. However, the problem here is that the Ottoman Empire in effect is treated as a passive arena rather than a pro-active agent such that what matters most are the actions of the European powers and subsequent changes in the balance of power that in turn led onto the inception of the First World War.

While Anievas also seeks to bring India and China into the analysis in his quest for a non-Eurocentric set of causes of the First World War, nevertheless a similar Eurocentric trope is applied here. Thus with the opening up of a massive power disparity between Europe and India/China, on the one hand, and the absolute decline of both these non-Western societies, on the other, so this led onto the restructuring of the direction and dynamics of inter-imperial rivalries between the European great powers. The Chinese power vacuum sucked Russia in and thereby re-channelled the direction of Russian imperialism, while simultaneously effecting a partial alleviation of European rivalries in the Balkans and the Ottoman Empire. Moreover, this also served to relieve the tensions between Austria-Hungary and Russia and enabled an entente in 1897 to secure the Balkan status quo, while also enabling a kind of ultra-imperialist moment of European great power cooperation through its collective intervention in the Boxer Rebellion. And finally, the decline of the Qing effectively sucked Russia into war with Japan over Manchuria that led to Russia's humiliating defeat which, in turn, led onto the 1905 Russian

revolution while simultaneously effecting a westward shift of Russian foreign policy. Accordingly, he concludes (2014, 95), 'the disintegrating Qing
Dynasty effected a dramatic reconfiguration of the European balance of
power'. But while this analysis does indeed chart the relevance of a North–
South vector in the analysis of the causes of the First World War, nevertheless it is the case that once again the actions of the European great powers
remain central to Anievas's narrative, with the decline of China, India and
the Ottoman Empire constituting, in effect, passive backdrops to the headlin-
ing story of European agency.[5] In essence, non-Western agency in its own
right is effectively ruled out of the analysis, thereby reconvening the standard
strictures of a Eurocentric approach, even if the spatial terrain has been most
usefully extended beyond the limited confines of Europe in the explanation
of the origins of the First World War.

     There are various other aspects concerning the issue of Eurocentrism,
though because these have been developed elsewhere in some detail (Hobson
2016), I shall confine my discussion to a few points. First, while Anievas
makes a compelling case for including the 'Bolshevik threat' when analysing
the inter-war period nevertheless the omission of non-Western agency constitutes a Eurocentric lacuna. While he is surely correct to highlight the issue
that the Bolshevik threat constituted in the minds of Western state leaders,
I argue that they were at least as worried by the 'Eastern threat'. Year 1919
was a significant moment, not just concerning Versailles and the fear over
the Russian Revolution, but also because it was this very year when the
anti-imperialist movements across the colonial world burst onto the scene of
global politics. For the first time Western hegemony in the world appeared
to be under direct threat. Moreover, this intersected with Versailles and the
Bolshevik Revolution. For it was Vladimir Lenin, more so than Woodrow
Wilson, who made so much of the idea of self-determination for the colonial societies, given that Wilson's pronouncements applied only to Eastern
Europe and even then he later expressed regret that he had articulated the
idea given the fillip that it had provided for the anti-imperialist nationalist
cause; and in any case, Wilson was a keen supporter of the League of Nations
Mandate System which allowed for the continuation of Western imperialism
(see Hobson 2012, 167–75; Levin 1973; Ambrosius 2002; Seymour 2012).
Thus whether Bolshevism was viewed in Lord Milner's terms as 'the greatest danger of the civilized world' as Anievas insists (2014a, 131), is a moot
point given that many Westerners, whether they be IR scholars such as Alfred
Zimmern and Gilbert Murray or political representatives at Versailles such as
Woodrow Wilson, Jan Smuts, Billy Hughes and Lord Robert Cecil, viewed
the 'Eastern (anti-colonial) threat' that emerged with a vengeance in 1919
as a colossal challenge to Western hegemony and white racial supremacy
(Hobson 2012, chapter 7); notwithstanding the point that the Bolshevik and

'Eastern' threats tended to be treated holistically as a combined twin-threat in the minds of many Westerners.

Thus in Anievas's narrative we encounter an uneven treatment of the North-South vector. For its presence in the pre-1914 era is inversely related to its exclusion concerning the inter-war period. Once again, then, this returns us to the Eurocentric problem that was highlighted above in that it is the European arena which is treated as the real theatre of agency. This is perplexing because Japan was a formative actor in the Second World War and, of course, its invasion of Pearl Harbor in 1941 was a key factor that brought the United States into the war and thereby changed its dynamic altogether. And as even Niall Ferguson (2009) argues, arguably the Second World War began with the war between China and Japan in 1937. Thus the omission of the North–South vector is doubly perplexing given that it could be such a fruitful area of analysis both for a non-Eurocentric approach, on the one hand, and as a means to flesh out his important conceptual analysis of the development of world politics, on the other. And to sum up the overall discussion I conclude that while Anievas makes a bold attempt at bridging Europe with Asia in a non-Eurocentric way, nevertheless in the end it seems that arriving at the non-Eurocentric promised land constitutes a bridge too far. That said, though, as I argue in the next section, Anievas's work on the rise of the West does succeed in delivering on his non-Eurocentric promise, though the question then becomes whether he has had to sacrifice Trotskyist integrity in the process.

ALEXANDER ANIEVAS AND KEREM NIŞANCIOĞLU'S WORK ON THE 'RISE OF THE WEST': BUILDING A NON-EUROCENTRIC BRIDGE OF THE WORLD

As discussed at the beginning of this chapter, one of the key ways in which the *non-Eurocentric* agenda within neo-Trotskyist IR is being advanced is via the location of the process of UCD in the pre-industrial era. To this end, Anievas and Nişancioğlu have developed a framework for rethinking the rise of Western capitalism in a global context. Here I examine two of their journal articles (Anievas and Nişancioğlu 2013; Nişancioğlu 2014), and I also draw on their excellent 2015 book, *How the West Came to Rule* (Anievas and Nişancioğlu 2015). Their essential strategy is effectively to get behind the moment when UCD is conventionally thought to have cut in by making the claim that the rise of Western capitalism can only be understood through the application of UCD in various non-Western contexts. Given that my own work is situated within a non-Eurocentric problematique and given its many similarities with the recent work of Anievas and Nişancioğlu (see Hobson 2004; 2011), I might be forgiven for applauding their efforts in this regard and for declaring that they have indeed succeeded in advancing a non-Eurocentric approach! Nevertheless, the issue at stake is whether they have thrown the Trotskyist-baby out with the Eurocentric bathwater by insisting that the existence of various external whips of necessity pre-date the era of capitalist industrialisation. Here it seems to me that in advancing a more nuanced analysis of pre-industrial UCD they have succeeded in retaining Trotskyist integrity.

In their 2013 article, they set out the strictures of a non-Eurocentric approach, critiquing orthodox Marxism, found for example in the work of Robert Brenner, for its internalist approach that they rightly see as symptomatic of Eurocentrism (see also Blaut 2000, 45–72; Bhambra 2007, chapter 6; Tansel 2015; Anievas and Nişancioğlu 2015, chapter 2). For as I have also argued, Eurocentrism focuses on the 'exceptionalism' of Europe and it is this that generates the idea of the Eurocentric 'logic of immanence' wherein the breakthrough into modernity is seen as but an historical inevitability as a result of Europe's innate ability to self-generate into capitalist modernity (Hobson 2004, chapter 1). And they rightly point out that only by factoring in externalist logics that are issued from the non-Western world can we begin to overcome Eurocentrism. In their explanation of the rise of Europe they focus on three extra-European sources in the origins of the rise of the West: the benefits of the Mongol Empire and the unintended consequences of the Black Death (wherein the bubonic plague was transmitted along the sinews of this empire); the enabling effects of the Americas; and the enabling and constraining effects of the Ottoman Empire. I shall take each briefly in turn.

The Mongols were important, they argue, in that they unified the Eurasian economy thereby enabling trade to diffuse all the way across from China in the East to Europe in the West. Indeed, the *Pax Mongolica* provided a conducive environment not just for the diffusion of long-distance trade but also for the diffusion of the more advanced non-Western ideas, institutions and technologies from East to West. This interconnected space, however, exhibited a proliferation of different modes of production: the tributary mode in the east, nomadic in the Steppes and feudalism in Europe. But each society's conditions of existence were imbricated in this nascent interdependence that the *Pax Mongolica* enabled (see Anievas and Nişancioğlu 2015, chapter 3). Accordingly, they argue that nomadic expansionism constituted an archaic form of UCD, which in turn enabled the development of Europe via the fillip that enhanced inter-continental trade provided (though simultaneously it impeded growth in China).

They also focus on the effects of the spread of the Black Death. The origins of the bubonic plague stem back to China (in 1331), before it diffused across to Christendom courtesy of the trade routes that were stimulated by the *Pax Mongolica*. When the plague hit Christendom it had a major transformative impact, serving to raise wages (given the decimation of the working population) and shifting social relations towards the peasants. The seigniorial reaction that this prompted differed across Christendom. In contrast to the situation in France where the state sided with the peasantry as part of its efforts to enhance its power vis-à-vis the landlords, nevertheless in England, where the state was much more intimately tied in with the aristocracy, the latter was able to consolidate and enclose peasant landholdings thereby promoting the development of market forces and agrarian capitalism. And here they mention a point that they develop later: that England's isolation from the geopolitical turmoil of the continent enabled the consolidation and unification of the state and ruling class (Anievas and Nişancioğlu 2015, chapter 4).

They also develop an argument that narrates the transatlantic sources of European capitalism, all of which is most useful and none of which I find problematic so far as a non-Eurocentric approach is concerned (Anievas and Nişancioğlu 2015, 97–100). The key point is that the Americas, in their argument, constitute an *enabling* force for the advancement of European development. Here, however, I shall consider and interrogate the third vector that they emphasise: Ottoman/Habsburg rivalry during the Long Sixteenth Century. The Ottoman Empire was heavily imbricated within the 'European' balance of power, serving ultimately to prevent a Habsburg unification of Christendom thereby enabling the reproduction of a pluralist multiple-polity system. Here special emphasis is accorded to the origins of capitalism in England. Specifically, they argue that in strong contrast to much of the continent, England enjoyed a buffer from the Ottoman military threat such that this 'breathing space' enabled an unprecedented coherence of English customs, laws and the market. Coupled with the point that this buffer enabled the English state to avoid building a large standing army meant that the aristocracy could concentrate on commercial activities rather than providing military service. Here it is also worth noting Nişancioğlu's argument that it was the Ottoman 'whip of necessity' which socialised and conditioned the development of English capitalism (2014, 344–6).

The key question that all this throws up is whether this argument breaks with, or retains, Trotskyist integrity. I shall take each of the different arguments in turn. First, they claim in effect that the impact of the Mongol Empire was double-edged. Thus, so far as the *Pax Mongolica* provided a conducive environment within which transcontinental trade could flourish, coupled with its ability to diffuse non-Western inventions from the East to West, so it constituted a kind of helping or enabling hand that comprised the antithesis of the external geopolitical whip of necessity; or what in their book they refer to as a 'gift of external opportunity' (Anievas and Nişancioğlu 2015, 73, 76). However, they also focus on the impact of the spread of the Bubonic Plague which, *inter alia*, provided a permissive environment for the rise of English agrarian capitalism. This, once again, points to an enabling external hand rather than an external whip of geopolitical necessity. Finally, they focus on the impact of the Ottoman Empire wherein the first instance, the fact that its place in the European state system prevented the latter's transcendence by a Habsburg suzerainty once again equates the Ottoman impact with a helping hand, since the maintenance of the anarchic European system was conducive to the later development of capitalism. Finally, it is clear that it was the very *absence* of an Ottoman whip of external necessity that enabled the development of English capitalism. Moreover, they argue that across much of the continent, where the Ottoman whip of external necessity did cut in, the development of capitalism was stifled. This seems to be precisely the inverse logic to that which we would expect from an approach which seeks to place the Ottoman whip-hand at the centre of the causal origins of agrarian capitalism in England. For despite Nişancioğlu's (2014, 333) insistence that '[t]he various forms of unevenness entailed both an Ottoman "whip of external necessity" and a European "privilege of backwardness" which I argue were crucial pre-conditions for the eventual emergence of capitalism within Europe', it seems clear that it was precisely its *absence* that accounts for the English transition.

However, it would be unfair to entirely dismiss their brave efforts at demonstrating the presence of an Ottoman whip of external necessity in particular and various geopolitical whips more generally as existing in the pre-British industrial era. To this end the following claims are significant. First, the Ottoman whip enabled the development of European agrarian capitalism as a necessary but not sufficient condition because it redirected the geopolitical centre of gravity away from England and, equally, the Dutch in their breakaway from the Habsburgs. So, while English development did not, in this sense, constitute a fully combined development, the argument they make in the book is that it was rather a particular *outcome* of combined development: 'the developmental outcomes of an intersocietal condition rooted in the uneven relation of England to the Euro-Ottoman geopolitical milieu' (Anievas and Nişancioğlu 2015, 119). Second, they show in their book the effects of the Ottoman whip in provoking a structural shift away from traditional Mediterranean trade routes towards the Atlantic which thereby provided immense economic opportunities for North-Western states (notably the Dutch and English). And, furthermore, that Ottoman geopolitical policies both intentionally and unintentionally proved a crucial contributing factor in the origins and expansion of the Reformation throughout Europe. In addition, they argue that the geopolitical whip of external necessity was crucial to both the making of the Dutch Revolt and the English Civil Wars/Glorious Revolution—both of which, of course, preceded British industrialisation by almost two centuries. Moreover, in chapter 7 in their discussion of Dutch colonisation in South Asia, they reveal the geopolitical and commercial rivalries (i.e.

the whip) among the Portuguese, English and Dutch in the sixteenth and seventeenth centuries, which drove Dutch merchants to increasingly take control over the production process in the colonies and southern India, thus leading to the transformation of extant social relations in a capitalist direction. These are all significant instantiations of geopolitical pressures, though it is notable that they do not conform to the precise Trotskyist definition of the whip of external necessity insofar as they were regional rather than fully global.

However, this opens up the point that UCD is multi-factored, sometimes comprising an external whip of geopolitical necessity (especially after the British industrial revolution) and at other times comprising largely an enabling logic (as is often the case before British industrialisation). This is reinforced in the conclusion to their book where they suggest that there were huge differences in the forms that UCD take over time. That is, UCD articulates differentially across time and across modes of production. They, correctly in my view, concede that UCD takes on its most intensive form once European capitalism has emerged, thereby confirming the orthodox Trotskyist position. Poignantly, they claim with respect to pre-industrial UCD that '[t]he external pressures did not systematically require societies to take on the developmental achievements of more advanced societal forms. However, such intersocietal pressures did necessitate changes in the social reproduction of societies' (Anievas and Nişancioğlu 2015, 101). All of which means that we need to think not simply about 'uneven development' but also about how the combination process and the 'whip of external necessity' are themselves deeply uneven processes that articulate differentially in different eras. Or, to paraphrase Trotsky (1970, 15), we need to recognise that *combined* 'historical development of different countries and continents is itself uneven'.

All in all, I conclude that their more careful empirical treatment of pre-industrial UCD suggests that they have in fact produced a fascinating and viable neo-Trotskyism which simultaneously breaks fundamentally with Eurocentrism. That their arguments are not only insightful, with which I am in full agreement I might add, but also they are in my view to be congratulated for a superb achievement.

MATIN'S *RECASTING IRANIAN MODERNITY*: A NON-EUROCENTRIC APPROACH TO UCD THAT RETAINS TROTSKYIST INTEGRITY

Matin's *Recasting Iranian Modernity* is the first neo-Trotskyist IR book-length treatment that explores non-Eurocentric world history, simultaneously spanning the pre-industrialisation era and the period that concludes at the end of the twentieth century. Unlike the other books and articles discussed above, this one traces UCD as a key socialising phenomenon in both the modern (post-1850) and pre-modern eras. Picking up on the point above concerning the nature of UCD in the pre-modern era, Matin posits an interesting claim. As noted above, Anievas and Nişancioğlu suggest that while UCD was indeed important in the pre-modern era nevertheless its constraining intensity was of a much lower scale to that which is associated with modern capitalism. Matin, though also insistent that UCD operates before European industrialisation, poses this problem in the following way:

> In the pre-capitalist epoch ... uneven and combined development occurs within an international context where in the absence of a globally dominant capitalist logic, the interactive nature of unevenness does not *regularly* generate forms of combined development that involve a fundamental transformation of the social fabric of the interacting polities. In other words, general reproductive processes of the interactive societies do not undergo qualitative change. (Matin 2013c, 29)

In thereby retaining a good deal of Trotskyist integrity from the outset by refusing to extrapolate back in time the precise nature of modern capitalist UCD, he prefers to talk about the pre-modern process of *geopolitical* rather than capitalist accumulation. The key difference between modern and pre-modern UCD is that in the latter case societies are largely similar in economic terms (*contra* Anievas and Nişancioğlu 2013; 2015) but politically differentiated. Thus, the process of UCD applies mainly at the political level, leading to what he calls 'amalgamated state-formations'. Of particular interest here, however, is his claim that this should not be understood as meaning that pre-capitalist forms of combined development are of lesser historical significance than capitalist ones. While this is an important point that reinforces the pertinence of the existence of UCD prior to the temporal watershed of c.1850, nevertheless an orthodox Trotskyist might well rest assured safe in the knowledge that the primacy of UCD and the unique existence of the whip of external capitalist-geopolitical necessity in the modern capitalist era remains intact owing to the fact that it is modes of production (rather than political modes of domination) under conditions of economic unevenness that lie at the core of their preferred conception of UCD. In short, nothing that Matin argues about pre-industrial UCD disturbs orthodox Trotskyist integrity.

One of the favoured old chestnuts of Marxism lies in the fetishised conception of the 'bourgeois revolution'. Matin certainly breathes fresh critical life into this concept by departing from the standard internalist, methodological nationalist approach that is offered by the vast majority of Marxists. Chapter 3 hones in on what he refers to as the Iranian 'revolution of backwardness' via his analysis of the Constitutional Revolution (1906–1911). Taking on those Marxists who relate this in terms of (albeit an abortive) bourgeois revolution he shows how Iran lacked the existence of a sufficiently strong bourgeoisie at the time. Instead, he argues that this revolution reflected the process of 'defensive accumulation' and 'defensive modernization', which was a response to Iran's backwardness in the face of external capitalist-geopolitical pressures under conditions of uneven and combined development. This led to a peculiar amalgamation wherein this revolution modernised Iran's political structure via the adoption of a written constitution and the initiation of a parliament, to wit: this revolution 'superimposed the political institutions of capitalist-based liberal democracy on a substantively non-capitalist socio-economic structure, [thereby constituting a] peculiar amalgamation [which] was the *first acute expression* of Iran's experience of *modern* uneven and combined development' (Matin 2013c, 146, emphases added). A similar approach is applied in chapter 4 to what he calls 'nationless nationalism', where he focuses on Raza Khan's reforms and Mossadeq's revolt (covering the period from 1921 to 1953). There he argues against conceiving the phenomenon of nationalism as something that causally emerges internally within states by showing how Khan's 'defensive modernization' was pursued under the whip of external necessity.

It is also interesting to note that chapters 5 and 6 point up a role for non-Western agency, the presence of which can provide a counter to Eurocentrism which reifies Western agency in world politics. To this end, Matin argues that the Shah's reaction to various non-Western developments—specifically the peasant revolutions in China and Latin America—led to the implementation of a passive revolution in Iran which entailed the initiation of extensive land reforms. In chapter 6 he shows how Iranian Muslim intellectuals like Ruhollah Khomeini and especially Ali Shariati proactively and creatively combined Western and Islamic discursive and ideological resources and ideas to craft the potent new ideology/discourse of 'revolutionary Islam', which outperformed all secular/leftist (Western) competitors and became the hegemonic form of the revolution. Moreover, the Islamic revolution had and continues to have a significant impact in terms of reconfiguring not only the region but also the global order not least because it became the source of ideological-political inspiration for almost all subsequent 'political Islamist' movements across the world including, in a paradoxical way, ISIS—the effects of which are relayed in our Western newspapers and on our TV screens on a daily basis today.

Finally, let me turn to Matin's treatment of Marxist theory. One of the interesting aspects of his book lies in Matin's ability to overcome some of the blind-spots of orthodox Marxism. Matin and others are critical of the internalist approach that marks standard Marxist work. In their book, Anievas and Nişancioğlu (2015, chapter 2) take Robert Brenner to task for his endogenous approach (see also Tansel 2015). However, Matin produces a critique

of Brenner but with a novel twist, arguing that Brenner's account of the rise
of capitalism in England factors in empirically various external logics—for
example, the Norman Conquest—though Matin's complaint is that none of
this enters into Brenner's theoretical schema (Matin 2013c, 53–54). Even
so, of course, such external logics that Brenner points to empirically are all
intra-European, thereby confirming or dovetailing with the critique levied by
Anievas and Nişancıoğlu (2015) and Tansel (2013).

Of particular import to my own argument is that in Matin's final chapter he
claims that not only is it necessary to revise the basic premises of Marxism
so that it can take into account the international causes of social change
but, moreover, that there are numerous cues for this found in various scattered comments in Marx's writings. There is the well-known claim made
in *Capital* where Marx claims that the moments of primitive accumulation
of capital began outside of Europe in the colonies (a claim reminiscent—or
pre-emptive—of the decolonial writings of the likes of Quijano (2000) and
Mignolo (2000)). For this qualifies the generic point that the origins of capitalist development outside of the West lay with the export of capital to the
colonies throughout the world courtesy of European imperialism. There is
also the first draft of a letter that Marx wrote to Vera Zasulich towards the
end of his life which in essence pointed up the international origins of social
change. In this way, Matin lays out the challenge to conventional Marxism
more generally, suggesting clearly in turn that whatever Eurocentric cues
there are in Marx's basic theory these need not constitute an impediment to
reformulating Marxism on non-Eurocentric lines; that is, a non-Eurocentric
Marxism is not a non-sequitur. And to return to the argument made above,
it seems clear that while Matin certainly demonstrates the salience of UCD
prior to British industrialisation, nevertheless its modality was such that it
does not disturb orthodox Trotskyist integrity. Accordingly, I conclude that
he too provides a superb non-Eurocentric inflection of Trotskyism which
simultaneously retains Trotskyist integrity in particular as well as Marxist
integrity more generally.

CONCLUSION

Although I have questioned the success of Anievas's attempt at overcoming
non-Eurocentrism in his undeniably important 2014 book, nevertheless I have
argued that the work which he has undertaken with his co-author, Kerem
Nişancıoğlu (2015), clearly succeeds in this objective. I have also argued
that their nuanced analysis of pre-industrial UCD enables them to retain
Trotskyist integrity. In support of their argument I would like in this conclusion to produce a non-Eurocentric conception of UCD which, like theirs',

retains orthodox Trotskyist integrity (even though at the risk of sounding like I am contradicting myself I should confess that my Marxist credentials are hardly impeccable!). My argument is that there was no singular global logic to UCD in the pre-industrial era and that instead it operated at various regional and trans-regional levels, on the one hand, and that it took a more informal *modus operandi*, on the other.

One obvious candidate here would be the Middle East. The long historical relations between 'Europe' and Islam would at first sight appear to fit the bill. Standard (Eurocentric) histories often place much emphasis on the early Islamic pretensions to conquer Europe. And given the non-Eurocentric claim that Islam was more advanced than Europe at least until 1500 (if not until the eighteenth century) then taken together this might well appear as a strong potential instance of an Islamic whip of external necessity. One of the most oft-cited examples of this constitutes the Muslim attempt at conquering Europe in 733. But the problem here is that this instance was not in fact one of an attempted conquest of 'Europe' (or rather of Christendom) for the mundane reality was that this was simply a raiding party that comprised a small band of Muslims intent on stealing the gold from the wealthy shrine of St. Martin's. And it was repelled by Charles Martel not by the deployment of the shock cavalry, as we are conventionally told, but rather by a hail of arrows and javelins. In general, it was not the gaining of Western Christendom that the Muslims were interested in, particularly given its backward nature, but Eastern Christendom—especially Constantinople. It is partly for this reason that the 'defeats' incurred at Tours and Poitiers were ignored in the Muslim histories whereas the defeat at Constantinople in 718 CE was openly lamented. Marc Bloch's observation, therefore, remains pertinent: that of all the 'enemies of Western Europe, Islam was certainly the least dangerous.... For a long period neither Gaul nor Italy, among their poor cities, had anything to offer which approached the splendour of Baghdad or Cordova' (Bloch 1961, 3). So, despite the perceptions of the Western half of Christendom there was no *objective* Islamic whip of external necessity.

I would, however, argue that while Middle Eastern Islam did not pose an objective geopolitical threat to Western Christendom, nevertheless, the Christians chose to perceive Islam as a major threat and it did not take long before they acted upon it in no uncertain terms. For it was precisely this perception that launched the 'first round' of the Crusades between 1095 and 1291. Moreover, it was during the era of the Crusades that the Christians began to enquire into the secrets of Islamic civilisation, with Spanish and Portuguese monarchs in particular employing Jews to translate the Islamic scientific texts (because to employ Muslim translators at the time of the Crusades would have appeared contradictory to their mission and in any case, it would have given the game way that after all, the Christians were looking to emulate the superior knowledge of the 'barbarous' civilisation that they were at war with). As a result of all this the acquiring of Islamic knowledge played a massive role in stimulating the Renaissance and later on the Scientific Revolution (Hobson 2004, chapter 8). And this partly state-led combination process was complemented by the Crusaders themselves who learned much about Islamic civilisation when fighting there and brought back various ideas upon their return. Three points by way of conclusion here are notable: first, that Islam was perceived as a threat does not confirm the material, objective presence of an Islamic external whip of necessity. Second, Islam turned out to comprise an enabling rather than constraining factor in the development of Western Europe; a point that remained the case right down to the sixteenth century at the very least. Third, though clearly not an objective whip, nevertheless that it was perceived as one which prompted a combination process suggests that there was an *informal* Islamic whip of external necessity. What then of the Ottoman Empire as constituting a potential candidate for an external whip of necessity? Here we need look no further than the arguments of Anievas and Nişancioğlu (2015) which provide a rich source in this respect as already noted.

Another potential candidate for a non-Western external whip of necessity would be the Mongol Empire. Certainly it entered into geopolitical conflict with significant swathes of what later came to be called Eastern Europe in general, and Russia in particular. Arguably though, the impact of Mongolian interactions with Russia was to effect a shift away from the mercantile centre of Kievan Russia towards the autocratic centre of Novgorod which, though certainly a highly significant shift, is nevertheless one that does not accord with a Mongolian whip of external necessity. And, in any case, nothing in what Anievas and Nişancioğlu (2015, chapter 3) have argued for in relation to the Mongol Empire would evidence such a presence. Once again, a more likely interpretation is that the 'Europeans' perceived, or constructed, the Mongols as a threat. Strengthening Christendom as a response did occur but it was a function of a constructed rather than an objective threat. So I conclude that there was an *informal* rather than an objective Mongol whip of external necessity.

All in all, then, it is hard to register even in the most relevant regional cases, the existence of an *objective* external whip of necessity, never mind the presence of a singular global whip, in the pre-industrial era. Which is most probably why, in the end, applying the logic of UCD to the rise of the West is certainly plausible but not something that can be conflated with the presence of a *global* pre-industrial whip of external necessity. Thus, by allowing for the presence of a pre-industrial presence of UCD in the absence of a pure, objective external whip of geopolitical necessity, means that orthodox Trotskyists need not worry about non-Eurocentric efforts at identifying the presence of UCD *prior* to capitalist industrialisation but why, at the same time, they might reflect further on the need to develop a genuinely non-Eurocentric take on Trotskyist IR and world history by considering the informal non-Western whips of necessity, safe in the knowledge that this need not entail a break with Trotskyist integrity. Accordingly, the onus of the burden, I believe, now falls on orthodox Trotskyists to break with Eurocentrism.

NOTES

1. I would like to thank both of the editors for their excellent suggestions though, of course, I remain responsible for the final product.

2. I also accept the point that Trotsky was somewhat ambivalent about this, implying that UCD had played a role in stimulating Russian development well before the time of the British industrial revolution, as indicated in the first chapter of *The History of the Russian Revolution*. I am grateful to Alex Anievas and Kamran Matin for this insight.

3. Nevertheless, Trotsky did note with respect to Russia that UCD operated as far back as the eleventh century (Matin 2013c, 17).

4. See especially: Callinicos and Rosenberg (2010), as well as several of the other chapters in Anievas (2010).

5. For excellent discussions of war in the context of Eastern agency, see Barkawi (2006) and Laffey and Barkawi (2006).

Chapter 14

The Stakes of Uneven and Combined Development

David L. Blaney and Naeem Inayatullah

Exploration and colonisation brought Europeans into increasing contact with far-flung peoples. Some were difficult to incorporate into received categories of difference, offering special interpretive problems and spurring intellectual efforts to manage difference within the nascent human sciences (Hodgen 1964, chapter 9; Pagden 1982; in relation to international relations (IR), see Inayatullah and Blaney 2004, chapter 2, and international political economy (IPE), see Blaney and Inayatuallah 2010, chapter 2). With the extension of empires and the rising availability of experiences with, and 'knowledge' of, different societies, Enlightenment thinkers developed 'philosophical and historical methods to rethink and account for the diversity of ways of living and the historical development of societies' (Mantena 2010, 13). Most important, we have argued (Blaney and Inayatullah 2010, 46), Enlightenment social theory performs a temporal displacement: societies different from the Europeans are exiled into a developmentally prior past with Europe placed at the pinnacle of human achievement. In short, space is converted into time (see Anievas and Matin, this volume).

Marx, as heir to this tradition, offers a similarly totalising and assimilative project, where he, as Teodor Shanin (1983, 4) puts it, uses a '[d]iversity of stages' to explain 'the essential diversity of forms'. We flag Marx's Eurocentrism (Blaney and Inayatullah 2010, chapter 6), and we suggest that this is an integral, not contingent, feature of his work: it is built right into his method such that Marx's musings about the empirical specificity of Russian or other non-Western European modes of production or trajectories serve as observations that are difficult to integrate seamlessly into the logic of capital. We see the recovery of Trotsky's UCD as one in a line of efforts, briefly reviewed below, to integrate what is not seamless into large theoretical abstractions about capitalism.

Anievas and Matin (this volume) indicate that UCD allows scholars to capture what is often erased: 'alterity, hybridity, and non-linear forms of development' and 'the central role' of 'extra-European societies ... in the making of world history'. They pit the work of the contributors to *Historical Sociology and World History* against the practice of 'methodological internalism' where scholars conceive of 'the birth of the modern world [as] endogenously and autonomously emerging within Europe'. These dominant narratives and 'theoretical understandings of world history' unfold 'with non-European societies and agents largely absent'. Embracing UCD eschews incorporating difference only via a 'comparative method', that treats 'the distinct forms and paths of European development ... as ideal-type abstractions and/or normative benchmarks' that serve as a universal register within which all difference can be managed. Trotsky's UCD directs us to a theoretical understanding of world history as 'intersocietal' that, by the editors' testimony, prompts us to see the direction of 'human development' as governed by processes that are 'neither unilinear nor homogenous/homogenising but interactively multilinear'. We read their claim that recovery of Trotsky's UCD involves 'a fundamental redefinition of the very logic and concept of development', linked they say to 'a 'more-than-one' ontological premise', as an even bolder and somewhat doubtful claim about UCD. We believe that invoking ontological difference points beyond the intersocietal interactions that are the mainstay of UCD and, as we will argue, towards thinking about cultural encounters across more radical differences.

We nonetheless recognise the power of UCD as a mode of ethical/political engagement and also acknowledge our own kinship with efforts to break the spell of atomistic or 'internalist' explanations of development that implicitly or explicitly justify inequality and domination (Inayatullah and Blaney 2004, chapter 4; 2015; 2016). Armed with the 'intersocietal' as 'unit of analysis' (Anievas and Nişancioğlu 2015, 53), UCD highlights the interrelations necessary to understanding structured inequalities but repressed by those who order their thinking according to an atomistic political economy. Stressing that parts cannot exist apart from wholes draws us also to negate claims that insist either that parts can be understood by severing them from wholes or that parts bear full responsibility for their position in the (repressed) whole. UCD appears as among a family of social theoretical perspectives that reveal the whole that is presumed and repressed by methodological individualism and other atomised unit-level doctrines.

We believe this is an important and powerful move, though the contributors to this volume underplay this political/ethical moment in their work, emphasising instead the relative superiority of UCD to competing modes of historical sociology (see Hobson 2011 and this volume; the editors' introduction, Brown, Makki, Evans and Cooper in this volume). Authors stress that

UCD uniquely allows us to hold together fairly grand theoretical abstractions about capitalism or human development with the dictates of the messy and seamless empirical realities of actually existing historical processes. Other modes of historical sociological inquiry, we are told, falsely attribute primary causal power to intra-societal factors, thereby vindicating a story of heroic and unique European agency, or degenerate into culturalism/relativism when they construct extra-European agency as an internal capacity to generate multiple modes of capitalism or modernity. In short, by erasing the more central and ubiquitous 'intersocietal' interactions, competing modes of inquiry are judged guilty of factual, conceptual and explanatory failures.

Despite this characterisation of the failures of Eurocentric scholarship, we believe a political/ethical concern about assigning responsibility for one's fate—as oppressor or oppressed, as developmental success or failure—remains embedded in UCD scholarship. Where the contributors to historical sociology and world history ascribe 'a certain unity' to either capitalism or human development writ large as 'an intelligible (albeit contradictory) object of analysis' that they are empowered to describe and explain (Anievas and Nişancioğlu 2015, 9), we sense that the authors also hold onto capitalism or human development as processes of achievement and creation as well as oppression and destruction for which moral responsibility might be (and usually is) assigned. To avoid charges of European superiority, then, they believe they must assign agential responsibility or any claims of human historical achievements widely, dispersing the causal processes generating capitalism and modernity (or any 'development') beyond any individual society's bounds. The impulse to dissolve claims of European super-agency and diffuse agency to non-European actors also implies non-European complicity for oppression and destruction. The recovery of extra-European agency may be important, but may not fully capture what we see to be at stake in claims about the achievements and destructiveness of capitalist or colonial modernity. It is not just whose sweat, intelligence, creativity, or subjugation was involved but, to invoke the editors' reference to multiple ontologies, whose cosmologies, histories and forms of life were suppressed, subsumed or destroyed by a process that seems to have been centred but not localised in certain European powers.

Drawing on Robbie Shilliam's work and our own efforts, we want to focus less attention on the combined and unequal material processes that distinguish capitalism (or maybe human development). We would focus more on the constitutive role of cultural encounters that perhaps offered prospects of mutual learning but resulted instead in processes of cultural subordination and degradation. Invoking the language of culture refers us to the human capacity to construct, inhabit and aesthetically express forms of life. An emphasis on culture highlights the weight of linguistic and visual representations in shaping human existence into forms of life, including their role in constituting groups' specific identity in relation to others and to the cosmos. We see the interactions stressed by UCD as encounters of different, if always also overlapping, visions and traditions (see Inayatullah and Blaney 2004, introduction). In our view, then, the claims of European universalism that fuelled cultural subordination and degradation are not simply a mis-description of historical realities or a faulty theoretical conception but a constitutive feature of the encounters that shaped capitalist modernity. We believe that the form of the attack on Eurocentrism mobilised in this book underplays this constitutive role and therefore misses an opportunity to stake out a stronger anti-colonial position that indicts the cultural erasures central to modernity. The point is not that cultural destruction is unique to the modern period, but that modern imperialism is consistently hostile to difference. A serious anti-colonial stance would involve reimagining IR as a site for the study of difference and recovering erased voices as collaborators in political and ethical reflection.[1]

We move towards that final claim in the remainder of this essay. We discuss two earlier attempts by Marxist scholars to redress the erasures of extra-European realities risked by stage theories or historical narratives driven by the imperatives of the logic of capital. The idea of the articulation of modes of production and Dipesh Chakrabarty's critique of historicism share with this volume's contributors the motive of recovering the role of extra-European actors in the construction of capitalism. Despite interesting insights, these efforts display problems that help us think about the limits of UCD's challenge to European colonial ideology. Two stand out. First, we see no necessity to the claim that attending to the *differentia specifica* of capitalism is Eurocentric. Second, we believe that replacing the logic of capitalism with a notion of human development risks effacing the presence of multiple cosmologies and forms of life in the encounters making and made by capitalist modernity. In closing, we draw on our work and the work of Robbie Shilliam to suggest alternative formulations that highlight the cultural encounters and destruction specific to capitalist modernity as a way of moving to a stronger anti-colonial stance.

MARXISM AND THE CHALLENGE OF NON-EUROPEAN DIFFERENCE

The rise of dependency and World-System Theories placed the problem of the periphery at the centre of debates about the logic of capitalism. Were the concrete conditions in capitalism's peripheries a sign that capitalist relations had yet to fully overcome backwardness (as in Bill Warren's somewhat later book [1981] and Marx's essays on India) or was underdevelopment a function of dependency relations central to capitalism as a (combined and uneven) system (Foster-Carter 1978, 1–2)? A growing number of contributors to this debate were practicing anthropologists, who struggled to reconcile their field notes and their theoretical conceptions of peripheral social formations with a claim about the global spread of the logic of capitalism. Marxist scholars generally, as Foster-Carter (1978, 3) suggests, were bedevilled by their observation that many of the features of Third World social formations were recognisable as remnants of earlier modes of production, as residual to the main game and destined for eclipse by developmental forces. Yet, these differences seemed crucial to the social formation and were quite resilient. Drawing on Anievas and Matin's introduction to this volume, a comparative method trading in Eurocentric ideal-types founders when confronted with the facts of 'alterity' and 'hybridity'.

The formulations designed to negotiate this paradox, as Foster-Carter reports them, seem precursors of those contemporary practitioners of UCD that centre their work on the uneven and combined character of capitalism. The earlier debates likewise began with the assumption that conditions in the Third World were 'indeed capitalistic', that is, part of a combined historical system, but that the 'whole' is both 'structured and differentiated'. And the differences from the logic of capital displayed in its centres are not 'exogenous to capitalism', but 'an intrinsic and structured part of the wider system' (Foster-Carter 1978, 3, here paraphrasing Laclau). Various writers, 'working over a wide variety of sources of material and levels of analysis', redefined capitalism's unfolding as contradictory processes of 'dissolution and conservation' (as in Poulantzas), where, as in Meillassoux, 'pre-capitalist social forms are "being undermined and perpetuated at the same time"' (Foster-Carter 1978, 3). The concrete social formations might be described then as different and hybrid, but not beyond the grasp of Marxist tools to comprehend.

But these tools needed to be refined. Many in economic anthropology turned to the Althusserian language of 'articulation' which they used to 'indicate relations of linkage and effectivity between different levels of all sorts of things' (Foster-Carter 1978, 5). And they resisted simplistic teleological claims about successive modes of production by suggesting that specific social formations need to be understood as in 'process'—as having a trajectory defined by their 'own periodization' (Foster-Carter 1978, 6), an intriguing term that might prefigure contemporary UCD's emphasis on multilinear development trajectories, but might militate against use of the term development itself.[2]

But, as Foster-Carter (1978, 9–10) argues, the 'articulation' formulation largely remained an 'internal' account of the trajectory of a social formation, and, as some UCD scholars also emphasise (Anievas and Nişancioğlu 2015, 31), downplays the central role of coercion and violence in institutionalising capitalism across space. It also leaves us with an 'inside/outside' puzzle

(Foster-Carter 1978, 11, 14): Is capitalism transferred having been fully formed elsewhere, so that capitalism is exogenous to Third World social formations with their articulated modes as the 'deformed progeny'? Or are the social formations that emerge historically to be understood as 'relational and interactional', so that Trotsky's language of 'combination' becomes pertinent? Or is it somehow both? The internecine debates among UCD scholars seem to turn on a roughly similar 'inside-outside' issue of when and how something might be counted as 'combined' (Davidson, Buzan and Lawson, Allinson, Hobson and Anievas and Matin, all in this volume), including dissension over whether uneven and combined development is specific to capitalism.

Dipesh Chakrabarty's later intervention similarly resists Eurocentric historicism and, on this basis, merits reference in the editor's introduction. But we find a hint of a notably different ontological understanding. Chakrabarty (2000, 7, 29) indicts European historicism not simply as a misrepresentation of the facts of history or a mistaken theoretical conception, but as a force that 'enabled European domination' by placing the rest of the world into a position of backwardness relative to a purportedly universal Europe. In this reading, Marx himself is culpable in European domination given his characterisation of 'European history [as] an entelechy of universal reason'. But, Chakrabarty (2000, 47) reminds us, Marx and Marxist thought were central to the Subaltern Studies movement and, in parallel to the contributors to this volume, he attempts to recover some elements of Marxist historiography as a resource for the postcolonial project while resisting other Eurocentric formulations.

Chakrabarty re-reads Marx's historiographical reflections to indicate commitment to both a grand theory rooted in the logic of capital and sensitivity to the messier specificity of historical processes. He quotes Marx in *Grundrisse* (1973, 460–61) to suggest that the logic of capital points us also 'to the real history of the relations of production'—to 'empirical' realities 'which point towards a past lying behind this system'. We find here, Chakrabarty (2000, 63) claims, reference both to 'the universal and necessary history we associate with capital', forming 'the backbone of the usual narrative of transition to the capitalist mode of production', and moments of difference. Thus, a second and competing history opens us to different elements in the past: antecedent to capital, which might be part of a story of its ancestry but are not strictly necessary for the 'being' of capital (Chakrabarty 2000, 64).

It is not clear how much space Chakrabarty opens for 'alterity' or the 'multilinear' processes UCD wishes to recognise with this move. In somewhat tortured language and confirming our suspicion that alterity is about to be effaced, Chakrabarty (2000, 64) explains that the contemporary 'being' of capital faces elements of past societies that are not posited by capital in the form that they assume in its 'own life process'. These 'older forms' must be transformed, subjugated, converted or appended to (or into) the logic of capital. Social practices we may find in the present, that we might associate with capitalism, like the exploitation of unfree labour, are not necessarily 'central to capital's reproduction', yet they 'are not pasts separate from capital'. Rather, 'they inhere in capital and yet interrupt and punctuate the run of capital's own logic'.

The language of 'inhere in', 'interrupt', and 'punctuate' reinforces the temptation to override the details of history with the logic of capitalism. As Chakrabarty (2000, 65) stresses, the messy historical process of capital's 'becoming' need not 'be thought of as a process outside of and prior to its "being"'. Holding together the messy historical process of its becoming and its being destroys

> the usual topological distinction of the outside and the inside that marks debates about whether or not the whole world can be properly said to have fallen under the sway of capital. Difference, in this account, is not something external to capital. Nor is it something subsumed into capital. It lives in intimate and plural relation to capital. (Chakrabarty 2000, 65–6)

Where non- or a-capitalist elements cannot be relegated to the outside of the unit constituted by capitalism, they function within this 'combined' historical capitalism to constantly and only interrupt 'the totalising thrusts' of the 'being' of capital. Though the narrative of the logic of capital is thereby interrupted by the diversity of historical elements that make it up as a combined unit, as Chakrabarty also suggests, '[c]apital brings into every history some of the universal themes of the European Enlightenment'. The opening to a diversity of historical becoming is quite limited when this diversity always only works to 'modify' the totalising thrusts of the logic of capital (Chakrabarty 2000, 66–7, 70–1; see a similar critique in Matin 2013a, 363–5).

But what kind of space is there for difference or multilinear processes if the 'becoming' only modifies the being of capital? It seems that the dialectical unfolding of the logic of capital can be interrupted but not refused. In language we favour, this is a cultural encounter of modern capitalism and various other modes of life, the outcome and direction of which is already known, though the details of the transition to capitalism are messy.

BEYOND INTERSOCIETAL INTERACTIONS TO CULTURAL ENCOUNTERS

Contemporary UCD scholars also attempt to negotiate this inside/outside of capitalism problem, resisting formulations where 'the rest' seem only to modify capitalism's being or logic. Rosenberg (2013a, 2013b) and Hobson (2011 and this volume) translate this issue as a problem of Eurocentrism. Excessive emphasis on modes of production, particularly the distinctively 'combined' and 'uneven' complexly articulated capitalist social formations unfolding in various parts of the world, lends aid and comfort to Eurocentric scholars with their comparative methodological internalism. More precisely perhaps, emphasising the 'being' of capital, in Chakrabarty's terms, requires a 'logic of immanence' that trades in capitalism's 'exceptional qualities' (Hobson 2011, 154). With capitalism so centred, Europe appears as 'sui generis': 'capable of self-generated or independent auto-development' (Hobson 2011, 154). Recourse not to capitalism, but to 'human development' as our object of analysis (as in Hobson 2011 and this volume; Rosenberg 2013b; and Anievas and Nişancioğlu 2015) perhaps does inoculate us against placing non-Europeans outside of our historical narratives, since there seems no outside to human development.[3] Yet, it is unclear to us that attending to the *differentia specifica* of capitalism or modernity necessarily aids and abets Eurocentricism, as we shall suggest below. Resolving this inside/outside problem by displacing the logic of capitalism with the logic of human development is worrisome. What we see as cultural encounters of differing modes of life now appear as entangled in universal processes of human development, albeit with multilinear trajectories.[4]

We imagine a protest: Trotsky's UCD offers us a vision of a more-than-one ontology. We want to take that idea seriously and see where it leads us. When we restore extra-European forms of life to our stories, we find distinctly non-developmental cosmological visions. Some envision and reproduce the cosmos as cyclical. Others envision social life as marching backward to recover a harmony, now fractured by human oppressions (Shilliam 2015, introduction). Others may orient themselves around reproducing a minimally surplus-producing form of life (Blaney and Inayatullah 2010, chapter 6). James Tully (1993, 138–9) suggests that the modern 'problem space', defined by Locke and inherited by Marx, presumes a mode of political 'society' and advancing human productive capacities. Other forms of life are erased from our reckonings of human existence and hence suitably colonised and destroyed in the name of human advance. It is a small step to imagine the 'problem space' of human development as 'intersocietal' interactions.

Perhaps we (and Tully) nostalgically ignore that developmental processes go on behind the backs of our extra-European actors. But we do not ignore the interactions and mutual influences. Starting with the idea of more-than-one ontology leads us to highlight the centrality of cultural encounters: the possibilities of learning, but also of subordination, assimilation and destruction. Restoring these modes of life to our stories of cultural encounter also might be a protest against the way modern notions of development, including UCD in our estimation, assimilate all under their register, and how the processes or forces unleashed attempt to subordinate and destroy other forms of life in the name of development.[5]

Ashman (cited by Hobson 2011, 156) and Davidson (this volume) share this concern: embracing human development as the object of analysis risks missing the historical specificity of capitalist modernity. Perhaps different than them, we would stress the risk of missing the constitutive centrality of Eurocentrism in not only legitimating European dominance, but also in enabling capitalist modernity's assimilative and destructive project.[6] The language of 'combined' or 'uneven' hardly captures the constitutive impact of dividing of humanity into advanced and backward, universal and particular. Whether focusing its historical materialist lens on the unevenness of capitalism or human development as an uneven and combined process, we fear that the attempt to marry 'alterity' and 'development' puts UCD on capitalist modernity's side in cultural encounters. Indeed, its historical sensibility is itself a product of modernity (Lundborg 2016, 103–4, 110).

A different emphasis better captures the constitutive or enabling role of modernity/colonialism/capitalist and its creative, violent and fracturing consequences. Robbie Shilliam's article on the 'Atlantic Vector', though cited by the editors as within the UCD tradition, is remarkably diffident. Like UCD, his move to make Atlantic slavery central to any discussion of the 'differentiation of European and Western hemispheric trajectories' replaces a story of the 'rise of capitalism, nation, and class within England or Europe' with a deep appreciation of the 'international sociality' at the heart of New World social formations and identities (Shilliam 2009a, 72). But he resists embracing UCD's rather abstract grand narrative, opting instead for regionally grounded and more penetrating notion of 'creolization': more 'organically linked to Atlantic slavery', more attuned to the specific political grammar, forms of social organisation and racial meta-identities involved and, therefore a 'more apposite concept for exploring New world development' (Shilliam 2009a, 71, 83). His survey of the rich literature on Atlantic slavery suggests that the 'international sociality' constituted by Atlantic slavery might lead us to see a 'combined' space, but that this was a 'paradoxical and frictional union' (Shilliam 2009a, 83).

Read in relation to his later work, we might read this interconnection less as a combined process of human development, however tension-filled our notion of development might be, and more as a process both of cultural erasure and destruction and the establishment of a new, hierarchically structured modern order. Shilliam (2015, chapter 1) describes the modern era wrought by colonialism as establishing a fundamental breach or fracture in human relationality: Europeans and their modern science locate them in a position separate from (outside and above) the others they can know and presume to govern. The consequences of this act of separation includes the relations of power and production we might characterise as combined and uneven development, but these are intertwined with a deep fracturing of human relationality—a violence at once epistemological and ontological.[7]

Drawing on Shilliam's terms, we would argue that a distinctive modern/capitalist political and economic grammar coalesces in certain sites in Western Europe (though not autonomously or without Eastern influences to be sure) and in relation to broader spaces beyond Europe. This political and economic grammar works to fragment the world by effacing other grammars and social relations and subjecting people and peoples within Europe and beyond to systems of domination. To translate into terms we have used elsewhere, we understand capitalism as cultural, political economy as cultural political economy, and interaction as cultural encounter, offering myriad possibilities of violence and subjugation, assimilation, complicity, and, we hope, mutual learning (Inayatullah and Blaney 2004; Blaney and Inayatullah 2010). And we would stress, along with Shilliam (we believe) and Chakrabarty that these colonial/capitalist political and economic grammars are not simply false explanations or representations but practices of knowledge central to and constitutive of cultural encounters as moments of learning and violence.

It is worthy and helpful to denaturalise the Eurocentrism of IR by widening the frame so that it incorporates the extra-European. But if we widen the frame by embracing 'human development', we downplay and potentially reinforce the very practices of exclusion and erasure central to notions of development that made modern cultural encounters so violent and destructive. A different sort of engagement seems to be required if IR is to be cultivated as a deeper anti-colonial practice. This engagement would not displace into the past those effaced by the cultural encounters that constitute modernity—as superseded by capitalist or human development. Rather, these visions and traditions would be available as sources of historical understanding, as contributions to political and ethical reflection in the present and as alternative possibilities as we imagine how we might live in relation with others.

NOTES

1. We make this case in Inayatullah and Blaney (2004) and Blaney and Inayatullah (2010).

2. This reading resonates with authors like Nederveen Pieterse and Arturo Escobar, referenced in the introduction, as critiques of Eurocentric scholarships, but not as critics of developmental cosmologies.

3. Others like Davidson (this volume) challenge the extension of the logic of uneven and combined development to any social forms beyond capitalism. Though,

as the editors have warned us, there are a range of formulations possible within the frame of UCD, including the idea that particular modes of production produce their own 'historically-bound forms and dynamics of UCD', our impulse is to resist any invocation of the idea of 'human development'.

4. Lundborg (2016, 103–4, 110, 113–14) lays something like this charge at the feet of historical sociologists, including those who protest against Eurocentric histories. Brown's answer (this volume) to a similar charge from Bhambra (2011) illustrates the way that multilinear trajectories of development are substituted for a simple stage theory without, however, displacing a generally modernist claim that history has a developmental direction.

5. Our sense is that the 'savage' serves as the constitutive outside of human development (see Blaney and Inayatullah 2010). Rosenberg's efforts (2010, 171–75) to place hunting and foraging societies within UCD largely confirms our sense. Hunting and gathering societies move towards the 'international' only when processes of vertical stratification and differentiation are unleashed. And still these moves beyond hunting and gathering bands are 'many steps' removed from an '"international" political system'.

6. See, however, Anievas and Nişancioğlu 2015, 123–9.

7. Note the resemblance to the critique of the coloniality of power and knowledge found in Escobar (2012) and Quijano (2007).

Conclusion

Rethinking Historical Sociology and World History

Beyond the Eurocentric Gaze

Alexander Anievas and Kamran Matin

Historical sociology and world history are distinct academic fields with a shared concern for large-scale historical processes of social transformation. Historical sociology has focused on providing 'historically sensitive, yet generally applicable' accounts of the emergence of capitalist industrial societies, or capitalist modernity more generally (Hobson, Lawson, Rosenberg 2010, 1). World history, especially since its rebirth in the late twentieth century, has in turn sought to 'establish a historical context for the integrated and interdependent world of modern times' (Bentley cited in Mazlish 1998, 386). Moreover, both frameworks partly emerged as a reaction to the nationalist and comparative methodologies of their home-disciplines of sociology and comparative history from which they have self-differentiated.

Yet, despite the similarity of historical sociology and world history's intellectual genesis and the significant overlap between their basic analytical concerns, there remains relatively little dialogue and explicit intellectual exchange between the two fields. One obvious reason for this mutual neglect is the scepticism that the practitioners of world history, like all historians, tend to have towards the types of grand-scale theory characteristic of historical sociology. However, there is arguably a deeper reason for this disconnect between historical sociology and world history. It concerns different conceptions of 'the international' in the two fields.

As an internally diverse research programme, historical sociology's intellectual vocation closely resonates with the tradition of classical sociology more broadly. That tradition anchored its theory of modern social orders in a dialectically configured tripartite framework consisting of (social) *structure*, *history* and *totality*. The basic premise is that human agency, its possibilities and constraints, and hence the results of its conduct, are shaped by their necessary implications in specific configurations of social relations and political orders, which themselves are historically congealed constellations of prior exercises of human agency (*structure*); that these structures are intrinsically historical in that they both differ in, and change over, time (*history*); and that an adequate account of the historical evolution of human societies ought to avoid compartmentalising social reality involved in the modern disciplinary division of knowledge. For the real-world referents of disciplinary sciences are organically and intrinsically interrelated (*totality*) (Rosenberg 2016, 295–96).

Thus, the epithet 'historical' in historical sociology arguably indicates a restorative reaction to contemporary sociology's shift towards more abstract and ahistorical forms of theorisation which deviated from classical sociology's original intellectual project (e.g. Parsons 1991). Indeed, this was the circumstance to which historical sociology emerged as a response in the 1970s and 1980s. While in this early stage historical sociology sought to expand upon classical sociology's historical and spatial scope, in part by moving beyond the methodological internalism of that tradition, it largely rested on a proto-realist conception of states and geopolitics (e.g. Skocpol 1979; Mann 1986; Tilly 1992). Later, during the 1990s and early 2000s, historical sociology emerged at the critical fringes of disciplinary International Relations (IR) as an explicit critique of realist IR's reification and fetishisation of 'the international' demonstrating the variety of historically distinct forms of international relations, which was in turn derived from spatio-temporally specific forms of social structures (e.g. Rosenberg 1994; Spruyt 1994; Teschke 2003). Thus, the *fin de siècle* historical sociology not only challenged contemporary sociology but also involved an indirect critique of its immediate precursor.

It is however the most recent contributions to historical sociology that have laid the fundamental intellectual foundations for a mutually beneficial dialogue with world history, a goal with which this volume has been centrally concerned. For these latest works of historical sociology in IR have been seeking to complete the dialectics of the earlier literature's focus on the social substratum of international relations by demonstrating the causal and constitutive significance of 'the international' for the rise and development of specific social orders. To this end, uneven and combined development has emerged as an important intellectual idiom in which this latest strand of historical sociology has been articulated.[1] For as the contributions to this volume have shown in their different ways, the framework of uneven and combined development involves an explicit theoretical and methodological recognition and comprehension of 'the international' as a distinct but organic dimension of the social world.

Crucially, the plural and relational ontology that underpins uneven and combined development both resonates with the key concerns of world history and addresses its main limitations: namely, Eurocentrism and methodological imprecision. For even though contemporary world history was a reaction to the universalist assumptions of earlier approaches to world history, which constructed their basic categories by extrapolating from the European experience, much of the literature has nevertheless not been able to fully overcome the problem of Eurocentrism at its source; with some approaches even partially reproducing it through an insufficiently radical break from civilisational analysis in which western civilisation supplied the 'ideal types' through which other civilisations were studied (Gran 1996; McNeill 1995; Geyer and Bright 1995). This Eurocentric tendency was reinforced by the new world history's focus on 'trans-civilizational' phenomena as opposed to 'inter-societal' ones. The former, it must be noted, arise *despite* societal multiplicity while the latter occur *because of* it. This focus therefore reproduced the 'diffusionist' analytical trope of earlier forms of world history, which methodologically downplayed the role of violent encounters and confrontations in history, a circumstance that reached unprecedented levels with the emergence of colonialism and capitalist modernity.

The centrality to world history of the concept of civilisation—broadly understood as a culturally shaped 'style of life'—also involved the problem of methodological imprecision (McNeill 1995, 16). For 'civilization'—the central unit of analysis for much of existing scholarship on world history—remains conceptually inchoate: it is socioculturally diverse and politically conflictual internally, and spatially amorphous externally. This problem underpins a number of key and still unresolved questions regarding the spatial delimitations of cultures and civilisations. William McNeill has sought to address this problem by positing the 'common subjections to rulers' (McNeill 1995, 16) as the fundamental integrative element of civilisations as internally diverse units. This overtly political conception of civilisation brings world history close to historical sociology. However, the methodological value-added of this move is diluted by some world history approaches' loyalty to an 'ecumenical' global analytical framework. Indeed, as the editors of a major work on world history note, 'the lust for coverage is world history's deadliest sin and has constantly to be restrained' (Embree and Gluck 1997, xvii). While it would be surely haphazard to claim that *all* of contemporary world history remains trapped within the Eurocentric cage given the wealth of recent studies explicitly seeking to break with Eurocentrism (see, *inter alia,* Gran 1996; Bayly 2004), the intellectual sources of the problem nonetheless persist.

There are, of course, no easy solutions to such a deeply engrained, political and institutionalised dilemma. Yet, we argue that the framework of uneven and combined development can provide a theoretical 'first-step' to address these problems. It confronts the issue of Eurocentrism by replacing classical sociology's ontologically singular conception of the social with a plural social ontology, which has radical implications for the mode of concept formation and method of explanation. Uneven and combined development also provides a methodological procedure that unites the advantages of a holistic perspective with the methodological rigour of historical sociology. This is so because the three constitutive elements of the approach are invested with distinct yet interrelated methodological functions: 'unevenness' directs attention to both the wider conjunction of different developmental temporalities and dynamics in which the society under investigation, or a given feature thereof, is implicated, and the specific historical pressures, constraints and opportunities that this circumstance generates; 'combination' highlights the particular sociological fusions that arises from this intersocietal condition; and 'development' foregrounds the distinct dynamics of socio-historical change that results from these two interactive circumstances (Rosenberg in this volume). In other words, uneven and combined development dialectically supplants the Eurocentric universalist terms of traditional world history approaches and the particularistic assumptions of classical sociology through a strategic theoretical and analytical emphasis on 'the international'. And it does so by recasting social contexts as 'neither bounded to a particular society, nor universal in scope, but rather delineated in and through a specific society's interaction with other, differentially developed societies' (Shilliam 2009b, 5). To varying degrees of systematicity and explicitness, this intellectual position is discernible in all the contributions to this volume.

In conclusion, we would like to emphasise that while we believe uneven and combined development is a highly fertile and vital research programme we are also keenly aware that it is also a young project and will definitely benefit from further reflexive engagements and critical refinement. For instance, a recurrent criticism of the contemporary IR literature on uneven and combined development has been that it is too abstract and preoccupied with (meta)theoretical questions (Teschke 2014). Addressing this issue is a key aim of this volume. But there are also more substantive issues such as the normative and political dimensions of uneven and combined development raised by David Blaney and Naeem Inayatullah in the last chapter. And, indeed, the precise political and normative implications of uneven and combined development are a significant topic in need of much further debate and discussion.[2]

Moreover, while it would be incorrect to criticise uneven and combined development as intrinsically antithetical to analytically capturing and articulating agential processes (cf. Teschke 2014)—as many of the above contributions well demonstrate—a more direct engagement with the question of precisely how 'lived agency' relates to structure in different historical epochs from the perspective of uneven and combined development is a promising avenue for future research. So too is the issue of whether uneven and combined development entails a distinct approach to history-writing itself: a unique way of thinking about history as a particular 'form of knowledge and experience' which, in different times and places, provides differential frameworks for conceiving the relations between past, present and future, as well as demarcations in time and space (Davenport 2016, 263). For if historical consciousness can be said to constitute, as Andrew Davenport suggests (2016), a distinctively modern form of the relationship to 'the past' itself inextricably tied to the rise of modern sovereign authorities—and thus by extension the fractured space of 'the international'—then what might the framework of uneven and combined development mean for critical reflecting upon the *(geo)political meaning* of history in rethinking the relation of past, present and future?

While this volume has been oriented around an engagement *with* history, perhaps the next step is a critique *of* history, to which we believe the perspective of uneven and combined development might indeed prove useful. In one way or another, we hope that this volume can act as catalyst for further critical and constructive debate around the various issues raised here and throughout the volume in opening up new and exciting avenues for future research.

NOTES

1. For an extensive bibliography visit www.unevenandcombined.com.
2. For a brief discussion of some of these issues, see Anievas and Nişancioğlu (2015, 274–82).

Bibliography

Abou-El-Haj, Rifaat Ali. 1991. *Formation of the Modern State: The Ottoman Empire Sixteenth to Eighteenth Centuries*. New York: SUNY Press.

Abu-Lughod, Janet L. 1989. *Before European Hegemony: The World System A.D. 1250–1350*. Oxford: Oxford University Press.

Adas, Michael. 1990. *Machines as the Measure of Men: Science, Technology and Ideologies of Western Dominance*. Ithaca: Cornell University Press.

Adelman, Jeremy. 1992. "The Social Bases of Technical Change: Mechanisation of the Wheatlands of Argentina and Canada, 1890 to 1914." *Comparative Studies in Society and History* 3(2): 271–300.

Adelman, Jeremy. 1994. *Frontier Development: Land, Labour, and Capital on the Wheatlands of Argentina and Canada, 1890–1914*. Oxford: Oxford University Press.

Allen, Chris. 1995. "Understanding African Politics." *Review of African Political Economy* 22(65): 301–20.

Allinson, Jamie. 2016. *The Struggle for the State in Jordan: The Social Origins of Alliances in the Middle East*. London: I.B. Tauris.

Allinson, Jamie C. and Alexander Anievas. 2010a. "The Uneven and Combined Development of the Meiji Restoration: A Passive Revolutionary Road to Capitalist Modernity." *Capital & Class* 34(3): 469–90.

Allinson, Jamie C. and Alexander Anievas. 2010b. "Approaching the 'International': Beyond Political Marxism." In *Marxism and World Politics: Contesting Global Capitalism*, edited by Alexander Anievas, 197–214. London: Routledge.

Allinson, Jamie C. and Alexander Anievas. 2009. "The Uses and Misuses of Uneven and Combined Development: An Anatomy of a Concept." *Cambridge Review of International Affairs* 22(1): 47–67.

Ambrosius, Lloyd E. 2002. *Wilsonianism*. Houndmills: Palgrave Macmillan.

Amin, Samir. 1976. *Unequal Development: An Essay on the Social Formations of Peripheral Capitalism*. New York: Monthly Review Press.

257

Amin, Samir. 1989. *Eurocentrism.* London: Zed Books.

Amin, Samir. 2011. *Global History: A View from the South.* Cape Town: Pambazuka Press.

Amitai, Reuven. 2010. "Armies and Their Economic Basis in Iran and the Surrounding Lands, c. 1000–1500." In *The New Cambridge History of Islam*, edited by David O. Morgan and Anthony Reid, 539–60. Cambridge: Cambridge University Press.

Anderson, Benedict. 1991. *Imagined Communities: The Origin and Spread of Nationalism.* London: Verso.

Anderson, Perry. 1996 [1974]. *Passages from Antiquity to Feudalism.* London: Verso.

Anderson, Perry. 1992. English Questions. London: Verso.

Anderson, Perry. 1984. "Modernity and Revolution." *New Left Review* I/144: 96–113.

Anderson, Perry. 1976–1977. "The Antinomies of Antonio Gramsci." *New Left Review* I/100: 1–78.

Anderson, Perry. 1976. *Considerations on Western Marxism.* London: New Left Books.

Anderson, Perry. 1974. *Lineages of the Absolutist State.* London: New Left Books.

Anievas, Alexander and Kerem Nişancioğlu. 2013. "What's at Stake in the Transition Debate? Rethinking the Origins of Capitalism and the 'Rise of the West'." *Millennium: Journal of International Studies* 42(1): 78–102.

Anievas, Alexander and Kerem Nişancioğlu. 2015. *How the West Came to Rule: The Geopolitical Origins of Capitalism.* London: Pluto Press.

Anievas, Alexander, ed. 2010. *Marxism and World Politics: Contesting Global Capitalism.* London: Routledge.

Anievas, Alexander. 2013. "1914 in World Historical Perspective: The 'Uneven' and 'Combined' Origins of the First World War." *European Journal of International Relations* 19(4): 721–46.

Anievas, Alexander. 2014a. *Capital, the State, and War: Class Conflict and Geopolitics in the Thirty Years' Crisis, 1914–1945.* Ann Arbor: University of Michigan Press.

Anievas, Alexander. 2014b. "International Relations between War and Revolution: Wilsonian Diplomacy and the Making of the Treaty of Versailles." *International Politics* 51(5): 619–47.

Anon. 1783. *Consequences (Not before Adverted to): That Are Likely to Result from the Late Revolution of the British Empire.* London: Printed for the author and sold by G. Wilkie, Debrett, Walter.

Armstrong, W. 1985. "The Social Origins of Industrial Growth: Canada, Argentina and Australia, 1870–1930." In *Argentina, Australia and Canada: Studies in Comparative Development 1870–1965*, edited by D.C.M. Platt and Guido di Tella, 76–94. London: The Macmillan Press Ltd.

Arnold, Jeanne, ed. 2004. *Foundations of Chumash Complexity. Perspectives in California Archaeology, Volume 7.* Los Angeles: Cotsen Institute.

Arrighi, Giovanni, Iftikhar Ahmad and Miin-wen Shih. 1999. "Western Hegemonies in Historical Perspective." In *Chaos and Governance in the Modern World System*, edited by Giovanni Arrighi and Beverly J. Silver, 217–70. Minneapolis: University of Minnesota Press.

Arrighi, Giovanni, Takeshi Hamashita, and Mark Selden. 2003. *The Resurgence of East Asia: 500, 150 and 50 Year Perspectives*. London: Routledge.

Arrighi, Giovanni. 2007a. "Globalization and Uneven Development". In *Frontiers of Globalization Research: Theoretical and Methodological Approaches*, edited by Ino Rossi, 185–201. New York, NY: Springer.

Arrighi, Giovanni. 2007b. *Adam Smith in Beijing*. London: Verso.

Arrighi, Giovanni. 2009. "China's Market Economy in the Long-Run." In *China and the Transformation of Global Capitalism*, edited by Ho-Fung Hung, 22–49. Baltimore: Johns Hopkins University Press.

Ashman, Sam. 2009. "Capitalism, Uneven and Combined Development and the Transhistoric." *Cambridge Review of International Affairs* 22(1): 29–46.

Ashman, Sam. 2010. "Capitalism, Uneven and Combined Development and the Transhistoric." In *Marxism and World Politics: Contesting Global Capitalism*, edited by Alexander Anievas, 183–96. London: Routledge.

Avcıoğlu, Doğan. 1968. *Türkiye'nin Düzeni [The Structure of Turkish Society]*. Ankara: Bilgi.

Avery, D. 1979. *Dangerous Foreigners: European Immigrant Workers and Labour Radicalism in Canada, 1896–1932*. Toronto: McClelland and Stewart.

Babones, Salvatore J. 2005 "The Country-Level Income Structure of the World Economy." *Journal of World-Systems Research* 11(1): 29–55.

Bacon, Francis. 1960. *The New Organon and Related Writings,* edited and introduced by Fulton H. Anderson. New York: Bobbs-Merrill.

Bailey, Anne M. and Josep R. Llobera. 1981. *The Asiatic Mode of Production: Science and Politics*. London: Routledge.

Balsvik, Randi Rønning. 1985. *Haile Selassie's Students: The Intellectual and Social Background to Revolution, 1952–1977*. East Lansing: African Studies Center, Michigan State University.

Banaji, Jairus. 2011. *Theory as History: Essays on Modes of Production and Exploitation*. Chicago: Haymarket.

Barder, Owen. 2012a. "David Cameron's 'Golden Thread' Theory of Development Is a Little Too Convenient." *The Guardian*, 27 August. Accessed 19 November 2015. http://www.theguardian.com/global-development/poverty-matters/2012/aug/27/david-cameron-development-theory-convenient.

Barder, Owen. 2012b. "Complexity, Adaptation and Results." *Centre for Global Development Blog*, 9 July. Accessed 19 November 2015. http://www.cgdev.org/blog/complexity-adaptation-and-results.

Barkawi, Tarak and Mark Laffey. 2006. "The Postcolonial Moment in Security Studies." *Review of International Studies* 32(2): 329–52.

Barkawi, Tarak. 2006. *Globalization and War*. Lanham: Rowman & Littlefield.

Barker, Colin. 2006. "Beyond Trotsky: Extending Combined and Uneven Development." In *100 Years of Permanent Revolution: Results and Prospects*, edited by Bill Dunn and Hugo Radice, 72–87. London: Pluto.

Barkey, Karen. 2008. *Empire of Difference: The Ottomans in Comparative Perspective*. Cambridge: Cambridge University Press.

Barnes, Gina L. 2001. *State Formation in Korea*. Richmond: Curzon Press.

Bartusis, Mark C. 1997. *The Late Byzantine Army: Arms and Society, 1204–1453.* Philadelphia: University of Pennsylvania Press.

Batatu, Hanna. 1978. *The Old Social Classes and the Revolutionary Movements of Iraq: A Study of Iraq's Old Landed Classes and of Its Communists, Ba'thists, and Free Officers.* Princeton: Princeton University Press.

Bauman, Zygmunt. 1992. *Intimations of Postmodernity.* London: Routledge.

Bayly, Christopher A. 2004. *The Birth of the Modern World, 1780–1914.* Oxford: Blackwell.

Bayly, Richard. 1896. "Diary of Colonel Bayly: 12th Regiment. 1796–1830." The Army and Navy Co-operative Society. Accessed 28 December 2015. http://archive.org/details/diarycolonelbay00baylgoog.

Be'eri, Eliezer. 1970. *Army Officers in Arab Politics and Society.* London: Praeger.

Beaujard, Phillippe. 2005. "The Indian Ocean in Eurasian and African World-Systems Before the Sixteenth Century." *Journal of World History* 16(4): 411–65.

Bendix, Richard. 1967. "Tradition and Modernity Reconsidered." *Studies in Comparative Society and History* 9(3): 292–346.

Benjamin, Walter. 1969. *Illuminations: Essays and Reflections.* London: Schocken Books.

Bergesen, Albert J. 2013. "The New Surgical Colonialism: China, Africa and Oil." In *Sociology and Empire,* edited by George Steinmetz, 300–18. Durham: Duke University Press.

Berki, R.N. 1971. "On Marxian Thought and the Problem of International Relations." *World Politics* 24(1): 80–105.

Berktay, Halil. 1987. "The Feudalism Debate: The Turkish End—Is 'Tax – vs. – Rent' Necessarily the Product and Sign of a Modal Difference?" *Journal of Peasant Studies* 14 (3): 291–333.

Berktay, Halil. 1990. *The 'Other' Feudalism: A Critique of 20th Century Turkish Historiography and Its Particularisation of Ottoman Society.* Birmingham: University of Birmingham.

Bernard, William Dallas. 1844a. *Narrative of the Voyages and Services of the Nemesis, from 1840 to 1843, Volume 1.* London: H. Colburn.

Bernard, William Dallas. 1844b. *Narrative of the Voyages and Services of the Nemesis, from 1840 to 1843, Volume 2.* London: H. Colburn.

Bertram, Christopher. 1990. "International Competition in Historical Materialism." *New Left Review* 183: 116–28.

Bhabha, Homi. 1994. *The Location of Culture.* London: Routledge.

Bhambra, Gurminder K. 2011. "Talking among Themselves? Weberian and Marxist Historical Sociologies as Dialogues without 'Others'." *Millennium: Journal of International Studies* 39(3): 667–81.

Bhambra, Gurminder K. 2010. "Historical Sociology, International Relations and Connected Histories." *Cambridge Review of International Affairs* 23(1): 127–43.

Bhambra, Gurminder K. 2007. *Rethinking Modernity: Postcolonialism and the Sociological Imagination.* Houndmills: Palgrave Macmillan.

Bieler, Andreas, Ian Bruff and Adam David Morton. 2015. "Antonio Gramsci and 'the International': Past, Present and Future." In *Antonio Gramsci,* edited by Mark McNally, 137–55. London: Palgrave Macmillan.

Bigo, Didier and R.B.J. Walker. 2007. "Political Sociology and the Problem of the International." *Millennium: Journal of International Studies* 35(3): 725–39.

Blair, Tony. 2001. "Speech to Labour Party Conference 2 October 2001, Brighton." *The Guardian*, 2 October. Accessed 21 November 2015. http://politics.guardian. co.uk/speeches/story/0,11126,590775,00.html.

Blaney, David L. and Naeem Inayatullah. 2010. *Savage Economics: Wealth, Poverty, and the Temporal Walls of Capitalism*. London: Routledge.

Blaut, James M. 1993. *The Colonizer's Model of the World*. London: Guilford.

Blaut, James M. 2000. *Eight Eurocentric Historians*. London: Guilford.

Bloch, Marc. 1961. *Feudal Society, Volume I*. Chicago: Chicago University Press.

Bocco, Ricardo and Tariq M.M. Tell. 1994. "*Pax Britannica* in the Steppe: British Policy and the Transjordanian Bedouin." In *Village, Steppe and State: The Social Origins of Modern Jordan*, edited by Eugene L. Rogan and Tariq M.M. Tell, 108–27. London: British Academic Press.

Bois, Guy. 1985 [1978]. "Against the Neo-Malthusian Orthodoxy." In *The Brenner Debate: Agrarian Class Structure and Economic Development in Pre-Industrial Europe*, edited by T.H. Aston and C.H.E. Philpin, 107–18. Cambridge: Cambridge University Press.

Bond, Patrick, ed. 2013a. *BRICS in Africa: Anti-imperialist, Sub-Imperialist or in Between?* Durban: Centre for Civil Society, University of Kwa-Zulu-Natal.

Bond, Patrick, ed. 2013b. "BRICS: 'Anti-imperialist' or Sub-Imperialist'?" *Links: International Journal of Socialist Renewal*. Accessed 7 April 2016. http://links. org.au/node/3265#_ftnref18.

Boratav, Korkut. 1983. *Bölüşüm Sorunları ve İktisat Politikaları [Problems of Economic Distribution and Economy Policies]*. Istanbul: Belge Yayınları.

Bosworth, Edmund. 2010. "The Steppe Peoples in the Islamic World." In *The New Cambridge History of Islam*, edited by David O. Morgan and Anthony Reid, 19–77. Cambridge: Cambridge University Press.

Bozeman, Ada. 1994. *Politics and Culture in International History: From the Ancient Near East to the Opening of the Modern Age*. New Brunswick: Transaction Publishers.

Brennan, Timothy. 2014. *Borrowed Light, Volume I: Vico, Hegel, and the Colonies*. Stanford: Stanford University Press.

Brenner, Robert. 1985. "Agrarian Class Structure and Economic Development in Pre-Industrial Europe." In *The Brenner Debate: Agrarian Class Structure and Economic Development in Pre-Industrial Europe*, edited by T.H. Aston and C.H.E. Philpin, 10–63. Cambridge: Cambridge University Press.

Brenner, Robert. 1982. "The Agrarian Roots of European Capitalism." *Past and Present* 97: 16–113.

Brenner, Robert. 1976. "Agrarian Class Structure and Economic Development in Pre-Industrial Europe." *Past & Present* 70: 30–75.

Brewer, Anthony. 1990. *Marxist Theories of Imperialism: A Critical Survey*. London: Routledge, 2nd Edition.

Brittlebank, Kate. 2003. "Tales of Treachery: Rumour as the Source of Claims that Tipu Sultan Was Betrayed." *Modern Asian Studies* 37(1): 195–211.

Bromley, Simon. 1994. *Rethinking Middle East Politics: State Formation and Development*. Cambridge: Polity Press.

Brown, William. 2013. "Sovereignty Matters: Africa, Donors and the Aid Relationship." *African Affairs* 112(447): 262–82.

Brown, William. 2009. "Reconsidering the Aid Relationship: International Relations and Social Development." *The Round Table* 98(402): 285–301.

Brown, William. 2006. "The Commission for Africa: Results and Prospects for the West's Africa Policy." *Journal of Modern African Studies* 44(3): 349–74.

Bulcha, Mekuria. 1988. *Flight and Integration: Causes of Mass Exodus from Ethiopia and Problems of Integration in the Sudan*. Uppsala: Institute of African Studies African Studies.

Bull, Hedley. 1966. "Society and Anarchy in International Relations." In *Diplomatic Investigations*, edited by Herbert Butterfield and Martin Wight, 35–50. London: Allen and Unwin.

Burawoy, Michael. 1989. "Two Methods in Search of Science: Skocpol versus Trotsky." *Theory and Society* 18(6): 759–805.

Burawoy, Michael. 1985. *The Politics of Production: Factory Regimes under Capitalism and Socialism*. London: Verso.

Burckhardt, Jacob. 1990 [1860]. *The Civilization of the Renaissance in Italy*. London: Penguin.

Buzan, Barry and George Lawson. 2015. *The Global Transformation: History, Modernity and the Making of International Relations*. Cambridge: Cambridge University Press.

Buzan, Barry and George Lawson. 2014a. "Capitalism and the Emergent World Order." *International Affairs* 90(1): 71–91.

Buzan, Barry and George Lawson. 2014b. "Rethinking Benchmark Dates in International Relations." *European Journal of International Relations* 20(2): 437–62.

Buzan, Barry and Richard Little. 2000. *International Systems in World History: Remaking the Study of International Relations*. Oxford: Oxford University Press.

Cahen, Claude. 2001. *The Formation of Turkey: The Seljukid Sultanate of Rūm, Eleventh to Fourteenth Century*. Essex: Longman.

Cahen, Claude. 1968. *Pre-Ottoman Turkey: A General Survey of the Material and Spiritual Culture and History, c. 1071–1330*. London: Sidgwick & Jackson.

Calhoun, Craig. 1982. *The Question of Class Struggle: Social Foundations of Popular Radicalism during the Industrial Revolution*. Chicago: University of Chicago Press.

Callinicos, Alex. 2010. "The Limits of Passive Revolution." *Capital and Class* 34(3): 491–507.

Callinicos, Alex. 2007. "Does Capitalism Need the State System?" *Cambridge Review of International Affairs* 20(4): 533–49.

Callinicos, Alex and Justin Rosenberg. 2010. "Uneven and Combined Development: The Social-Relational Substratum of 'the International'? – An Exchange of Letters." In *Marxism and World Politics*, edited by Alexander Anievas, 149–82. London: Routledge.

Cameron, David. 2005. "New Hope for Britain. New Hope for the World." Speech to the Centre for Policy Studies, London, 8 November. Accessed 22 November 2015. http://conservative-speeches.sayit.mysociety.org/speech/600212.

Cameron, David. 2012. "Transcript of David Cameron's Q&A at New York University." New York University, 15 May. Accessed 22 November 2015. https://www.gov. uk/government/speeches/transcript-of-david-cameron-qa-at-new-york-university.

Carmody, Padraig. 2011. *The New Scramble for Africa*. Cambridge: Polity.

Carothers, Thomas and Diane de Gramont. 2013. *Development Aid Confronts Politics: The Almost Revolution*. Washington DC: Carnegie Endowment for International Peace.

Césaire, Aimé. 1972. *Discourse on Colonialism*. New York: Monthly Review Press.

Chakrabarty, Dipesh. 2000. *Provincializing Europe: Postcolonial Thought and Historical Difference*. Princeton: Princeton University.

Chaliand, Gérard. 2006. *Nomadic Empires: From Mongolia to the Danube*. London: Transaction Publishers.

Chase-Dunn, Christopher. 2013. "BRICS and A Potentially Progressive Semiperiphery." Accessed 7 April 2016. http://www.pambazuka.org/governance/brics-and-potentially-progressive-semi-periphery.

Chase-Dunn, Christopher, Alessandro Morosin, and Alexis Álvarez. 2015. "Social Movements and Progressive Regimes in Latin America: World Revolutions and Semiperipheral Development". In *Handbook of Social Movements across Latin America*, edited by Paul D. Almeida and Allen Cordero, 13–24. Dordrecht: Springer.

Chase-Dunn, Christopher and Bruce Lerro. 2014. *Social Change: From the Stone Age to the Present*. Boulder: Paradigm Publishers.

Chase-Dunn, Christopher, Roy Kwon, Kirk Lawrence and Hiroko Inoue. 2011. "Last of the Hegemons: U.S. Decline and Global Governance." *International Review of Modern Sociology* 37(1): 1–29.

Chase-Dunn, Christopher and Kelly Mann. 1998. *The Wintu and Their Neighbors: A Very Small World-System in Northern California*. Tucson: University of Arizona Press.

Chase-Dunn, Christopher and Thomas D. Hall. 1997. *Rise and Demise: Comparing World-Systems*. Boulder: Westview Press.

Chatterjee, Partha. 2013. "Marxism and the Legacy of Subaltern Studies." Paper presented at *Historical Materialism* Conference, New York, NY, 26–28 April. Accessed 4 April 2016. https://www.youtube.com/watch?v=xbM8HJrxSJ4.

Chernilo, Daniel. 2010. "Methodological Nationalism and the Domestic Analogy: Classical Resources for Their Critique." *Cambridge Review of International Affairs* 23(1): 87–106.

Cheynet, Jean-Claude. 2006. *The Byzantine Aristocracy and Its Military Function*. Aldershot: Ashgate Pub.

Chŏn Sŏktam. 1949. *Chosŏn kyŏngjesa* [Economic History of Chosŏn]. Seoul: Pangmun ch'ulp'ansa.

Christian, David. 2004. *Maps of Time: An Introduction to Big History*. Berkeley: University of California Press.

Christie, James and Nesrin Degirmencioglu, eds. 2016. *Cultures of Uneven and Combined Development*. Leiden: Brill, forthcoming.

Chrysostomides, Julian. 2009. "The Byzantine Empire from the Eleventh to the Fifteenth Century." In *Cambridge History of Islam, Volume I*, edited by Kate Fleet, 6–50. Cambridge: Cambridge University Press.

Cohn, Bernard S. 1996. *Colonialism and Its Forms of Knowledge: The British in India*. Princeton: Princeton University Press.

Commission for Africa. 2005. *Our Common Interest: Report of the Commission for Africa*. London: Commission for Africa.

Congreve, Sir William Lieut Col. 1827. *A Treatise on the General Principles, Powers, and Facility of Application of the Congreve Rocket System, as Compared with Artillery (etc.)*. London: Longman.

Cooper, Frederick. 2014. *Africa in the World: Capitalism, Empire, Nation-State*. Cambridge: Harvard University Press.

Cooper, Frederick. 2002. *Africa Since 1940: The Past of the Present*. Cambridge: Cambridge University Press.

Cooper, Frederick and Randall Packard, eds. 1997. *International Development and the Social Sciences: Essays on the History and Politics of Knowledge*. Berkeley: University of California Press.

Cooper, Luke. 2013. "Can Contingency Be 'Internalised' into the Bounds of Theory? Critical Realism, the Philosophy of Internal Relations, and the Solution of 'Uneven and Combined Development'." *Cambridge Review of International Affairs* 26(3): 573–97.

Cooper, Luke. 2015. "The International Relations of the 'Imagined Community': Explaining the Late Nineteenth-century Genesis of the Chinese Nation." *Review of International Studies* 41(3): 477–501.

Cotterell, Arthur. 2009. *Western Power in Asia: Its Slow Rise and Swift Fall, 1415–1999*. Singapore: John Wiley & Sons.

Crossley, Pamela Kyle. 2010. *The Wobbling Pivot, China since 1800: An Interpretive History*. Chichester: John Wiley & Sons.

Crossley, Pamela Kyle. 1991. *Orphan Warriors: Three Manchu Generation and the End of the Qing World*. Princeton: Princeton University Press.

Crummey, Donald. 2000. *Land and Society in the Christian Kingdom of Ethiopia: From the Thirteenth to Twentieth Century*. Urbana: University of Illinois Press.

Dabashi, Hamid. 2006. *Theology of Discontent: The Ideological Foundation of the Islamic Republic in Iran*. New Brunswick: Transaction Publishers.

Dai, Yingcong. 2004. "A Disguised Defeat: The Myanmar Campaign of the Qing Dynasty." *Modern Asian Studies* 38(1): 145–89.

Danley, Mark H. and Patrick J. Speelman, eds. 2012. *The Seven Years' War: Global Views*. Boston: Brill.

Davenport, Andrew. 2016. "The International and the Limits of History." *Review of International Studies* 42(2): 247–65.

Davenport, Andrew. 2013. "Marxism in IR: Condemned to a Realist Fate?" *European Journal of International Relations* 19(1): 27–48.

Davidson, Neil. 2016 [2009/2010/2011]. "The Necessity of Multiple Nation-States for Capital." In *Nation-States: Consciousness and Competition*, 187–245. Chicago: Haymarket Books.

Davidson, Neil. 2015a. "The First World War, Classical Marxism and the End of the Bourgeois Revolution in Europe." In *Cataclysm 1914: The First World War and the Making of Modern World Politics*, edited by Alexander Anievas, 302–65. Leiden: Brill.

Davidson, Neil. 2015b. *We Cannot Escape History: States and Revolutions*. Chicago: Haymarket Books.

Davidson, Neil. 2015c. "Alasdair MacIntyre's Lost Sociology." In *Sociological Amnesia: Cross-currents in Disciplinary History*, edited by Alex Law and Eric R. Lybeck, 159–79. Farnham: Ashgate.

Davidson, Neil. 2015d. "Is Social Revolution Still Possible in the Twenty-First Century?" *Journal of Contemporary Central and Eastern Europe* 23(2–3): 105–50.

Davidson, Neil. 2012. *How Revolutionary were the Bourgeois Revolutions?* Chicago: Haymarket Books.

Davidson, Neil 2009. "Putting the Nation Back into 'the International'." *Cambridge Review of International Affairs* 22(1): 9–28.

Davidson, Neil. 2006. "From Uneven to Combined Development." In *100 Years of Permanent Revolution: Results and Prospects*, edited by Bill Dunn and Hugo Radice, 10–26. Pluto Press, London.

Davidson, Neil. 2005. "The Scottish Path to Capitalist Agriculture, 3: The Enlightenment as the Theory and Practice of Improvement." *Journal of Agrarian Change* 5(1): 1–72.

Davidson, Neil. 2003. *Discovering the Scottish Revolution, 1692–1746*. London: Pluto.

Day, Richard B. and Daniel Gaido, eds. 2009. *Witnesses to Permanent Revolution: The Documentary Record*. Leiden: Brill.

Day, Thomas. 1783. *Reflections upon the Present State of England and the Independence of America*. Piccadilly: John Stockdale.

De Vries, Jan. 2013. "Reflections on Doing Global History." In *Writing the History of the Global,* edited by Maxine Berg, 32–47. Oxford: Oxford University Press.

Department for International Development (DfID). 2011. *Bilateral Aid Review: Technical Report*. London, DfID. Accessed 22 November 2015. https://www.gov.uk/government/uploads/system/uploads/attachment_data/file/214110/FINAL_BAR_20TECHNICAL_20REPORT.pdf.

Deuchler, Martina. 2015. *Under the Ancestors' Eyes: Kinship, Status and Locality in Premodern Korea*. Cambridge: Harvard University Asia Center.

Deuchler, Martina. 1992. *The Confucian Transformation of Korea: A Study of Society and Ideology*. Cambridge: Harvard University Asia Center.

Deutscher, Isaac. 1954. *The Prophet Armed. Trotsky 1879–1921*. Oxford: Oxford University Press.

Deutscher, Isaac. 1984. *Marxism, Wars and Revolutions*. London: Verso.

Dharampal. 1971. *Indian Science and Technology in the Eighteenth Century: Some Contemporary European Accounts*. Goa: Other India Press.

Di Cosmo, Nicola. 1999. "State Formation and Periodization in Inner Asian History." *Journal of World History* 10(1): 1–40.

Diakonoff, Igor M. 1991. "Early Despotism in Mesopotamia." In *History of the Ancient World: Early Antiquity*, translated and edited by Philip Kohl, 84–97. Chicago: University of Chicago Press.

Diehl, Charles. 1957 [1920]. *Byzantinium: Greatness and Decline*. New Brunswick: Rutgers University Press.

Dirlik, Arif. 1994. "The Postcolonial Aura: Third World Criticism in the Age of Global Capitalism." *Critical Enquiry* 20(2): 328–58.

Dirlik, Arif. 1999. "Is There a History after Eurocentrism?: Globalism, Postcolonialism, and the Disavowal of History." *Cultural Critique* 42: 1–34.

Divitçioğlu, Sencer. 1967. *Asya Üretim Tarzı ve Osmanlı Toplumu [The Asiatic Mode of Production and Ottoman Society]*. Istanbul: Publications of the Faculty of Economics of Istanbul University.

Donham, Donald. 1999. *Marxist Modern: An Ethnographic History of the Ethiopian Revolution*. Berkeley: University of California Press.

Donham, Donald. 1992. "Revolution and Modernity in Maale: Ethiopia from 1974 to 1987." *Comparative Studies in Society and History* 34: 28–57.

Donham, Donald. 1986. "Old Abyssinia and the New Ethiopian Empire: Themes in Social History." In *The Southern Marches of Imperial Ethiopia: Essays in History and Social Anthropology*, edited by Donald Donham and Wendy James, 37–44. Cambridge: Cambridge University Press.

Donham, Donald, Wendy James, Eisei Kurimoto and Alessandro Triulzi, eds. 2002. *Remapping Ethiopia: Socialism & After*. Athens: Ohio University Press.

Dorman, Sara Rich. 2015. "New Year; New Questions." *Democracy in Africa Blog,* Accessed 21 November 2015. http://democracyinafrica.org/new-year-new-questions-sara-rich-dorman/.

Duara, Prasenjit. 1995. *Rescuing History from the Nation: Questioning Narratives of Modern China*. Chicago: University of Chicago Press.

Duddridge, James. 2015. "How Much Does Africa Matter? Defining the UK's Africa Policy under the Coalition Government. Minister for Africa's Speech on UK's Africa Policy." Chatham House, 23 March. Accessed 20 November 2015. https://www.gov.uk/government/speeches/minister-for-africas-speech-on-uks-africa-policy.

Duffield, Mark and Vernon Hewitt, eds. 2009. *Empire, Development and Colonialism: The Past in the Present*. Woodbridge: James Currey.

Duncan, John. 2000. *The Origins of the Chosŏn Dynasty*. Seattle: University of Washington Press.

Dunn, Bill and Hugo Radice, eds. 2006. *100 Years of Permanent Revolution: Results and Prospects*. London: Pluto Press.

Eckert, Carter J. 1991. *Offspring of Empire: The Koch'ang Kims and the Colonial Origins of Korean Capitalism, 1876–1945*. Seattle: University of Washington Press.

Eisenstadt, S.N. 2000. "Multiple Modernities." *Daedalus* 129(1): 1–29.

Eley, Geoff. 2015. "Germany, the Fischer Controversy, and the Context of War: Rethinking German Imperialism, 1880–1914." In *Cataclysm 1914: The First World War and the Making of Modern World Politics,* edited by Alexander Anievas, 23–46. Leiden: Brill.

Elster, Jon. 1986. "The Theory of Combined and Uneven Development: A Critique." In *Analytical Marxism*, edited by John Roemer, 54–63. Cambridge: Cambridge University Press.

Elvin, Mark. 2002. "Braudel and China." In *Early Modern History and the Social Sciences: Testing the Limits of Braudel's Mediterranean,* edited by John A. Marino, 225–54. Kirksville: Truman State University Press.

Elvin, Mark. 1973. *The Pattern of the Chinese Past*. Stanford: Stanford University Press.

Embree, Ainslie T. and Carol Gluck. 1997. "Introduction." In *Asia in Western and World History: A Guide for Teaching*, edited by Ainslie T. Embree and Carol Gluck, xv–xviii. New York: An East Gate Book.

Emmanuel, Arghiri. 1972. *Unequal Exchange: A Study of the Imperialism of Trade.* London: Monthly Review Press.

Engels, Frederick. 2005 [1895]. "Engels to Schmidt, 12 March 1895." In *Collected Works, Volume 50*, 564–65. London: Lawrence and Wishart.

Ephrat, Daphna. 2002. "Religious Leadership and Associations in the Public Sphere of Seljuk Baghdad." In *The Public Sphere in Muslim Societies*, edited by Miriam Hoexter, Shmuel Eisenstadt, and Nehemia Levtzion, 31–48. New York: SUNY Press.

Escobar, Arturo. 2012. *Encountering Development*. Princeton: Princeton University Press, 2nd Edition.

Fairbank, John K. 1978. "Introduction: The Old Order." In *The Cambridge History of China Volume 10: Late Ch'ing 1800–1911, Part 1*, edited by John K. Fairbank, 1–34. Cambridge: Cambridge University Press.

Fanon, Frantz. 1963. *The Wretched of the Earth*. London: MacGibbon and Kee.

Federici, Silvia. 2004. *Caliban and the Witch: Women, the Body and Primitive Accumulation*. New York: Autonomedia.

Ferguson, James. 2005. "Decomposing Modernity: History and Hierarchy After Development." In *Postcolonial Studies and Beyond*, edited by Ania Loomba, Suvir Kaul and Jed Esty, 166–81. Durham: Duke University Press.

Ferguson, Niall. 2009. *The War of the World*. London: Penguin.

Ferguson, Niall. 2003. *Empire: How Britain Made the Modern World*. Harmondsworth: Penguin.

Findley, Carter V. 2004. *The Turks in World History*. Oxford: Oxford University Press.

Fine, Ben. 2010. *Theories of Social Capital: Researchers Behaving Badly*. London: Pluto Press.

Fischbach, Michael. R. 2000. *State, Society and Land in Jordan*. Leiden: Brill.

Fisseha, Abebe. 2000. "Education and the Formation of the Modern Ethiopian State, 1896–1974." PhD dissertation, University of Illinois at Urbana-Champaign.

Fodor, Pál. 2009. "Ottoman Warfare, 1300–1453." In *Cambridge History of Turkey, Volume I*, edited by Kate Fleet, 192–226. Cambridge: Cambridge University Press.

Fogarty, John. 1985. "Staples, Super-Staples and the Limits of Staple Theory: The Experiences of Argentina, Australia and Canada Compared." In *Argentina, Australia and Canada: Studies in Comparative Development 1870–1965*, edited by D.C.M. Platt and Guido di Tella, 19–36. London: The Macmillan Press Ltd.

Fogel, Joshua A. 1988. "The Debates over the Asiatic Mode of Production in Soviet Russia, China and Japan." *American Historical Review* 93(1): 56–79.

Foster-Carter, Aidan. 1978. "The Modes of Production Controversy." *New Left Review* 107: 1–25.

Frank, Andre Gunder. 2014. *Reorienting the 19th Century: Global Economy in the Continuing Asian Age*, edited and introduced by Robert A. Denemark. Boulder: Paradigm Publishers.

Frank, Andre Gunder. 1998. *ReOrient: Global Economy in the Asian Age*. Berkeley: University of California Press.

Frank, Andre Gunder. 1966. "The Development of Underdevelopment." *Monthly Review* 18(4): 17–31.

Frankopan, Peter. 2009. "Land and Power in the Middle and Later Period." In *A Social History of Byzantium*, edited by John Haldon, 112–42. Oxford: Blackwell.

Frieden, Jeffrey. 2006. *Global Capitalism: Its Rise and Fall in the Twentieth Century*. New York: Norton.

Friedman, D. 1989. "Industrialisation and the State: Argentina in the Late Nineteenth and Early Twentieth Centuries." Paper presented to the Latin American Studies Association XV International Congress, Miami, Florida.

Friedman, Thomas. 2005. *The World is Flat: A Brief History of the Twenty-First Century*. New York: Farrar, Straus and Giroux.

Fukuda Tokuzō. 1925 [1904]. *Kankoku no keizai soshiki to keizai tani*. Tōkyō: Dōbunkan.

Gabay, Clive. 2015. "New Year; New Questions." *Democracy in Africa Blog*. Accessed 21 November 2015. http://democracyinafrica.org/new-year-new-questions-clive-gabay/.

Gallagher, John and Ronald Robinson. 1953. "The Imperialism of Free Trade." *The Economic History Review* 6(1): 1–15.

Gallagher, Julia. 2013. *Britain and Africa under Blair: The Pursuit of the Good State*. Manchester: Manchester University Press.

Gaonkar, Dilip Parameshwar. 1999. "On Alternative Modernities." *Public Culture* 11(1): 1–18.

Gerber, Haim. 1987. *The Social Origins of the Modern Middle East*. Boulder: Lynne Rienner.

Gerschenkron, Alexander. 1962. *Economic Backwardness in Historical Perspective*. Cambridge: Harvard University Press.

Geyer, Michael and Charles Bright. 1995. "World History in a Global Age." *The American Historical Review* 100(4): 1034–60.

Gibbon, Edward. 1907 [1776]. *The History of the Decline and Fall of the Roman Empire, Volume 5*. London: Oxford University Press.

Gibbons, Herbert Adams. 1916. *The Foundation of the Ottoman Empire: A History of the Osmanlis Up to the Death of Bayezid I (1300–1403)*. Oxford: Clarendon.

Giddens, Anthony. 1990. *The Consequences of Modernity*. Cambridge: Polity.

Giddens, Anthony. 1985. *The Nation-State and Violence: A Contemporary Critique of Historical Materialism, Volume II*. Cambridge: Polity.

Gilpin, Robert. 1981. *War and Change in World Politics*. Cambridge: Cambridge University Press.

Go, Julian and George Lawson. 2016. "For a Global Historical Sociology." In *Global Historical Sociology*, edited by Julian Go and George Lawson, forthcoming. Cambridge: Cambridge University Press.

Go, Julian. 2011. *Patterns of Empire*. Cambridge: Cambridge University Press.

Goffman, Daniel. 2002. *The Ottoman Empire and Early Modern Europe*. Cambridge: Cambridge University Press.

Golden, Peter B. 1992. *An Introduction to the History of the Turkic Peoples: Ethnogenesis and State Formation in the Medieval and Early Modern Eurasia and the Middle East*. Weisbaden: O. Harrassowitz.

Goldstone, Jack. A. 2008. *Why Europe? The Rise of the West in World History 1500–1850*. Boston: McGraw Hill.

Goldstone, Jack. A. 2002. "Efflorescences and Economic Growth in World History: Rethinking the 'Rise of the West' and the Industrial Revolution." *Journal of World History* 13(2): 323–89.

Goldstone, Jack. A. 1991. *Revolution and Rebellion in the Early Modern World*. Berkeley: University of California Press.

Goody, Jack. 1996. *The East in the West*. Cambridge: Cambridge University Press.

Gowan, Peter. 1999. *The Global Gamble: Washington's Faustian Bid for World Dominance*. London: Verso.

Gramsci, Antonio. 1971. *Selections from the Prison Notebooks of Antonio Gramsci*. London: Lawrence & Wishart.

Gran, Peter. 1996. *Beyond Eurocentrism: New View of Modern World History*. Syracuse: Syracuse University Press.

Gran, Peter. 1987. "Late Eighteenth-Early-Nineteenth-Century Egypt: Merchant Capitalism or Modern Capitalism?" In *The Ottoman Empire and the World Economy*, edited by Huri Islamoğlu-Inan, 27–42. Cambridge: Cambridge University Press.

Green, Jeremy. 2012. "Uneven and Combined Development and the Anglo-German Prelude to World War I." *European Journal of International Relations* 18(2): 345–68.

Greenfield, Richard. 1965. *Ethiopia: A New Political History*. London: Pall Mall Press, 1965.

Grell-Brisk, Marilyn. 2015. "Beyond the Long Twentieth Century: China in Sub-Saharan Africa and the Changing Dynamics of the World System." Institute for Research on World Systems (IROWS) Working Paper #105. Accessed 7 April 2016. http://irows.ucr.edu/papers/irows105/irows105.htm.

Group of 8 (G8). 2005. "The Gleneagles Communiqué." July. Accessed 21 November 2015. http://www.g8.utoronto.ca/summit/2005gleneagles/communique.pdf.

Gruffydd Jones, Branwen, ed. 2006. *Decolonizing International Relations*. Lanham: Rowman & Littlefield.

Habib, Irfan, ed. 2002. *Confronting Colonialism: Resistance and Modernization under Haidar Ali and Tipu Sultan*. London: Anthem Press.

Haldon, John. 1993. *The State and the Tributary Mode of Production*. London: Verso.

Haldon, John. 1991. "The Ottoman State and the Question of State Autonomy: Comparative Perspectives." *Journal of Peasant Studies* 18(3–4): 18–108.

Hall, Martin. 1999. "Review: International Relations and Historical Sociology: Taking Stock of Convergence." *Review of International Political Economy* 6(1): 101–9.

Hall, Thomas D. 1991. "Civilizational Change: The Role of Nomads." *Comparative Civilizations Review* 24: 34–57.

Halliday, Fred. 2002. "For an International Sociology." In *Historical Sociology of International Relations,* edited by Stephen Hobden and John M. Hobson, 244–64. Cambridge: Cambridge University Press.

Halliday, Fred. 1999. *Revolutions and World Politics: The Rise and Fall of the Sixth World Power*. London: Macmillan.

Halliday, Fred. 1987. "State and Society in International Relations: A Second Agenda." *Millennium: Journal of International Studies* 16: 215–29.

Halliday, Fred and Maxine Molyneux. 1981. *The Ethiopian Revolution.* London: Verso.

Hamarneh, Mustafa B. 1985. "Social and Economic Transformation of Transjordan, 1921–1946." PhD Diss., Georgetown University.

Hanes, W. Travis and Frank Sanello. 2002. *Opium Wars: The Addiction of One Empire and the Corruption of Another.* Naperville: Sourcebooks.

Harvey, Alan. 2003. *Economic Expansion in the Byzantine Empire, 900–1200.* Cambridge: Cambridge University Press.

Harvey, David. 2005. *A Brief History of Neoliberalism.* New York: Oxford University Press.

Harvey, David. 2003. *The New Imperialism.* Oxford: Oxford University Press.

Harvey, David. 2001. *Spaces of Capital: Towards a Critical Geography.* Edinburgh: Edinburgh University Press.

Hasan, Mohibbul. 1971. *History of Tipu Sultan.* Calcutta: Aakar Books, 2nd Edition.

Havinden, Michael and David Meredith. 1993. *Colonialism and Development: Britain and its Tropical Colonies, 1850–1960.* London: Routledge.

Hawley, Amos. 1950. *Human Ecology: A Theory of Community Structure.* New York: Ronald Press Co.

Haywood, John. 2006. *Atlas of World History.* Sheriffs Lench: Sandcastle Books.

Headrick, Daniel R. 1981. *The Tools of Empire: Technology and European Imperialism in the Nineteenth Century.* New York: Oxford University Press.

Heywood, Colin. 2000. "Filling the Black Hole: The Emergence of the Bithynian Atamanates." In *The Great Ottoman Turkish Civilization, Volume I,* edited by Kemal Çiçek, Ercüment Kuran, Nejat Göyünç, and İlber Ortaylı, 108–13. Istanbul: Yeni Türkiye.

Hilton, Rodney. 1990. "Introduction." In *The Brenner Debate: Agrarian Class Structure and Economic Development in Pre-Industrial Europe,* edited by T.H. Ashton and C.H.E. Philpin, 1–9. Cambridge: Cambridge University Press.

Hirst, Paul. 1985. *Marxism and Historical Writing.* London: Routledge and Kegan Paul.

Hobsbawm, Eric. 1996. *The Age of Revolution 1789–1848.* New York: Vintage Books.

Hobsbawm, Eric. 1987. *The Age of Empire, 1875–1914.* London: Weidenfeld and Nicolson.

Hobsbawm, Eric. 1962. *The Age of Revolution, 1789–1848.* London: Abacus.

Hobden, Stephen and John M. Hobson, eds. 2002. *Historical Sociology of International Relations.* Cambridge: Cambridge University Press.

Hobson, John M. 2016. "The Lacuna of *Capital, the State, and War?* The Lost Global History and Theory of Eastern Agency." *International Politics,* forthcoming.

Hobson, John M. 2012. *The Eurocentric Conception of Wold Politics: Western International Theory, 1760–2010.* Cambridge: Cambridge University Press.

Hobson, John M. 2011. "What's at Stake in the Neo-Trotskyist Debate? Towards a Non-Eurocentric Historical Sociology of Uneven and Combined Development." *Millennium: Journal of international Studies* 40(1): 147–66.

Hobson, John M. 2004. *The Eastern Origins of Western Civilisation*. Cambridge: Cambridge University Press.

Hobson, John M. 1998. "The Historical Sociology of the State and the State of Historical Sociology in International Relations." *Review of International Political Economy* 5(2): 284–320

Hobson, John M. 1997. *The Wealth of States*: *A Comparative Sociology of International Economic and Political Change*. Cambridge: Cambridge University Press.

Hobson, John M., George Lawson, and Justin Rosenberg. 2010. "Historical Sociology." In *The International Studies Encyclopaedia,* edited by Robert A. Denemark, 3357–75. London: Wiley-Blackwell.

Hodgen, Margaret T. 1964. *Early Anthropology in the Sixteenth and Seventeenth Centuries*. Philadelphia: University of Pennsylvania.

Hodgson, Geoffrey. 2014. "What is Capital? Economists and Sociologists Have Changed Its Meaning–Should it be Changed Back?" *Cambridge Journal of Economics* 38(5): 1063–86.

Hodgson, Marshall G.S. 2009. *The Venture of Islam, Volume 2: The Expansion of Islam in the Middle Periods*. London: University of Chicago Press.

Horrowitz, David. 1969. *Imperialism and Revolution: A Radical Interpretation of Contemporary History*. New York: Random House.

Huang, Yasheng. 2008. *Capitalism with Chinese Characteristics*. New York: Cambridge University Press.

Hudson, Pat. 2014. *The Industrial Revolution*. London: Bloomsbury Publishing.

Hung, Ho-Fung. 2015a. *The China Boom*. New York: Columbia University Press.

Hung, Ho-Fung. 2015b. "China Steps Back." *New York Times: The Opinion Pages*. Accessed 7 April 2016. *http://www.nytimes.com/2015/04/06/opinion/china-steps-back.html?_r=0*.

Huntington, Samuel. 1968a. "The Bases of Accommodation." *Foreign Affairs* 46(4): 642–56.

Huntington, Samuel P. 1968b. *Political Order in Changing Societies*. London: Yale University Press.

Idahosa, Pablo L.E. and Bob Shenton. 2004. "The Africanist's 'New' Clothes." *Historical Materialism* 12(4): 67–113.

Imber, Colin. 2009. *The Ottoman Empire, 1300–1650: The Structure of Power*. Basingstoke: Palgrave Macmillan.

Imber, Colin. 1987. "The Ottoman Dynastic Myth." *Turcica* 19: 7–27.

İnalcık, Halil. 2000. *The Ottoman Empire: The Classical Age, 1300–1600*. London: Phoenix Publishers.

İnalcik, Halil, ed. 1994. *An Economic and Social History of the Ottoman Empire 1300–1914*. Cambridge: Cambridge University Press.

İnalcık, Halil. 1992. "Comments on 'Sultanism': Max Weber's Typification of the Ottoman Polity." *Princeton Papers in Near Eastern Studies* 1: 49–72.

İnalcık, Halil. 1977. "The Emergence of the Ottomans." In *Cambridge History of Islam, Volume I*. edited by P.M. Holt, Ann K.S. Lambton, and Bernard Lewis, 263–92. Cambridge: Cambridge University Press.

İnalcık, Halil. 1976. "The Rise of the Ottoman Empire." In *A History of the Ottoman Empire to 1730*, edited by M.A. Cook, 10–53. Cambridge: Cambridge University Press.

İnalcık, Halil. 1954. "Ottoman Methods of Conquest." *Studia Islamica* 2: 103–29.

Inayatullah, Naeem and David L. Blaney. 2016. "Global Capitalism, Inequality and Poverty." In *International Relations Theory Today*, edited by Toni Erskine and Ken Booth. London: Polity.

Inayatullah, Naeem and David L. Blaney. 2015. "A Problem with Levels: How to Engage a Diverse IPE." *Contexto Internacional* 37: 889–911.

Inayatullah, Naeem and David L Blaney. 2004. *International Relations and the Problem of Difference*. New York: Routledge.

Innis, Harold A. 1995. *Staples, Markets and Cultural Change: Selected Essays*. Montreal & Kingston: McGill-Queen's University Press.

Inoue, Hiroko, Alexis Álvarez, E.N. Anderson, Kirk Lawrence, Teresa Neal, Dmytro Khutkyy, Sandor Nagy and Christopher Chase-Dunn. 2016. "Comparing World-Systems: Empire Upsweeps and Non-Core Marcher States Since the Bronze Age." Institute for Research on World Systems (IROWS) Working Paper 56. Accessed 7 April 2016. http://irows.ucr.edu/papers/irows56/irows56.htm.

Inoue, Hiroko, Alexis Alvarez, Eugene N. Anderson, Andrew Owen, and Christopher Chase-Dunn. 2015. "Urban Scale Shifts Since the Bronze Age: Upsweeps, Collapses and Semiperipheral Development." *Social Science History* 39(2): 175–200

Inoue, Hiroko, Alexis Álvarez, Kirk Lawrence, Anthony Roberts, Eugene N. Anderson and Christopher Chase-Dunn. 2012. "Polity Scale Shifts in World-Systems Since the Bronze Age: A Comparative Inventory of Upsweeps and Collapses." *International Journal of Comparative Sociology* 53(3): 210–29.

Ireton, Barrie. 2014. *Britain's International Development Policies: A History of DFID and Overseas Aid*. Basingstoke: Palgrave Macmillan.

Islamoğlu-Inan, Huri and Çağlar Keyder. 1977. "Agenda for Ottoman History." *Review (Fernand Braudel Center)* 1(1): 31–55.

Islamoğlu-Inan, Huri, ed. 1987. *The Ottoman Empire and the World Economy*. Cambridge: Cambridge University Press.

Issawi, Charles. 1988. *The Fertile Crescent, 1800–1914: A Documentary Economic History*. Oxford: Oxford University Press.

Issawi, Charles. 1982. *The Economic History of the Middle East and North Africa*. New York: Columbia University Press.

Issawi, Charles. 1980. *The Economic History of Turkey 1800–1914*. Chicago: University of Chicago Press.

Jaim, H.M. Iftekhar and Jasmine Jaim. 2011. "The Decisive Nature of the Indian War Rocket in the Anglo-Mysore Wars of the Eighteenth Century." *Arms & Armour* 8(2): 131–38.

Janin, Hunt. 1999. *The India-China Opium Trade in the Nineteenth Century*. Jefferson: McFarland.

Jones, Eric. 1981. *The European Miracle: Environment, Economies and Geopolitics in the History of Europe and Asia*. Cambridge: Cambridge University Press.

Jones, Susan Mann and Philip A. Kuhn. 1978. "Dynastic Decline and the Roots of Rebellion." In *The Cambridge History of China, Volume 10: Late Ch'ing*

1800–1911, Part 1, edited by John K. Fairbank, 107–62. Cambridge: Cambridge University Press.

Jones, Terry and Kathryn A. Klar, eds. 2007. *California Prehistory: Colonization, Culture and Complexity*. Lanham: Rowman and Littlefield.

Kafadar, Cemal. 1995. *Between Two Worlds: The Construction of the Ottoman State*. Berkeley: University of California Press.

Karatasli, Sahan Savas and Sefika Kumral. 2015. "World-Hegemonic Ascendancy and National Liberation Movements in Comparative Perspective." Paper presented at the *American Sociological Association* 2015 Annual Meeting.

Kasaba, Reşat. 2009. *A Moveable Empire: Ottoman Nomads, Migrants, and Refugees*. Seattle: University of Washington Press.

Kelsall, Tom with David Booth *et al.* 2013. *Business, Politics and the State in Africa: Challenging the Orthodoxies on Growth and Transformation*. London: Zed Books.

Kennedy, Paul. 1989. *The Rise and Fall of the Great Powers: Economic Change and Military Conflict from 1500–2000*. London: Fontana Press.

Keyder, Çağlar. 1987. *State and Class in Turkey: A Study in Capitalist Development*. London: Verso.

Keyder, Çağlar. 1976. "The Dissolution of the Asiatic Mode of Production." *Economy and Society* 5(2): 178–96.

Keyder, Çağlar and Huri Islamoğlu-Inan. 1987. "Agenda for Ottoman History." In *The Ottoman Empire*, edited by Huri Islamoğlu-Inan, 42–62. Cambridge: Cambridge University Press.

Khoury, Philip S. and Joseph Kostiner, eds. 1990. *Tribes and State Formation in the Middle East*. Los Angles: University of California Press.

Kiel, Michael. 2009. "The Incorporation of the Balkans into the Ottoman Empire, 1353–1453." In *Cambridge History of Turkey, Volume 1*, edited by Kate Fleet, 138–91. Cambridge: Cambridge University Press.

Kiely, Ray. 2012. "Spatial Hierarchy and/or Contemporary Geopolitics: What Can and Can't Uneven and Combined Development Explain?" *Cambridge Review of International Affairs* 25(2): 231–48

King, Chester. 1978. "Prehistoric and Historic Archeology." In *Handbook of North American Indians, Volume 8: California*, edited by Robert F. Heizer, 58–68. Washington, DC: Smithsonian Institution.

Kirch, Patrick V. 1984. *The Evolution of Polynesian Chiefdoms*. Cambridge: Cambridge University Press.

Knei-Paz, Baruch. 1978. *The Social and Political Thought of Leon Trotsky*. Oxford: Clarendon Press.

Koselleck, Reinhart. 2002. *The Practice of Conceptual History: Timing History, Spacing Concepts*. Stanford: Stanford University Press.

Köprülü, Mehmet Fuat. 1999. *Some Observations on the Influence of Byzantine Institutions on Ottoman Institutions*. Ankara: Türk Tarih Kurumu.

Köprülü, Mehmet Fuat. 1992a. *The Origins of the Ottoman Empire*. New York: SUNY Press.

Köprülü, Mehmet Fuat. 1992b. *The Seljuks of Anatolia: Their History and Culture According to Local Muslim Sources*. Salt Lake City: University of Utah Press.

Kroeber, Alfred L. 1976 [1925]. *Handbook of the Indians of California.* New York: Dover Publications

Lacher, Hannes and Julian Germann. 2012. "Before Hegemony: Britain, Free Trade, and Nineteenth-Century World Order Revisited." *International Studies Review* 14(1): 99–124.

Laclau, Ernesto. 2014. *The Rhetorical Foundations of Society.* London: Verso.

Laclau, Ernesto. 1971. "Feudalism and Capitalism in Latin America." *New Left Review* 1(67): 19–37.

Landau, Jacob M., ed. 1984. *Atatürk and the Modernization of Turkey.* Leiden: Brill.

Landes, David. 1998. *The Wealth and Poverty of Nations: Why Some Are So Rich and Some So Poor.* New York: Norton.

Landsberg, Chris. 2011. "Diffused Continentally; Undermined Abroad?" Paper presented at the seminar, *African Agency: Implications for IR Theory*, City University, London, 14 September 2011. Accessed 21 November 2015. www.open.ac.uk/ socialsciences/bisa-africa/files/africanagency-seminar4-landsberg.pdf.

Latham, Michael E. 2000. *Modernization as Ideology: American Social Science and 'Nation Building' in the Kennedy Era.* Chapel Hill: University of North Carolina Press.

Lattimore, Owen. 1980. "The Periphery as Locus of Innovations." In *Centre and Periphery: Spatial Variation in Politics*, edited by Jean Gottmann, 205–8. Beverly Hills: Sage.

Lawson, George. 2010. "The 'What', 'When' and 'Where' of the Global 1989." In *The Global 1989: Continuity and Change in World Politics*, edited by George Lawson, Chris Armbruster and Michael Cox, 1–20. Cambridge: Cambridge University Press.

Lee, Ki-baik. 1984. *A New History of Korea.* Cambridge: Harvard University Press.

Lefort, Rene. 1983. *Ethiopia: An Heretical Revolution?* London: Zed Press.

Lenin, Vladimir I. 1964 [1916]. "Imperialism, the Highest Stage of Capitalism: A Popular Outline." In *Collected Works, Volume 22*, 185–303. Moscow: Foreign Languages Publishing House.

Levine, Donald. 1965. *Wax and Gold: Tradition and Innovation in Ethiopian Culture.* Chicago: Chicago University Press.

Levin, N. Gordon. 1973. *Woodrow Wilson and World Politics.* Oxford: Oxford University Press.

Lewis, Bernard. 2002. *The Emergence of Modern Turkey.* London: Oxford University Press.

Lewis, Norman N. 1987. *Nomads and Settlers in Syria and Jordan, 1800–1980.* Cambridge: Cambridge University Press.

Lindner, Rudi Paul. 2009. "Anatolia, 1300–1451." In *The Cambridge History of Turkey*, edited by Kate Fleet, 102–37. Cambridge: Cambridge University Press.

Lindner, Rudi Paul. 2007. *Explorations in Ottoman Prehistory.* Ann Arbor: University of Michigan Press.

Lindner, Rudi Paul. 1983. *Nomads and Ottomans in Medieval Anatolia.* Bloomington: Research Institute for Inner Asian Studies, Indiana University.

Linklater, Andrew. 1990. *Beyond Realism and Marxism: Critical Theory and International Relations.* London: Macmillan.

Lockwood, Matthew. 2005. *The State They're In: An Agenda for International Action on Poverty in Africa.* Burton-on-Dunsmore: ITDG Publishing.

Looker, Robert and David Coates. 1986. "The State and the Working Class." In *The Rise of the Modern State*, edited by James Anderson, 91–114. Brighton: Harvester.

Louis, Roger W.M. 1976. *Imperialism: The Robinson and Gallagher Controversy.* New York: New Viewpoints.

Lowry, Heath W. 2003. *The Nature of the Early Ottoman State.* New York: State University of New York Press.

Löwy, Michael. 2006a. "The Marxism of *Results and Prospects.*" In *100 Years of Permanent Revolution: Results and Prospects,* edited by Bill Dunn and Hugo Radice, 27–34. London: Pluto Press.

Löwy, Michael. 2006b. *Fire Alarm: Reading Walter Benjamin's "On the Concept of History."* London: Verso.

Löwy, Michael. 1981. *The Politics of Combined and Uneven Development: The Theory of Permanent Revolution.* London: Verso.

Lugard, Frederick. 1965 [1921]. *The Dual Mandate in British Tropical Africa.* London: Frank Cass.

Lundborg, Tom. 2016. "The Limits of Historical Sociology: Temporal Borders and the Reproduction of the 'Modern' Political Present." *European Journal of International Relations* 22(1): 99–121.

MacDonald, J.S. 1963. "Agricultural Organisation, Migration and Labour Militancy in Rural Italy." *The Economic History Review* 16(1): 61–75.

Makki, Fouad. 2015. "Reframing Development Theory: The Significance of the Idea of Uneven and Combined Development." *Theory & Society* 44(5): 471–97.

Makki, Fouad. 2011. "Empire and Modernity: Dynastic Centralization and Official Nationalism in Late Imperial Ethiopia." *Cambridge Review of International Affairs* 24(2): 265–86.

Mamdani, Mahmood. 1996. *Citizen and Subject: Contemporary Africa and the Legacy of Later Colonialism.* Princeton: Princeton University Press.

Mandel, Ernest. 1970. "The Laws of Uneven Development." *New Left Review* 1(59): 19–40.

Mann, Michael. 2013. *The Sources of Social Power, Volume IV: Globalizations, 1945–2011.* Cambridge: Cambridge University Press.

Mann, Michael. 2012. *The Sources of Social Power, Volume III: Global Empires and Revolution, 1890–1945.* Cambridge: Cambridge University Press.

Mann, Michael. 1993. *The Sources of Social Power, Volume II: The Rise of Classes and Nation States 1760–1914.* Cambridge: Cambridge University Press.

Mann, Michael. 1988. *States, Wars and Capitalism: Studies in Political Sociology.* Oxford: Oxford University Press.

Mann, Michael. 1986. *The Sources of Social Power, Volume I: A History of Power from the Beginning to AD 1760.* Cambridge: Cambridge University Press.

Mantena, Karuna. 2010. *Henry Maine and the Ends of Liberal Imperialism.* Princeton: Princeton University.

Mantienne, Frédéric. 2003. "The Transfer of Western Military Technology to Vietnam in the Late Eighteenth and Early Nineteenth Centuries: The Case of the Nguyễn." *Journal of Southeast Asian Studies* 34(3): 519–34.

Markakis, John. 1987. *National and Class Conflict in the Horn of Africa*. Cambridge: Cambridge University Press.

Markakis, John. 1984. "Material and Social Aspects of National Conflict in the Horn of Africa." In *Proceedings of the Seventh International Conference of Ethiopian Studies*, edited by Sven Rubinson, 751–57. Uppsala: Scandinavian Institute of African Studies.

Markakis, John. 1974. *Ethiopia: Anatomy of a Traditional Polity*. Oxford: Clarendon Press.

Marini, Ruy Mauro. 1972. "Brazilian Subimperialism." *Monthly Review* 23(9): 14–24.

Marshall, Hodgson. 1993. *Rethinking World History: Essays on Europe, Islam, and World History*. Cambridge: Cambridge University Press.

Masud, Muhammad Khalid and Armando Salvatore. 2009. "Western Scholars of Islam on the Issue of Modernity." In *Islam and Modernity: Key Issues and Debates*, edited by Muhammad Khalid Masud, Armando Salvatore, and Martin Bruinessen, 36–53. Edinburgh: Edinburgh University Press.

Marx, Karl. 1993 [1885]. *Capital: A Critique of Political Economy, Volume II*. Harmondsworth: Penguin.

Marx, Karl. 1990 [1867]. *Capital: A Critique of Political Economy, Volume I*. Harmondsworth: Penguin.

Marx, Karl. 1987. *Pre-Capitalist Formations*. London: Lawrence and Wishart.

Marx, Karl. 1976 [1867]. *Capital: A Critique of Political Economy, Volume I*. Harmondsworth: Penguin/New Left Review.

Marx, Karl. 1975 [1844]. "Draft of an Article on Frederick List's Book, *Das Nationale System Der Politischen Oekkonomie*." In *Collected Works, Volume 4*, 265–93. London: Lawrence and Wishart.

Marx, Karl. 1974 [1867]. *Capital: A Critique of Political Economy, Volume I*. London: Lawrence and Wishart.

Marx, Karl 1973 [1857–1858]. *Grundrisse: Foundations for the Critique of Political Economy*. Harmondsworth: Penguin Books/New Left Review.

Marx, Karl. 1859. "Preface to a Contribution to a Critique of Political Economy." Accessed 9 April 2016. http://www.marxists.org/archive/marx/works/1859/critique-pol-economy/preface.htm.

Marx, Karl and Friedrich Engels. 1973 [1848]. "Manifesto of the Communist Party." In *The Revolutions of 1848. Political Writings, Volume I*, edited and introduced by David Fernbach, 67–98. Harmondsworth: Penguin.

Matin, Kamran. 2013a. "Redeeming the Universal: Postcolonialism and the Inner Life of Eurocentricism." *European Journal of International Relations* 19(2): 353–77.

Matin, Kamran. 2013b. "International Relations in the Making of Political Islam: Interrogating Khomeini's 'Islamic Government'." *Journal of International Relations and Development* 16: 455–82.

Matin, Kamran. 2013c. *Recasting Iranian Modernity: International Relations and Social Change*. London: Routledge.

Matin, Kamran. 2007. "Uneven and Combined Development in World History: The International Relations of State-Formation in Premodern Iran." *European Journal of International Relations* 13(3): 419–47.

Mazlish, Bruce. 1998. "Comparing Global History to World History." *The Journal of Interdisciplinary History* 28(3): 385–95.

McDaniel, Tim. 1991. *Autocracy, Modernization, and Revolution in Russia and Iran.* Princeton: Princeton University Press.

McNally, David. 1981. "Staple Theory as Commodity Fetishism: Marx, Innis and Canadian Political Economy." *Studies in Political Economy* 6: 35–63.

McNeill, John and William McNeill. 2009 [2003]. *The Human Web: A Bird's-eye View of World History.* London: W.W. Norton and Co.

McNeill, John R. and William H. McNeill. 2003. *The Human Web: A Bird's-eye View of World History.* New York: Norton.

McNeill, William H. 1995. "The Changing Shape of World History." *History and Theory* 34(2): 8–26.

Melville, Charles. 2009. "Anatolia Under the Mongols." In *Cambridge History of Turkey, Volume I*, edited by Kate Fleet, 51–101. Cambridge: Cambridge University Press.

Mengistie, Habtamu. 2004. *Lord, Ze`ga and Peasant: A Study of Property and Agrarian Relations in Rural Eastern Gojjam.* Addis Ababa: Addis Ababa University Press.

Mielants, Eric H. 2008. *The Origins of Capitalism and the 'Rise of the West'.* Philadelphia: Temple University Press, 2nd Edition.

Migdal, Joel S. 1994. "The State in Society: An Approach to Struggles for Domination." In *State Power and Social Forces: Domination and Transformation in the Third World,* edited by Joel S. Migdal, Atul Kohli and Vivienne Shue, 7–37. Cambridge: Cambridge University Press.

Mignolo, Walter D. 2000. *Local Histories/Global Designs.* Princeton: Princeton University Press.

Miller, Owen. 2016. "The Transformation of the Chosŏn Economy in the Open Port Period, 1876–1910." In *Routledge Handbook of Modern Korean History,* edited by Michael Seth, 81–94. Abingdon: Routledge.

Miller, Owen. 2011. "Haebang chŏnhu Chŏn Sŏktam ŭi yŏksahak: kŭndae kungmin kukka ro ihaeng kwa malksŭjuŭi yŏksahak." In *Cheguk kwa minjok ŭi kyoch'a ro,* 225–54. Seoul: Ch'aekkwa hamkke.

Miller, Owen. 2010. "The Idea of Stagnation in Korean History from Fukuda Tokuzō to the New Right." *Korean Histories* 2.

Miller, Owen. 2007. "The Merchants of the Myŏnjujŏn: Guild and Government in Late Chosŏn Korea." PhD Diss., University of London.

Mitchell, Timothy. 1988. *Colonising Egypt.* Cambridge: Cambridge University Press.

Moore, Robert Ian. 1997. "The Birth of Europe as a Eurasian Phenomenon." *Modern Asian Studies* 31(3): 583–601.

Morgan, David J. 1980. *The Official History of Colonial Development—Volume One: The Origins of British Aid Policy 1924–1945.* London: Macmillan.

Morris, Ian. 2010. *Why the West Rules for Now.* London: Profile.

Mukherjee, Pablo. 2010. *Postcolonial Environments.* London: Palgrave Macmillan.

Mundy, Martha and Richard Saumarez Smith. 2007. *Governing Property, Making the Modern State: Law, Administration and Production in Ottoman Syria.* London: I. B. Tauris.

Munro, Innes. 1789. *Munro, Innes. Narrative of the Military Operations, on the Coromandel Coast, Against the Combined Forces of the French, Dutch, and Hyder Ally Cawn, from the Year 1780 to the Peace in 1784; In A Series of Letters.* London: T. Bensley.

Myers, Ramon and Yeh-chien Wang. 2002. "Economic Developments, 1644–1800." In *Cambridge History of China, Volume 9: The Ch'ing Empire to 1800, Part 1,* edited by Willard Peterson, 563–646. Cambridge: Cambridge University Press.

Myrdal, Gunnar. 1963. *Economic Theory and Underdeveloped Regions.* London: Methuen & Co. Ltd.

Nagdy, Mohamed and Max Roser. 2015. "International Trade." Accessed 4 April 2016. http://ourworldindata.org/data/global-interconnections/international-trade.

Nalbantoğlu, Hasan Ünal. 1978. "Prekapitalist Küçük Sanayi ve Tüccar Sermayesine Bağımlılığı [Precapitalist Small Industry and its Dependence on Merchant Capital]." In *Sanayide Küçük Üretim: Toplumsal ve Mekânsal Boyutlar [Small Production in Industry. Social and Spatial Dimensions].* Ankara: Chamber of Architects.

Narasimha, Roddam. 1999. "Rocketing from the Galaxy Bazaar." *Nature* 400(6740): 123.

Narasimha, Roddam. 1985. "Rockets in Mysore and Britain, 1750–1850 A.D." National Aeronautical Laboratory and Indian Institute of Science, Project Document DU 8503. Accessed 10 April 2016. http://www.nal.res.in/pdf/pdfrocket.pdf.

Nederveen Pieterse, Jan. 2001. *Development Theory: Deconstructions/Reconstructions.* London: Sage.

Needham, Joseph. 1987. *Science and Civilisation in China: Volume 5, Chemistry and Chemical Technology, Part 7, Military Technology: The Gunpowder Epic.* Cambridge: Cambridge University Press.

Needham, Joseph. 1971. *Science and Civilisation in China: Volume 4, Physics and Physical Technology, Part 3, Civil Engineering and Nautics.* Cambridge: Cambridge University Press.

Needham, Joseph. 1969. *The Grand Titration: Science and Society in East and West.* London: Allen and Unwin.

Nilsen, Alf Gunvald. 2015. "Passages from Marxism to Postcolonialism: A Comment on Vivek Chibber's *Postcolonial Theory and the Specter of Capital.*" *Critical Sociology.* OnlineFirst.

Nişancioğlu, Kerem. 2014. "The Ottoman Origins of Capitalism: Uneven and Combined Development and Eurocentrism." *Review of International Studies* 40(2): 325–47.

Nisbet, Robert. 1969. *Social Change and History: Aspects of the Western Theory of Development.* New York: Oxford University Press.

North, Douglass C., John Joseph Wallis, and Barry R. Weingast. 2009. *Violence and Social Orders: A Conceptual Framework for Interpreting Recorded Human History.* Cambridge: Cambridge University Press.

Novack, George. 1972. *Understanding History: Marxist Essays.* New York: Pathfinder.

Nugent, Walter. 1992. *Crossings: The Great Transatlantic Migrations, 1870–1914.* Bloomington: Indiana University Press.

O'Brien, Patrick K. 2006. "Mercantilist Institutions for the Pursuit of Power with Profit: The Management of Britain's National Debt, 1756–1815." Working Papers No. 95/06. London School of Economics, Department of Economic History.

O'Brien, Patrick K. 2010. "Deconstructing the British Industrial Revolution as a Conjuncture and Paradigm for Global Economic History." In *Reconceptualizing the Industrial Revolution*, edited by Leonard N. Rosenband, Merritt Roe Smith, and Jeff Horn, 21–46. Cambridge: MIT Press.

O'Leary, Brendan. 1989. *The Asiatic Mode of Production*. Oxford: Wiley-Blackwell.

Oh, Youngchan. 2008. "The Governing Authority of Lelang." Paper presented at 'Korea and the Han Commanderies Workshop', Korea Institute, Harvard University, Cambridge, USA.

Oikonomides, Nicolas. 2002. "The Role of the Byzantine State in the Economy." In *The Economic History of Byzantium from the Seventh Through the Fifteenth Century*, edited by Angela E. Laiou, 973–1058. Washington: Dumbarton Oaks.

Ollman, Bertell. 2003. *Dance of the Dialectic: Steps in Marx's Method*. Chicago: University of Illinois Press.

Osterhammel, Jürgen. 2014 [2009]. *The Transformation of the World: A Global History of the Nineteenth Century*. Princeton: Princeton University Press.

Paek Nam'un. 1989 [1933]. *Chōsen shakai keizaishi* [Socio-Economic History of Korea], Korean edition translated from Japanese by Pak Kwangsun. Seoul.

Pagden, Anthony. 1982. *The Fall of Natural Man: The American Indian and the Origins of Comparative Ethnology*. Cambridge: Cambridge University.

Pai, Hyung-il. 2000. *Constructing 'Korean' Origins: A Critical Review of Archaeology, Historiography, and Racial Myth in Korean State Formation Theories*. Cambridge: Harvard University Asia Center.

Pak, S.K. and S.I. Pak. 1988. "Chosŏn hugi chaejŏng ŭi yakhwa sijŏm e kwanhan koch'al." *Tongbang hakchi* 60.

Pakenham, Thomas. 1991. *The Scramble for Africa: 1876–1912*. London: Abacus/ George Weidenfeld & Nicolson.

Palais, James B. 1998. "Progress or Stasis in Korean Society." In *Views on Korean Social History*, 1–21. Seoul: Institute for Modern Korean Studies.

Palais, James B. 1996. *Confucian Statecraft and Korean Institutions: Yu Hyongwon and the Late Choson Dynasty*. Seattle: University of Washington Press.

Palais, James B. 1991. *Politics and Policy in Traditional Korea*. Cambridge: Harvard University Asia Center.

Palais, James B. 1984. "Confucianism and the Aristocratic/Bureaucratic Balance in Korea." *Harvard Journal of Asiatic Studies* 44(2): 427–68.

Palais, James B. 1982. "Land Tenure in Korea: Tenth to Twelfth Centuries." *Journal of Korean Studies* 4: 73–205.

Palmer, Bryan D. 1983. "Town, Port and Country: Speculations on the Capitalist Transformation in Canada." *Acadiensis* 12(2): 131–39.

Pang Kie-chung. 2005. "Paek Namun and Marxist Scholarship during the Colonial Period." In *Landlords, Peasants and Intellectuals in Modern Korea*, edited by Pang Kie-chung and Michael D. Shin, 245–308. Ithaca: Cornell East Asia Series.

Parmar, Inderjeet. 2005. "'I'm Proud of the British Empire': Why Tony Blair backs George Bush." *Political Quarterly* 76(2): 218–31.

Parsons, Talcott. 1991 [1951]. *The Social System*. London: Routledge.

Pasha, M. Kamal. 2010. "Untimely Reflections." In *International Relations and Non-Western Thought: Imperialism, Colonialism and Investigations of Global Modernity*, edited by Robbie Shilliam, 217–38, London: Routledge.

Passé-Smith, John T. 1993. "Could It Be That the Whole World Is Already Rich? A Comparison of RGDP/pc and GNP/pc Measures." In *Development and Underdevelopment: The Political Economy of Inequality*, edited by M.A. Seligson and J.T. Passé-Smith, 103–18. Boulder: Lynne Reiner.

Perdue, Peter C. 2010b. "The First Opium War: The Anglo-Chinese War of 1839–1842." MIT Open Courseware. Accessed 28 December 2015. http://ocw.mit.edu/ans7870/21f/21f.027/opium_wars_01/ow1_essay01.html.

Perdue, Peter C. 2010a. *China Marches West*. Cambridge: Harvard University Press, 2nd Edition.

Perdue, Peter C. 1996. "Military Mobilization in Seventeenth and Eighteenth-Century China, Russia, and Mongolia." *Modern Asian Studies* 30(4): 757–93.

Peregrine, Peter N. 1992. *Mississippian Evolution: A World-System Perspective. Monographs in World Archaeology, Number 9*. Madison: Prehistory Press.

Petrov, Leonid. 2006. "Turning Historians into Party Scholar-Bureaucrats: North Korean Historiography from 1955–58." *East Asian History* 31: 101–24.

Piketty, Thomas. 2014. *Capital in the Twenty-First Century*. Cambridge: Belknap Press.

Poggi, Gianfranco. 1965. "A Main Theme of Contemporary Sociological Analysis: Its Achievements and Limitations." *The British Journal of Sociology* 16(4): 283–94.

Pomeranz, Kenneth. 2000. *The Great Divergence: China, Europe, and the Making World Economy*. Princeton: Princeton University Press.

Porter, Andrew and Robert Holland, eds. 1988. *Theory and Practice in the History of European Expansion Overseas: Essays in Honour of Ronald Robinson*. London: Frank Cass.

Porteus, Tom. 2008. *Britain in Africa*. London: Zed Books.

Post, Ken and Phil Wright. 1989. *Socialism and Underdevelopment*. London: Routledge.

Pye, Lucian W. 1981. "Foreword." In *Shanghai: Revolution and Development in an Asian Metropolis*, edited by Christopher Howe, xi–xvi. Cambridge: Cambridge University Press.

Quataert, Donald. 1994. "The Age of Reforms, 1812–1914." In *An Economic and Social History of the Ottoman Empire 1300–1914*, edited by Halil İnalcık, 749–943. Cambridge: Cambridge University Press.

Quigley, Carroll. 1979. *The Evolution of Civilization*. Indianapolis: Liberty Press.

Quijano, Anibal. 2007. "Coloniality and Modernity/Rationality." *Cultural Studies* 21: 168–78.

Quijano, Aníbal. 2000. "Coloniality of Power and Eurocentrism in Latin America." *International Sociology* 15(2): 215–32.

Rahmato, Dessalegn. 2008. *The Peasant and the State: Studies in Agrarian Change in Ethiopia, 1950s–2000s*. Custom Publishing.

Rahmato, Dessalegn. 1988. "Political Power and Social Formation Under the Old Regime: Notes on Marxist Theory." In *Proceedings of the Eighth International*

Conference of Ethiopian Studies, Volume I, edited by Taddese Beyene, 463–78. Addis Ababa: Institute of Ethiopian Studies.

Rahmato, Dessalegn. 1984. *Agrarian Reform in Ethiopia*. Uppsala: Scandinavian Institute of African Studies.

Rawlinson, John, L. 1967. "China's Failure to Coordinate Her Modern Fleets in the Late Nineteenth Century." In *Approaches to Modern Chinese History*, edited by Albert Feuerwerker, Rhoads Murphey and Mary Clabaugh Wright, 105–32. Cambridge: Cambridge University Press.

Reeve, John. 2011. "British Naval Strategy: War on a Global Scale." In *Strategy in the American War of Independence: A Global Approach*, edited by Donald Stoker, Kenneth J. Hagan, and Michael T. McMaster, 73–99. London: Routledge.

Retta, Zewde. 2000. *Ye Ertra Guday be Kedamawi Haile Selassie Mengist: 1941–1963* [The Eritrean Case during the Reign of Haile Selassie I: 1941–63]. Addis Ababa: Central Printing Press.

Riper, A. Bowdoin Van. 2007. *Rockets and Missiles: The Life Story of a Technology*. Baltimore: Johns Hopkins University Press.

Robinson, Ronald, John Gallagher, and Alice Denny. 1981. *Africa and the Victorians: The Official Mind of Imperialism*. London: Macmillan.

Robinson, Ronald. 1972. "Non-European Foundations of European Imperialism: Sketch for a Theory of Collaboration." In *Studies in the Theory of Imperialism*, edited by Roger Owen and Bob Sutcliffe, 117–42. London: Longman.

Robinson, Ronald. 1986. "The Excentric Idea of Imperialism, With or Without Empire." In *Imperialism and After: Continuities and Discontinuities,* edited by Wolfgang J. Mommsen and Jürgen Osterhammel, 267–89. London: Allen & Unwin.

Robinson, William I. 2015. "The Transnational State and the BRICS: A Global Capitalism Perspective." *Third World Quarterly* 36(1): 1–21.

Rock, Michael T. 1993. "'Twenty-Five Years of Economic Development' Revisited." *World Development* 21: 1787–801.

Rogan, Eugene L. 2002. *Frontiers of the State in the Late Ottoman Empire: 1850–1921*. Cambridge: Cambridge University Press.

Rogan, Eugene L. 1994. "Bringing the State Back: The Limits of Ottoman Rule in Jordan, 1840–1910." In *Village, Steppe and State: The Social Origins of Modern Jordan*, edited by Eugene L. Rogan and Tariq M.M. Tell, 32–57. London: British Academic Press.

Rogers, J.M. 1976. "Waqf and Patronage in Seljuk Anatolia: The Epigraphic Evidence." *Anatolian Studies* 26: 69–103.

Romagnolo, David. J. 1975. "The So-Called Law of Uneven and Combined Development." *Latin American Perspectives* 2(1): 7–31.

Rosenberg, Justin. 2016. "Confessions of a Sociolator." *Millennium: Journal of International Studies* 44(2): 292–99.

Rosenberg, Justin. 2013a. "Kenneth Waltz and Leon Trotsky: Anarchy in the Mirror of Uneven and Combined Development." *International Politics* 50(2): 183–230.

Rosenberg, Justin. 2013b. "The 'Philosophical Premises' of Uneven and Combined Development." *Review of International Studies* 39(3): 569–97.

Rosenberg, Justin. 2010. "Basic Problems in the Theory of Uneven and Combined Development, Part II: Unevenness and Political Multiplicity." *Cambridge Review of International Affairs* 23(1): 165–89.

Rosenberg, Justin. 2007. "International Relations—the 'Higher Bullshit': A Reply to the Globalization Theory Debate." *International Politics* 44(4): 450–82.

Rosenberg, Justin. 2006. "Why Is There No International Historical Sociology?" *European Journal of International Relations* 12(3): 307–40.

Rosenberg, Justin. 2005. "Globalization Theory: A Post-Mortem." *International Politics* 42(1): 2–74.

Rosenberg, Justin. 1996. "Isaac Deutscher and the Lost History of International Relations." *New Left Review* I/215: 3–15.

Rosenberg, Justin. 1994. *The Empire of Civil Society: A Critique of the Realist Theory of International Relations.* London: Verso.

Rostow, W.W. 1960. *The Stages of Economic Growth: A Non-Communist Manifesto.* Cambridge: Cambridge University Press.

Rowe, William. 2002. "Social Stability and Social Change." In *Cambridge History of China, Volume 9: The Ch'ing Empire to 1800, Part 1,* edited by Willard Peterson, 473–562. Cambridge: Cambridge University Press.

Ruggie, John G. 1982. "International Regimes, Transactions and Change: Embedded Liberalism in the Postwar Economic Order." *International Organization* 36(2): 379–415.

Runciman, W.G. 1997. *A Treatise on Social Theory, Volume III: Applied Social Theory.* Cambridge: Cambridge University Press.

Runciman, W.G. 1989. *A Treatise on Social Theory, Volume II: Substantive Social Theory.* Cambridge: Cambridge University Press.

Runciman, W.G. 1983. *A Treatise on Social Theory, Volume I: The Methodology of Social Theory.* Cambridge: Cambridge University Press.

Sabaratnam, Meera. 2011. "The Manacles of (Uneven and Combined) Development: Can We Be Released?" Paper presented at British International Studies Association Conference.

Said, Edward W. 1978/2003. *Orientalism.* London: Penguin.

Sandbrook, Richard. 2005. "Africa's Great Transformation." *Journal of Development Studies* 41(6): 1118–25.

Schaeffer, Robert K. 2012. *Red, Inc.: Dictatorship and the Development of Capitalism in China, 1949 to the Present.* Boulder: Paradigm Publishers

Schmidt, Ray. 1981. "Canadian Political Economy: A Critique." *Studies in Political Economy* 6: 65–92.

Schneider, Jane. 1977. "Was There a Pre-Capitalist World-System?" *Peasant Studies* 6(1): 20–9. Reprinted in *Core/Periphery Relations in Precapitalist Worlds*, edited by Christopher Chase-Dunn and Thomas D. Hall, 45–66. Boulder: Westview Press.

Schwartz, Herman. 2000 [1994]. *States versus Markets: The Emergence of a Global Economy.* London: Palgrave Macmillan, 2nd Edition.

Selwyn, Ben. 2011. "Trotsky, Gerschenkron and the Political Economy of Late Capitalist Development." *Economy and Society* 40(3): 421–50.

Service, Elman. 1971. *Cultural Evolutionism: Theory and Practice.* New York: Holt, Reinhart and Winston.

Seth, Michael. 2011. *A History of Korea from Antiquity to the Present.* Lanham: Rowman and Littlefield.

Sewell, William. 2005. *Logics of History: Social Theory and Social Transformation.* Chicago: University of Chicago Press.

Seymour, Richard. 2012. *The Liberal Defence of Murder.* London: Verso.

Shanin, Teodor. 1990. "The Question of Socialism: A Development Failure or an Ethical Defeat?" *History Workshop Journal* 30(1): 68–74.

Shanin, Teodor. 1983. "Late Marx: Gods and Craftsman." In *Late Marx and the Russian Road: Marx and 'the Peripheries of Capitalism',* edited by Teodor Shanin, 3–39. New York: Monthly Review.

Shaw, Martin. 2000. *Theory of the Global State: Globality as an Unfinished Revolution.* Cambridge: Cambridge University Press.

Shaw, Stanford J. 1976. *History of the Ottoman Empire and Modern Turkey: Volume 1, Empire of the Gazis: The Rise and Decline of the Ottoman Empire 1280–1808.* Cambridge: Cambridge University Press.

Shilliam, Robbie. 2015. *The Black Pacific: Anti-Colonial Struggles and Oceanic Connections.* London: Bloomsbury.

Shilliam, Robbie. 2009a. "The Atlantic as a Vector of Uneven and Combined Development." *Cambridge Review of International Affairs* 22(1): 69–88.

Shilliam, Robbie. 2009b. *German Thought and International Relations: The Rise and Fall of a Liberal Project.* London: Palgrave Macmillan.

Shilliam, Robbie. 2004. "Hegemony and the Unfashionable Problematic of Primitive Accumulation." *Millennium: Journal of International Studies* 33(1): 59–88.

Shin, Sangwon. 2015. "Socio-Economic Changes and the Fluctuation in the Nobi Population in Choson Korea After the Imjin War (1592–1598)." MA Diss., SOAS, University of London.

Shinder, Joel. 1978. "Early Ottoman Administration in the Wilderness: Some Limits on Comparison." *International Journal of Middle East Studies* 9(4): 497–517.

Simpson, Gerry. 2004. *Great Powers and Outlaw States: Unequal Sovereigns in the International Legal Order.* Cambridge: Cambridge University Press.

Skocpol, Theda. 1994. *Social Revolutions in the Modern World.* Cambridge: Cambridge University Press.

Skocpol, Theda. 1979. *States and Social Revolution: A Comparative Analysis of France, Russia and China.* Cambridge: Cambridge University Press.

Skocpol, Theda. 1973. "A Critical Review of Barrington Moore's *Social Origins of Dictatorship and Democracy.*" *Politics and Society* 4(1): 1–34.

Smith, Neil. 2008. *Uneven Development: Nature, Capital and the Production of Space.* Athens: University of Georgia Press.

Smith, Neil. 2006. "The Geography of Uneven Development." In *100 Years of Permanent Revolution: Results and Prospects,* edited by Hugo Radice and Bill Dunn, 180–95. London: Pluto.

Smith, Richard. 2009. *Premodern Trade in World History.* Abingdon: Routledge.

Solberg, C.E. 1973. "The Tariff and Politics in Argentina, 1916–1930." *The Hispanic American Historical Review* 53(2): 260–84.

Solberg, C.E. 1987. *The Prairies and the Pampas: Agrarian Policy in Canada and Argentina 1880–1930.* Stanford: Stanford University Press

Solberg, C.E. 1985. "Land Tenure and Land Settlement: Policy and Patterns in the Canadian Prairies and the Argentine Pampas." In *Argentina, Australia and Canada: Studies in Comparative Development 1870–1965*, edited by D.C.M. Platt and Guido di Tella, 53–75. London: Macmillan Press Ltd.

Spivak, Gayatri. 1994. "Can the Subaltern Speak?" In *Colonial Discourse and Post-Colonial Theory: A Reader*, edited by Patrick Williams and Laura Chrisman, 66–111. New York: Columbia University Press.

Spruyt, Hendrik. 1994. *The Sovereign State and its Competitors: An Analysis of Systems Change.* Princeton: Princeton University Press.

Stedman Jones, Gareth. 1984 [1971]. *Outcast London: A Study in the Relationships between Classes in Victorian Society.* Harmondsworth: Penguin Books.

Steel, David. 2010. "A Combined and Uneven Development Approach to the European Neolithic." *Critique of Anthropology* 30(2): 131–51.

Stinchcombe, Arthur. 1978. *Theoretical Methods in Social History.* New York: Academic Press.

Stoker, Donald, Kenneth J. Hagan, and Michael T. McMaster, eds. 2011. *Strategy in the American War of Independence: A Global Approach.* London: Routledge.

Stone, Norman. 1983. *Europe Transformed, 1878–1919.* London: Fontana.

Strikwerda, Carl. 1999. "Tides of Migration, Currents of History: The State, Economy, and Transatlantic Movements of Labour in the Nineteenth and Twentieth Centuries." *International Review of Social History* 44(3): 367–94.

Sugar, Peter F. 1993. *Southeastern Europe Under Ottoman Rule: 1354–1804.* London: University of Washington Press.

Sunar, Ilkay. 1987. "State and Economy in the Ottoman Empire." In *The Ottoman Empire and the World Economy*, edited by Huri Islamoğlu-Inan, 63–88. Cambridge: Cambridge University Press.

Sweezy, Paul Marlor. 1954. *The Transition from Feudalism to Capitalism: A Symposium.* London: Science and Society.

Tansel, Cemal Burak. 2015. "Deafening Silence? Marxism, International Historical Sociology and the Spectre of Eurocentrism." *European Journal of International Relations* 21(1): 76–100.

Tareke, Gebru. 2009. *The Ethiopian Revolution: War in the Horn of Africa.* New Haven: Yale University Press.

Temple, Robert. 2007. *The Genius of China: 3,000 Years of Science, Discovery, and Invention.* Rochester: Inner Traditions.

Tenbruck, Friedrich. 1994. "Internal History of Society or Universal History?" *Theory, Culture and Society* 11(1): 75–93.

Teschke, Benno. 2014. "IR Theory, Historical Materialism, and the False Promise of International Historical Sociology." *Spectrum: Journal of Global Studies* 6(1): 1–66.

Teschke, Benno. 2005. "Bourgeois Revolution, State Formation and the Absence of the International." *Historical Materialism* 13(2): 3–26.

Teschke, Benno. 2003. *The Myth of 1648: Class, Geopolitics, and the Making of Modern International Relations.* London: Verso.

Tezcan, Baki. 2011. "The New Order and the Fate of the Old: The Historiographical Construction of an Ottoman *Ancien Regime* in the Nineteenth Century." In

Tributary Empires in Global History, edited by Peter Fibiger Bang and C.A. Bayly, 74–95. Eastbourne: Palgrave Macmillan.

Tezcan, Baki. 2010. *The Second Ottoman Empire: Political and Social Transformation in the Early Modern World*. Cambridge: Cambridge University Press.

Thomas, Peter D. 2009. *The Gramscian Moment: Philosophy, Hegemony and Marxism*. Leiden: Brill.

Thompson, William, R. 1999. "The Military Superiority Thesis and the Ascendancy of Western Eurasia in the World System." *Journal of World History* 10(1): 143–78.

Tibebu, Teshale. 1995. *The Making of Modern Ethiopia, 1896–1974*. Rutgers: Red Sea Press.

Tilly, Charles. 2004. *Contention and Democracy in Europe, 1650–2000*. Cambridge: Cambridge University Press.

Tilly, Charles. 1992. *Coercion, Capital and European States, A.D. 990–1990*. Oxford: Wiley-Blackwell, Revised Edition.

Tilly, Charles. 1984. *Big Structures, Large Processes, Huge Comparisons*. New York: Russell Sage Foundation.

Tiruneh, Andargatchew. 1993. *The Ethiopia Revolution, 1974–1987: A Transformation from an Aristocratic to a Totalitarian Autocracy*. Cambridge: Cambridge University Press.

Togan, Isenbike. 1991. "Ottoman History by Inner Asian Norms." *Journal of Peasant Studies* 18(3–4): 185–210.

Tooze, Adam. 2015. "Capitalist Peace or Capitalist War? The July Crisis Revisited." In Cataclysm 1914: The First World War and the Making of Modern World Politics, edited by Alexander Anievas, 66–95. Leiden: Brill.

Toynbee, Arnold. 1946. *A Study of History* (Somervell Abridgement). Oxford: Oxford University Press.

Trotsky, Leon D. 2007 [1930–1932]. *The History of the Russian Revolution*. Chicago: Haymarket Books.

Trotsky, Leon. 1997 [1930–1932]. *The History of the Russian Revolution*. London: Pluto.

Trotsky, Leon D. 1980b [1913]. "Stojan Novakovic." In *The Balkan Wars, 1912–1913*, edited by George Weissman and Duncan Williams, 82–89. New York: Monad Press.

Trotsky, Leon D. 1980a [1926]. "Speech to the Seventh (Enlarged) Plenum of the ECCI." In *The Challenge of the Left Opposition (1926–27)*, edited by Naomi Allen and George Saunders, 258–64. New York: Pathfinder.

Trotsky, Leon D. 1979 [1940]. "A Serious Work on Russian Revolutionary History." In *Writings of Leon Trotsky Supplement (1934–40)*, edited by George Breitman, 857–59. New York: Pathfinder.

Trotsky, Leon D. 1977 [1930–32]. *The History of the Russian Revolution*. London: Pluto.

Trotsky, Leon D. 1976b [1938]. "Revolution and War in China." In *Leon Trotsky on China*, edited by Les Evans and Russell Block, 578–91. New York: Monad.

Trotsky, Leon D. 1976a [1937]. "Not a Worker's State and Not a Bourgeois State?" In *Writings of Leon Trotsky [1937–38]*, edited by Naomi Allen and George Breitman, 60–71. New York: Pathfinder, 2nd Edition.

Trotsky, Leon D. 1974b [1928]. *The Third International after Lenin*. London: New Park.

Trotsky, Leon D. 1974a [1925]. "Where Is Britain Going?" In *Collected Writings and Speeches on Britain, Volume 2*, edited by R. Chappell and Alan Clinton, 1–123. London: New Park.

Trotsky, Leon D. 1973 [1931]. "The Spanish Revolution and the Dangers Threatening It." In *The Spanish Revolution (1931–39)*, edited by Naomi Allen and George Breitman, 111–34. New York: Pathfinder Press.

Trotsky, Leon D. 1972c [1933]. "Japan Heads for Disaster." In *Writings of Leon Trotsky [1932–33]*, edited by George Breitman and Sarah Lovell, 287–94. New York: Pathfinder.

Trotsky, Leon D. 1972b [1924]. "For the Internationalist Perspective." In *Leon Trotsky Speaks*, 198–208. New York: Pathfinder.

Trotsky, Leon D. 1972a [1933]. "Uneven and Combined Development and the Role of American Imperialism: Minutes of a Discussion." In *Writings of Leon Trotsky [1932–33]*, edited by George Breitman and Sarah Lovell, 116–20. New York: Pathfinder.

Trotsky, Leon. 1970 [1928]. *The Third International After Lenin*. New York: Pathfinder.

Trotsky, Leon. 1969 [1907]. *1905*. Paris: Éditions de minuit.

Trotsky, Leon. 1967 [1930–32]. *History of the Russian Revolution, Volume I*. London: Sphere.

Trotsky, Leon. 1962. *The Permanent Revolution/Results and Prospects*. London: New Park Publications.

Trotsky, Leon. 1960 [1930–32]. *The History of the Russian Revolution*. New York: Pathfinder.

Trotsky, Leon D. 1949. "Karl Marx." In *Leon Trotsky Presents the Living Thoughts of Karl Marx*, 1–45. London: Cassell.

Trotsky, Leon D. 1937. *The Revolution Betrayed: What Is the Soviet Union and Where Is It Going?* New York: Pathfinder.

Trotsky, Leon. 1918. *Our Revolution*. Translated by Moissaye J. Olgin. New York: Henry Holt and Company.

Tully, James. 1993. *An Approach to Political Philosophy*. Cambridge: Cambridge University.

Turan, Osman. 1970. "Anatolia in the Period of the Selçuks and the Beyliks." In *Cambridge History of Islam, Volume I*, edited by P.M. Holt, Ann K.S. Lambton, and Bernard Lewis, 231–62. Cambridge: Cambridge University Press.

Turchin, Peter. 2009. "A Theory of the Formation of Large Empires." *Journal of Global History* 4: 191–217.

Turner, Bryan S. 1978. *Marx and the End of Orientalism*. Sydney: Allen & Unwin.

van der Linden, Marcel. 2007. "The 'Law' of Uneven and Combined Development: Some Underdeveloped Thoughts." *Historical Materialism* 15(1): 145–65.

van der Pijl, Kees. 2015. "The Uneven and Combined Development of International Historical Sociology." In *Theoretical Engagements in Geopolitical Economy (Research in Political Economy Volume 30A)*, edited by Radhika Desai, 45–83. Bingley: Emerald Group Publishing Limited.

van der Pijl, Kees. 2013. *The Discipline of Western Supremacy: Modes of Foreign Relations and Political Economy, Volume III*. London: Pluto.

van der Pijl, Kees. 2010a. *The Foreign Encounter in Myth and Religion: Modes of Foreign Relations and Political Economy, Volume II*. London: Pluto.

van der Pijl, Kees. 2010b. "Historicising the International: Modes of Foreign Relations and Political Economy." *Historical Materialism* 18(2): 3–34.

van der Pijl, Kees. 2007. *Nomads, Empires, States: Modes of Foreign Relations and Political Economy*. London: Pluto Press.

Vayda, Andrew P. 1967. "Pomo Trade Feasts." In *Tribal and Peasant Economies*, edited by George Dalton, 494–500. Garden City: Natural History Press.

Vico, Giambattista. 1984. *New Science of Giambattista Vico: Unabridged Translation of the Third Edition*. Translated by T.G. Bergin and M.H. Fisch. Ithaca: Cornell University Press.

Voegelin, Ermine W. 1942. "Culture Element Distributions: Northeast California." *University of California Anthropological Records* 7(2): 47–252.

Vryonis, Speros. 1969. "The Byzantine Legacy and Ottoman Forms." *Dumbarton Oaks Papers* 23/24: 251–308.

Vryonis, Speros. 1975. "Nomadization and Islamization in Asia Minor." *Dumbarton Oaks Papers* 29: 41–71.

Wade, Abdoulaye. 2008. "Time for the West to Practice What It Preaches." *Financial Times*. Accessed 7 April 2016. http://www.ft.com/cms/s/0/5d347f88-c897–11dc-94a6–0000779fd2ac.html#axzz458jDSZdT.

Waites, Bernard. 1999. *Europe and the Third World: From Colonisation to Decolonisation, c.1500–1998*. London: MacMillan.

Wallerstein, Immanuel. 1974. *The Modern World System, Volume I: Capitalist Agriculture and the Origins of the European World-Economy in the Sixteenth Century*. New York: Academic Press

Wallerstein, Immanuel. 1976. "Semiperipheral Countries and the Contemporary World Crisis." *Theory and Society* 3(4): 461–83.

Wallerstein, Immanuel. 1980. *The Modern World-System, Volume II: Mercantilism and the Consolidation of the European World-Economy, 1600–1750*. New York: Academic Press.

Wallerstein, Immanuel. 1984. "The Quality of Life in Different Social Systems: The Model and the Reality." In *The Politics of the World-Economy*, edited by Immanuel Wallerstein, 147–58. Cambridge: Cambridge University Press.

Wallerstein, Immanuel. 1989. *The Modern World-System, Volume III: The Second Era of Great Expansion of the Capitalist World-Economy, 1730s–1840s*. San Diego: Academic Press.

Wallerstein, Immanuel. 2002. "The West, Capitalism and the Modern World System." In *China and Historical Capitalism: Genealogies of Sinological Knowledge*, edited by Timothy Brook and Gregory Blue, 10–56. Cambridge: Cambridge University Press.

Wallerstein, Immanuel. 2011. *The Modern World-System, Volume IV: Centrist Liberalism Triumphant, 1789–1914*. Berkeley: University of California Press.

Waltz, Kenneth N. 1986. "Reflections on *Theory of International Politics*: A Response to My Critics." In *Neorealism and its Critics*, edited by Robert Keohane, 322–46. New York: Columbia University Press.

Waltz, Kenneth N. 1979. *Theory of International Politics*. Reading: Addison-Wesley.

Waltz, Kenneth N. 1998. "Interview with Ken Waltz, Conducted by Fred Halliday and Justin Rosenberg." *Review of International Studies* 24(3): 371–86.

Warner, Carolyn M. 1999. "The Political Economy of 'Quasi-Statehood' and the Demise of 19th Century African Politics." *Review of International Studies* 25(2): 233–55.

Warner, Carolyn M. 2001. "The Rise of the State System in Africa." *Review of International Studies* 27(5): 65–89.

Warren, Bill. 1981. *Imperialism: Pioneer of Capitalism*. New York: Verso.

Warwick Research Collective. 2015. *Combined and Uneven Development: Towards a New Theory of World-Literature*. Liverpool: Liverpool University Press.

Watkins, M.H. 1963. "A Staple Theory of Economic Growth." *The Canadian Journal of Economics and Political Science* 29(2): 141–58.

Watson, Adam. 1992. *The Evolution of International Society: A Comparative Historical Analysis*. London: Routledge.

Wei, Lingling and Bob Davis. 2015. "China Forgoes Veto Power at New Bank to Win Key European Nations' Support." *Wall Street Journal*. Accessed 7 April 2016. http://www.wsj.com/articles/china-forgoes-veto-power-at-new-bank-to-win-key-european-nations-support-1427131055.

Wertheim, Willem. 1974. *Evolution and Revolution: The Rising Waves of Emancipation*. Harmondsworth: Penguin Books.

Wickham, Chris. 2005. *Framing the Early Middle Ages: Europe and the Mediterranean, 400–800*. Oxford: Oxford University Press.

Wight, Martin. 1966. "Why Is There No International Theory?" In *Diplomatic Investigations*, edited by Herbert Butterfield and Martin Wight, 17–34. London: Allen and Unwin.

Wilks, Mark. 1869. *Historical Sketches of the South of India, in an Attempt to Trace the History of Mysoor: From the Origin of the Hindoo Government of That State, to the Extinction of the Mohammedan Dynasty in 1799*. Madras: Higginbotham and Co., 2nd Edition.

Williams, David and Tom Young. 2009. "The International Politics of Social Transformation: Trusteeship and Intervention in Historical Perspective." In *Empire, Development and Colonialism: The Past in the Present,* edited by Mark Duffield and Vernon Hewitt, 102–15. Woodbridge: James Currey.

Wittek, Paul. 2012. *The Rise of the Ottoman Empire: Studies in the History of Turkey, Thirteenth-Fifteenth Centuries*. New York: Routledge Chapman & Hall.

Wittfogel, Karl. 1957. *Oriental Despotism: A Comparative Study of Total Power*. London: Yale University Press.

Woldegiorgis, Dawit. 1989. *Red Tears: War, Famine, and Revolution in Ethiopia*. Trenton, NJ: Red Sea Press.

Wolf, Eric R. 1982. *Europe and the People Without History*. Berkeley: University of California Press.

Wong, R. Bin. 2002. "The Search for European Differences and Domination in the Early Modern World: A View from Asia." *The American Historical Review* 107(2): 447–69.

Wood, Ellen Meiksins. 1995. *Democracy Against Capitalism: Renewing Historical Materialism*. Cambridge: Cambridge University Press.

Wood, Ellen Meiksins. 2002. *The Origin of Capitalism: A Longer View*. London: Verso.

Woods, Ngaire. 2005. "The Shifting Politics of Foreign Aid." *International Affairs* 81(2): 393–409.

Wright, Erik Olin. 1983. "Review: Is Marxism Really Functionalist, Class Reductionist, and Teleological?" *American Journal of Sociology* 89(2): 452–59.

Yi Ch'ŏngwon. 1935. "Chosŏnin sasang e issŏsŏ ui 'Aseajŏk' hyŏngtae e taehaya." *Tonga Ilbo* [On The 'Asiatic' Forms Present in Korean Thought], 30 November.

Yi Pungman. 1948. *Yijo sahoe kyongjesa yon'gu* [A Study in the Socio-Economic History of the Yi Dynasty]. Soul: Taesŏng Publishing.

Yoffee, Norman. 1991. "The Collapse of Ancient Mesopotamian States and Civilization." In *The Collapse of Ancient States and Civilizations*, edited by Norman Yoffee and George Cowgill, 44–68. Tucson: University of Arizona Press.

Young, John. 2006. *Peasant Revolution in Ethiopia: The Tigray People's Liberation Front, 1975–1991*. Cambridge: Cambridge University Press.

Zachariadou, Elizabeth. 1978. "Observations on Some Turcica of Pachymeres." *Revue des études byzantines* 36(1): 261–67.

Zewde, Bahru. 2014. *The Quest for a Socialist Utopia: The Ethiopian Student Movement, c. 1960–1974*. London: James Curry.

Zewde, Bahru. 2002. *Pioneers of Change in Ethiopia: The Reformist Intellectuals of the Early Twentieth Century*. Athens: Ohio University Press.

Zewde, Bahru. 1991. *A History of Modern Ethiopia, 1855–1974*. Addis Ababa: Addis Ababa University Press.

Zewde, Bahru. 1984. "Economic Origins of the Absolutist State in Ethiopia, 1916–1935." *Journal of Ethiopian Studies* 17: 1–24.

Zmolek, Michael Andrew. 2013. *Rethinking the Industrial Revolution: Five Centuries of Transition from Agrarian to Industrial Capitalism in England*. Leiden: Brill.

Zurcher, E.J. 1993. *Turkey: A Modern History*. London: I.B. Taurus.

Index

11 September attacks (9/11), 27, 163
1848 Revolutions, 46
absolutism, 1, 49, 193
Adelman, Jeremy, 136–43
Africa, 13, 50, 127, 149–69, 177, 179,
    187, 195, 199, 202, 215, 216,
    218;
  East, 156–57;
  North, 25;
  Sub-Saharan, 18;
  West, 156, 158
African Union, 164
ahistoricism, 14, 219, 242
akhis, 79, 80, 85, 86
Akkadian empire, 213
Alexander II, 48
al-Fayiz, Sattam, 105
Algeria, 101, 199
Allinson, Jamie, 12, 38, 59, 146–47n3,
    176, 244
alternative modernities, 16n5
amalgamated state-formations, 232
American War of Independence
    (1775–83), 117
Americas, 22, 44, 50, 228, 229;
  See also 'New World'
Amin, Samir, 58, 70n5, 97
Anatolia, 12, 75–78, 80–82, 84, 85, 86,
    87, 89, 90, 94, 100
Anderson, Perry, 2, 32, 69n2, 70n4

Anglo-Japanese Alliance, 176
Anievas, Alexander, 14–15, 33–34, 35,
    37, 38, 39, 44, 51, 146–47n3,
    168n3, 176, 214, 219, 221, 223,
    224–27, 227–31, 232, 233, 234,
    236, 240, 243
anti-colonialism/anti-colonial, 106, 161,
    199, 202, 224, 226, 242, 248
Arabian Peninsula, 104
Argentina, 47, 127–28, 131, 135–36,
    137, 139, 141–46
aristocracy, 46, 60, 62, 65–66, 68, 69,
    70n10, 75, 81, 83, 185, 229
Arrighi, Giovanni, 114, 215
Asante, 155, 157
Asia, 12–13, 25, 28, 43, 54, 55, 76,
    113–14, 115–16, 117, 123, 124,
    125, 127, 154, 227;
  Central, 76;
  East, 50, 53, 54, 55, 66, 115, 117,
    178, 215;
  Inner, 12, 75, 76–78, 82, 84, 85, 86,
    89;
  Minor, 76–77, 81;
  South and Southeast, 177, 215,
    230–31.
  See also Asia Pacific
Asian Infrastructure Investment Bank,
    215, 216–17, 218
Asia Pacific, 224

askeri, 74, 75, 84, 88, 89
Austria, 101.
  See also Austria-Hungary
Austria-Hungary, 48, 225
Australia, 146n1, 178

backwardness, 16n6, 23, 33, 45–46,
  48–59, 53–57, 69, 96, 106,
  188–90, 193–97, 200, 202–3,
  203n3, 233, 242, 244;
  advantages of, 41, 207;
  consciousness of, 189;
  'Privilege of historic', 23–24, 26,
    28–29, 40, 44, 47, 188, 208,
    214, 230
Bacon, Francis, 19
balance of power, 155, 225–26, 229
Balkan Wars (1912–13), 225
Battle of Köse Dağı (1243), 80
Battle of Manzikert (1071), 76
Battle of Pollilur (1780), 122, 123
Bauman, Zygmunt, 20
Bayezid I, 77
Bayly, Christopher, 47, 50
bedouin, 95, 98, 102, 103–4, 105,
  107, 108
Bendix, Richard, 3
Berlin Conference (1884–85), 225
Bhambra, Gurminder, 111, 112, 249n4
bifurcated states, 158–59
Bithynia, 75, 77, 82, 84, 86
Black Death, 228, 299
Bois, Guy, 44–45
Bolivarian Alliance for the Peoples of
  Our America (ALBA), 215, 218
Bolshevik threat, 226
Bolshevism, 226.
  See also Bolshevik threat
Bond, Patrick, 216, 217
bourgeoisie, 21–22, 38, 46, 99, 201,
  233.
  See also capitalist class;
    'petty-bourgeois'
Boxer Rebellion (1899–1901), 225
Brazil, 14, 178, 215–16

Brenner, Robert, 132–33, 147n3, 203n4,
  228, 233–34
BRICs, 182, 215–18
Britain, 12–13, 27, 43–46, 50–51, 101,
  113–14, 114–19, 119–21, 124,
  125n5, 136, 149–69, 169n8, 178,
  181, 182, 183n4, 206, 215.
  See also British Empire; England
British East India Company, 117, 126n3
British Empire, 161, 224
Bromley, Simon, 90
Bronze Age, 212, 214
Buddhism, 62, 66
Burawoy, Michael, 33, 36, 51–52
Buzan, Barry, 13–14, 93, 244
Byzantine Empire, 12, 26, 74–77, 78,
  80–83, 84, 85, 86–87, 89

caging, 84, 91n4
Caliphate, 90
Callinicos, Alex, 39
Canada, 127–31, 135–40, 142–46
Cape of Good Hope, 120
Capital: Critique of Political Economy
  (1867), 42, 44, 70n6, 125n1, 234
capitalism, 8, 10, 13, 15, 21, 24–25,
  27, 28, 35, 36–37, 39, 40, 41–47,
  49, 51, 55, 56, 58, 59, 67, 94, 95,
  112, 114, 115–16, 130, 133–34,
  139, 152, 186–88, 191, 201, 207,
  214, 215–17, 221, 223, 232, 239,
  241, 242–48, 248n3;
  agrarian, 229–3;
  colonial, 161, 191;
  industrial, 11, 12, 23, 35, 36–37, 44,
    45, 46, 47, 137, 151, 221, 223;
  monopoly, 49;
  origins of, 1, 10, 21, 43–44, 132–33,
    220, 221, 227–31, 234, 247;
  state, 215.
  See also capitalist modernity
capitalist class, 22, 58, 115, 214
capitalist modernity, 10, 14–15, 44, 53,
  57, 147, 187, 189–90, 194, 228,
  242, 247, 251, 253

Carnatic Wars (1744–1763), 117
Catalonia, 43, 44
Cecil, Lord Robert, 226
centred globalism, 175, 180–81, 183
Chamberlain, Joseph, 160
Chase-Dunn, Christopher, 10, 14,
    205–6, 208–10, 215–16
Chatterjee, Partha, 94
Chenghis Khan, 77
Chile, 146, 178
China, 12–14, 19, 24, 26–28, 31, 36,
    43–44, 49, 52, 54–55, 60–61,
    63–64, 66, 68, 76, 113–15,
    120, 123, 125n2, 154, 167,
    174, 176–77, 179–81, 199, 206,
    215–18, 224–28, 233
Chŏn, Sŏktam, 55–56
Chosŏn Dynasty, 55, 60, 61, 64, 65–68
Christianity, 153, 193
city-states, 45, 175, 205–6, 208, 212–14
civilisation, 25, 26, 53, 124, 153, 173,
    236, 253.
    See also civilisational analysis
civilisational analysis, 253
class conflict and struggle, 21, 45, 46,
    58, 59, 60, 66–67, 68–69, 89,
    97, 135
class differentiation, 46, 61
class formation, 13, 113, 115, 128, 134,
    138, 140
classical political philosophy, 3
Cold War, 27, 162, 163, 180, 199–200,
    201
colonial modernity, 6, 241
combined and uneven development,
    8–9, 33, 248
commerce, 68, 69, 118, 153, 154, 155,
    193, 195.
    See also commercialisation
commercialisation, 67, 115, 197, 200
Commission for Africa, 149, 164–66
Commodore Perry, 176
communism, 25, 42, 57, 174;
    primitive, 42, 55, 58
Communist Manifesto (1848), 21, 22

Community of Latin American and
    Caribbean States (CELAC), 218
Confucianism, 62, 66
Confucius, 48, 66
Congreve, William Jr., 124
Congreve rocket, 121–24
conservatism, 174, 209
Constantine XI Palaiologos, 83
the Constitutional Revolution
    (1906–11), 232
constructivism, 20
contradictions of sociological
    amalgamation, 86
convergence/divergence, 54, 57, 58,
    59, 69
Cooper, Fredric, 157, 159, 162, 165,
    168
core-periphery, 14, 175, 177–78, 180,
    200, 205–6, 208, 210–11, 213,
    215, 217
corvée labour, 59, 65, 67, 69
creolisation, 247
critical theory, 20
Crusades, 42, 76, 78, 81, 235–36
cultural encounters, 15, 240–42, 245–48
customary rule, 159

Dalai Lama, 118
Davidson, Neil, 7, 8, 11, 219, 220, 221,
    244, 247, 248n3
Dead Sea, 106
decentred globalism, 182
decolonisation, 179, 194–95
democracy, 18, 163, 164, 174, 181, 196,
    198, 233
dependent development, 127, 129
despotic power, 97
devşirme, 74, 75, 80, 83, 87
diplomacy, 69, 151, 162, 166
domestic analogy, 4
Durkheim, Émile, 3, 19
Dutch Revolt of 1566, 44, 240

'Eastern Question', 93–110
'Eastern threat', 226

Economic Backwardness in Historical Perspective (1962), 23

Egypt, 90, 101, 104, 106–7, 156, 177

The Empire of Civil Society (1994), 33

Engels, Friedrich, 21, 41, 42

England, 1, 10, 21–22, 23, 24, 42, 43, 44–46, 47, 50, 97, 114–15, 133, 140, 195, 229–30, 234, 247

English Civil Wars (1642–51), 230

Enlightenment, 34, 41, 112, 172, 187, 239, 245

Escobar, Arturo, 8, 248n2, 249n7

Ethiopia, 14, 49, 155, 161, 185–203

Ethiopian revolutions, (1974/1991), 14, 185–203

ethnicity, 74, 90, 194, 198

Eurocentrism, 1, 2, 4–6, 10, 11, 14, 15, 16n3, 26, 41, 43–44, 53, 54–55, 56, 68, 94, 95–96, 111–13, 114, 115, 116, 121, 125, 150, 152, 154, 171–72, 202, 207, 219–37, 239, 241, 242–44, 246–47, 248, 248n2, 249n4, 252–53

Europe, 1, 5, 6, 10, 12, 14, 19, 23, 26, 27, 28, 36, 38, 42, 43–45, 53, 54, 56, 60, 67, 81, 82, 85, 86, 93, 94, 96, 97, 100, 101, 111, 114, 116, 122, 125, 129, 134, 135, 137, 144, 152, 155, 156, 172, 174, 176, 187, 193, 202, 203n4, 206, 207, 212, 214, 215, 217, 220, 221–23, 224–25, 226, 227, 228, 230, 234, 235–36, 239, 240, 244, 246, 247, 248;
    Central and Eastern, 139, 178, 224, 225, 226, 236
    North Western, 44, 221, 223
    South Eastern, 81
    Western, 23, 43–44, 100–101, 134, 207, 219, 221–23, 235–36, 239, 248

Europe and the People without History (1982), 70n5

Eurozone, 18

Evrenos, Gazi, 82

exchange networks, 14, 205, 210, 212–13

Fall of Constantinople (1453), 88

fascism, 39, 174;
    Italian, 156

fellahin, 98, 107, 108

feminism, 20

feudalism, 21, 42, 44–45, 50, 55, 56, 60, 94, 96, 97, 139, 144, 176, 194, 228.
    See also feudal mode of production

feudal mode of production, 45, 58, 70n4, 132

financialisation, 215

First World War (1914–18), 30n7, 47, 49, 94, 106, 109, 136, 160, 178, 179, 224–26

forces of production, 41, 46, 135, 136, 174

Fordism, 39

foreign investment, 215, 217

foreign policy, 75, 83, 84, 149, 163, 226.
    See also diplomacy

Foster-Carter, Aidan, 243–24

Fourth Anglo–Mysore War (1798–99), 122

Fourth International, 32

France, 18, 42, 43, 44–45, 46, 47, 97, 101, 116, 117, 137, 157, 229

'free trade', 153, 166, 179

French Revolution, 101, 189

G8, 149, 164

G20, 182

Gallagher, John, 152, 153, 154, 168n4

geography, 69n2, 86, 97, 129, 165, 173, 211

geopolitics, 20, 76, 80, 115, 118, 207, 252

Germany, 27, 42, 43, 46, 47, 156–57, 160, 174, 181.
    See also Prussia

Gerschenkron, Alexander, 22–23, 207

Ghana, 159

ghulam, 78–79
Gilpin, Robert, 16n8
global governance, 182
globalisation, 181, 216, 222
global modernity, 14, 172, 175–79,
    181–83, 183n1, 183n4, 188
global transformation, 171–72, 174–78,
    180–83, 183n1, 183n4
Glorious Revolution (1688–89), 230
Gold Coast, 157, 162
Goldstone, Jack, 2
Gramsci, Antonio, 38–39
great powers, 27, 46–47, 176, 180,
    225, 226
Grundrisse (1857–58), 244
Gulhane Rescript of 1839, 101–2

Haidar Ali, 117, 122
Haiti, 177
Haldon, John, 58, 70n7, 97
Halliday, Fred, 16n8, 193
Han Dynasty, 61
Harvey, David, 35
Hashemite monarchy, 49
Hegel, Georg Wilhelm Friedrich, 203n3
hegemony, 38–39;
    British, 113, 117, 118, 125;
    Chinese, 61;
    European, 206;
    'legalised', 179, 180;
    US, 215, 217;
    Western, 179–80, 187
Hideyoshi, Toyotomi, 66
Hideyoshi invasions of 1592–98, 66, 67
historical sociology (sub-field), 1–16,
    33–34, 53, 57, 93, 95, 109, 129,
    131, 208, 240–41, 251–55
historicism and historicity, 5, 52, 57, 244.
    See also ahistoricism;
        transhistoricity; 'ultra-historicist'
historiography, 244;
    Korean 11, 53, 54–56, 69n3, 70n12;
    Ottoman 73, 74, 93–94, 95
The History of the Russian Revolution
    (1932), 31, 36, 40, 48, 237n2

Hobson, John M., 10, 14–15, 43–44,
    114, 125n2, 244
House of Bourbon, 116
House of Hanover, 116
House of Osman, 85
How the West Came to Rule (2015), 38,
    227–31
hub theory, 209
Hughes, Billy, 226
Hung, Fo-Fung, 217
Huntington, Samuel, 23
hybridity, 1, 8, 90, 94, 240, 243

ideology, 66, 69, 82, 86, 90, 96, 187,
    201, 202, 233, 242
Ilkhanid Empire 76, 77, 87
imperialism 47, 150, 152, 153, 167,
    168n4, 171–72, 178;
    British, 113, 125;
    European, 101, 234;
    formal, 154, 180, 222;
    informal, 155;
    Japanese, 53;
    liberal, 13;
    modern, 242;
    practices of, 177;
    Russian, 225;
    sub-, 216;
    Western, 226;
    world, 49.
    See also social imperialists
İnalcık, Halil, 86
India, 14, 43–44, 50, 156, 171, 176,
    183n4, 215, 224–26, 231, 242.
    See also Indian subcontinent
Indian Ocean, 26, 100, 117
Indian subcontinent, 117, 122, 124
industrialisation, 27, 36, 45, 47, 49–50,
    118, 124, 129–30, 136, 143, 153,
    172, 175, 178, 179, 183n3, 200,
    220, 224;
    British, 171, 219–20, 230–31, 234;
    capitalist, 272–8, 45–46, 52, 151,
    222, 228, 237;
    'catch-up', 33;

Chinese, 28;
de-, 171;
European, 219, 223, 232;
German, 174;
late, 43, 188;
Russian, 22, 48, 223
Industrial Revolution, 21, 23, 189, 231, 237n2
infrastructural power, 94, 101, 104
intergovernmental organisations (IGOs), 179–80
International Marxist Group, 32
International Monetary Fund, 217–18
International Political Economy (IPE), 239
International Relations (IR), 1, 2, 3–4, 7, 11, 14, 15n1, 16n2, 16n3, 16n8, 17, 20, 25, 26, 29–30, 33–34, 94, 95, 109, 111, 125, 183n3, 219–21, 224, 226, 239, 242, 248, 252, 254
international sociality, 247
International society, 171, 177, 179–82;
Western-colonial, 171, 177;
Western-global, 171, 179–80
interpolity interaction, 14, 205–6, 209–10
intersocietal and international systems, 1, 4, 113, 133, 146n3, 151, 172, 221
iqta, 79, 80, 88
Iran, 27, 36, 177, 199, 208, 220–21, 223, 233.
See also the Constitutional Revolution (1906–11)
Iraq, 49, 106, 107, 109
Islam, 27, 73, 74, 78, 79, 86, 90, 193, 235–36;
heterodox, 79;
revolutionary, 233
Islamic, 235–36
Italian Risorgimento, 39
Italy/Italian city-states, 39, 43, 45, 47, 143–44, 191, 195, 235
Ivan the Terrible, 48

Janissaries, 80, 87, 88

Japan, 14, 43, 46–48, 53–58, 60–64, 66, 68–69, 69n, 176–81, 195, 215, 225, 227
Jones, Gareth Stedman, 51
Jordan, 12, 38, 100, 101, 104, 105, 106, 107–9

kadıs, 79, 80
Kant, Immanuel, 203n3
Karak Revolt of 1910, 104, 106
Khomeini, Ruhollah, 233
khuwwa, 12, 98–99, 101–2, 103–6, 107, 109–10
Kim, Kwangjin, 55
Kingdom of Mysore, 12, 117, 119, 122, 124, 126n3
kin-ordered mode of production, 70n5
Knei-Paz, Baruch, 16n6
Korea, 11, 53–73;
North, 54, 56, 61, 69n3;
South, 54, 56, 69n3, 180
Koryŏ Dynasty, 60, 63–67, 70n15

Labour Party (UK), 163, 169n5.
See also New Labour
Lagos, 157
Land Code of 1858, 99, 101–2, 105, 106, 107–8
Lattimore, Owen, 209, 212
law, 26, 65, 77, 79, 87, 88–89, 102, 105, 158, 164, 166, 169n10, 179, 200
Lawson, George, 13–14, 93, 244
League of Nations, 160, 226
Lenin, Vladimir Ilyich, 22, 47, 196, 226
liberalism, 149, 165, 172, 174, 180;
neo-, 180, 216
Lineages of the Absolutist State (1974), 70n4
List, Frederick, 42
Löwy, Michael, 32, 59

MacDonald, J. S., 138, 144
Macedonia, 213
Madagascar, 155
Mahdi Rebellion of 1881–84, 157

Malaya, 178
Manchuria, 61, 225
Mandate System, 226
Mann, Michael, 2, 101, 210, 213
marcher states, 14, 205–6, 213–14
Marx, Karl, 3, 19, 21, 22, 34, 35, 39,
    41–42, 44, 45, 54, 55, 56, 57,
    70n6, 96, 110n3, 125n1, 137,
    146n3, 200, 222, 234, 239, 242,
    244, 246
Marxism, 16n7, 20, 21–24, 31, 32–33,
    34–35, 39, 50, 54, 55–56, 57, 68,
    73–74, 96–97, 112, 131, 146nf3,
    168n4, 188, 196, 199, 224, 228,
    232, 233, 234–35, 242–45, 247;
    classical, 7, 32, 33, 35.
    See also Marxism-Leninism
Marxism-Leninism, 196, 198, 199, 201
Matin, Kamran, 14–15, 38, 208, 219,
    221, 223, 231–34, 240, 244
Mau Mau Uprising (1952–60), 162
means of production, 74, 75, 88, 90, 96,
    87, 105, 139, 141, 145
medresse, 79, 80
Mehmet II, 83, 88, 89
Meiji Restoration (1868), 48, 99
mercantilism, 115, 116, 153
merchants, 66, 68, 70n10, 84, 100, 115,
    116, 130, 138, 141, 231
Mesopotamia, 174.
    See also Mesopotamia system
Mesopotamia system, 213
methodological internalism/nationalism,
    1, 3, 4–5, 10, 15, 19, 20, 29, 54,
    73, 74, 90, 94, 95, 186, 222, 228,
    232, 233, 240, 246, 252
Michael VIII Palaeologus, 82
Middle East, 12, 28, 49, 73, 93,
    95, 235
migration, 13, 38, 75–78, 81–82, 84–85,
    89, 118, 135–36, 138, 142,
    144–45, 147, 163, 180, 293;
    Great Atlantic, 13, 135
Mihal, Köse, 82
Ming Empire, 25, 66

mode of power, 14, 172, 174–77,
    179–82, 183n2, 183n3
mode of production, 9, 35, 36, 37, 42,
    54, 57–58, 70n4, 70n5, 91n2,
    94, 97, 132, 146–47n3, 206, 221,
    228, 231, 232, 239, 242, 243,
    246, 249n3;
    articulation of, 8, 243–44
Modernisation Theory, 22, 73, 179
Molyneux, Maxine, 193
Mongolia, 118, 120
Mongols, 65, 76–77, 206, 228, 236
Morgenthau, Hans, 203n3
Moritani, Katsumi, 55
Mughal Empire, 25, 117
Muhammad Ali, 100, 101
multiple modernities, 5–6
Murad I, 87–88
Murray, Gilbert, 226
musha', 98, 102, 107–8
Mysorean rocket, 12, 111–26

Napoleonic Wars (1803–15), 118, 120
nationalism, 106, 124, 163, 172, 176,
    190, 193, 194, 199, 233.
    See also 'nationless nationalism'
'nationless nationalism', 233
nation state, 26, 57, 101, 115, 179, 189,
    194, 214
Ndebele Rebellion of 1896, 157
Needham, Joseph, 120
Nemesis, 120–21, 121–22
Neo-Gramscianism, 20
Netherlands, 43–44, 46, 206, 214
New Development Bank (NDB),
    215, 218
New Economic Partnership for African
    Development, 164
New Labour, 163–65, 169n5
New Left Review, 32
New Partnership for Africa's
    Development (NEPAD), 216
'New World', 13, 118, 127, 140, 247
New Zealand, 146n1, 178
Nicaragua, 177, 179

Nigeria, 159, 162–64
Nile Valley, 156, 157
Nişancıoğlu, Kerem, 12, 33–34, 35, 37, 38, 39, 44, 51, 95, 110n2, 215, 219, 221, 223, 227–31, 232, 233, 234, 236
nomadic mode of production, 70n4, 78, 86
nomads and nomadism, 12, 26, 42, 50, 75, 76–78, 82, 84, 86, 94, 96, 98, 102, 105, 107, 110, 208. *See also* nomadic mode of production
non-Western agency, 10, 94, 224, 226, 233, 237n5, 241, 242, 246
Norman Conquest of 1066, 42, 234

Ollman, Bertell, 35
Opium Wars (1839–42/1856–60), 12, 113, 114, 118, 119–21, 126n5, 176
Orientalism, 54, 73, 90, 186
Ottoman Empire, 12, 44, 49, 73–91, 93–110, 154, 177, 179, 224–26, 228–30, 236

Paek, Namun, 55
Palaeolithic Age, 14, 205
Palais, James, 60, 66, 67, 70n14–15
Palestine, 107
Parsons, Talcott, 3
Passages from Antiquity to Feudalism (1974), 70n4
passive revolution, 39, 223
patrimonial authority, 74, 75, 78, 89, 90. *See also* patrimonialism
patrimonialism, 174
Pax Mongolica, 214, 228–29
peasantry, 38, 42, 49, 74, 75, 78, 86, 90, 191, 192, 198, 199, 200, 229
permanent revolution, 6, 16n7, 31–32, 33, 51
Peter the Great, 41, 48
'petty-bourgeois', 196
Philippines, 178
Pieterse, Nederveen, 8, 248n2

Poggi, Gianfranco, 3
Poland, 83
Political Economy (discipline), 127, 129, 131; bourgeois, 39; classical, 34
Political Marxism, 13, 41, 44, 128, 131–32, 147n3
The Politics of Combined and Uneven Development (1981), 32
Polo, Marco, 26
Pomeranz, Kenneth, 114, 119
Portugal, 43, 47, 157, 231, 235
postcolonialism, 5–6, 20, 30, 68, 94, 111–12, 218, 244
poststructuralism, 6, 20
poverty, 55, 163, 197; global, 149
primitive accumulation, 12, 45, 94, 96, 99, 105, 109, 110, 135, 234; 'mimetic', 94, 96, 98, 102; 'socialist', 196
'problematic of the international', 1–16, 18–21
proletariat, 50–51, 140, 141, 145. *See also* working class
pronoia, 81–82, 83, 88
Prussia, 46

Qing Dynasty, 176, 213, 226
Quataert, Donald, 102
Quigley, Carrol, 207

race and racism, 172, 180, 216, 217, 226, 247
Rasid Pasha, Mehmet, 103, 104
rational statehood, 172, 183n3
Realism (International Relations theory), 4, 16n2, 20, 223, 252
reaya, 74, 75, 84, 88, 89
reciprocal minisystems, 209
relationality, 247–48
relations of production, 13, 44, 73–74, 100, 101, 107, 109, 131, 137, 244
Renaissance, 1, 26, 236;

post-, 193
revolution, 16n8, 21–22, 24, 27, 39,
    52, 174, 186, 189, 190, 202, 203,
    203n2, 215, 216, 224, 233;
    from above, 49;
    'against backwardness', 200, 202–3;
    'of backwardness', 232–33;
    bourgeois, 21, 22, 38, 39, 45, 51, 56,
        201, 232–33;
    counter-, 39;
    socialist, 6, 21, 51
The Revolution Betrayed (1937), 39
rise of the West, 1, 19, 26, 214, 221,
    223, 227, 228, 236
Robinson, Ronald, 150, 152–54,
    156–59, 161, 165, 168, 168n4
Rogan, Eugene, 101, 109
Roman Empire, 19, 61, 80, 89, 213
Rosenberg, Justin, 7, 9, 10, 11, 16n8,
    33, 36, 37, 39–41, 51, 113, 146n3,
    150, 168n2, 173, 179, 203n1,
    207, 208, 219, 221, 222, 223,
    246, 249n5
Rostow, Walt, 22, 23
ruling class, 29, 39, 42–43, 58, 62, 63,
    69, 70n14, 74, 75, 82, 83, 88,
    89–90, 96, 97, 99, 116, 229
Runcimen, W. G., 2
Russia, 6, 9, 14, 21–22, 23–24, 26, 27,
    31, 37, 38, 40, 43, 48–49, 50–51,
    52, 55, 99, 101, 133, 178, 181,
    188, 207, 215, 225–56, 236,
    237n3, 239

Samoa, 178
samurai, 97, 176
Sargon of Akkad, 213
Saudi Arabia, 27, 181
Scotland, 43, 46, 140, 220
scramble for Africa, 13, 153, 156–57,
    177
Second Anglo–Mysore War (1780–84),
    122
Second Battle of Chuenpee (1841), 121
Second International, 6, 23, 41, 51

Second World War (1939–45), 20, 32,
    114, 177, 202, 217, 227
seigniorial reaction, 229
Seljuk Empire, 12, 73, 75, 76, 77,
    78–80, 81, 82, 84, 87, 89
Senegal, 217
Seth, Michael, 61, 62, 70n13
SetPol Research Working Group, 214
settler colonies, 13, 127, 128, 129, 130,
    134, 135, 145, 146, 176, 177
Seven Years' War (1754–63), 117
Shanghai Cooperation Organisation, 192
sharecropping, 105–6, 107, 108, 110, 144
Shariati, Ali, 233
Shilliam, Robbie, 94, 203n3, 219, 241,
    242, 247–48, 254
Siam, 118
Siege of Seringapatam (1799), 122, 124
Sierra Leone, 149, 163
Silla Dynasty, 60, 62–64, 70n12, 70n13
Singapore, 180
Sino-Nepalese War of 1788–92, 119
Skocpol, Theda, 3, 20, 22
slavery, 55–56, 59–60, 63, 71n17, 97,
    155, 157;
    anti-, 153, 179;
    Atlantic, 247
Smith, Adam, 34
Smuts, Jan, 226
social democracy, 174;
    Russian, 38
social imperialists, 160
socialism, 6, 21, 172, 174, 196, 199
social property relations, 13, 128, 129,
    132, 133, 137, 139, 140, 141–42,
    145, 147n3, 200
sociocultural evolution, 14, 205, 209
Solberg, C. E., 127–28, 136, 139,
    141–44
Song Dynasty, 64, 123
South Africa, 14, 156–57, 162, 164,
    215–16
South America, 43
sovereignty, 64, 101, 177, 180, 192, 195;
    parcellized, 97

Spain, 43, 146, 235
The Stages of Economic Growth: A Non-Communist Manifesto (1960), 22
Stalin, Joseph, 55
Stalinism, 31
staples theory, 127, 128, 129, 131, 136
state formation, 54, 59–60, 64, 68, 89, 116–17, 155, 171;
    absolutist, 193;
    adaptive model of, 125;
    early, 61;
    Korean, 11, 53–71;
    Mysorean, 122;
    nomadic, 71;
    non-European, 12;
    Ottoman, 73–91
states system, 1, 46, 94, 95
Stone Age, 209
Subaltern Studies, 244
Sudan, 156–57
Suez Canal, 156
Suleyman the Magnificent, 83, 100
Sultan Bayezid I, 77, 88
Sultanism, 32, 56, 89
Sultan Orhan, 83
Sumer, 26, 213–14, 219
Syria, 12, 90, 101, 103, 106, 107, 109

Taiwan, 55, 120, 180
Tamerlane, 208
Tang Dynasty, 63
Tanzimat reforms, 99, 103, 104
tax-farming, 100
Tenbruck, Friedrich, 20
Thomas, Hall, 206
Three Kingdoms, 62–63, 70n11
Tibet, 118
Tilly, Charles, 3
tımar system, 74, 75, 80, 83, 85, 88
Tipu Sultan, 122, 124
Tönnies, Ferdinand, 3
totality, 35, 59, 75, 133, 251–52
trade, 19, 26, 28, 38, 59, 61, 66, 69, 70n13, 79, 100, 115, 118, 119–20,

129–30, 132, 144, 153, 155, 159, 160, 164, 166, 167, 169n8, 172, 173, 178, 179, 206, 209–10, 211, 212, 214, 228, 229, 230.
    See also 'free trade'
transhistoricity, 35–41
Transjordan, 94
tribelets, 210
tributary empires, 43, 105, 191, 206, 213–14
tributary mode of production, 12, 42, 54, 58, 70n5, 77, 84, 88, 89–90, 94, 96–97, 228;
    'fractured', 94, 96
Trotsky, Leon, 1, 6–11, 15, 16n6–8, 17, 18, 21–25, 25–27, 30, 30n3, 31–34, 36–37, 39–41, 46, 47–49, 50, 51, 52, 96, 98, 99, 111–13, 116, 121, 128, 131, 133–34, 146n3, 188, 203n1, 205, 207, 208, 209, 212, 214, 219, 220, 221, 223, 231, 237n2, 237n3, 239, 240, 244, 246
Trotskyism, 7, 15, 32, 33, 219–20, 224, 234
Tully, James, 246
Tunisia, 155
Turkey, 48–49, 199
Turkmenistan, 178

Uganda, 156
Ukraine, 18, 26, 83
ulema, 79, 84, 86, 87, 89, 90
'ultra-historicist', 222
underdevelopment, 165, 213, 242
uneven development, 8, 10, 11, 26, 28, 29, 34, 35, 39, 40, 41, 41–47, 52, 99, 173, 189, 205, 231
United States, 14, 22, 23, 28, 39, 44, 49, 137, 138, 143, 146, 177, 181, 182, 193, 195, 206, 215, 217, 218, 227
universalism, 5, 10–11, 55, 242, 253, 254
urbanisation, 36, 52
Uruguay, 146
uymaq, 208
Uzbekistan, 178

van der Pijl, Kees, 2, 33
Vico, Giambattista, 112
Vietnam, 23, 199
Vietnam War (1955–75), 23
Vikings, 19, 26
Virgin Islands, 178

wage labour, 35, 110, 139, 140, 143, 198
Wallerstein, Immanuel, 2, 209
Waltz, Kenneth, 20–22, 173
Wang Kŏn, 64
waqfs, 79
warfare, 63, 86–87, 100, 118, 209, 210, 212
Warren, Bill, 242
Washington consensus, 218
Weber, Max, 19, 203n3
Weberianism, 6
West Indies, 160–61
whip of external necessity, 6, 23, 24, 26, 28, 29, 40, 41, 95, 96, 98, 99–102, 105, 110, 113, 116, 120, 122, 125, 174, 220, 228, 230–31, 233, 235, 236
Wight, Martin, 3

Wilson, Woodrow, 226.
    See also Wilsonian diplomacy
Wilsonian diplomacy, 168n3
Wolf, Eric, 58, 70n5, 168n2
Wood, Ellen Meiksins, 30n4
Woolwich Arsenal, 124
working class, 22, 31, 32, 38, 45–46, 50–51, 140, 162, 190
World History (discipline), 2, 15, 219, 241, 251–55
World Social Forum, 218
World-Systems Analysis, 14, 30, 205–18
Wright, Erik Olin, 30n4

Xi, Zhu, 66

yangban class, 60, 65, 66–67, 68, 70n10, 71n17
Yi, Ch'ŏngwon, 55, 56
Yi, Pungman, 55, 56, 57
Yi, Sŏnggye (King T'aejo), 65, 66
Yuan Dynasty, 65

Zimbabwe, 163
Zimmern, Alfred, 226

About the Contributors

Jamie Allinson is a lecturer in politics and international relations at the University of Edinburgh, UK. He is the author of *The Struggle for the State in Jordan: The Social Origins of Alliances in the Middle East* (2016).

Alexander Anievas is an assistant professor of international political economy at the University of Connecticut, USA. He previously held research fellowships at the University of Oxford and Cambridge. He is the author of *Capital, the State, and War: Class Conflict and Geopolitics in the Thirty Years' Crisis, 1914–1945* (2014), for which he was awarded the Sussex International Theory Prize, and co-author (with Kerem Nişancıoğlu) of *How the West Came to Rule: The Geopolitical Origins of Capitalism* (2015). He is currently working on a manuscript (with Richard Saull) entitled *Legacies of Fascism: Race and the Far-Right in the Making of the Cold War*.

David L. Blaney is the G. Theodore Mitau Professor of Political Science, Macalester College, Saint Paul, Minnesota, USA. He writes on the political and social theory of international relations and global political economy. His two books (co-authored with Naeem Inayatullah), *International Relations and the Problem of Difference* (2004) and *Savage Economics: Wealth, Poverty, and the Temporal Walls of Capitalism* (2010), explore international relations/political economy as a cultural project constructing a modern Western identity that makes it complicit with colonialism. He is beginning work on a book, *Justifying Suffering*, exploring the political economy tradition from Smith to neoclassical economics and contemporary rationalist IPE.

William Brown is a senior lecturer in government and politics at the Open University, UK. His research is in the field of international relations with a particular focus on Africa, and on the international politics of development aid. William Brown was a founder of the British International Studies Association (BISA) Working Group on Africa and International Studies. Recent work has focussed on the issue of sovereignty in aid relations and African agency. The latter work includes the book *African Agency in International Politics* co-edited with Sophie Harman and a number of articles. Previous research has included work on IR theory and Africa as well as contemporary political developments. He has written in particular on aid relations between UK/EU and Africa including a history of European Union relations with Africa: *The European Union and Africa: Restructuring North-South Relations*. He has also co-edited a number of textbooks and written extensively for the Open University, including *International Relations: Continuity and Change in Global Politics* and *Ordering the International*.

Barry Buzan is a fellow of the British Academy, Emeritus Professor in the LSE Department of International Relations and a senior fellow at LSE IDEAS, UK. He was formerly Montague Burton Professor in the Department of International Relations, LSE. Among his books are, with Richard Little, *International Systems in World History* (2000); with Ole Wæver, *Regions and Powers* (2003); *From International to World Society?* (2004); with Lene Hansen, *The Evolution of International Security Studies* (2009); *An Introduction to the English School of International Relations* (2014); and, with George Lawson, *The Global Transformation: History, Modernity and the Making of International Relations* (2015).

Christopher Chase-Dunn is a distinguished professor of sociology and director of the Institute for Research on World-Systems at the University of California, Riverside, USA. He has written *Rise and Demise: Comparing World-Systems* (with Thomas D. Hall), *The Wintu and Their Neighbors* (with Kelly Mann) and *The Spiral of Capitalism and Socialism* (with Terry Boswell). He is the founder and former editor of the *Journal of World-Systems Research*. Chase-Dunn is currently doing research on global party formation and antisystemic social movements. He also studies the rise and fall of settlements and polities since the Stone Age as well as the trajectory of global state formation.

Luke Cooper is a lecturer in politics at Anglia Ruskin University, UK. He has a broad range of research interests, spanning historical sociology, international history and global politics, with a specific concern for historical materialist approaches within these fields. His empirical research is currently focused on national identity and nationalism across the *longue durée*. He is a member of the British International Studies Association (BISA), the BISA Workgroup on Historical Sociology in International Relations and the Workgroup on Uneven and Combined Development.

Neil Davidson lectures in sociology with the School of Social and Political Sciences at the University of Glasgow, UK. He is the author of *The Origins of Scottish Nationhood* (2000), *Discovering the Scottish Revolution* (2003), for which he was awarded the Deutscher Prize, *How Revolutionary Were the Bourgeois Revolutions?* (2012) and *Holding Fast to an Image of the Past* (2014). Davidson has also co-edited and contributed to *Alasdair MacIntyre's Engagement with Marxism* (2008), *Neoliberal Scotland* (2010) and *The Longue Durée of the Far-Right* (2015).

Jessica Evans is a PhD student in political science at York University, Toronto, Canada. Her research interests broadly include migration, international historical sociology, political economy, labour organisation and 'late development'. Her current research attempts to understand the relationship between international migration and variable labour market and national state formation in the late nineteenth century.

Marilyn Grell-Brisk is a PhD candidate in sociology at the University of Neuchatel, Switzerland. Her PhD project focuses on the dual impact of China's rise and its re-engagement with Sub-Saharan Africa vis-à-vis global economic stratification. She has spent time at the Arrighi Center at Johns Hopkins University and is a regular participant at the Institute for Research on World-Systems' Working Group at the University of California, Riverside. She received her master's degree in political science at the University of Lausanne. Her undergraduate degree is in government with a leadership sequence which she completed at Claremont McKenna College. Her primary interests are in world-systems theory, development, Marxist and critical thought, comparative historical sociology and China's involvement with Sub-Saharan Africa and the Global South.

John M. Hobson is a professor of politics and international relations at the University of Sheffield (UK) and is a fellow of the British Academy. His theoretical and empirical work is situated in the vortex of global historical sociology, international relations/IPE and postcolonialism. He has published eight books, the latest of which is *The Eurocentric Conception of World Politics: Western International Theory, 1760–2010* (2012). His current research charts the formation and development of the world economy in a non-Eurocentric IPE context.

Naeem Inayatullah is a professor of politics at Ithaca College, USA. His work locates the Third World in international relations and global political economy. With David Blaney, he is the co-author of *Savage Economics: Wealth, Poverty, and the Temporal Walls of Capitalism* (2010) and *International Relations and the Problem of Difference* (2004). He is the editor of *Autobiographical International Relations* (2011), and co-editor of *Interrogating Imperialism* (2006) and *The Global Economy as Political Space* (1994). Recent journal articles include 'Liberal Fundamentals', *Journal of International Relations and Development* (2012) and 'The Dark Heart of Kindness', *International Studies Perspectives* (2012).

George Lawson is an associate professor in international relations at the London School of Economics and Political Science, UK. His books include: *Global Historical* Sociology, edited with Julian Go (2016); *The Global Transformation: History, Modernity and the Making of International Relations* (2015), with Barry Buzan; *The Global 1989: Continuity and Change in World Politics*, edited with Chris Armbruster and Michael Cox (2010); and *Negotiated Revolutions: The Czech Republic, South Africa and Chile* (2005). He is currently working on a monograph entitled *Anatomies of Revolution*.

Fouad Makki is an associate professor of development sociology at Cornell University, USA. His research areas include social theory, the historical sociology of modernity, and international political economy. His most recent publications include: 'Reframing Development Theory: The Significance of the Idea of Uneven and Combined Development', *Theory and Society* (2015); 'Post-Colonial Africa and the World Economy', *Journal of World-Systems Research* (2015); 'Development by Dispossession: *Terra Nullius* and the Social-Ecology of New Enclosures in Ethiopia,' *Rural Sociology* (2014).

Kamran Matin is a senior lecturer in international relations at Sussex University (UK), management committee member of *Centre for Advanced International Theory* and a co-founder and co-director of the Sussex Working Group on Uneven and Combined Development. His publications on historical sociology and premodern state formation, postcolonial theory, political Islam and modern Iranian history have appeared in *European Journal of International Relations*, *Journal of International Relations and Development* and *Middle East Critique*. He is the author of *Recasting Iranian Modernity: International Relations and Social Change* (2013).

Owen Miller is a lecturer in Korean Studies at SOAS, University of London (UK) where he teaches Korean history. He was previously a research fellow at

Robinson College, University of Cambridge, where he worked on developing an atlas of Korean history. Owen received his PhD from SOAS in 2007 for a thesis on merchant-government relations in late nineteenth-century Korea. More broadly, his research interests include: the transition from pre-capitalist to capitalist societies in Northeast Asia; the social and economic history of nineteenth- and twentieth-century Korea; urban history; Korean nationalist and Marxist historiographies; and the economic history of North Korea.

Kerem Nişancioğlu is a lecturer in international relations at the School of Oriental and African Studies, University of London, UK. His research focuses on Eurocentrism in international relations, and how this Eurocentrism can be subverted in both theory and history. In particular, his research has explored the ways in which non-European societies have been constitutive of European social relations in the early modern period. He is the co-author (with Alexander Anievas) of *How the West Came to Rule: The Geopolitical Origins of Capitalism* (2015).

Justin Rosenberg is a professor of international relations at the University of Sussex (UK) and co-convenor of the Sussex Working Group on Uneven and Combined Development. His previous publications include *The Empire of Civil Society* (1994) and *The Follies of Globalisation Theory* (2000).